W9-DEX-335

the Molsons

John Molson

the Molsons
Their Lives & Times
1780-2000

Karen Molson

FIREFLY BOOKS

A FIREFLY BOOK

Published by Firefly Books Ltd. 2001

First Printing

National Library of Canada Cataloguing in Publication Data

Molson, Karen
The Molsons : their lives and times: 1780-2000

Includes bibliographical references and index.
ISBN 1-55209-418-9
1. Molson family. 2. Molson, John, 1763-1836—Family. 3. Molson Companies—History.
4. Businessmen—Canada—Biography. I. Title

HC112.5.M64M64 2001 338.092′271 C2001-930718-7

U.S. Cataloging-in-Publication Data
(Library of Congress Standards)

Molson. Karen.
The Molsons : their lives and times: 1780-2000 / Karen Molson – 1st ed.
[464] p. : photos.; cm.
Includes bibliographic references and index.
Summary: The epic history of one of Canada's oldest and most important families and their company.
ISBN 1-55209-418-9
1. Molson family. 2. Businesspeople—Canada—Biography. I. Title.
338/.04/09222 B 21 2001

Published in Canada in 2001 by
Firefly Books Ltd.
3680 Victoria Park Avenue
Willowdale, Ontario M2H 3K1

Published in the United States in 2001 by
Firefly Books (U.S.) Inc.
P.O. Box 1338, Ellicott Station
Buffalo, New York 14205

Cover design: Interrobang Graphic Design Inc. & George Walker
Graphic design and layout: George Walker

Printed and bound in Canada by Friesens, Altona, Manitoba

The Publisher acknowledges the financial support of the Government of Canada through the Book Publishing Industry Development program for its publishing activities.

For
Lindsay, Josie, Paul and Alison
with love

Acknowledgments

First of all, I am ineffably grateful to researchers Hilbert Buist and Jenny Doyle, who shared my reverence and passion for history. Tirelessly and scrupulously they sought answers to increasingly obscure questions, squinting at microfiche screens, lugging heavy tomes, identifying files of fragile yellowed documents. Alone or paired, some of us travelled to and from places including Montreal, Kingston, Mount Forest, Coteau du Lac and England. Needless to say, without their invaluable assistance this project would have taken many more years.

I am likewise indebted to Ian Bowering, Trevor Neilson, Stephen Paterson and Lorna Hart, whose work helped illuminate the big picture and provided countless small insights.

Twenty years ago, writer-researcher Alastair Sweeny helped me believe my dream was achievable. At university, professor Bob Hogg was particularly supportive and helpful. Some years later, writer Sandra Gwyn's "non-fiction novel" *The Private Capital* inspired me, and her kind letters to me honed my determination to tell the Molson story.

I thank Mabel Tinkiss Good, who worked for many years as the family archivist at Molson's brewery, sorting and organizing documents, thus making my quests that much easier. Mrs. Good's daughter, Kelly Good, kindly shared her mother's notes and papers with me.

I am also deeply indebted to those who helped in innumerable ways, including specific research, transcriptions and translations, and to those who offered hospitality, interest and support:

Beverly Birks, Penny Blades, Phyllis and Colin Brockett, Richard Carruthers, Joyce Clinton, James Dalziel, Marie Demarais, Marie-France Deragon, Sarah Doyle, John Durnford, Claude Ethier, Susan Edlington, Bob Elsdale, Dr. Stanley Frost, Lindsay Fry, Dr. Victor Goldbloom, Roberta and Grey Haddock, Ken Hague, Susan and Hugh Hamilton, Victor Isganaitis, Bill and Lois Irvine, Leyone Jutras, Valerie Knowles, Rob and Debra Latham, Ed Lawrence, Frank Leeson, Doreen Lindsay, Jack and Anne Loader, Margit and Gerry Lunn, Karen MacIntosh, Alan Molson, Christine and Jack Molson, Paulette Montreuil, Peter Nelson, Derrick and Sheila Oakes, David Oliver, Christine Peringer, Marylyn Peringer, Percival Molson Ritchie, Allison Robichaud, Alison Rolland, Ralph Ruhs, Ernie Skutezsky, Colonel William Sutherland, Richard Sutton, Tom Thompson, Randy Weekes, Greg Weil, Dorothy Weitzenbauer, Josie Weitzenbauer, Ralph Weitzenbauer, Miss Lorelei Williams, Ken Woodbridge, and Earl Zuckerman.

This biography is neither sanctioned nor official, authorized nor unauthorized. I am grateful to have consistently enjoyed the full cooperation of family members, who have unhesitatingly shared their memories and mementos with me. I felt welcomed by each and all, and am proud to be related to them:

Ian and Daphne Angus, John Angus, Lucille and David Ashdown, Phyllis and Colin Brockett, Olive Dodes, Meredith Fisher, Mary Molson Iversen, Stuart Iversen, Celia LaFleur, Jack and Anne Loader, Naomi Molson Longden, Lorna McDougall, Clive and Diana Meredith, Helen Meredith, Alan Molson, CJG (Jack) Molson, Christine and Jack Molson, Connie Molson, David and Claire Molson, Eric H. Molson, Hartland de M. Molson, Ian Molson, John Molson, Nancy Paterson Molson, Nicola Jane (Nicky) Molson, Robin and Carolyn Molson, Robert and Margaret Molson, Stephen T. Molson, Willie Molson, Mary Molson Nesbitt, Maggie Oliphant, Derrick and Sheila Oakes, Margaret Payton, Lin Russell, Marnie Russell, Michael Stewart, Jane Sullivan, David Sullivan, Peggy Willis and Edward and Isabel Winslow-Spragge.

Some of the people and institutions to whom I'd like to extend further my appreciation include: Andy Roy and Myriam Cloutier, Mount Royal Cemetery, Montreal; Elizabeth Kennell, Pam Miller, Conrad Graham, Joan McKim, Suzanne Morin and Nora Hague at the McCord Museum, Montreal; Dr. Stanley Frost, Tom Thompson and Earl Zuckerman at McGill University, Montreal; Tom Royce and Norman Leveritt of the Gentlemen's Society, in Spalding, Lincolnshire; Stephen Salmon and Michel Brisebois, National Archives Canada; the board and staff members at Canadian Heritage of Quebec, Montreal; David Andrews, Ginn Photographic, Ottawa; Margaret Turner, Quebec Family History Society, Montreal; Paul Berry, Canadian Currency Museum, Ottawa; Denzel Palmar, Aileen Kopacka, and Susie and Celly Gorman, Royal Montreal Golf Club; Giselle and Bob Hall, and John Thompson, of the Forest and Stream Club, Dorval; and Stéphane Lamontagne, Old Port of Quebec, Quebec City.

I extend affection to Nimali, Hattie and Dale at the Sun Café in Lincoln, Lincolnshire.

I thank my husband and family, for their love and patient belief.

I thank my publishers, Lionel Koffler and Michael Worek, for offering me this opportunity, and editors Wendy Thomas and Dan Liebman for shepherding the manuscript to its completion.

Contents

Photo sections appear following pages 64, 224 and 384

Sarah Molson

Molson Family Tree

The Canadian Molson family can trace seven generations back to John Molson Senior, who emigrated from England to Canada in 1782. The family tree presented on the next pages records a relatively small number of Molson descendants, being limited, largely, to those family members who appear in the book.

The purpose of the family tree is to help readers understand the relationship between family members. This is especially important because the Molsons often used the same Christian names generation after generation. An additional complication is created by the marriages between first cousins, a practice that causes complicated genealogies. Finally, the large families (six and seven children were common) in the early generations present a considerable number of players on the stage at one time.

As will become apparent after looking at the tree, the key to understanding the genealogy is to follow the lineage of John Molson Senior's and Sarah Vaughan's three children–John II, Thomas and William. From these three men, two of whom married first cousins, spring all the Molsons who appear in the book.

The Molson Family Tree

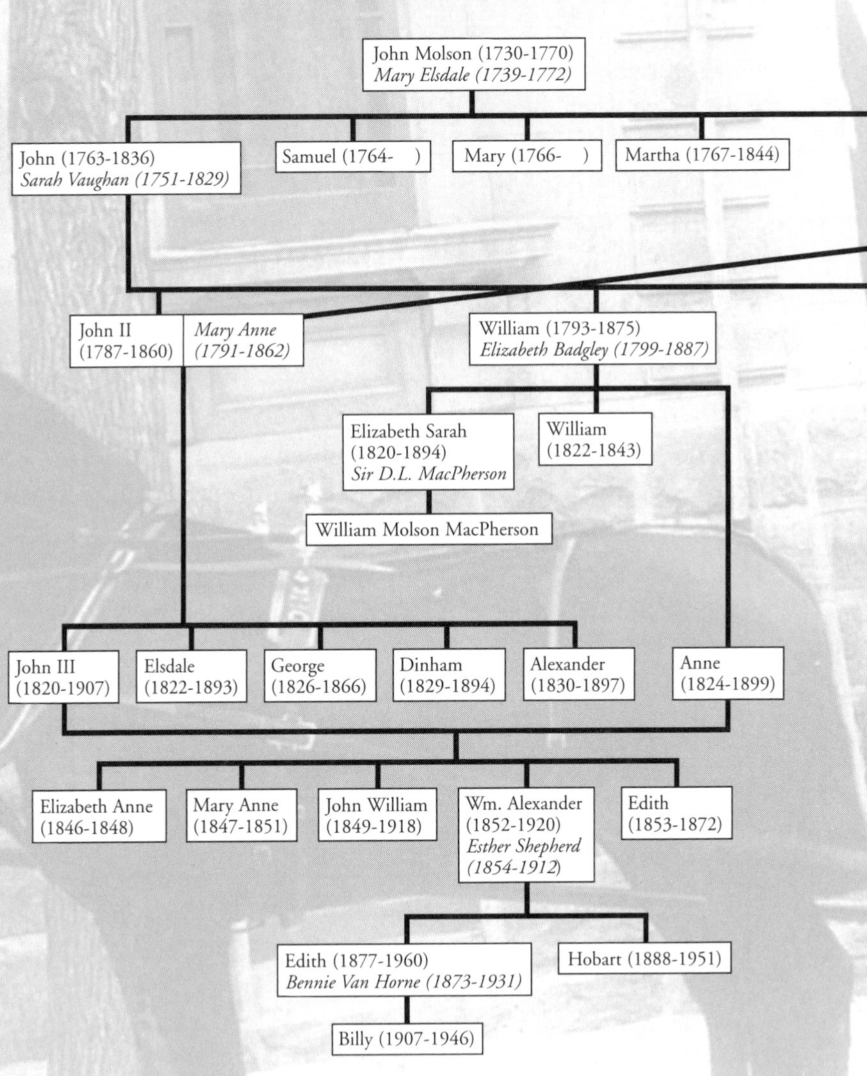
John Molson (1730-1770)
Mary Elsdale (1739-1772)
John (1763-1836)
Sarah Vaughan (1751-1829)
Samuel (1764-)
Mary (1766-)
Martha (1767-1844)
John II (1787-1860)
Mary Anne (1791-1862)
William (1793-1875)
Elizabeth Badgley (1799-1887)
Elizabeth Sarah (1820-1894)
Sir D.L. MacPherson
William (1822-1843)
William Molson MacPherson
John III (1820-1907)
Elsdale (1822-1893)
George (1826-1866)
Dinham (1829-1894)
Alexander (1830-1897)
Anne (1824-1899)
Elizabeth Anne (1846-1848)
Mary Anne (1847-1851)
John William (1849-1918)
Wm. Alexander (1852-1920)
Esther Shepherd (1854-1912)
Edith (1853-1872)
Edith (1877-1960)
Bennie Van Horne (1873-1931)
Hobart (1888-1951)
Billy (1907-1946)

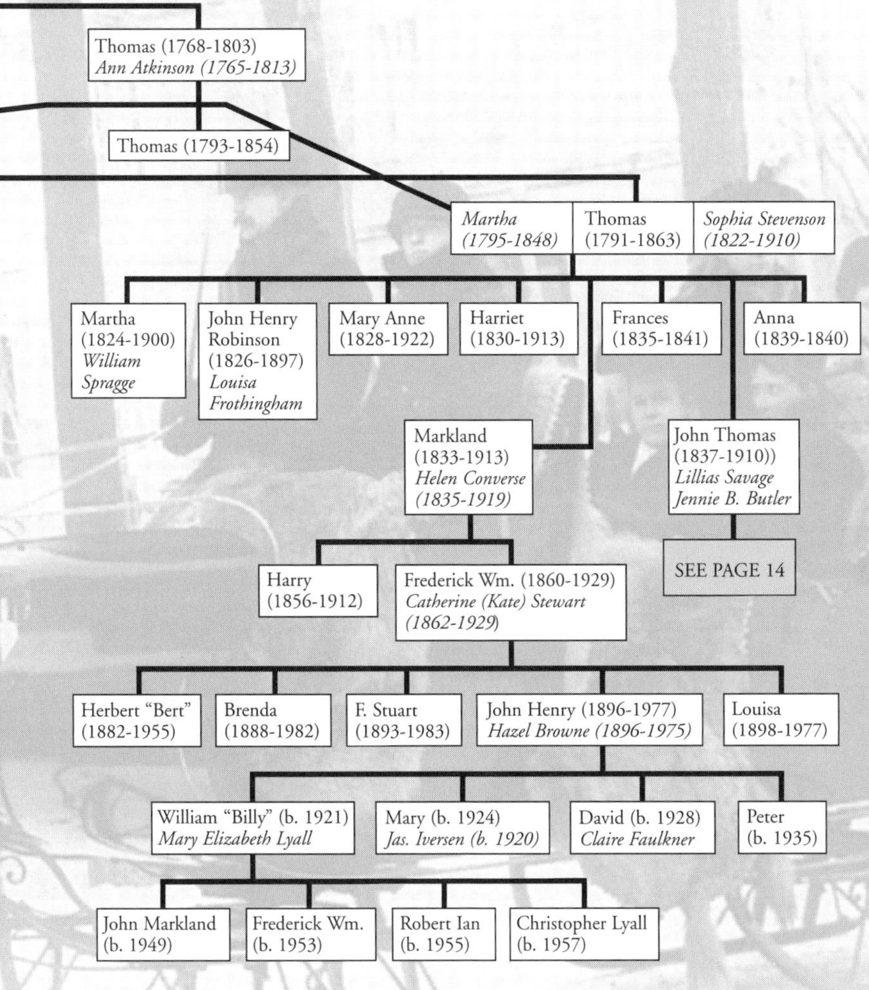

Thomas (1768-1803)
Ann Atkinson (1765-1813)
Thomas (1793-1854)
Martha (1795-1848)
Thomas (1791-1863)
Sophia Stevenson (1822-1910)
Martha (1824-1900) *William Spragge*
John Henry Robinson (1826-1897) *Louisa Frothingham*
Mary Anne (1828-1922)
Harriet (1830-1913)
Frances (1835-1841)
Anna (1839-1840)
Markland (1833-1913) *Helen Converse (1835-1919)*
John Thomas (1837-1910)) *Lillias Savage* *Jennie B. Butler*
SEE PAGE 14
Harry (1856-1912)
Frederick Wm. (1860-1929) *Catherine (Kate) Stewart (1862-1929)*
Herbert "Bert" (1882-1955)
Brenda (1888-1982)
F. Stuart (1893-1983)
John Henry (1896-1977) *Hazel Browne (1896-1975)*
Louisa (1898-1977)
William "Billy" (b. 1921) *Mary Elizabeth Lyall*
Mary (b. 1924) *Jas. Iversen (b. 1920)*
David (b. 1928) *Claire Faulkner*
Peter (b. 1935)
John Markland (b. 1949)
Frederick Wm. (b. 1953)
Robert Ian (b. 1955)
Christopher Lyall (b. 1957)

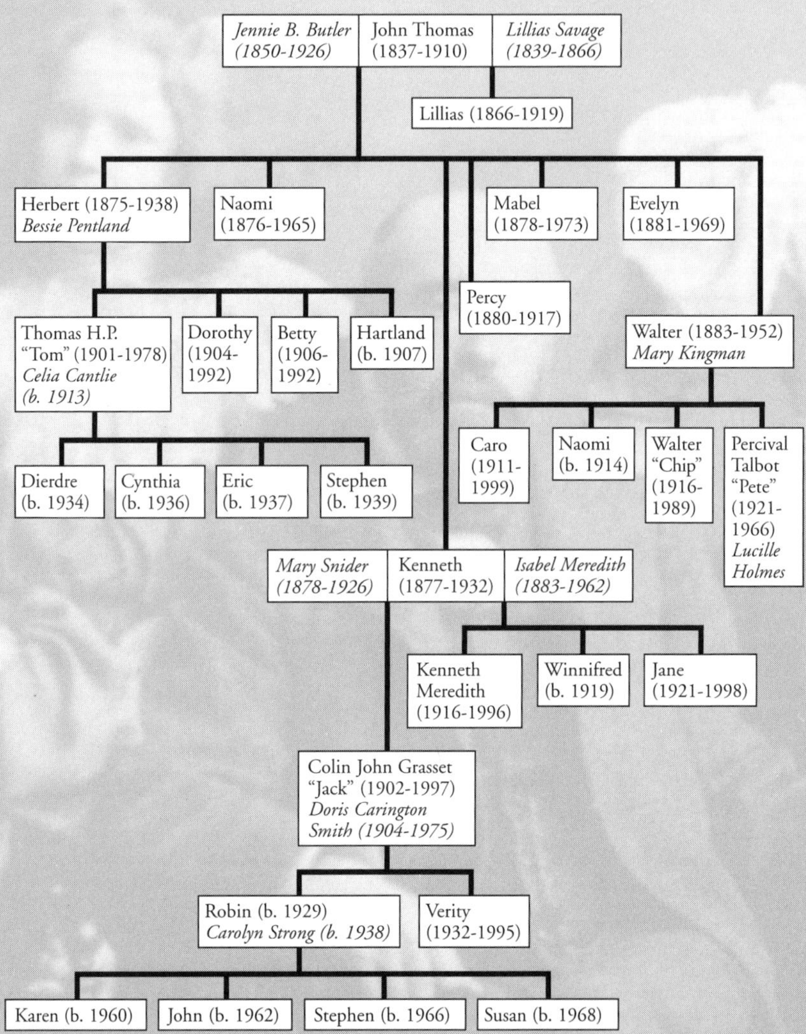

Jennie B. Butler (1850-1926)
John Thomas (1837-1910)
Lillias Savage (1839-1866)
Lillias (1866-1919)
Herbert (1875-1938) *Bessie Pentland*
Naomi (1876-1965)
Mabel (1878-1973)
Evelyn (1881-1969)
Percy (1880-1917)
Walter (1883-1952) *Mary Kingman*
Thomas H.P. "Tom" (1901-1978) *Celia Cantlie (b. 1913)*
Dorothy (1904-1992)
Betty (1906-1992)
Hartland (b. 1907)
Caro (1911-1999)
Naomi (b. 1914)
Walter "Chip" (1916-1989)
Percival Talbot "Pete" (1921-1966) *Lucille Holmes*
Dierdre (b. 1934)
Cynthia (b. 1936)
Eric (b. 1937)
Stephen (b. 1939)
Mary Snider (1878-1926)
Kenneth (1877-1932)
Isabel Meredith (1883-1962)
Kenneth Meredith (1916-1996)
Winnifred (b. 1919)
Jane (1921-1998)
Colin John Grasset "Jack" (1902-1997) *Doris Carington Smith (1904-1975)*
Robin (b. 1929) *Carolyn Strong (b. 1938)*
Verity (1932-1995)
Karen (b. 1960)
John (b. 1962)
Stephen (b. 1966)
Susan (b. 1968)

Preface

All that is good and great about the family should not be underground.
John HR Molson, 1897

The idea to write this book first inspired me thirty years ago, when as a little girl I listened to my grandfather tell me about his grandparents and realized what remarkable people our ancestors were. As a teenager I asked many questions of relatives, took notes and recorded my grandfather's memories on audiotape. In the years that followed I was delighted to find that hundreds of years of family history had been saved and preserved in numerous archives, both public and private.

A biographer's purpose, whether reaching into an archival box for a file or squinting into the darkness of an ancient cellar, is to discover the truth. And while passing judgment is not necessary, the responsibility of drawing conclusions is a serious one. It is not until one has assembled all the flotsam and jetsam (those things which, considered singly, seem meaningless) that the subjects' lives begin to assume shape, form and direction.

As a writer and a family member, I felt I was in a unique position to write a literary history. I could explore the family's collective consciousness from within, as well as plumb for facts from without. I was certain I didn't want to write a business history or a panegyric. But what, exactly? The men and women who'd lived and died had left marks and mysteries behind. How they fascinated me! To do them justice, I would try to cast their true characters into a narrative of real events; to create a colourful and noisy pilgrimage through a panorama of time, a Canadian crusade from the past to the present.

Archival material spanning the Molson family's seven generations in Canada is abundant, even overwhelming. Tens of thousands of items such as letters, diaries, deeds, artifacts and photos harbour veritable treasures and yield secrets from the past. Libraries and public archives harbour vast resources, including books, newspapers, periodicals, business records, census records, copies of land transactions, and maps. From the beginning I aimed to cast a huge net of curious inquiry, to be assured that nothing would be left uninspected. I was much gratified to be able to work with some tireless, enthusiastic researchers.

I travelled to as many sites as possible in which the events in this book took place. While moving through the spaces my ancestors used to inhabit, I was ever-conscious of the existence of the past around me. I gazed at the enduring landscapes, and contemplated the St. Lawrence, a river of water enclosing a river of time. After a while it seemed an utterly natural process to present glimpses of my ancestors' lives in the present tense. I found that through the tangible, I could effortlessly reach the intangible.

More than two hundred great-grandchildren can trace their ancestry back to the Lincolnshire orphan who emigrated to Montreal in 1782. John Molson Senior was eighteen when he came to Canada, fair-haired and easy-mannered. He considered every decision carefully. His attention to detail was remarkable; his vision, shrewd and keen. He kept his coins in an old grain chest. He recorded every penny earned, lent, given away or spent. He saved copies of every letter he wrote, to keep with each one he received. He did not have to exhort his sons to do the same; they–and their children, in turn–either learned or inherited his fastidious habits.

I am grateful they did.

Introduction

When the sun begins to set behind Mount Royal at the end of the day, the past and the present converge in the old city. The shadows, longer and wider now, drift from the street once known as St. Mary's to the river edge. They connect the intangible with the tangible, the things that stay the same with those that change. I plumb the past in order to find John Molson, my great-grandfather's great-grandfather, who in the seventy-three years he lived (1763–1836) was always seeking the future. We meet each other here at the brewery.

The huge buildings on Nôtre Dame Street dwarf the people, bound to myriad destinations. There was a time when a little log brewery was all that was here, when the road passed many empty fields before reaching the old walled city, when long strip farms and *seigneuries* lay one after another to the east. To get here, we have taken the highway from Ontario and negotiated a series of lane-changes downtown before taking a lucky turn and finding ourselves on Nôtre Dame Street. Molson's Brewery dominates blocks on the right and left. We pull into a parking lot where the sign says "Visitors" and are greeted by an attendant.

The river is not visible from here, although it is only a hundred yards away. We are introduced to our escort, who guides us past a set of iron gates and then through a side door that clicks behind us. Underground, a light switch is located, and we walk past rows of shelves lined with machine parts: cylinders, taps, spigots, valves and jointed pipe pieces–an array of obsolete equipment that seems to stretch to infinity.

Dug in the eighteenth century for cool storage of beer and ale, the old cellar crouches under the stone, steel and cement structure that encompasses this modern brewery. We stop in front of a door and our escort searches for the right key, shaking the others loose from it on the ring. The thrum of some far-off machinery is faintly heard, muffled by walls and ceilings. I look up. The outline of the original log brewhouse above us is just discernible.

The door opens. Something makes me catch my breath. It is impossible not to feel impressed by those who measured the twenty- by forty-foot space with yardsticks, who shovelled this cavity from the earth, who lifted these flat stones from wooden-wheeled barrows and slapped on the mortar with trowels, who groined the ceiling so it could withstand the weight of the great fermenting vats, who applied the first coats of whitewash, who stood in the very space we stand in now.

I scrape a handful of earth together and squeeze it. This redolent handful–this sandy, musty, damp earth that absorbed the splashes and spills of beer over the years–harbours its secrets. Just on the other side of the thin gauze of history are the rows of hogsheads braced on stillions lining either side of the room, brimming with ale and the promise of riches. I look up and experience this room that, for its first hundred years, was wreathed in shadows, the air always pungent with the scent of malt and sweet wort.

"And so", John Molson concluded with grim relief, "we escaped with nothing only what was on our backs."

Chapter One

Aweighing Anchor

Thursday, May 2, 1782

THE OLD MERCHANT ship doesn't look seaworthy. She bobs uneasily in the water, dwarfed by the gilt-edged vessels *H.M.S. Victory* and *Preston* which loom above her on either side. A length of frayed hawser is all that holds the vessel to the mooring. Her jib boom is poorly secured; her mizzen and studding-sails are tattered and randomly patched. A faded British flag sags at her stern. Eighteen-year-old John Molson looks over the ship he will be sailing on, summoning enough resolution to overcome his dismay.

John turns to the older man beside him. "I trust you have prepared your will, Mr. Pell."

No ocean-going vessel is immune to virulent fevers, which can rage unchecked on board. The sight of a ship anchored in quarantine, or burned to the water's edge in an attempt to contain a new outbreak, is a spectre so common that it elicits only murmurs in passing.

As the sun rises, activity is illuminated along the old harbour. Crewmen from the superior vessels are attending to last-minute tasks, deckhands are checking pumps, sailors are climbing into the rigging to secure knots. Burly stevedores haul the last barrels of salt on board. The air smells of fresh dung, seaweed and pitch. Sheep and goats are prodded up the planks, while crates of chickens and ducks are passed from one hand to the next. John notices that their merchant ship is nominally equipped for defence. He watches as she is loaded with goods destined for Quebec and Montreal, including sacks of grain, barrels of flour, crates of groceries and bolts of cloth. The fleet of eight naval ships will protect the merchant vessel during the long voyage ahead.

Officers and captains stand by gravely, effulgent in their wide tricorn hats. Golden fringes swing from their epaulettes, and polished buckles on their shoes wink in the morning light. Referred to by Captain Horatio Nelson as the "Quebec Fleet," the vessels at Portsmouth Harbour are preparing to set sail for the voyage across the Atlantic. Even with good weather, it will take them at least four weeks to reach the Gulf of St. Lawrence, and at least three more to reach Quebec.

John Molson and his two companions–the older man at his side and his son–don't want to draw attention to themselves. Captains are obliged by law to check passengers' names against lists of "wanted" individuals circulated by the admiralty, and James Gibbins is one of those names. His indebtedness has necessitated both his emigration and the adoption of aliases for himself and James Junior who is near Molson's age. Here at the wharf, at any moment a messenger-at-arms might appear with a warrant, looking for Gibbins. As long as he remains in England he is at risk of being imprisoned. While thieves serve their time and are released eventually, debtors, considered worse, are locked up until their debts are paid, which for most means a lifetime of confinement. To make things grimmer still, the overcrowding and filth in the jails provoke epidemics of fever and typhus. In 1782 debtors account for the vast majority of inmates in British penal institutions. Gibbins is desperate not to become one of them.

Molson is careful to refer to Gibbins, who is actually the brother-in-law of his uncle, as "Mr. Pell," whenever he speaks to him, mentions him in his letters home, or writes about him in his private diary of that sea voyage.

John is well aware of the harshness of the times. Hangings and public floggings are relatively common. In the town of Lincoln, such punishments are scheduled for the next market day after Assize Court dates, to bring out a good crowd.

A gloomy old hulk anchored not far from where they stand reminds John of James Gibbins's possible fate. It is a prison ship groaning with human ballast–those wet and miserable wretches for whom even Newgate prison had no more room.

James is nervous. The dockyard commander has walked by them twice, the vessel they are to board (of which neither its name nor its cargo has been recorded) looks shabby and decrepit, and there is no captain around who has claimed to command her. Gibbins urges that they board anyway. The crowds are beginning to thin; the three seem to be the only passengers travelling on this ship, and if they loiter on the wharf any longer he is afraid someone will start asking them questions.

Below deck, in a sour-smelling room, they find some crew members stowing away chests and buckling provisions in place.

"Where's our captain, then?" Molson asks. No one answers; one fellow, with his back to the passengers, shrugs his shoulders and carries on with his work.

By mid-morning, the eight ready vessels in the Quebec fleet have set sail. John and the Gibbinses watch with mounting frustration as the perfect wind dies down and the perfect tide turns.

"At this rate, we may never get there at all," James says darkly.

"Perhaps it's just as well, sir, on a vessel as sorry as this," James Junior adds quietly.

"Aye, there's enough trouble with all the rogues out there, without the means around us to brace a storm or two," John agrees. But he is pacing impatiently.

One of the crew members overhears him and looks up. "They say that Yankee pirate John Paul Jones is at sea–"

"There are cannon lashed to this deck, to be sure, but not enough hands to man them!" injects another.

"I should not worry about pirates being interested in this old bucket. One look at her and they'd guffaw, or maybe wish us luck," Gibbins says wryly.

The men grow quiet as the sun rises higher in the sky and the morning edges toward noon. In frustration, they pace in their cramped quarters. The rest of the fleet has already vanished over the horizon. Sailors and mates have long ago completed all their duties. Even the cook is getting short-tempered.

"One of you ought to summon the dockyard commander," he barks. Molson and James Gibbins exchange glances.

"Someone could start searching for the captain on shore," Gibbins suggests doubtfully. "Does anyone know his name?"

Seagulls briefly alight on the mooring piles. All human activity around the dock has subsided. The travellers curse their luck and wish themselves on another–any other–sailing ship.

To young John Molson, the county of Lincolnshire had offered little in the way of advancement. After his parents had died–his father in 1770, his mother in 1772–old widower Samuel Elsdale, the boy's maternal grandfather, had been named guardian and executor. This meant that until he reached his majority, still two and a half years away, John operated at the whim of his conservative grandfather. The Industrial Revolution was well under way. The old order was dying. England was changing.

Molson's maternal uncle Robinson Elsdale, a retired captain of the merchant vessel *Duke of Ancaster* and former privateer, was the one who had first suggested to John that he consider North America.

When John announced that he was going to emigrate, Samuel was incensed. His trust that his eldest grandson would share the responsibility of managing the estate and take over the care of his siblings was sabotaged. "Have you no respect for the family name?" he'd demanded.

Having a respectable line of forebears went hand in hand with the system of landed estates. The surname "Molson" and its variant spellings had evolved over centuries. An armorial ensign had been acknowledged in medieval times. The earliest recorded ancestor, Thomas de Multon (also spelled "de Moulton"), migrated to Yorkshire from France in the eleventh century, after the first of the Crusades. He moved south (possibly in search of more fertile land) to the Fen region. He was later named Sheriff of Lincolnshire and was granted land in that county. For twenty years he fell in and out of favour with kings and was twice imprisoned. In 1215 de Multon was one of the landowners who demanded from King John the concessions laid down in the Magna Carta, and from 1224 until his death in 1240 he sat as a Justice in Westminster. According to unverifiable legend, another de Multon was arrested for being a highwayman and was hanged in York Tower later that century.

By the end of the fourteenth century the "de" in the name had been lost. Standardized spellings for most surnames weren't found in those days of widespread illiteracy. In one Court of Chancery document dated 1531, the same gentleman's name appears variably spelled as Moulton, Moldson, Moldeson, Malson, Malsham and Molson.

In 1627 Sir Thomas Moulson built a church in Hargrave, Cheshire, with a school adjoining it "for the education and instruction of youth in grammar and virtue." A panel was erected in 1774 above the door of the church, which reads: "Thomas Moulson of ye citty of London, Alderman, built this Chapell upon his owne cost and charge, Ano. Dni. 1627."

The Molsons of Canada trace their ancestry directly to a Thomas Molson from Cantley, Yorkshire, who married his cousin Margaret Moulson in 1598. Their youngest son, Thomas, also spelled his surname Molson. Thomas Junior left Cantley for fertile Crowland, Lincolnshire, around 1600; his eldest son, Thomas Molson (there are no middle names to help distinguish the Thomases), would settle in nearby Cowbit, then move to Peakhill.

Near the end of the seventeenth century, Thomas Molson of Peakhill inherited, at the death of his first wife, Sarah, the manor house known as Snake Hall. He remarried (to Mary Wincely), and their son, John Molson, was born at Snake Hall in 1699. In 1727 this young man married Martha Baker; their eldest surviving son, born in 1730, was also called John Molson. He, in turn, married Mary Elsdale in 1759. Mary's dowry, worth a thousand pounds (including land in nearby Pinchbeck), reveals that her father, Samuel, clearly approved of the match.

Owning freehold land entitled an adult male in the family to write "Gentleman" after his name. One's prosperity and status were directly affected by the size of one's property, as were marriage prospects, educational opportunities, political power and the assumption of social responsibility. Thus, many of the Molsons, like other members of the gentry, became deputy lieutenants, militia captains, clergymen, magistrates and justices of the peace. In 1726, for example, John Molson, son of Thomas Molson, was made a church warden and a justice of the peace, and in

1731 he became an overseer of the Moulton Grammar School.

In 1770 John's son, known as "John of Snake Hall," died. His widow lived only two more years, leaving five children: John, Samuel, Mary, Martha and Thomas.

John's parents are buried under Moulton All-Saints Church, one on either side of the baptismal font in the narthex. Slate memorial tablets were installed in the floor above them. By the light of the oil lamps hanging from chains in the arches, John could read the inscriptions etched on them:

> *In memory of John Molson, Gentleman, whose friendship was steady and sincere, and as he lived respected, so he died lamented. June 4, 1770, aged 40 years. In memory of Mary Elsdale, the widow of John Molson, Gentleman, who departed this life, Sept. 21st 1772, aged 33 years … In Brief to speak her praise, let this suffice, She was a wife most loving, modest, wise. Of children careful, to her neighbours kind, A worthy mistress, & of lib'ral mind.*

Orphaned at the age of eight, John was primary heir to the fertile land on which the family and their tenant farmers grew sugar beets, turnips and potatoes, and grazed longwool sheep. Not only were there no restrictions of entail upon the legacy passed to young John, including Snake Hall, but he was to inherit all his father's estates in Moulton, Peakhill and Cowbit. To three of John's younger siblings, their father left various tracts of land in the parishes of Moulton, Pinchbeck, Whaplode, Cowbit and Holbeach. If any of them were to predecease their eldest brother, their share would pass to him.

Only one son, Samuel, was treated differently. "My father in law Mr. Samuel Elsdale hath faithfully promised me to take care of and provide for my beloved son Samuel Elsdale Molson," wrote John of Snake Hall in his will. "I do therefore only give & bequeath unto my said beloved son Samuel Elsdale Molson the legacy or sum of one hundred pounds to be paid to my said trustees … to place the 100 pounds out at interest upon the best security that can be procured for the same for the use & benefit of Samuel." No record exists of Samuel's birth, baptism, marriage or death. There is but one mention in a letter–by a brother-in-law who referred to him as "a queer feelow"–and we can only speculate that Samuel was disabled in some way. Samuel Elsdale would leave this grandson cash, land and the furniture in the room in which he slept.

The Elsdales, as well known in Lincolnshire as the Molsons, had lived on their own prosperous estates at Surfleet since the arrival of old Samuel's grandfather, John Elsdale, in the early eighteenth century. Some sources reveal variant spellings, including monument inscriptions in Surfleet Parish Church which use "Elsdaile" throughout. When land in Lincoln County was ordered "enclosed" by Acts of Parliament in 1767, Samuel Elsdale was one of the commissioners appointed to replan the layout of local parishes, create new roads and divert waterways. Like the Molsons and other Lincolnshire families living on estates, they had their own brew house, steeping their own barley and casking their own ale. In addition to being landowners and farmers, many Elsdales were strong proponents of universal education, a very liberal attitude for the time. Samuel's two earnest and scholarly grandsons (sons of Robinson Elsdale) became Trinity dons at Oxford, the younger a published poet.

While an easier camaraderie than in most households existed between the Molson and Elsdale family members and their servants, within the families themselves a certain reserve prevailed. Their children were expected to uphold dignified conduct at all times and apply themselves to tasks with diligence. If one of the Molson children spoke out of turn or acted otherwise disrespectfully, threepence would be forfeited from their modest allowance. Both households kept careful records of expenses and income, down to the last farthing.

In 1774 Samuel Elsdale Senior remarried, finding five young children an exhausting responsibility for a septuagenarian. By 1776, at the age of twelve, John Molson was sent to boarding school in nearby Surfleet, where "gentlemen are liberally boarded and expeditiously forwarded in those branches of education their future prospects may require, on terms so reduced as to meet the views of the most economical." When he returned to Snake Hall for holidays, his grandfather charged room and board for the boy and his horse. For all expenses, including educational, young John was required to initial entries in an imposing ledger. When he came of age, John would find that at the direction of his grandfather one thousand, three hundred seventy-two pounds, eleven shillings, twopence and three farthings had been deducted from his inheritance for his upkeep.

By midday, reeking of strong drink, the captain at last stumbled on board. But the tide was coming in, and immediate attempts to sail the ship out of the harbour failed. Tacking was ineffective. The hapless vessel was forced to return and await the tide. It was dusk before she unfurled her sails and set her bowsprit for the long voyage across the ocean. They sailed throughout the night, and the following morning caught up with the convoy, which was waiting for the ship. The commodore on board the *H.M.S. Preston* immediately summoned the tardy captain aboard for "a sevear check for delaying him."

For almost a fortnight, the weather was all the crew and passengers could hope for. To pass the time, the passengers played backgammon and quoits. At night, the three companions slept on hammocks below deck with the crew, and during the day they satisfied their hunger with hard biscuits called "midshipmen's nuts," cheese found in the larder, and salt pork and sausages from barrels. The cook allowed them rations but refused to prepare meals for the three. One day they tried to prepare plum dumplings in a big cauldron on deck, but a sudden swell caused the deck to tilt and the pot turned over, spilling its contents out of a scupper hole and into the sea.

The commodore's tongue-lashing to the captain didn't have a long effect. Molson noted in his diary that the captain was frequently drunk. "An idle, diletary man," John wrote later, "and an obstinate fellow of a Scotchman who would hearken to nobody's advice scarce at all." When the captain wasn't drunk, he was indifferent, alienating his few passengers and apparently his crew as well. One day Molson found him passed out on deck near the jib boom. The ship would frequently fall back from the fleet, so that the other vessels were out of sight for hours at a time. The air in the hold became fouler every day, heavy with the mingled scents of body odour, vomit and stagnant bilge water. Although the passengers could make their way to the deck and fresh air during the day, there was no escaping the stench during the bitterly cold night.

At first Molson bore the discomforts with stoicism and a sense of adventure, having been prepared by his uncle for what to expect. With the sailors he indulged in the occasional bumper of beer flavoured with lime juice, Captain James Cook's recently discovered preventive against scurvy. He welcomed the feeling of gaining his "sea legs," relished the sharp taste of salt in the air, and soon found, as he gazed out to sea on the clearest days, that he wasn't looking east anymore.

"Noon on the 17th of May a heavy gale of wind came on," John wrote in his diary. Perhaps as a result of the weather, the vessel sprang a leak in an upper deck midship, and in less than an hour four feet of water inundated the hold. As a signal of distress to the rest of the fleet the captain fired a cannon, but again the vessel had fallen too far behind. The other frigates were windward of them and the cannon shot landed in the sea unheard. As the gale whipped about them and the vessel swung wildly in the thrashing swell, the frantic captain ordered all the starboard cannon heaved overboard. All night long the passengers and crew worked together, bailing and repairing, securing the essentials, and keeping the ship from capsizing. Finally, in the morning, the gale abated.

> *We made sail again on the larboard tack and got in sight of the fleet at 11 A.M. and they shorten'd sail for us, and we came up with the frigate and made signal to speak [to] them ... Carpenter was despatched to inspect the sorry vessel ... He told us that the upper Works were very mean, and must be caulked or else the vessel could not live if any more bad weather came.*

Some perfunctory repairs were attempted, but three days later a second gale engulfed them. This time, clinging to the mizzen chains, John and the Gibbinses watched in horror as a young sailor lost his balance and tumbled overboard while attempting to relieve himself. Conditions made a rescue impossible. "We could do nothing but throw a few things overboard, which however would only have prolonged his misery, as the sea ran mountains high."

Once the second gale had subsided and they were again in sight of the fleet, water began to pour in near the stern. The ship's mate shouted that they were certain to sink. By the time the captain had conceded that they couldn't repair the leak on their own, the rest of the fleet was yet again out of sight, and the discharge of one of their remaining cannon resounded across an empty ocean. The captain snapped new orders to the crew. John and James Junior were placed in braces near the foresail. Crew rigged the sails to gain more speed. As daylight ebbed, the air grew colder. Tempers burst like ignited gunpowder, and bodies grew tired of bailing even as the water in the hold continued to rise. Eventually their ship made some headway toward the fleet.

Gibbins had been through enough. He faced the captain at the bow, unsheathed a dagger, and warned that if the commodore on board the *Preston* was not signalled at once for help, he would take over the ship himself. The captain ordered the signal flags hoisted. Finally, the merchant ship drew near enough to the waiting frigate that Gibbins lifted a speaking-trumpet over the water and began shouting into it. The commodore granted permission to the three passengers to continue their journey on board the *Preston.* "And so," John Molson concluded with grim relief, "we escaped with nothing only what was on our backs." The commodore offered accommodation to the captain and his crew on the condition that they would "scuttle the ship and sink her," but to the disappointment of the crew, the captain angrily refused.

Conditions aboard the sturdy frigate, while far safer and relatively comfortable, were not necessarily more civil. John was struck with horror one day to see a man receive two dozen lashes with the cat-o'-nine-tails for a "trivial mistake," while the captain looked on dispassionately.

One day a cry of alarm was raised. Heavy mist had thinned for a moment and the sinister-looking hulls of two ships–and then two more–could be seen bearing directly toward them. Molson wasn't the only one on board who thought they were facing an attack by the dreaded John Paul Jones. The entire fleet prepared to line themselves up in a battle formation. As John recorded:

> *All hands were beat to quarters, and every thing got ready to Receive them, all the Fleet being Lain too; two of them came considerably first, which we could plainly see to be Frigates; however when the Head most came within about half a league, the officers discovered one of them to be our frigate, and immediately the captain ordered the guns to be taken in and lashed as usual, the which I was sorry for as I should have liked to have seen something of the kind.*

Some time later, the first iceberg loomed startlingly white and smooth in the distance, a welcome sight after eight weeks of the relentless expanse of ocean. Gannets and a great auk became tangled in the rigging. The crew baited hooks with seabirds' entrails and dropped fishing lines into the water. Within minutes dozens of cod were hauled onto the deck. The ship's cook and his helpers deftly sliced off the heads and eviscerated the fish before throwing them into the hold to be salted.

The craggy coast of Newfoundland rose up suddenly from a mantle of fog. The scout ensconced in the foremast's rigging excitedly announced the sighting, and everyone crowded to the foredecks. Cheers erupted on board each ship, all the way to the battered old merchant vessel deserted by her passengers. A chorus of joyful "hurrahs" resounded across the water, from every bow to every stern, and each starboard to port.

"Being eighteen and on one's own in 1782 was both daunting and enviable. While the cycle of wars and social unrest continued in Europe, North America offered a new beginning, free from the shackles of tradition."

Chapter Two

The Log Brewery

JOHN MOLSON was awed by his first sight of the St. Lawrence River. He had never imagined an estuary could be this vast. An older sailor–whom John thought to be about his uncle Robinson's age–gestured past the *Preston's* salt-encrusted figurehead. The wind had died down.

"There's Anticosti Island. Keep watch, we'll pass so close you'll be able to chuck a biscuit on it."

Black specks shifting on the coastal rocks slowly turned into a colony of seals. "They say the Indians tame them. They teach them to follow like dogs." To the young immigrant the St. Lawrence River was a fantastic world. Finback and minke whales gathered around the fleet, much to the delight of the newcomers. Belugas appeared like marine phantoms, and harbour porpoises wove in and out between the ships.

Following the *Victory*, the *H.M.S. Preston* sailed close to the south shore of the river, toward the island of Bic. Nearer the shore, Molson gazed at coniferous trees of an astonishing size. The ships anchored near the island for the night. As the passengers fell asleep, an occasional "Hallooo!" punctuated the silence; two syllables of welcome lifting in an unfamiliar accent from canoes of Montagnais Indians gliding invisibly past.

Next morning the fleet took a local pilot on board to guide them past the shoals and sandbars upriver. The rhythmic singing of voyageurs heading to the trading post at Tadoussac echoed across the water. As the ship drew near the Ile d'Orléans, John could see swathes of terrain that had been cleared of timber. He began to notice the long, narrow strip farms and the low stone walls dividing fields and pastureland. John recognized by their colour which fields were sown with oats, flax, clover or barley. But the barley here–"barley big," he called it–was a far coarser form of barley than that grown in Lincolnshire.

Whitewashed farmhouses and their timbered, thatched outbuildings dotted the river's edge. Farther inland, the tin-covered spires of stone churches reflected the afternoon sunlight. The river gradually narrowed until even the white crosses that marked the coastal toll road could be seen from the ship.

Three days after picking up their pilot, the *Preston* and the rest of the fleet docked at Quebec. The city was a welcome, dramatic sight. At the foot of the rock escarpment, streets ran parallel and perpendicular. Stone houses with three and four storeys and steeply pitched roofs were built side by side. Blending majestically into the edge of the escarpment were the stone walls enclosing the fortress. Crowds gathered along the wharf and shoreline to be among the first to see and greet the new arrivals. Formerly indolent sailors sprang to, impatient to squander their wages.

John and the Gibbinses left the *Preston* with little regret. They laughed at each other as they stumbled to regain their "land legs." They asked for directions to an inn and were pointed past the cramped quarters of port labourers and artisans, past the cluster of nautical outfitters' shops. Wood frame homes with brightly coloured shutters seemed to light up rue St. Pierre, which gave way to an equally colourful merchant neighbourhood spanning Place Royale, with its larger and more elaborate structures. They stopped in at Le Chien d'Or and were recommended lodgings at the Neptune Inn. After eight weeks at sea, the expectation of a clean bed, some fresh meat and varied meals raised their spirits and renewed their optimism.

John and his companions slept fitfully that first night on land, no longer rocked to sleep amid the creaking of the wooden ship. They had one day to explore the maze of narrow roads, see the naval construction yard, walk along rue Sous-le-Fort and marvel at the cliffside. Their belongings from the merchant ship had been returned to them, and the following morning they boarded a schooner bound for Montreal.

Being eighteen and on one's own in 1782 was both daunting and enviable. While the cycle of wars and social unrest continued in Europe, North America offered a new beginning, free from the shackles of tradition. The Revolutionary War over, Britain offered incentives to immigrants who wished to invest in Quebec. Many had already come and foundered, worn down by the hard and fickle new land. Nor would force of character not be enough to secure a future here; luck, and the ability to speculate, would be equally important.

About six thousand people lived within and without Montreal's walls, making it smaller than Quebec City. John and the Gibbinses rented a house in the St. Mary's suburbs; soon James and his son found employment with the butcher Pierre Monarque. It was steady work, preparing fresh, cured and pickled meat. Ships always needed provisions to return to England, fur barons ate mightily at their celebratory dinners, and the garrison troops boasted hearty appetites.

Every day the cannon on Montreal's Citadel Hill was fired at dawn and noon. Summer market days were noisy and colourful. Pedlars came to sell their wares and farmers their produce, and the townspeople milled about in their finest clothes. English women sported huge hats and wore their best dresses over hoops and frilled petticoats. The colourful homespun clothing worn by many French *habitants* contrasted with the black robes of the Jesuit, Recollet and Sulpician priests. Some French women had adopted shawls, moccasins, beaded caps and other Indian garments. Scotsmen and Englishmen would occasionally be seen in *sabots*, the wooden shoes favoured by the *habitants*. On some days, bells seemed to toll incessantly. They were rung to summon worshippers to masses and mourners to funerals, for weddings and to announce the arrival of ships. All the bells ringing out together signalled a fire, when each man's duty was to bring two leather buckets and form chains from the fire to the river. On days when it didn't rain, the stench of urine and fecal and rotting matter was strong enough in the streets to cause stomachs to heave. Ladies as well as gentlemen carried snuffboxes or vinaigrettes with them, filled with aromatics to help them maintain equilibrium.

Privies led to underground stone drains that also collected the runoff from rain, yet the drains were inadequate to prevent floods, which rendered streets impassable for days. Rooting pigs and livestock fought over scraps thrown from the houses, and mud was everywhere. Because the St. Mary's suburbs sprawled east of the walled town, John missed the worst of it. Still, public sanitary conditions did not differ much from those in market towns at home. Some things were the same everywhere, it seemed. But there was definitely something that attracted him. It was more than the land itself, the underdeveloped strip farms along the river, or the mountain and its orchard-covered slopes that rose behind the town. John never tired of looking at the enigmatic St. Lawrence, which, while absorbing the moods of weather, light and wind, seemed to take on a new shade of turquoise every day.

On October 7, 1782, John wrote his first letter home:

> *To Samuel Elsdale, Spalding, in Lincolnshire*
>
> *Hon'd Grandfather,*
> *I remained verry happy till we arrived at Quebec which was on the 26th of June and the day following I went on shore, and after I had remained at Quebec a little time I went in a schoner to Montreal which is about 200 miles further up, where with the Blessing of God I purpose staying a winter; hoping at the same time you will not be displeased with me for so doing. The sea has fully answered my expectations for I am in as good health as ever I was in my life–I have made bold to draw for my Year's allowance of '82 as it will not arrive till about Christmas, and as the bankers in London would not give me credit at no where but Lisbon, therefore the merchants there will not give me any money till they see the draft is accepted which will not be till July or August 1783.*

The young man had hoped that being an ocean away from Samuel Elsdale would make financial transfers from his estate more businesslike and straightforward than they had been. Although he still wasn't willing to compromise his own convictions to appease his grandfather, he respected the old man.

In a letter written to his uncle Robinson on the same day, John's tone was much more relaxed and candid:

> *Dear Sir,*
> *I am come to a Resolution to settle in America therefore shall lose no time in beginning to do something for myself. Here is Land as good as any you have for little or nothing, and the prices of the Produce I shall send you in my next, which will be at the return of the vessel here present ... One reason for my not returning to England is my Grandfather always complains of scarcity of money, that I do not consider myself a proper person to settle with him–tho' do not consider you a proper person neither in that particular–but if anything goes contrary to your wishes you may have it in your power to intercede on my behalf; which I make no doubt but you will, as you always have done–hope you'll not find me ungrateful–James and we are all well. Mr Pell has treated me exceedingly civilly during my absence from you, but I hope I shall [have] it in my Power to make him amends hereafter ... The summer has not been particularly Hot nor disagreeable, tho' I am told it has been the coolest for some years past, and as for the winters do not dread at all as they have such Conveniences to keep a Person warm.*

Coming to North America was considered by many to be forsaking all pleasures of fine society, fashion and modern conveniences. Indeed, John was amazed to discover that farmers seemed unaware of agricultural practices now common in England. The habitants didn't rotate their crops, he noticed, and most didn't make cheese or butter. East of the suburbs, they dumped all their manure by cartloads into the river. Yet the rusticity of his new surroundings appealed to John.

Fall passed into winter. On the surface, there seemed in Montreal to be little enmity between the French and the English who shared a displeasure for the out-of-touch British-appointed bureaucracy. The Scots and French joked with each other that they had the same "stepmother country," or *"paye de belle mère."* Public meetings attracting a cross-section of inhabitants were common. Yet beyond *la politesse*, beneath the gestures of courtesy shown among Montreal's French- and English-speaking citizens, there lay an uneasy imbalance. Political, linguistic and religious differences were deepened by disparities in rank and class. The Scots in town were a tiny minority, yet they dominated the fur trade and most other business transactions, while the British, another minority, dominated the garrison and the legislative bodies. Extremes of poverty and wealth were evident. Just inside the Recollet Gate in the old fortification wall, some inhabitants were dying of starvation and disease while others were becoming rich beyond their expectations.

English servants, John reported, could be hired for six to eight dollars per month. "The Canadians come a great deal lower," he added, "but then they are poor creatures, and must have their smoking hours from morn till almost night, boys not excepted."

Molson confided only to his uncle Robinson that he had become a partner of Thomas Lloyd, an earlier emigrant from Whaplode, Lincolnshire. Lloyd, whose father had been headmaster for a time at young Molson's grammar school, had emigrated to Montreal after his wife died in childbirth. He was building a brewery, "a malting new to the ground" in the St. Mary's suburbs, at the foot of the "current" (rapids) for which the suburb was named. Through years of observation and experience in brewing beer in Lincolnshire, Molson was aware of how much could go wrong. As John explained to Robinson, he planned to wait and see if the brewery showed any promise in its first season before committing himself further.

A vast tract near today's Canada–U.S. border at Missisquoi Bay, the westerly bay of Lake Champlain (then considered part of British North America), had been subdivided by Henry Caldwell. Originally secured by a grant from the French king to a nobleman in 1740, the land had been sold twice since. Having heard about this "fine and rich" property, Molson, Lloyd and the Gibbinses rode south to see it for themselves. For only four guineas, John secured four hundred acres on a peninsula jutting into beautiful Lake Champlain. The contract required him to live there within a year and a day to begin cultivating it.

John wrote to his uncle Robinson:

> *I intend going into the United States in the spring and if there is a probability of doing better for myself shall settle there, if not shall return [to Canada] and begin to clear and cultivate the land I have already purchased … Should be glad if you would send me Word what my Grandfather thinks of my getting to America … I do not intend coming over to England to settle my Affairs, but shall give Mr. Ashley [the Molsons' solicitor in Spalding, Lincolnshire] and you my Power of Attorney. Have drawn on Mssrs. Gosling [bankers and dealers in bills of exchange] for 80 more, thinking my Grandfather cannot be against it as being little enough to serve me till my Affairs is settled; Hope therefore you will make your Interest in my Favour. Have wrote to my Grandfather and Mr. Ashley … the same Purpose.*

By the end of November all the ships had departed and work had come to an end. The inhabitants finished cutting and piling their wood, salting and smoking their meat, and storing their turnips and cabbages in cellars. The air smelled clearer, sweeter. As soon as the river froze all the way across, "roads" were marked by propping fir trees into banks of snow, and carriole races followed soon after. Officers and privates at the garrison performed amateur plays and concerts in assembly halls, and British soldiers staged plays by Shakespeare (in English) and Molière (in French.)

Most houses had several wood stoves that had chimneys but no dampers; the stoves had to be stoked constantly. It astonished John that people kept their houses so hot inside that they stripped down to their shirts. Furs were laid on the floors to help keep out the cold. Still, the fire in the iron stoves never lasted the whole night, and water standing in jugs froze before morning.

John worked with Lloyd at the little log brewery for most of the winter. In January 1783 they hired brewmaster John Wait. Unfortunately, no records of the early Lloyd-Molson maltings have been preserved. Neither Molson nor Lloyd was a novice to the brewing process, but here they found many unfamiliar variables, including the lack of good barley. It is likely that in their earliest experiments they used "barley big," and even oats.

In spring the transformation of the river was a remarkable sight. Within three weeks, the picture of horses, carriages and men travelling on the ice changed into a beautiful flowing river with ships in full sail and brightly painted canoes. John tasted his first maple syrup. Although he had continued to write letters home, when the first spring packets arrived they had not contained a reply from his grandfather.

John waited until July to write another polite letter to Samuel Elsdale. Again he asked for his annual allowance of £80 to be advanced to him, indicating in detail those living expenses and purchases for which the money was needed. He wrote to three more people in the villages of Moulton and Spalding to ask if they would intercede on his behalf. "I am convinced it will be money saved in the end," he rationalized, "and not injuring my fortune at present." But Samuel Elsdale was not to be persuaded that John knew what he was doing.

May 3, 1784

Lloyd and Molson's apprentice, sixteen-year-old Christopher Cook, is paid £4 sterling per month. Much is expected of him, and his employers –especially Molson–are stingy. John is only four years older than Cook, but the apprentice approaches his master with the deference appropriate to his position.

"It's the letter carrier, Mr. Molson. He says he has two letters for you, yet there is a farthing owing him from the last ... he would be obliged–"

"Langhorn, is it?"

"Sir?"

"Langhorn, the letter carrier. I owe him no such thing. Give him this for the present one." Molson hands Cook a penny. The lad hesitates.

"If you please, Sir ... There are two letters."

John unties his cloth trouser bag, reaches into it to finger another penny, and passes them both, pressed between his thumb and forefinger, into Cook's anxious hands.

A moment later the apprentice is back, holding two black-edged envelopes. "Mr. Langhorn says that upon want of a farthing he will not bring you any more letters."

"Then tell him to bring me no more letters," John responds.

Cook disappears again, and Molson looks down at the letters. Both the ink and the seal of the first are black. The handwriting is that of John's teenaged sister, Martha. John's hands tremble as he turns it over:

> *To John Molson, Montreal*
> *Surfleet November 24 1783*
>
> *Dear Brother,*
> *Before we rec'd your last letter we lost the best and truest friend we ever had. My Uncle Robinson Elsdale, died the 15 of October and left my Aunt and two sweet little boys as ever was seen, Sammy and Robinson. My poor Uncle lay'd ill about a month of Nervous Fever, was exceedingly sensible of his death, and took a very affecting leave of us all, and sent you his Blessing and a little of his advice. He thought your Affairs could not be settled without you, and I hope the intreaties of your Sisters & Brothers will have some weight. We beg you will come and see both yours and ours Affairs settled as we have no Friend on earth but you. Mr. Horton is dead and left no will poor Mrs. Horton is very much distressed. Mr. Muse is dead, Mr. Grundy is dead; and Mr. Tompson has got all his fortune. I hope you will excuse all mistakes when you now it comes from your*
> *Afft and Loving Sister,*
>
> *Martha Molson*

A letter from Martha's younger sister, Mary, is in the same post:

> *O My Dear Brother, I am sorry I cannot write of any thing that will Entertain you … of friends, I am unhappy to say we have very few left … Mrs. Boulton is dead …*

On learning of his uncle Robinson's death, John was torn between his deeply felt obligation to his sisters and his new life in North America. His disaffection is evident from a diary entry:

> *The solicitations of Brothers & Sisters who are so dear to me is sufficient inducement to bring me over to the Eastern side of the Atlantic (this at the greatest inconvenience) to see our affairs settled: But am sorry that Martha cannot find one friend in the world besides a Brother who is at a distance of 3000 miles.*

Eventually John penned the following to his sisters:

> *The inscriptions intimated from whose kind hands your letters came, but the Seals denoted something that made me dread the opening of them which on inspection found to my inexpressible Sorrow we have lost our once lov'd and for ever esteemed and best of Friends, our Uncle Robinson Elsdale ... [whom] may the Almighty take into his never ending Regions of Bliss.*
>
> *My Uncle's Blessings give me infinite Satisfaction but what a moving and affecting scene must it have been to see a loving Husband and father take his leave in this world of that Amiable Woman his wife ... the little boys ... the very thoughts of it make my heart run over at my eyes like a child that has received Correction. The subject is too melancholy to treat of it more largely ...*

Although the first season's maltings at the brewery were well received, Thomas Lloyd became discouraged. Not only had the business's start-up expenses exceeded its profit, but the partners had not even been able to pay their brewmaster, John Wait, his last wages due. Lloyd found the financial burden difficult. When he broached the subject to Molson, his underage (and therefore unofficial) partner perceived a chance to acquire the brewery at nominal cost.

Molson made Lloyd an offer; Lloyd accepted. The older man would leave Montreal in the spring to begin tilling John's property at Lake Champlain, thus fulfilling the terms of Caldwell's contract. All profits cleared by the farm would be Lloyd's. Molson would assume total responsibility for the brewery.

In a carefully planned series of actions in which Molson and Lloyd enlisted the sheriff's cooperation, Lloyd declared himself legally insolvent, and the brewery was put up for auction. Yet no public notice was given of the auction, held in December 1784, and the sheriff duly observed that no bidders attended. After John had passed his twenty-first birthday a few days later, a second auction was declared. Again no public notice was given; this time, Molson was the sole bidder. Thus, on a bright afternoon in January 1785, the little log brewery at St.

Mary's Current–upon the assumption of its £100 mortgage–became John Molson's.

John returned to England in June 1785. He was hoping he would be back in Montreal by the end of the shipping season in November, although the trip itself would be eight weeks each way. Taking all precautions, John visited a notary to have his first will drawn up, in which he bequeathed his land at Caldwell's Manor to Thomas Lloyd, and his little brewery to "James Pell." Gibbins was entrusted with the key to the padlocked premises. Molson sailed from New York on board the *Triumph,* not knowing he would be away from his new country for over a year.

Molson was anxious to explain that his intentions were reasonable and serious. The little brewery had the potential of becoming a sound business if only he could invest some

Chapter Three

Forty Bushels of Barley

John had hoped to return to Canada by the autumn of 1785, but financial and legal matters in Lincolnshire did not progress as quickly as expected. England felt both familiar and unfamiliar; he felt welcome and unwelcome. The friction that existed between John and his grandfather had worsened. When John indicated that he wanted to liquidate the estate he'd inherited on his twenty-first birthday, Samuel Elsdale, who at this point was living in Snake Hall with John's siblings, steadfastly avoided meeting with him.

John stayed in Surfleet during the summer and into the fall, with Gibbins's sister Ann (Robinson's widow), called Nancy by those closest to her. Only two years apart in age, John and Nancy appreciated each other's company. On Tuesdays, which were market days, they would ride into Spalding, taking the long way not only to avoid the tolls but to keep off the London Road, where the privies "were in a very bad state," the reeking bone yards, pigsties and cesspools drained into the river, and "an upper stratum of manure" prevailed.

John and Nancy occasionally paid their respects to Reverend John Dinham, who "had the living on Whaplode Drove." They bought bread from the baker in Spalding, William Molson, and visited John's uncle Thomas Molson, a grazier. Some days Morris dancers would give colourful displays in the courtyard of the Crown Inn. Attached to the riverside's Mermaid Inn were the Surfleet Maltings, where beer was brewed from barley that was brought directly to the bridge. Visitors were invited to sample the brews by imbibing from long glass tubes inserted into the barrels.

Every day the mail coach, called "Old Perseverance," arrived in Spalding and drew up to an assembled crowd outside the White Hart Hotel for letters and news from London. On Sundays, John and Nancy and her two young sons would attend either St. Nicholas and All Saints Church, in Surfleet, or nearby Moulton Chapel.

Living in Nancy's informal and affectionate household appealed to John. The servant was sympathetic, the children were an amusing distraction, and their mother was a faithful ally and confidante. They had merry times together as well as melancholy ones, for both John and Nancy had loved Robinson with all the devotion accorded to heroes. John wrote letters late at night after everyone else had gone to bed. One night, writing to Gibbins, he confessed that he'd wept:

> *Nancy and me being by ourselves this evening, our conversation fell upon the manner of my Uncle's taking leave of his friends and his particular desire to see us before his death drew tears from the Worthy Little Woman's eyes to a verry great degree, it caused some involuntary Tears to flow from mine tho' ashamed of such a weakness could not suppress 'em.*

Christmas passed and the new year came, but John made no headway with his grandfather. The Molsons' lawyer, Philip Ashley, didn't offer him much encouragement. Ashley had been loyal to Samuel Elsdale for years and knew well that the old man was resisting because he wanted his grandson to mortgage, not sell, Snake Hall. Without an income, Molson could not afford to hire his own solicitor to seek independent advice.

Nancy sympathized with John in his conflict with his grandfather. After all, Samuel Elsdale, her father-in-law, had never approved of her. In 1779, when Robinson had retired from privateering at thirty-five to marry Nancy, who was eighteen, almost all his family had regarded her with suspicion. John's sisters, Mary and Martha, were open in their disapproval of Nancy's youth and beauty–which they equated with promiscuity–and her ingenuousness. Later Martha's husband, John Rayment, was known to have remarked gravely, "I have far too much cause to say, she is a bad woman."

In January 1786, a letter from Gibbins brought news to John of the previous summer in Montreal. Gibbins related that other merchants in town were facing setbacks, and that some were even closing their businesses. As for himself, he had decided to take up residence with a widow named Mrs. Jacobs, and James Junior had moved into other premises. At the end of the letter, James offhandedly added, "The brewhouse has been broke into by a set of Dutchmen who stole the mill and haircloth [a stiff cloth woven of hair, used for filtering beer] but three of them have been hanged lately, and several more in Prison … "

This news at first added to John's discouragement, but then necessitated a new kind of resolve. In his reply to Gibbins he described more of the emotional turmoil he was going through at home:

> *I am now come to a full Resolution of Conquering that foolish and absurd Timidity & Bashfullness which (tho' ashamed to owe) in great measure prevents me [from] communicating my nonsense to a friend. All is vanity and vexation of spirit–have … since my arrival in England … not made myself popular by entering into every fool's company to be teased with their nonsense. Now do I miss that worthy man our friend, having nobody to advise me in my future prospects and intentions nobody that I can pour my heart to as a Friend. I have this reflection however left me: there are 2 fine little boys and his once much beloved & affectionate wife, on whom every encomium my pen can bestow would fall infinitely short of her Merits & Qualifications. However, not to task my friend any longer with my Nonsense …*

By February 1786 Molson had succeeded in his persistent attempts to arrange a three-way meeting with his grandfather and Philip Ashley. He was anxious to explain to both that his intentions were reasonable and serious. The little brewery had the potential of becoming a sound business if only he could invest some capital into expanding its operation.

John had made arrangements with his friend Jack Baxter to spend the rest of the winter in a "Coffee House lodging" in London. Neighbours near Surfleet were apparently beginning to gossip about an impending "match" between John and Nancy, for he had been living in the young widow's household for five months. London offered other attractions than protecting Nancy from the rumours. In the city, Molson spent time at Whitbread's Brewery to study its operation and inspect the newest equipment available.

London had many diversions to offer bachelors. In addition to plays at the Theatre Royal on Drury Lane, there were musical concerts at which the patrons dressed in all their finest fashions. Street performers set up their acts near roasted-chestnut vendors. John was much taken with London's cobbled streets, its crowds and its squalour.

In coffeehouses and on the streets talk was about the safety of hot-air balloons. A mime pretended to get carried off by one. Laughter erupted over the satirical antics of Punch and Judy in every puppet booth, and Punch's shrill, familiar voice rose over the laughing crowds while a collector passed a hat around. At Covent Garden the young men drank to the health of the royal family, and to the deliverance into safety of those faraway British loyalists in the Thirteen Colonies.

February 19, 1786

John and Jack weave their way along Charing Cross Road through the scattered people, tapping the cobblestones with the tips of their umbrellas.

"Why return to the Americas?" Jack is asking. "Everything you need is here."

Jack follows him over a mosaic threshold into a dimly lit bookshop. Molson picks up a book, *Theoretic Hints on an Improved Practice in Brewing,* by the British brewer John Richardson. He has heard about this man and his controversial new "scientific" methods of brewing.

"I told you. Land can be got for little or nothing."

I hear the laws are repugnant to an Englishman. The French have advantages over the English, is it not so?"

Molson laughs. "Aye. When they are branded for their crimes they must thrice repeat 'Vive le Roi' before the brand is removed, whereas the English are made to say 'God Save the King,' which takes far longer to say."

Jack Baxter frowns. "I, for one, am grateful to be an Englishman."

"God save the King," replies John, turning to raise an imaginary pint.

Baxter silently hands him Lord Chesterfield's *Letters to His Son,* a recently published compendium of advice and courtly manners. Molson purchases both books, and later packs them carefully with his belongings.

The news Molson had been waiting for came in March 1786. Philip Ashley had brokered an agreement that allowed Samuel Elsdale to continue living in Snake Hall while a mortgage was arranged. Ashley in turn had procured £300 in cash for Elsdale, and–to complete the mortgage–a commitment of five hundred more to follow. Optimistic, John ordered forty bushels of the finest English barley from Lincolnshire and booked a passage for his trip home to Montreal.

Thinking of his sisters, John wrote:

March 23, 1786
Guildhall Coffee House, London

Dear Martha and Mary,
As the separation of us once more is unavoidable at present, therefore hope you arm yourselves with all the fortitude in your power the fewness of your Friends who would take any interesting part in your affairs demand the greatest attention to be paid to those few existing … Mr. J. Ashley would do almost any service that may lie in his power. Mr. P. Ashley, Spalding, may also be very serviceable … but there is another Friend [he is referring to Nancy] I have not mentioned yet who perhaps may be the best Friend you have, her being the choice of one who was the greatest Friend we ever had & who was as good a judge of human heart as most men that exist & when you consider that opinion which at first rather sprung from external appearance … you need not have a dread of entering into the most open & generous friendship with the Worthiest of Women … which of all others is most likely to find the true Jewel of the Soul …

While John was away, news had reached Montreal that young Alexander Mackenzie had turned back from his quest for the Pacific, having encountered the remote Arctic Sea instead. Throughout the town and its suburbs French and English had mingled opinions: some said they'd known all along that reaching the Pacific by land couldn't be done; some said it was a victory anyway. Would he claim the reward? Would he try again? Was anyone ever meant to know if North America joined the Indian continent?

Closer to home, growing numbers of British Loyalists from the Thirteen Colonies were being transferred across the border under a flag of truce. Montrealers read that the American Patriots had compiled "black lists" and had enacted laws that made "the crime of adhering to Great Britain" punishable by flogging, imprisonment and even death. Stories of ill-treatment endured by Loyalists were interspersed with rumours of invasion. Everywhere, the promise of uncertainty was as familiar as the uncertainty of promise.

"I have hired a maid servant 4 dollars a month." Molson wrote in a letter a few days later. He considered, then decided against, elaborating about Mrs. Vaughan.

Chapter Four

Sarah's Story

April 29, 1786

ALONG THE SHORES of the St. Lawrence the last of the encrusted ice breaks free with a final thundering shudder and heads swiftly east in the river's turbulent wake.

The first spring fleet is always an incredible sight. Crowds come running to the landing place just below Sir John Johnson's grand house to greet the arrivals, see the new fashions from Europe, or sort through the mail. The landing process can take hours or even days, unless a strong northeast wind is blowing. Vessels often have to be pulled past St. Mary's Current by teams of oxen. Smaller craft are dispatched to ferry the passengers, trunks and packages.

Tradesmen, merchants, soldiers, fur traders, young families, ministers and travelling musicians are disembarking in Montreal. Some are here for a short time to work or do business, but most are arriving with the intention to settle. They lumber ashore, laden with their bulky possessions. Some stand on the muddy bank, bewildered.

Waiting among the hubbub and excited clamour at the river's edge is a tall, determined-looking woman in a cropped bonnet and a flowing gown of black muslin. She anxiously watches all those who are coming ashore. Sarah Vaughan is looking for work, but she has never before been employed. The fifth of seven children born to Northumberland gentleman-scholar Thomas Vaughan, Sarah knows how to order a household, how to sew, how to sing, how to converse modestly in drawing rooms. She thinks this is the roughest and most unrefined place she has ever seen.

Sarah was born in Harnham Moor, a hamlet "situated on a wooded eminence" near Morpeth, in Northumberland. Untouched by time for many hundreds of years, her home overlooked the site of an ancient Roman camp where pagan rituals were conducted regularly. Sarah might have watched midsummer's eve bonfires from her bedroom window in Harnham Hall, the sixteenth-century mansion-house in which she and her sisters and her brother were raised. Her ancestors rest near the gardens of Harnham Hall, in a sepulchre carved out of a high rock wall.

Sarah is the niece of the Earl of Lisburne and is a cousin, through her mother's family (the Aynsleys), to the Duke of Atholl. Among her ancestors she can name two authors, a poet and a judge. Her brother, Shaftoe Vaughan, is a successful London barrister. Sarah, however, is illiterate, because of the ideas of her Cambridge- and Oxford-educated father who, like many men of his class, deplored the idea of giving classical educations to their daughters.

In July 1775 Sarah had married David Tetchley at the Morpeth Parish. She emigrated with her husband to the United States, but for reasons unknown to us, she was estranged from him by 1785. Sarah fled to Montreal that summer, joining a small band of "friends of the government" travelling along the Richelieu River in a convoy of assorted craft. One state after another had passed laws stripping British Loyalists of their land and possessions and restricting their rights to work. Sarah, who didn't want to be found or followed by her husband, had joined her weary neighbours and come as far as Montreal, accepting temporary accommodations that had been set up for Loyalists at the barracks.

The British government had offered the refugees farm tools, seeds, livestock and land in Canada. Lots in the Eastern Townships were made available to them. Every head of a family was offered 100 acres; 50 to each single man. Being a married woman without a husband, Sarah had no legal right to file a claim.

Sarah confided in the former chaplain of the 84th Regiment (Royal

Highland Emigrants), one of the loyalists staying at the barracks. Never had she felt more alone or more lost, she told John Bethune. On this day in April, she is grateful he has escorted her here to the landing place, to ask returning Englishmen if they are in need of domestic help. Zealous in his faith and chivalrous in his manner, Bethune thinks a tolerable situation for her would be placement with a gentleman or a British family.

Now, Sarah watches a purposeful young man climb out of the bateau and gesture for a cart. He seems preoccupied, intent on balancing the boat while he prepares to unload some large bushels. His trousers and black coattails swish in the water. A horse, harnessed to a shallow two-wheeled cart, steps into the lapping waves. It is led on a tether by a man in homespun druggets, who grins when he recognizes Molson. As the men speak, John Bethune and Sarah step toward them. Molson turns around.

"Begging your pardon, sir, I am Reverend John Bethune. I believe we may be acquainted."

Molson extends his hand. "John Molson. I allow you do look familiar, sir."

"Permit me to introduce you to Mrs. Vaughan. The lady is looking for work. Have you need of a domestic servant or a housemaid?"

John sees a woman slightly taller than himself, plainly dressed, with a wide mouth turned down at the corners. Her gloveless hands are as pale as her face. A bonnet is tied under her pointed chin, a cascade of dark hair tucked within. John regards her for a moment, hesitates, then asks her some brief questions. Who is her family? How did she come to be here? What kind of work was she accustomed to? He makes note of her north country accent.

"I shall be in need of a housekeeper," he grudgingly acknowledges. "However, I can but pay you little."

Sarah steps toward the cart, lowering her head to hide a relieved smile, and reaches for a piece of rope to help lash the bushels to the boards.

"I have hired a maid servant 4 dollars a month," Molson wrote in a letter to Jack Baxter in London, a few days later. He considered, then decided against, elaborating about Mrs. Vaughan in this letter. He wanted his friend to appreciate the great bargain he had made, for Sarah had agreed to accept half the average wage for English servants in Montreal. "Canada, since the Peace, fills with people who have taken up arms in His Majesty's favour," John wrote. "Having forfeited their properties in the United States, they are waiting with impatience the provision the Govt. is making for them."

John and Sarah were never idle. John rented a log house, which was one of three close to the brewery but far outside town, furnished simply but adequately for his needs. A stone fire pit served as a cooking hearth, and next to it was a ladder that led to a loft where they stored their household grains and supplies. A saucepan, dripping pan and ladle were hung on pothooks.

Sarah settled into her role. Friday was washing day; on hot days she gathered the cool wrung-out shirts and linens and held them against her forehead before pegging them to the line. She dried chunks of beef and hung them with strings of apples on poles suspended from the ceiling.

Most townspeople used either public wells or the river for their water supply, while others purchased it from pedlars who came by with water carts. Molson had three-and-a-half-foot-diameter wooden conduits installed through which he could draw river water for the brewery, pumping it in by turning a crank shaft. When she wanted water for boiling meat or vegetables, Sarah would enter the brewery, fill two leather buckets and walk very slowly across the courtyard back to the house, careful not to let much spill. She never had to make more than two trips a day. Bathing was a once-a-week activity in summer, a once-a-fortnight event in winter. Water was thought to penetrate the pores and therefore to be dangerous to the health. Men and women sprinkled on scents or perfumes to mask unpleasant odours.

Summer, 1786

Happy is not a word Sarah uses, though surely she feels needed and secure; she has a place in a household, and her employer, though often distracted, is never unkind. In fact, a certain warmth seems to develop between them; an easy affection born of mutual respect grows as they work side by side. She finds herself at times helping in the brewery, scouring the equipment, lining up the mash oars, rakes and grain shovels, checking the hoses, arranging the weigh scales. Molson has discovered that Sarah is skilled as a brewster. She knows what she is doing, having often brewed beer at Harnham Hall. Now and then John enters her name in his wage book at the brewery, and sometimes in his accounts receivable.

Sarah looks forward more and more to John's coming home at night, when he sniffs the air appreciatively and declares that he feels like a king to be served her tasty, savoury puddings. Tolerant, pragmatic and patient, Sarah has simple needs. She doesn't complain or ask for very much, is deferential to John, is the kind of woman who rolls her sleeves up and doesn't have time to ponder things or gaze out the window. Her demeanour has none of the vapid coquettishness that John has encountered in younger English ladies. Her temperament suits his perfectly.

Molson is a difficult man to get to know. He never explains his inner convictions to anyone, believing actions should stand for themselves. He does not ask Sarah about her past. He keeps his emotions concealed, cultivating reserve and dignity. He does not permit anyone to see weakness in him. He is easily amused, but he makes no time for amusements. He never complains. At first he is disarmingly shy, but when Sarah can coax him into talking about brewing, his expression grows more animated and his answers more sure. Sarah listens. She senses he is no ordinary man. John Molson can see the future, and they both know he is destined for great things.

Sarah Vaughan is *l'éminence grise* in Molson's story. She hovers there, for she is modest, and lives her life as if knowing she will leave only traces of her own passing. Is she bashful, or merely amused? We can imagine her becoming wistful, as an older woman, recalling the day she followed John down to the cellar in the middle of an afternoon. There, her eyes adjusting to the sudden darkness, she caught him looking at her. She drew her shawl a little tighter about her shoulders a moment before he kissed her.

On July 28, 1786, John bought his first eight bushels of barley from a local farmer–a M. Barsalou–to augment the forty bushels he'd brought with him from England. It was a simple but significant purchase. That evening, by candlelight at the table, he opened his notebook and dipped his pen in the ink. Sarah watched over his shoulder as John formed a line of hurried–but grandiose–capitals across the page, an isolated burst of triumph:

MY COMMENCEMENT ON THE GRAND STAGE OF THE WORLD

The words reflected John Molson's complete confidence, pride and optimism. He knew that weeks and months of arduous work were about to begin. He also knew he had the ability to achieve his goal.

Brewing was still considered a mysterious and artful practice, although a new age of knowledge was beginning. Brewers like John Richardson were beginning to understand the biochemical reactions taking place at various stages of malting and brewing. Although a brewer's skills could improve with experience, his senses of smell, touch and taste, and his respect for the mysteries themselves made the difference between failure or success with his brew.

Molson knew that the quality of the raw ingredients was critically important. Hard, clean water, as well as good-quality barley, hops and yeast would make for consistently good taste.

It was important to choose the time for his trial malting very carefully, for barley could be germinated properly only in the colder months of the year. On the first of September, he began washing and sorting the grains. He steeped the barley in water for three days, watching carefully for the liquid to take on a characteristic reddish hue. He then had to spread the steeped barley, or malt, on the floor to dry and turn it occasionally to prevent mould. Over the next twenty-five days, he kept turning the malted grain, sometimes up to six times a day. He watched anxiously for changes in the weather, for he knew that a few warm days could destroy his malt.

To grind the malted barley, Molson harnessed a horse upon a treadmill. Rolling pairs of cylinders crushed the grain two or three times. On September 30, he lit the fire under the brewing kettle for his first time. With long-handled wooden ladles he transferred the boiling water into the mash tun, to which he added the ground barley malt, turning the mixture into "wort." The wort had to be manually mashed with wooden "oars." Hotter water was then added and stirred in. John would not have been able to explain how the malt starches converted to sugar, but he knew this step was complete when the liquid was sweet to taste. The wort was filtered down into a reservoir, called the underback, where it rested until the remaining fine particles of grain settled to the bottom. The resulting clear liquor was pumped back up to the brew kettle and once more heated to the boiling point.

At this stage Molson added hops to the liquid to give aroma and flavour, letting the mixture steep for about four hours. He ladled it into troughs so the mixture could flow into a "hop back." Then the liquid was strained, this time through a bed of clean straw, into cooling pans. Here, if the liquid was not cooled quickly enough, it would acidify, meaning that the whole lot might be soured.

Molson knew the wort was ready once the steam had cleared enough for him to see his exhausted reflection on the surface. He had had to work for fourteen consecutive hours to be ready for this moment. Now he released the liquor into fermenting casks. This was the critical point when he added the yeast, and if it fermented–if the wort's sugar content converted into alcohol and carbon dioxide–success was imminent. Molson was gratified when he took a deep breath and smelled the working yeast–a rich, thick fragrance with a hint of bitterness.

The finished brew was transferred to aging casks in the cool cellar, where it settled, naturally clarifying as it matured. Then it would be transferred once again, by spigot, funnel, leather pipes and hose, into the clean wooden kegs from which the beer would be sold.

It was vital to know the right time to keg the ale. The barrels might burst if active fermentation hadn't ceased; on the other hand, if kegged too late, the beer would turn stale and flat. The book that Molson had bought, *Theoretic Hints on An Improved Practice in Brewing*, was one of the first to recommend the use of a saccharometer to determine accurately the gravity of the beer, from which reading he would be able to determine its sugar and alcohol content. John had purchased a saccharometer in London.

Late at night Molson would usually still be at work. The whitewashed walls and ceilings inside the brewery reflected the light cast by the candles' tin reflecting backs. Labouring from 5 a.m. until well after dark left John exhausted. He kept on his apprentice, Christopher Cook, whom he paid £4 a month. Sarah continued to help as well, although before the summer was over her name (and record of any wages paid to her) ceased to appear in the account book.

When Jack Baxter's last letter arrived in early October 1786, Molson and Cook had already begun their second malting. Jack's flamboyant handwriting was unmistakable with its grand loops and swirls. Even after the many weeks the letter had spent in transit, a faint scent of powder still clung to its bleached white pages. Typical of Baxter, the tone was gossipy and imperious:

> *Dear Sir,*
> *... I see you have commenced a Housekeeper. I commend you but get some Old Woman in the House you do not wish to come within a Yard of, or else you will be wrong; I mean till such time as you provide yourself with a Rib ...*
> *I know James Gibbins alias Pell with 2 sons are fixed at Montreal and of course you must think I have a desire to hear of their welfare but you say not a word ... [I]f you write me again pray let me hear of them, or be assured I will send by first post to Montreal a few Hand Bills which shall make their Names Public.*
> *I am wishing you every success –*
> *Your ver hble servt*
> *J. Baxter*
> *London, 9th Sept. 1786*

Whether John found this letter offensive or insulting is a matter of speculation. Regardless, their acquaintance was not kept up after this note. Baxter's name disappeared from Molson's correspondence, and Gibbins's identity remained a secret throughout his life in North America.

Given the diversity of Scots, English and Indians and black slaves who attended, it was a relatively tolerant group of people who would have been unlikely to look upon Molson's domestic situation with much ill judgment.

CHAPTER FIVE

AN HONEST BREW

BEER WAS the favourite beverage of most Englishmen. Well-to-do families in particular recorded an enormous consumption of it. In the early eighteenth century tea was uncommon, and people would not drink water if they could get anything else. Beer was the safest beverage to drink, having been boiled several times. "Small beer" (weak beer) was taken with every meal and between meals by every member of the household. Workers in many professions indulged all day long. Benjamin Franklin described the daily beer-drinking in a London printing-house: "The men took a pint before breakfast, a pint with breakfast, a pint between breakfast and dinner, a pint at dinner, a pint at six, and a pint when work was knocked off."

During the last decades of the eighteenth century, "spirits" were considered the root of social corruption, yet beer remained, "to an Englishman, like mother's milk." The British War Office considered its purchase a necessity, ordering that six pints of small beer be allotted per day to each enlisted man. Porter was freely recommended by doctors to improve one's general health, and spruce beer (made without malt) was even known to help prevent scurvy. Governor Simcoe described in his diary why he promoted the building of a brewery in Upper Canada:

> *... in the hope that use of a wholesome malt liquor might be substituted by the lower classes, in the place of ardent spirits ... [it] would no doubt be a most desirable circumstance, that this substitute could be brought about, as tending to the improvement of morals, by cutting off so fruitful a resource of delirious excess, as the intemperate use of drams.*

In Montreal also, demand for beer was very high. Hard as they worked at the log brewery during their first season (1786–87), Molson, Sarah Vaughan and Christopher Cook were not able to produce more than four hogsheads (54-gallon barrels) of ale each week. Brewing cycles overlapped during the winter months, which meant constant work; altogether, they produced 6,900 gallons that thirty-week season, before warm weather forced production to stop.

At first, Molson was gratified and encouraged. In December he reported: "The speculation is now beginning to show in good ale and table beer ... My beer has the readiest sale." Beer had definite class distinctions (while officers quaffed imported London porters, the enlisted men tended to prefer Bristol and other dark ales), but Molson's beer crossed these lines. "My beer is universally well liked, beyond my most sanguine expectations. Cannot serve half my customers, and they [are] increasing every day."

By now, John and Sarah had begun to present themselves publicly as a couple. They attended church services led by the Reverend Bethune in temporary premises on Nôtre Dame Street. Molson had been raised on the doctrine of the Church of England, and Bethune, although a trained Anglican, was now ministering to Presbyterian Scots. Bethune and the Scots congregation offered the couple a blend of what each found reassuring. Though Molson missed the sepulchral reverence of Moulton All-Saints Church, with its boxed pews and ornate rood screen, and though Sarah missed the stony calm and ageless vista of Morpeth Chapel, they both appreciated the familiar words of the service.

In this congregation sat many of Montreal's most prominent citizens and powerful businessmen, including James McGill, a successful fur trader and member of the Beaver Club; the florid Thomas Busby, hotel-keeper; Joseph Frobisher, the founder of the North West

Company whose imposing "Beaver Hall" looked imperiously over the town; and young Alexander Mackenzie, the explorer.

The merchant Angus Shaw brought his half-Indian daughter to Bethune one Sunday to be baptized. He was not the first to do so. Given the diversity of Scots, English and (though they sat at the back) Indians and black slaves who attended, it was a relatively tolerant and liberal-minded group of people who would have been unlikely to look upon Molson's domestic situation with much ill judgment.

Although English officials, Scottish fur traders and British merchants accounted for only 10 percent of the population in the closing decade of the eighteenth century, they owned nearly half of all non-institutional land within the walls. Almost all trade in Montreal was owned and controlled by them. Sir John Johnson, the Superintendent of Indian Affairs, owned a two-storey stone villa two hundred yards west of the brewery and a stone mansion adjacent to the marketplace and wharf. Traders Isaac Todd and Alexander Henry would become justices of the peace; Joseph Frobisher and Molson's neighbour, John Richardson (no relation to the British brewer), would enter politics. William McGillivray, one of Frobisher's partners in the North West Company, also handled groceries, dry goods and hardware. Simon McTavish, nicknamed "The Marquis," was another partner. Each was attempting to stake pieces of prosperity for himself. Many were Molson's neighbours along St. Mary's Street, and all of them were Molson's customers.

It was soon obvious that not only were Molson's quantities of ale too small to generate much profit, but four hogsheads a week would never be enough to quench the thirst of Montreal. If his brewery was going to be successful, he would need to expand his operation and purchase bigger and better equipment.

By mid-October in his first brewing season, John dispatched a letter to the family solicitor, Philip Ashley, in Lincolnshire to ask about the promised funds. Another letter followed not long after, then another. As winter wore on without word from Ashley, John became more and more exasperated, and the tone of his letters grew sharper:

October 13, 1786

Dear Sir,
Have drawn on Messrs. Gosling for £50 at six weeks after sight. As my future credit in this place entirely depends on my present probity, hope Mr. Ashley will take the earliest opportunity of giving me credit to that amount on Messrs. Gosling ...

October 22, 1786

Dear Sir,
My expectations grow every day more sanguine on this speculation & I presume that it will in a short time prove very lucrative & not without sufficient reason. Money is the only thing I want [lack] for to carry it on with a degree of spirit and respectability which may in some measure deter any other person entering on same scheme ...

December 13, 1786

Dear Sir,
The speculation is beginning to show in good Ale and Table Beer can acquaint my friend that my beer has the readiest sale and orders are by one half more than can execute ... I depend upon it Canada will continue to improve as long as it belongs to the Crown of Great Britain ...

January 18, 1787

Dear Sir,
Have wrote since my leaving Graves End without receiving a Scrip from you, to accuse you of not writing would be more than can justify, but have rec'd letters from England. It's beyond a doubt, might have received from you. As [I] shall most certainly sell out everything in England in three years time send me at least five hundred pounds exclusive of my orders ...

February 7, 1787

Dear Sir,
Have nothing more to impart than have already communicated ... My continual theme is money, and money I must have ...

March 17, 1787

Dear Sir,
Have wrote till I am tired of writing without receiving an answer which can impart no other reason but your not having wrote any. Am confident you must have received my Epistles all or most of them. Every person here has letters regularly every month by New York packet & here I remain like a fool without being able to determine anything as have already informed you cannot half supply my customers. Every body keeps briefing in my ears shall make a fortune here. Had a person proffered to enter £500 in partnership with me & with enlarging my office there is no doubt but shall meet with an opposition. Tis already talked on & the only way to prevent it is to carry the business with spirit …

April 14, 1787

Dear Sir,
Shall be very concise with this Epistle as my prolifity avails nothing your not complying with my request will be my immediate ruin …

A packet service had opened up between New York and Montreal, so letters to and from England no longer had to be delayed by ice on the river. But it wasn't until May that John received the five hundred pounds he had been so impatient for. The draft arrived before he'd finished writing yet another furious letter to Ashley, this time accusing him of being "puerile" and adding (in formal, third-person singular), "Mr. Ashley has neglected giving me a scrip not through any ill design but rather that he does not wish me to become a resident of this country." The letter broke off and resumed with a calm conclusion: "Mr. Ashley's ready compliance with my request has been the means of the ale brewery being brought to perfection in Canada."

With funds now in hand, Molson immediately directed Captain Featonby of the *Everetta* to have a larger, seven-hogshead copper kettle shipped from England. He ordered the building of a stone malt house and had the existing log building converted into a brew house. Construction was completed before the new kettle arrived. Beneath the new malt house he had a cellar dug for storage.

Friday, September 7, 1787

"All this pomp, for Silly Billy." Simon McTavish lifts his walking stick and gestures at the colourful and crowded street scene in front of them.

Since word had reached the Lower Canada that His Royal Highness Prince William was coming for an official visit, advertisements for dancing lessons had begun to appear in the new weekly newspaper, the Montreal *Gazette.* Houses were whitewashed, and extra British flags were raised. Hairdressers arrived from Paris and London. The few milliners and tailors in town were overwhelmed with demand for the latest fashions.

"It's historic," Molson says in defence of the celebration. "First Royal visit to British North America."

McTavish scoffs. "This one's a princely role model, that he is. His favourite sport is wenching! 'Tis said he lives fer cockfights and duels."

"Is it not a pity he'll miss yours," murmurs a deep voice behind the pair. Abner Bagg, Esquire, from Durham County, cannot abide criticism of the British royal family.

The cavalcade leading the convoy is now in sight. Trumpets sound at the front of the procession; soldiers in scarlet and white tunics guard the edges of the route. Twenty-one-year-old Prince William is seated in a barouche pulled by six horses, the grandest outfit this town has ever seen. The party will be met at the Quebec Gate by the governor of Quebec, Lord Dorchester and his staff, clerical dignitaries and judicial officers. The Prince will be escorted to the Château Ramezay for a reception.

As the entourage disappears, the crowds disperse. But that night, as fireworks burst over the river, they're back for more celebrating.

The prince spends a week in Montreal, but most of the time feels so ill that he makes only the barest of appearances at the lavish dinners and formal balls held in his honour. On the last night of his tour, he is able to attend a dinner in his honour sponsored by the Brothers of Canada, of which John Molson is now a member.

Molson collection

John Molson Senior (1763-1836) came to Canada in 1782, and within months had invested in a "little log brewery" east of Montreal. By the time this portrait was painted in 1826, Molson had not only expanded the brewery several times, but also controlled a solid financial empire that included a line of steamships, a luxury hotel, a theatre, a foundry, and income properties in Montreal and Quebec City. At this time he was also a legislative councillor and the president of both the Bank of Montreal and the Montreal General Hospital.

Molson collection

Sarah Inseley Vaughan (1751-1829), born in Northumberland, England, came to Montreal in 1786 and worked for a time as John Molson's housekeeper. She also helped him in the brewery, where her name was recorded in account books as both wage-earner and customer. John and Sarah were married in 1801.

hn Molson Junior (1787-1860) and Mary Anne Molson, first cousins, were married in 1816. By 1837 John olson Junior had become a legislative councillor and the president of Canada's first railway. These portraits, 1830, were painted shortly before Mary Anne left her husband and sons to return home to England. Though e would later be reunited with her sons, she did not return to Canada until the year of her husband's death.

Molson collection

Thomas Molson (1791-1863), c. 1830, was the second (surviving) son of John Molson and Sarah Vaughan. As brilliant and eccentric as his brothers, he was also the most ambitious. This is the earliest known portrait of Thomas.

Molson collection

William Molson (1793-1875), c. 1830, age 36, was the youngest son of John Molson and Sarah Vaughan. He was originally chosen to inherit his father's brewery, but John Senior changed his mind and passed it instead to his grandson, John HR Molson. William would become head of the Molsons Bank.

Molson collection

Molson collection

Above left: Martha Molson Senior (1795-1848), c. 1840, married her cousin Thomas Molson in 1816. Often a fretful mother, she was also a pragmatic, stoical woman. Martha poses here for a Daguerreotype with two of her children, Anna and Markland. Anna would die soon after, of complications following measles.

Above right: Harriet Bousfield Molson (1830-1913), daughter of Thomas and Martha, married Alexander Clerk in 1858. Here the couple poses for a Daguerrotype at the time of their engagement.

Right: Markland Molson (1833-1913), the second surviving son of Thomas and Martha, was born while the family lived in Kingston, Ontario. This photo was taken in 1863, the year his father died. Markland and his brothers (John HR and John Thomas) would rarely see eye to eye in business matters. Ultimately Markland lost most of his fortune to unwise investments, but managed to keep The Pines, his sprawling, turreted summer home in Cacouna, on the St. Lawrence River.

National Archives Canada

Notman Photographic Archives, McCord Museum

Above: This 1867 photograph is the only one known to survive of John Molson III (1820-1907), eldest son of John Molson Junior. Known as John of Belmont Hall, he married his cousin Anne Molson, daughter of his uncle William. Vice-president and then president of Molsons Bank, John Molson III inherited his father's prominent forehead and his grandfather's resolute demeanour.

Top right: Lillias Savage (1839-1866), in a drawing by an unknown artist, c.1865. Lillias, a jeweller's daughter, became the first wife of John Thomas Molson. The couple honeymooned in Europe for six months, during which time Lily kept a diary. She died after giving birth to their only child, Lillias Savage Molson, in 1866.

Bottom right: "Missie Lillias Molson," here at age 3 in 1870, posed in Notman's studio with a stuffed bird. The only child of John Thomas Molson and Lillias Savage (who died in childbirth), she was raised by the Savage family, who called her "Baby." The Savages arranged for this photo to be taken for John Thomas, who was making plans to sail around the world in his private steam-yacht. When John Thomas remarried four years later, his wife, Jennie Baker Butler, welcomed Lillias into their household.

Notman Photographic Archives, McCord Museum

Notman Photographic Archives, McCord Museum

For many years, Sophia Stevenson Molson (1822-1910)–who married wealthy widower Thomas Molson in Port Hope, Ontario, in 1858–was ostracized by members of her husband's family. The couple mingled in titled company and travelled frequently to London, England, where, in 1860, their photographs were taken before they were presented at Windsor Castle.

Molson collection

Encouraged by his young, second wife to pursue a baronetcy, Thomas Molson (1791-1863) wrote cogent letters to members of Queen Victoria's royal court. However, he did not succeed in his petition for a title. Following his death in Montreal in 1863, a substantial estate was divided among his sons and daughters, and a modest income mailed semi-annually to Sophia, who moved back to Ontario but never remarried.

National Archives Canada

Above: John Thomas Molson (1837-1910), youngest son of Thomas and Martha, had a passion for yachting. He had a steam-yacht, *S. Y. Nooya,* designed and built for him in 1869, and he crossed the Atlantic from Liverpool, England, to Montreal in 1870. In the fall of 1871, John Thomas set off to sail the *Nooya* around the world and became the first person to do so in a private steam-yacht.

Top left: Martha Molson Junior (1824-1900), eldest daughter of Thomas and Martha, married William Prosperous Spragge in 1846. When, following Confederation in 1867, Spragge became head of the Indian Affairs Department, the couple and their children moved to Ottawa. This photo was taken by Topley in 1872.

Top right: Raised in Belmont Hall on Sherbrooke Street, Edith Molson (1853-1872) was the youngest child of John Molson III and his wife, Anne. With her brother, Wm. Alexander (1852-1920), preparing to study medicine at McGill, Edith also wanted to further her education. Thanks to her mother's effort on behalf of the Ladies' Educational Association, in 1871 Edith became one of the first women admitted to McGill. The following September Edith died of unrecorded causes. Her family commissioned this posthumous painting in 1874, based upon a Notman photograph taken in early 1872.

National Archives Canada

Molson collection

Notman Photographic Archives, McCord Museum

John Thomas Molson with his daughter Lillias, his second wife Jennie, and others, in sleigh, c. 1879. The family lived on Prince of Wales Terrace before moving to University Avenue in 1884. Their fancy cutter had front-turning steel runners and seats for extra passengers. Furs were provided for warmth. Brass bells were mounted on the horses' belly bands.

Notman Photographic Archives, McCord Museum

Above: Mr. and Mrs. John HR Molson, c. 1895. President of the family brewery and head of Molsons Bank, John HR Molson (1826-1897) was as enterprising and committed a businessman as his grandfather, John Molson Senior, had been. He also believed in living an exemplary life, and dictated words of wisdom to this effect to his next of kin while on his deathbed. He and his wife Louisa (nee Frothingham) were childless, having married after a courtship of nearly thirty years.

Right: Harry Markland Molson (1856-1912), painted by G. Horne Russell, circa 1910. Harry Molson was a generous benefactor in Montreal, and a member of the Forest & Stream Club and the Royal Yacht Club in Dorval. He led an unconventional private life. Before he drowned upon the sinking of the *Titanic* in April 1912, Harry Molson was vice-president of Molsons Bank.

National Archives Canada

Notman Photographic Archives, McCord Museum

The 1878 wedding of Dr. Wm. Alexander Molson (1852-1920) and Esther Shepherd, in Montreal, was commemorated by photographer William Notman in this composite image. Each of the subjects–including the bride's three sisters and her parents; the groom's mother Anne, grandmother Betsey, and brother J.W. Molson; and the minister, Reverend J.P. Dumoulin–posed separately in Notman's studio. Their images were then superimposed on the background of St. George's Church.

A few weeks after the prince and his entourage departed, on October 14, 1787, a midwife attended to Sarah Vaughan as she gave birth to a healthy boy. Molson, writing to each of his sisters and to Ashley in England, did not mention John Junior's birth. Announcing the birth would invite questions about Sarah, a matter of concern, for as long as David Tetchley lived he had legal right to claim any child of his wife's, regardless of biological facts. As for the father, when his son was a week old, the twenty-three-year-old Molson could only bring himself to boast: "Have almost paid my carpenters and Mason's bill, 600 Bushels Barley in hand, Hops for season, wood for fuel for winter, and one hundred pounds sterling in hand."

He had stocked up just in time. The autumn John Junior was born marked the beginning of one of the hardest winters in living memory. Postwar depression in the United States and the failure of the Canadian wheat crop quadrupled the cost of bread. Montreal's shortages were more severe than they were in Quebec, and many people died of starvation in spite of the public and private committees that fed more than 1,400 of the poor in the first two months of the new year.

Many who survived the grim winter of 1787–88 would remember it for the rest of their lives as "the hungry year." Sheep that had been kept for wool were boiled for mutton instead; the poorest would pass the bones around to be boiled and reboiled for soup. Tea was brewed from catnip and given to babies to soothe their stomachaches. By the spring, children were plucking the buds from basswood trees and fanning out into fields to devour the first heads of rye and barley from the stalks.

The privations suffered by his fellow citizens seemed not to touch John Molson and his enterprise. That winter the brewery doubled its output, necessitating a further expansion. Molson would not refer to anything negative in his letters home, but noted excesses of luxury: "Gentlemen and ladies here are so much addicted to pleasure and dress that to come in their way would be ruinous." He took care to keep his own lifestyle a modest one.

In 1788 John and Sarah's accommodation remained much the same, although they now had ox hides to spread on the floor in winter for warmth and their own latrine dug next to the house. A large hole had been hollowed out of their cellar to pack with ice from the river in winter. John noted proudly in his diary that their garden had yielded more produce every summer. He began experimenting with ways to keep vegetables from spoiling during the winter months.

The *Gazette* advertised seeds that had never been available in Canada before, and gardeners all over town quickly became competitive in comparing their crops. It was at this time that Molson began a practice he continued for years: he noted the date his first strawberries were ready to eat, pointing out more than once that Sir John's berries were slower to ripen. He took as much pleasure in recording his garden victories as he did marking each time the brewery production exceeded its previous output.

Molson purchased all the barley grown by the farmers to whom he'd given the initial six bushels of British seed the first spring. Although his business was growing, he did not consider himself a rich man, and he hadn't forgotten those desperate months only a few years earlier when he'd had to beg his solicitor to send him funds. When he sent another letter to Ashley in Spalding, he explained that he had decided to sell everything in England and invest the proceeds in the brewery:

> *To P. Ashley*
> *March 20, 1788*
>
> *Dear Sir,*
> *Am come to a final determination to sell the whole of my estate in the parishes of Moulton, Peakill and Cowbit and therefore wish you immediately after the receipt of this to proceed in that business … The reason for desiring to draw immediately on Gosling [Molson's English banker] is the gentlemen who had my bills last year have had advice from their correspondents in England to send them no more bills drawn in the country, which is known through this place, therefore nobody here will give me cash for my bills …*

When Sarah gave birth to their second child (a boy named Thomas, who lived only a few days), Molson again told no one in Lincolnshire. Martha wrote to tell her brother of the death of their grandfather, Samuel Elsdale, whom John had not spoken to or heard from in three years. Elsdale's obituary in *Gentleman's Magazine* praised his work on behalf of the orphans in his care, and the writer had an undisguised tone of wonder when he wrote:

> *He lived to be nearly 80 years old without having ever experienced pain or sickness. Until that age he had never taken a dose of physic, or been confined to the house by indisposition for a single hour; and, till his death, was never let blood, or suffered any other medical operation. It ought also to be added, that he was never intoxicated with liquor.*

John Molson's Yorkshire cousin was asked to act as executor of Elsdale's will, but had refused to do so. "In consequence," Martha lamented, "it is supposed all estate will be spent in Chancery." Martha, Mary and Samuel Elsdale Molson were named as beneficiaries in their grandfather's will; John had been "cut off with nary a sixpence." Samuel Elsdale had never forgiven him for emigrating to Canada.

In the late summer of 1789 talk quickened at the quayside in Montreal; there were reports and rumours that civil war had broken out in France. The *Gazette* published a letter which revealed that armed Parisians not only had "seized upon the Bastille" but also had triumphantly borne through the streets the severed heads of the institution's governor and the "Commandant des Invalides." The French population in Montreal, usually indifferent to politics, absorbed the news with foreboding. At least one Englishman was already thinking of profits. In a letter home late in October, John wrote: "The war, though detrimental to many, will be favourable to me ..." He underwent his third expansion. Sure enough, in one year his sales rose from 11,000 to more than 30,000 gallons of all types of beer and ale.

John and Sarah's third son, Thomas, was born on the first of September 1791. The Molsons were living comfortably but carefully.

Molson allowed Sarah (whom he now listed as "wife" in brewery account books) a stipend for household expenses. Some merchants were content to provide Molson with credit and have their accounts paid for in beer. He turned all his profits back into the brewery, financing expansions and new equipment as needed, then buying surrounding lots of land along the river front. The foundation for the great Molson company was being laid in the manner it continued for generations: with care, deliberation, hard work and prudence.

The shortage of money in general circulation did not present a problem for Molson, since the government paid him in gold and silver for the beer it purchased for the army.

Chapter Six

Family Business

Molson's brewery stood between the road to Quebec and the bank of the St. Lawrence River, giving him a doubly strategic position. His ready access to both transportation links enabled him to be among the first to hear any news coming from the east and to glimpse the vessels before they anchored nearer the town.

"I had an opportunity to see him by day standing in the gateway with his wooden shoes or Sabbots on, with his blue cap and gray tunic hailing habitants passing from the country into town, with grain for market," wrote neighbour Jedediah Dorwin. It would not be the only time his manner of dress was commented upon. Hector Berthelot wrote, "Old inhabitants recall seeing him ... wearing a blue tuque, sabots and a homespun suit. He stood at the door of his brewery and stopped all the farmers coming into town with grain in order to purchase it. *Le Père Molson* enjoyed great popularity among the French-Canadians because of his frank *bonhomie* and the honesty he showed in all his transactions with them."

In the summer of 1786, rafts had begun appearing on the river, with lumbermen using makeshift sails and long poles to convey their cargoes of potash, wheat or flour. Often the goods would be unloaded and dispersed into waiting wagons at St. Mary's Current. Near the end of the season, the rafts themselves were sold. The logs, lashed together with willow strips and wooden pins, formed platforms big enough to live aboard. The structures resembled houses without walls. Central areas were squared off and filled with sand to support cooking fires; extensive roofs were supported by beams. The first raft that John bought and dismantled (in September 1786) was of white pine. Soon he bought more rafts from lumber barons Philemon Wright, Alexander Simpson and Joel Stone. He also bought more land east of the brewery, and the dismantled rafts quickly rose into great heaps of lumber. He sold much of the wood, but not before setting a few beams aside. His mind was already busy with plans to build a house for his growing family, the materials of which would cost him nothing.

The *Constitutional Act* was passed in Britain in 1791, dividing British North America into Upper Canada and Lower Canada. Town criers announced the news in Montreal on December 26, and a formal celebratory dinner was held at the Château Ramezay. In an attempt to gain the trust of the French majority, Britain decreed that the seigneurial system and French civil law would be upheld in Lower Canada, while English common law would prevail in Upper Canada. Some English Montrealers were indignant when they heard that their town would not be included in Upper Canada, as they had believed it would be.

Upper and Lower Canada were to be represented by lieutenant governors who each presided over executive and appointed legislative bodies. Lower Canadians would have their first House of Assembly elections in June. The Assembly would be empowered to make laws for the "peace, welfare and good of the government of the province." To the British minority in Lower Canada, it seemed inevitable that their will would prevail at all levels. The French had other ideas.

June 22, 1792

This summer is particularly hot. Lieutenant Governor John Graves Simcoe, Mrs. Simcoe and their entourage have anchored east of town late this evening. Elections in Lower Canada are over, and Simcoe is heading to Upper Canada to oversee elections there. Having spent the winter in Quebec, the couple are on their way to Newark (Niagara-on-the-Lake), where Simcoe will preside over the first House of Assembly of Upper Canada.

Waiting to collect them on shore is Joseph Frobisher's phaeton, the fanciest four-wheeled vehicle in Montreal. The guests are assisted aboard, and soon the horses are clopping past the brewery in the humid darkness. Soldiers ride at the front. Lanterns hang from the upper four corners of the carriage.

Although virtually impassable in springtime, the road from Montreal to Quebec is said to be the best in North America in the 1790s. Twenty-nine post-houses are dotted along its length; each postmaster has several horses, four *calèches* to use in winter and four *carioles* for summer. Depending on the time of year, the journey takes travellers three to four days.

"They have passed safely," Sarah tells John, propping the window open in hopes that cool air might waft in. She hears one of the soldiers in the rear of the party exclaim: "There is but a sheet of brown paper between this place and hell!"

At Beaver Hall, Frobisher offers the Simcoes table beer that he'd been having regularly delivered from Molson for five years. His guests do not leave until long after midnight.

"The air was filled with fire flies," wrote Elizabeth Simcoe later, "which as the night was dark appeared beautiful, like falling stars."

By the time John and Sarah's last son, William, was born on the fifth of November 1793, John Junior was six years old and Tommy was three. Molson was already thinking about the kind of schooling he'd be able to provide for them. He feared at first that a proper education would not be obtainable unless he sent the boys abroad. While some children in town studied a basic curriculum offered by the seminary, most *habitants* simply went without. Molson hoped he could engage a good tutor so his boys could stay nearby, having all the advantages of a classical education as well as picking up business acumen.

February 28, 1794

News has arrived in Montreal that explorer Alexander Mackenzie has finally reached the Pacific Ocean overland and is now on his way home. A prayer is said for him at the Scotch Presbyterian Church. The mood after the service is lighthearted.

"Where will the wee lad go next?"

"Back to Scotland I expect to spend his reward …"

"Home to Montreal first."

"To drink his reward!"

"Did you send him on his way with a few casks of ale, Mr. Molson?" Angus Shaw asks jovially.

"That I did. Aye, they must be empty by now."

Molson is everybody's friend. There are few who don't know him or have kind things to say about him. Considering all that the young entrepreneur has gained during his first years establishing himself in Montreal, others will agree that luck and coincidence play a very minor part. Through insistence and persistence he has rebuilt the entire brewery, and is now about to rebuild it again. He has quadrupled the land he owns at St. Mary's Current and has invested in other properties in town. He is buying lumber, lending money. His little family is growing, and in eight years he has increased the brewery's sales and output by nearly 800 percent.

From time to time Molson developed coughs and ague. Sometime late in 1794 he contracted a particularly severe cough. Reputed remedies such as Andalusian water, Godfrey's Cordial, and Doctor Huxham's Tinctura of bark failed to have any effect. Doctor Loedel prescribed a regimen of restorative teas brewed from dried herbs.

Although his malady may not have been considered life-threatening, Molson was not being overcautious by updating his will with each illness.

At the end of the eighteenth century, misdiagnosed illnesses claimed many lives. He and Sarah had already lost one infant. Both John's parents had died before they'd entered their fourth decades. In 1794, an unchecked infection claimed the life of John's brother Samuel at thirty, and their sister Mary was to die two years later of puerperal fever, also at thirty, following a premature delivery of her second baby.

Molson was not yet thirty when he was appointed to sit on the Grand Jury Courts of the Quarter Sessions as a commissioner of the peace. In this position he performed specific judicial functions as well as a wide range of low-level legislative and administrative duties.

It was a natural step for Molson to have become a member of the local Masonic order. The close-knit fraternity provided businessmen with invaluable contacts and extended security to their families in an age before insurance. John not only benefited from his membership but also gave much of his time and talent to the order. In 1791, at the age of twenty-eight, Molson became grand master upon the formation of St. Paul's Lodge. He would become one of the order's best-remembered and most conscientious leaders.

John Molson was one of a handful of magistrates and a dozen police commissioners in Montreal. Under the new Act, they took their directions from the Legislative Council in Quebec. Unsurprisingly, this system made for slow resolutions and often weak administration.

In the Council's earliest sessions, few ideas were acted upon, to the frustration of many of Montreal's merchants. In 1796 John Richardson introduced a bill for construction of a canal at Lachine, but the proposal was dropped for lack of interest. Thirteen years of meetings and petitions would follow the motion to tear down the town's fortification walls, now an encumbrance. Molson's petition to build a public wharf in Montreal was continually opposed on the grounds that if he was permitted to build one, then everyone else "along the beach" would also want a wharf.

Montreal's drainage and sewage system remained primitive and unsanitary, streets were unlit at night, and the town had no police force. The community needed its own council, but although petitions were organized and meetings well attended, two more decades would pass before there was a municipal government.

The shortage of money in general circulation did not present a problem for Molson, since the government paid him in gold and silver for the beer it purchased for the army. Customers and merchants traded whatever was available: doubloons, French crowns, American "eagles," Halifax "dollars" or British pounds sterling. Those who were able to lend small amounts of cash, or endorse notes and drafts at discounts for later redemption at full value, could make interest of up to 20 percent, not taking into account the dangers of forgery and theft. After his first few successful brewing seasons, Molson dabbled in providing loans: £100 to George Stansfield, a tobacconist, and another £90 to Thomas Walker, a justice of the peace. These loans were the first recorded instances of Molson's early banking endeavours. In a few more years he and his sons would act as agents for investors.

In the 1790s the Canada Banking Company opened, and the country's first paper money was circulated. The government's intent was to finance debts owing to London that had accumulated over the years of economic crises and, at the same time, to stabilize the currency. But people preferred the tangible English pounds and shillings and the hodgepodge of currencies with which they had become familiar, and considered the new paper bills worthless.

Silver coins stamped with the head of Louis XV, the coin of the realm during the French regime, were becoming scarce. Molson began collecting them in a strongbox in his cellar and some years later, in his typically pragmatic fashion, took them to Mssrs. Smiley and Hendery, silversmiths, to be melted down and formed into flatware.

Molson eventually found English tutors for his sons. When John Junior turned seven, his father hired William Gunn and Robert Tait, paying the men's wages in beer. But the boy turned out to be a difficult charge, and the tutors unreliable. Inquiries were dispatched to William Nelson's boarding school at William Henry, a few miles downstream on the south shore. Nelson, a British naval officer who had come to Quebec in 1781, and his wife Jane, had established a boys' school. The Nelsons' ten children included Robert and Wolfred, who later became Patriote leaders in the 1837 rebellion.

William Henry, 17th August, 1796

Dear Sir,
With real pleasure I perused your favour of the 15th inst. My terms for every branch of school education, including stationery articles (printed & bound books only accepted) all reasonable shirt and stocking mending also, are twenty-five pounds currency per annum for Children under twelve years of age; those above, twenty-seven pounds ten shillings ... Payments always quarterly, as being most convenient for both parties. Young Gentlemen provide a mattress, with its suitable changes of bedding ... vacations twice a year; a fortnight each time at Whitsuntide and Christmas. But if parents wish their children should continue at the school, as some do, they are indulged with a few days amusement, and other relaxations, which several of the scholars have preferred to going home. No additional charge was ever made by me for those who continued at the house, on these occasions, so I mean not to commence with you; nevertheless, should my attention to your Child come up to your expectation, as I hope it will, should you intrust him to my care, then indeed a little keg of your excellent ale would be esteemed a very genteel present for the usual vacation; a charge of itself of such little importance, that I really would be ashamto make. I am very
respectfully,
Dear Sir,
your obed't humble servant
W. Nelson

John Junior's first letter to his father was doubtless penned under the gaze of his schoolmaster:

William Henry, 10th October, 1796

Hon'd Papa,
It is with pleasure I write you these few lines to inform you that I am well in health and happy in my situation. I have according to your orders begun to learn Latin which at first I found rather difficult, but is now become much easier because I am made to take a great deal of pains with it. As the cold weather is coming on I should be glad if you would send me a few pairs of socks, and what else you may think proper

> *for winter. Please to give my humble duty to Mamma, and love to my brothers being,*
>
> *Dear Papa,*
> *Your most dutiful Son*
> *John Molson*

For all his sternness, William Nelson was a patient, conscientious guardian:

> *The very night of the day you bid us farewell by the waterside Master John was awakened out of his sleep by a violent fit of coughing, and right soundly did he call out … the cold hung about him and was superior to our usual family applications, which induced me to have recourse to Dr. Carter, who was of opinion that if the cold was not removed, it would, in all probability, fix in his breast for the greatest part of the winter. He was so successful as to remove our apprehensions much sooner than could be expected, and the troublesome cough seems to be entirely conquered.*

Like many boys, John Junior was constantly testing the boundaries of his abilities:

> *William Henry, 2nd May, 1797*
>
> *Dear Papa,*
> *Lest you should think I have been unmindful of you, please to understand my silence was caused by a hurt I got on my arm through one of my wrestling pranks. Playing and capering with my Comrades I soon found I could upset a bigger boy than myself, which tempted me to go a step farther with a bigger boy still, and down upon the ground I came with a souse which made the hurt I have mentioned. I hope you will not be angry with me since I tell you the whole truth. Beside I was kept a prisoner in the house and was made to take physick into the bargain which I found worse than any other punishment my Master could lay on me. Indeed I mean to shun such tricks in future, that I may have my belly full of play when I earn it, and this I mean to enjoy, for I come on not badly in my Learning. I have begun French too, which with my Latin and other duty, take up all my school time. I mean to be good to please you and Mamma, as well as to need no physick, which I do not, nor cannot bring myself to like. Please to kiss my Brothers for me, and fear not but I will bind myself by being,*
>
> *Dear Papa!*
> *Your most obedient and dutiful son,*
> *John Molson*

It was at school that John Junior had his first unfortunate experience of theft:

> *Lammas, 1797*
>
> *Hon'd Papa,*
> *I do not know how to begin about the seven copper pieces, because I was almost altogether unfortunate in them. My leathern purse was tied up well, and thrust into a corner in my pocket for the greater security, for I did not think it would have been safe in my trunk till after many bitter tears, I saw my folly in not trusting to it. You must understand I went a bathing with my Friend and school fellow, George Nelson, and when we had been a few minutes in the water three French boys came and staid among our clothes; but soon after we came out, they took themselves away, and on our return home we found our pockets had been rummaged. This is the whole truth of the matter, which my Master commanded me to tell you; for no other way is it possible for me to account for the loss of my purse. You will forgive my young wisdom since I have repented many hundreds of times for keeping so much money in my [purse] at a time. My Masters present their compliments and bid me inform you that they will try to make a good boy of me.*

On September 5, 1797, William Nelson reported to John Molson Senior: "Your son, Mr John, is as hearty as a Buck, but will handle his fists in an affair of 'Honour' at all events, a matter we must wink at now & then. In his daily business he acquits himself very well."

The "affair of honour" may well have been that John was taunted by schoolmates about his illegitimate parentage. It wasn't the first time nor would it be the last that he used his fists to try to settle disputes. Among the things he learned from school was to value his privacy fiercely. He seemed to adopt a stern reserve, to become disdainful, more uncompromising. The person he ultimately sought to please was his father and to him he was always solicitous, making suggestions, determined not to disappoint.

Nelson put it most diplomatically:

> *The character I formerly gave you of this Little Boy's daily experience shews to have been well founded; surely no boy of his standing can give stronger marks of being endowed in more than a common manner with spirit to make a resolute way through the world; his rights in it,*

> *he will have and hold, or he is not John Molson, Junior.*
> *John is a manly little Fellow, and I hope to find you satisfied with him when I have the pleasure to see you for a glass of your madeira ale ... I think he is a good Lad too, but the most spirited one you can imagine. No fear of his fighting his way through the world. As my remarks are true I shall be sorry to hear they prove offensive.*

Nelson's remarks did not offend Molson Senior, who wrote to his son with a series of remonstrances, such as: "You are much obliged to Mr. Nelson for making you take a great deal of pains, as it will be ultimately a great advantage to you to be a man of education instead of a Blockhead." At the bottom of one of his last letters to Molson, Nelson added a comment that is perhaps even more revealing: "John Molson, Junior, is a man ["man" underlined three times] whatever his Father may think to the contrary."

Chapter Seven

Dancing Shoes For Johnny

Apart from going to the Scottish Presbyterian Church on Sundays, Sarah rarely left home. She avoided concerts and social events, complaining that they were sure to be no more than fashion parades. The truth was, her low profile was maintained at Molson's insistence. John continued to fear that if Tetchley were to find Sarah, he would have claimed both her and the children.

John and Sarah were aware that had they been married, her acceptance in the community would have been taken for granted. Instead, the fact that she had lived with him for nearly ten years and had borne him three children was considered in fine society to be scandalous: men raised their eyebrows, and their wives avoided speaking to her. Among the Scots, however, their marital arrangement was accepted. Many of the fur traders had themselves entered into tacitly accepted arrangements with Indian women–*mariage à la façon du nord*–and then married white women later; most continued to support their Indian children.

Molson wasn't an easy man to live with. Sarah had to tolerate John's complete absorption in each of his projects, his absolute convictions about everything, his parsimonious ways. He was strong-willed, and usually right, although he seldom considered her feelings when making decisions. Yet there is no doubt that he loved her, and that his home and family were extremely important to him.

John Molson had been trained to be emotionally reserved. He was a far-seeing, pragmatic, but not particularly sensitive man. His concept of privacy was inviolable and applied to all matters in his life outside of business. By 1801 he had still not told anyone in Lincolnshire about Sarah or their children.

Deliverance came in the form of a letter. In March of 1801, Molson learned that David Tetchley had died. He lost no time contacting Reverend Mountain to have their marriage banns read. On the seventh of April, Reverend Jacob Mountain, the first Bishop of Quebec, came to Molson's house to marry John and Sarah. Mountain was the rector at Christ Church (then usually known as the Protestant Episcopal Church, or the English Church), whose congregation in 1801 occupied the old Jesuit chapel just north of the Place d'Armes. One reason John and Sarah chose to marry in the Anglican tradition was that John had had a falling-out with the Reverend John Young, the minister at the Presbyterian Church.

Molson's marriage contract was carefully chosen to protect Sarah and at the same time leave no doubt about their children's parentage. It was their attempt not to deny, but to somehow overcome the fact of the boys' illegitimacy:

> *Personally were present John Molson, Brewer, of the one part and Sarah Insley Vaughan, Singlewoman of the same place, and having declared that a Marriage by God's permission between them the said parties … are long desirous to recognize the long mutual affection they have had for each other by reason whereof and in contemplation of their future marriage they had issue of three children namely John Molson … Thomas Molson … and William Molson … which said Children in case the said intended marriage shall take effect the said John Molson and the said Sarah Insley Vaughan do hereby legitimate as their lawful Children and Heirs with all legal and hereditary rights as fully and amply and affectionately as if the said Children had been born in lawful wedlock.*

Christ Church records read: "Molson, John, 38, brewer and Vaughan, Sarah Insley, 39 [sic], 7 April 1801, Witnesses: Charles Blake, J.A. Gray, George Stansfield, James Hughes."

John's last will, worded to protect Sarah as best he could, referred to her as "Sarah Insley Vaughan, or Kitley, or any other name by which she may be known," thus ensuring that she could be a beneficiary. On every record kept that listed Sarah's age–family bibles and, now, their marriage certificate–John had entered different dates. In fact, Sarah was eleven years older than John, and by the time they were married she was nearing fifty.

Not long after his marriage, Molson hired Isaac Shay, a carpenter, to build a new house. It was to be a plain but commodious two-storey, constructed on the most recent lot he'd purchased from old Pierre Monarque, who owned much of the land surrounding the brewery. Molson had gained another forty feet of frontage along the river. The timbers he'd set aside from the rafts became lumber for walls, floors, roof, shingles, bed frames and tables.

Sarah worried about the boys–by now fourteen, ten, and eight–no matter the season. In the summer, when chores were done, they wanted to leap over the timber rafts; in the winter, she feared they would venture too near the ice. The movement of St. Mary's Current in front of the brewery meant that this section of the river never completely froze. Nearer town the ice was thicker. Trees marked off ice paths, where the boys often went to watch the British officers engage in curling, the new sport introduced from Scotland, in which teapot-shaped weights made of iron were slid along the river's ice.

John Junior, restless to undertake adult responsibilities, had already begun an informal apprenticeship at the brewery. Tommy was more headstrong, curious and inventive, and loved attention. He and John were rivals in many respects. Of the two, Thomas was more agile. He mastered the ability to jump out of an empty hogshead and land in another without touching the sides, a feat that became known as *"le Molson."* William, the youngest, filled blank pages in his father's account books with pencilled drawings. To encourage his interest, Molson engaged artist William Berczy to give William drawing lessons. Thomas had a calm nature and was conscientious, and of the three most attached to Sarah. Tutors would remark that all three boys were gifted with arithmetic.

The turn of the century at last saw some improvements being made in town. In 1800 an engineer paved Nôtre Dame and St. Paul streets with flagstones, and in 1801 the first Montreal water works company was formed by Joseph Frobisher. For more than thirty years, the town of Montreal had been served by stone drains that ran beneath the main roads. Built as storm sewers, they were connected to many privies or latrines to speed waste on its way into the river. Water was still pumped from domestic wells or hauled from the river to be sold door-to-door from carts. (Molson drew all his water from the river and pumped it into the brewing kettle before boiling it.) Some wells, dug too close to the latrines, had become contaminated. As well, nearly every spring the river overflowed its banks and the runoff coursed through the streets, flooding warehouses with water and sewage and causing rats to invade homes on higher ground.

Joseph Frobisher, recently retired from the North West Company, had hoped the Montreal Water Works Company would augment his fortune and solve the town's water supply problem. Men with picks and shovels worked all summer digging trenches. Then the pipes were laid. Two thousand hollowed-out pine trunks, banded together with iron hoops, conveyed water from the western side of Mount Royal down to the town. Sixty-three subscribers paid £3 a year for clean water to be piped directly to their homes. But to Frobisher's great dismay, the scheme was a business failure. Customers became fed up as the pipes constantly leaked, dried out in hot weather, and burst in the winter.

While Frobisher's losses were mounting, John was enjoying his new house, tending to the brewery in the winter and dealing in timber in the summer. Timber was suddenly in even greater demand, now that Napoleon had cut off England's regular supply.

Molson never enjoyed being idle. In the summer, when it was too warm for brewing, he had time to sort out his ideas. During the long tranquil days, he could build his dreams into reality. One of the things he'd been considering was expanding into spirits. He had first attempted distilling whisky in 1799, with a still he bought from

McBeth & Williams. He was amply satisfied with the results. In 1801 he hired a neighbour, Pierre Barsalou, to build a stillhouse adjacent to the main brewery building. A copper still ordered that spring from England was installed, and over the next three years the boys and their father taught themselves how to distill spirits and make whisky. Recipes were easy to find, but the process was distinctly different from brewing. Results were carefully recorded, mistakes remedied and changes incorporated.

Although it promised to be more lucrative, distilling was not as socially acceptable a practice as brewing. Beer was considered by most British to be a necessity of life, while spirits were looked on as "American" and the root of many social evils. Molson soon abandoned his experiment without recording his reasons–a rare lapse in a man who was meticulous in his record keeping. The stillhouse was dismantled in 1804 to make space for a stable.

Simon McTavish died suddenly that summer. The cause was unclear and became a subject of local speculation. McTavish had been one of Molson's ten steadiest customers at the brewery since 1790. The fifty-four-year-old fur trader–who had commissioned a grandiose stone dwelling on Mount Royal–had often stopped at Sullivan's Coffee House for a pint of Molson's table beer.

Molson was also beginning to invest in real estate. In the winter of 1802 he bought the Old Coffee House and three "dwelling houses" on Capital Street from Thomas Sullivan for £1,200. The tavern was ideally located in the market. He leased the tavern first to J.P. Belfast, who continued to operate it as a meeting-place and inn. Included in the lease was the condition that "all Beer of every description made use of in the house hereby leased shall be procured from the Brewery of the said John Molson or his heirs save & except all foreign beer."

December 15, 1805

A jovial, celebratory mood prevails at the Coffee House this evening. News of Nelson's great victory at the Battle of Trafalgar has reached town today. Dancing and cheering are making the floors tremble upstairs, and a supper is being prepared for everyone on the main floor. Suddenly Samuel Gerrard, the Montreal merchant and banker, calls for silence. He holds a packet of papers in his hand and looks stricken.

Gerrard has just received a copy of Admiral Collingwood's dispatch, and as he reads aloud the account of Nelson's heroics in the stages of battle, more cheers break out. His listeners are not prepared for his next words: "regrets to announce … the death of Admiral Lord Nelson."

Shocked stillness follows the news; then men cry out, women begin to weep. Immediately Gerrard leaps up on a chair.

"Ladies and gentlemen! Your attention, if you please! I propose … I propose the erection of a monument to our hero's honour."

The people push forward to sign their names to a subscription list. A rousing "For he's a jolly good fellow" fills the room. Within minutes, £800 is pledged for the erection of Montreal's first public monument.

Before the end of the new century's first decade, John Molson had bought a half interest in a farm at Long Point, another farm at St. Catharines, and an orchard in the St. Lawrence suburb. He had hired labourers and engaged a personal gardener, Alexander MacKenzie, who was able to coax the plumpest clusters of grapes, the largest watermelons and the finest flavoured muskmelons from Montreal's soil. MacKenzie was paid partly in beer and partly in cash.

By 1806 the Molsons had four live-in servants (three women and a man) who did all the washing, cooking, sewing and cleaning necessary in the household. Early in 1806 John spent five shillings on a new hat, had his watch mended for fifteen shillings, and gave one shilling and threepence to "Johnny for pocket money." John Junior, now eighteen, was boarding at Mr. Rogue's college out of town.

For all the years the servants and their families stayed with Molson, his commitment to them was generous. Household account books record many expenditures for their personal needs: combs, shoes, medical treatments, gloves and hats. A pension was allotted to one woman whose husband had died. Molson paid for baptisms of servants' children, as well as their education fees, doctors' visits and various articles of clothing. The children are listed by their first names only; when, in the years that their education expenses cease, those same names–Alexander, Charly, Martin, Gordon and Peggy–appear one by one as wage-earners on the staff list. "Dancing shoes for Johnny and Sandy" were purchased in 1810, as well as "playthings for Martin." Perhaps because he didn't have a daughter of his own, Peggy was Molson's favourite. He made arrangements for Peggy (the daughter of an employee identified only as Mrs. Gray) to be sent to a boarding school and bought her countless pairs of shoes, bonnets and ribbons, music books, bolts of black velvet and a new dress to wear to a ball. When young Johnny died in the fall of 1811, John spared no expense; the costs included a coffin, a hearse, the rector's fees, clerk and pallbearers' fees and burial cards, as well as mourning attire for himself, Johnny's brother Sandy, Mrs. Gray and Peggy, all of which amounted to more than £450.

Until 1807 Molson's brewery had virtually no competition. Although many breweries had opened and closed before 1782 in Montreal, it was not until 1807 that James Mason Goddard opened what was later called the Black Horse Brewery across from the King's Wood Yard. A year later, Miles Williams was operating another brewery on College Street, near Dupré Lane. James Dunn built a malting house in Chaboillez Square in 1810, followed by Thomas Dawes in Lachine in 1811. None of these enterprises seemed to make an impact on Molson's sales, which continued to rise year after year. During the winter of 1808–09 Molson's monthly beer sales rose to £7,000.

For many years following the turn of the century, Molson listed "James Pell" among a dozen other names under the heading "Doubtful Debts." An amount (£3) was listed beside Pell's name. Abandoning the pseudonym for the first time, Molson wrote in a letter home: "Mr. Gibbins has used me very ill, and I have parted with him."

Names such as Sir John Johnson, Joseph Frobisher, Judge Ogden, James Caldwell and Joseph "Pappinault" fill the pages of the brewery sales book. Only two women are listed: Miss Ermatinger; and Mrs. Finlayson, a widow who continued to attend the Scottish Presbyterian church with her two sons.

Alexander Skakel had asked to be paid in beer as payment for tutoring John's younger sons and several of the servants' children. Similarly, Benaiah Gibb the tailor, Isaac Shay the carpenter, and doctors Henry Blake and Charles Loedel were happy to accept ale as payment for services. The army, listed in the account books as "government," continued to be Molson's steadiest source of revenue. This reliable income enabled Molson to pay all the farmers promptly for hops and barley, invest in more real estate, lend money to others, and–eventually–to begin a banking establishment, finance steamships, build a grand hotel and theatre, step into politics, become a philanthropist, and fund a pioneer railway.

Chapter Eight

Steamships

Wednesday, November 1, 1809

The air is crisp and the trees are dappled with colour as the paddle wheels flanking Canada's first steamship churn into the St. Lawrence. To the amusement of the crowd assembled on shore and the hurrahs of their children, the six-horse-power engine clanks and groans as the eighty-five-foot vessel inches away from land. The *Accommodation's* two funnels are clouded by chugging coughs of thick black smoke that fill the air.

In addition to the ten passengers on board the *Accommodation* with Captain John Jackson and six crew are the Molson sons, William, Thomas and John Junior. Their father, standing on deck, is dressed in his best hat and suit; and for the first time that many can remember, Sarah stands next to him, one hand grasping the railing, the other holding her new hat from flying off.

Many of the people lining the shore scoffed at John's idea a year ago. Others are merely curious. Few admit believing such a feat is possible on this river. The shouts from the crowd convey the range of opinions.

"Bravo!"

"Amazing!"

"She'll never make it!"

"I could walk to Quebec faster than you'll get there!"

Unsure whether to nod or wave, Molson cloaks his mild embarrassment with the compromise of a formal lift of his hand, holding it still for a moment. He brings his hand down again and clenches his fists with satisfaction.

Ever since he'd heard about the maiden voyage of Robert Fulton's *North River Steam Boat* (later to be named *Clermont*) on the Hudson River in 1807, John Molson had toyed with the idea of bringing steam navigation to the St. Lawrence. He knew that Fulton's steam engine had been built in England, but he believed that the same engine parts could be fashioned at Les Forges du St-Maurice, a well-established local ironworks, at far less cost.

In 1808 he learned that the inventor brothers John and James Winans had launched a second steamship–called the *Vermont*–on Lake Champlain. There was no time to lose. John was afraid that if he didn't act quickly, someone else would.

Montreal's indifference presented Molson with his greatest obstacle. Not many believed that a steam engine would be powerful enough to overcome the currents and winds of the St. Lawrence. Yet one day in December 1808 two men who had heard about John's idea came to the brewery, one an experienced shipbuilder and the other an engineer. They offered their labour in exchange for shares in ownership of the vessel. They stayed and talked with John long into the night, and before they left the three men had agreed to draw up a partnership deal. At Molson's request they signed their names in black ink on the nearest paper at hand: the flyleaf of the brewery account book. Their names were John Jackson and John Bruce. Their labour would be calculated at the rate of seven shillings and six pence per day.

In January of 1809 an entry in the young brewer's notebook read, "Paid for 17 knees and 6 crooked pieces for the steam boat as per John Bruce's order £2.8.6." At the end of the month, Molson travelled by sleigh to Trois-Rivières to visit iron master Matthew Bell at Les Forges du St-Maurice. The ancient ironworks had been run by a succession of leaseholders who rented the premises from the government. At the turn of the century, the company's inventory included stoves, cauldrons, axle-boxes, cast iron ploughshares, anvils, frying pans, andirons, firebacks, tart plates, hammers and lidded basins. When Molson met with him, Bell must have been stupefied to hear what the brewer wanted: a forty-ton steam engine that would turn two water-wheels, which would propel an eighty-five-foot vessel on the St. Lawrence.

By the end of March, Jackson and Bruce had laid the framework for the hull at the beach in front of the brewery. Never one to rely on others when he could do it himself, Molson established his own small foundry next to his lumberyard so that he could have some tools and engine parts made to specifications on site.

Every day that spring and summer, a crew of workmen began at dawn and didn't stop until long after dusk. John was always one of the last to leave the beach, striding toward home in the dark, his lantern swinging from his hand. The question was on everyone's mind: would Molson be able to repeat the *Vermont's* success on the mighty St. Lawrence? In June the *Vermont* steamed its way up the Richelieu River to St. Johns. Molson took John Junior to see it–and spoke at length with the ship's chief engineer, twenty-year-old Ziba Pangborn.

By August, when the *Accommodation* was ready for her trial launch, costs and labour had come to nearly £2,000. Ten weeks before the steamship's maiden voyage to Quebec, a few curious Montrealers turned up to witness what was later called *la chaloupe fumée* ("the smoky launch"). Nevertheless, the trial launch was judged a success, and a few weeks later handbills made their way around the coffeehouses and taverns in Montreal, advertising the *Accommodation's* first trip to Quebec. Twenty berths were available in each of two rooms–the large one for men. Rows of beds lined each side, and on the table in the centre meals were served by day and possessions laid at night. Only ten passengers were persuaded to sign up.

"Ten are better than none," John said to Jackson and Bruce, who were disappointed and impatient to see some remuneration.

When the *Accommodation* anchored for the night twenty miles downstream from Montreal, Captain Jackson calculated her speed had been approximately five knots. By mid-afternoon the next day they reached Trois-Rivières, where the crew welcomed aboard some ironworkers from Les Forges du St-Maurice. These men had sailed and poled their way down the St. Maurice River to see for themselves the ship for which they'd fashioned the huge engine. Then, when the ship arrived in Quebec, locals streamed out from town to greet them. The Quebec *Mercury* expressed their wonder: "This is the first vessel of the kind that has ever appeared in this harbour. She is continually crowded with visitants … No wind nor tide can stop her."

The Montreal *Gazette's* account of the same event, however, echoed a continuing skepticism: "It is obvious that her machinery, at present, has not sufficient force for this River; but there can be no doubt of the possibility of perfectionating it, so as to answer every purpose for which it is intended."

The passage upstream to Montreal the following week tested the crew's ingenuity and seamanship. The wheels turned and the paddles stroked into the water as steadily as before, but now progress was maddeningly slow. No one had anticipated the vast amount of fuel needed for the return journey; soon the crew had to stop to purchase more wood. Four days passed before they reached Trois-Rivières, and by then even the supply of food was dwindling. Molson sent Captain Jackson ashore with John Junior to buy provisions for the passengers, who, aware of the great efforts being made on their behalf, remained loyally cheerful. A letter to the *Gazette*, signed by three of them, reads in part:

> *As the Public may be biassed to the prejudice of the STEAM BOAT in consequence of the length of her passage from Quebec, we do hereby give it as our opinion, that the reason of it is attributable only to an error in the calculation of the quantity of fuel she would require … which is indispensably necessary to produce the full effect of her machinery … We feel a pleasure in acknowledging that the accommodations are excellent, the entertainment good, and well served, and that the others on board evinced the greatest to render the passengers comfortable and happy and we, therefore, wish most complete success to an undertaking, on which much labour and money have been expended, and which ensures to both Ladies and Gentlemen, a cheap, comfortable, and expeditious mode of travelling between Quebec and Montreal.*

Over the next several weeks, the *Accommodation* made two more trips to Quebec. Although there were still echoes of mockery in the oft-heard criticisms of her ponderous headway, obnoxious noise and unpleasant smell, the sight of the steamboat had become a symbol of progress. For the first time, one could calculate how much time a vessel would take to arrive at its destination.

From a financial point of view, however, the *Accommodation* was not a success. In its first season, building and operating had cost Molson almost £4,000 and only a few hundred were earned. He wasn't the least bit discouraged. After the ship's second season (for which he had added two masts strung with auxiliary sails, and a "camboose" or cabin), Molson agreed to buy back Jackson's and Bruce's shares. He also drafted a petition, which was published in the *Gazette* as a prerequisite to its presentation to the Legislature. "The said John Molson," it read in part, "considering the utility that will accrue to the public from having such a vehicle for the conveyance of passengers from Quebec and Montreal … purposes to build a new boat which shall have the desired effect." The petition went on to apply for the exclusive privilege of operating steamboats on the St. Lawrence for fifteen years. Meanwhile he intended to put the present boat in the best possible shape for the summer 1811 so that "she shall be able to effect her voyage from Montreal to Quebec and back to Montreal in eight days and be ready to return, except in case of accident or extraordinary head winds."

Robert Fulton apparently had a monopoly on the Hudson River, and John wrote to the American entrepreneur for advice. Fulton replied with an offer to form a partnership for running a fleet on the St. Lawrence. A new ship, with specifications included, was part of his proposal. These Molson would simply adapt as his own.

While his petition was being considered in Quebec, Molson sailed for England, where he was to stay for the winter. His intention was to order a more powerful steam engine for his second ship. "I am on the eve of my departure for England, [and] I have left the business in the hands of those whom I have the greatest confidence in," John wrote in October to Fulton. "If anything is done I will advise you."

Those in whom Molson had "the greatest confidence" were his sons. In light of their father's new enterprise, the responsibilities of the two eldest sons had been directed to the brewery. All that winter, John Junior and Tommy worked at steeping barley, laying mash, ordering supplies for the dwelling-house, and making deliveries. John Junior paid close attention to the passage of his father's monopoly bill, which was being delayed in the House of Assembly by procedural requirements. William did as his brothers bade him, attending school and helping their mother at home. "Everything is agreeable at the house," John Junior assured his father in early January. "My dear Mother wishes you the greatest possible prosperity in your undertaking, and every success in your voyage. She complains of being very lonesome on acct. of your absence ... Thomas is industrious and healthy, William is still at school and I believe he can go the whole season as we will endeavour to do without him, he is growing fast and is nearly as tall as I am."

Molson was right to be confident of his sons. With their help, he had seen his production and sales rise to 54,000 gallons by 1796 and had overseen a fifth expansion by 1809. Under the supervision of the two eldest, the brewery produced 75,000 gallons of ale and beer the winter of 1810–11.

Once he'd received word that his father was returning, John Junior read the column in the *Gazette* regularly with great anticipation to check the names of ships arriving at the port of Quebec. He wrote John Senior a letter that was forwarded to him on the third of July. He was anxious that his father be kept informed of his lobbying efforts on behalf of the steamboat monopoly bill. Joseph Papineau and Denis-Benjamin Viger had put forward Molson's request for monopoly. The letter reveals the care with which John attended to his father's interests during his absence, as well as his balanced sense of political consciousness and obligation:

> *Your safe arrival has been the greatest satisfaction to us all after a long look out and having heard so many reports of all kinds. The exclusive privilege of navigating steamboats has not been obtained though it passed the lower house and I dare say you will hear how it was before you come up. The members of the lower house wish me to notify in the newspapers again for the next session and they will do their endeavors to pass it. S. Sewell, Esq, came up here before the bill entered the house and did not ask or speak to anybody to do it in his place. I took*

> *advice and found it was necessary to go down to Quebec to get the petition and bill drawn with T. Ross, Esq, and I gave it to J. Papineau, Sr., Esq, who corrected it for the house and promised to do the needful but circumstances obligated him to leave on a sudden without me being able to see him. Therefore I waited upon his son who lived in the same house with B.D. Viger who (the former) being not at home the latter said that he had taken the papers and would do what was necessary which he did with the greatest dispatch and proved successful on his part. Bellet, Esq, one of the members carried the bill to the Upper House where they threw it out. This gentleman having shown every attention I thought best to mention him to you as perhaps it may be necessary to call upon him to thank him for his attention which may be of service if you should have so much time … I sent him a [Hogshead] porter agreeable to an order from his last winter and I neglected to send the bill and write to him by the vessel that took it which if you see him you can mention.*

While in England, John had bought two steamship engines from Boulton and Watt, both intended for his new ship, the *Swiftsure.* The engines cost a staggering £5,850, but this new steamship was going to be the largest in the world. For six long months he went over plans, attended meetings with James Watt and consulted with engineers. The attempt to execute his dream became frustrating and exhausting. John complained to Ann Elsdale in a letter from London that he had "had enough of ships & shipping to hate each of them."

When John returned home in the summer of 1811, the *Accommodation's* dismantling began. Her cabin was carefully removed to be towed across the river on a raft, eventually to be turned into Molson's summer cottage. Any parts of the ship that could be reused were set aside. By autumn, the keel of the new steam vessel was laid at nearby Logan's Shipyard. By the time she was completed the 140-foot steamship contained comfortable accommodations for 150 passengers and another 350 could fit in her steerage. The *Swiftsure* offered both a gentlemen's and a ladies' cabin, captain's quarters and a private stateroom. Painted white, and decorated with pilastres, cornices, curtains and mirrors, the *Swiftsure* seemed both a miracle of achievement and a vision of elegance.

In the winter of 1811–12, most of Montreal feared that another war was imminent. The United States was bristling over British impositions and restrictions on international trade. The news that Napoleon had signed an alliance with the Americans against Britain made an invasion of Montreal suddenly seem likely.

Americans saw attacking Canada as their only means to retaliate against Britain. Their navy would not fare well in a sea battle, and besides, Canada would be such an easy acquisition. Public fervour against Britain grew as election time neared. Promising to declare war, James Madison was elected president for a second term. Thomas Jefferson announced that "the acquisition of Canada this year as far as the neighbourhood of Quebec, will be a mere matter of marching." The secretary of war, William Eustis, believed the United States could "take Canada without soldiers." Underestimating the loyalty of the people of the Canadas, he added, "We have only to send officers into the Provinces, and the people, disaffected toward their own Government, will rally round our standard."

In June of 1812 war was declared. Montrealers spent an uneasy summer, and many wanted to flee. At the outset, the odds looked bad: Americans had nearly five times as many soldiers, and of the Canadian militia the vast majority were inexperienced, badly trained or not trained at all. However, most were proficient in handling small arms, a rural necessity. Battalions of British soldiers arrived in Montreal and left for various posts along the river and farther west along the border. The low and muffled roll of a drum could be heard all the way to St. Mary's Current from the Montreal barracks, where military drilling carried on incessantly.

Montreal itself was on the American agenda as a priority target for attack. Before the year was over, troops advanced as far as Cornwall before, to their great surprise, they were driven back. In spring the same American regiment, augmented to three thousand troops, tried a second approach. They got as far as the western shore of Lake Champlain before the British launched another successful counterattack.

Just as war was regarded as a noble necessity, compulsory military service was an expected fact of life for every fit young or middle-aged man in British North America. As the summer wore on in Montreal, more and more men began to take up their duties. Sentry posts were set up at all entrances to the city. There, boys as young as fourteen could be seen, many of them resting on muskets too heavy to lift. Information was gathered from dispatches and repeated by soldiers passing through. Most of the fighting was going on in Upper Canada. The news was both good and bad: Canadian general Isaac Brock had captured Detroit, taking an American general and his soldiers prisoner. The Americans had been driven back at Queenston Heights, but both Brock and his second-in-command, Lt. Col. John MacDonnell, had been killed.

September 20, 1812

It is late in the evening when captured American general William Hull and his troop of soldiers are marched through Montreal on their way to Quebec from Detroit. John Molson and John Junior are among the many Montrealers who have assembled to see them. The streets through which the procession passes are illuminated by torches and lanterns. The sights and sounds infect the charged air with British patriotic spirit. The band of the King's Regiment precedes the general's carriage, behind which the captured men are escorted on foot. It is Montreal's first direct contact with the enemy. It is the first time John Junior has seen such a display of standards rippling, so many men assembled in tunics of scarlet cloth and brass buttons.

The handsome, impatient Joseph Papineau, a lawyer and representative of Montreal's west ward, has command of the company leading the American prisoners. As the procession passes the St. Paul Street barracks, the band of the King's Regiment mockingly starts up the tune "Yankee Doodle," and Papineau suddenly steps out of line.

"I will not be induced to be a party to treat prisoners with discourtesy!" he bellows.

The music sputters out.

"My duty to my country does not require this of me!"

On this day, caught up in the honour and energy of these events around them, John Molson and John Junior sign up to fight the enemy.

Molson Senior will purchase a commission, secure his uniform and personal supplies, and wait for his summons. It comes by messenger, in February 1813. Sarah regrets seeing him go.

In spite of the threats and concerns of military manoeuvres close by, life in Montreal continued much as it had before. Ships arrived and departed; farmers laid out their wares on market days; the cannon's fire still marked noon. Businesses in fact were busier than ever. Molsons continued to sell more beer, and work progressed on the *Swiftsure.*

The *Swiftsure's* maiden voyage took place on May 1, 1813. Attending the launch were Sir John Johnson; Horatio Gates, importer of groceries and liquors; Judge Joseph Odgen, a member of the lower Canadian courts; Molson's neighbour Pierre Monarque; and fur-trader-turned-entrepreneur Joseph Frobisher. None of these men would ever forget this day, the biggest event in Montreal since the visit of Prince William twenty-five years earlier. Even Sir George Prevost, governor-in-chief of British North America and commander of British forces in North America, set time aside on his way to Upper Canada (where the siege of Fort Megis had just begun at Lake Erie), arriving with his wife to take part in the ceremony. Reverend J. Douglas Borthwick described the scene:

> *On a bright Thursday afternoon, the sun shining clearly down on Mariopolis and St. Helen's Isle, 300 of the best families of Montreal assembled together to witness the launching of this wonderful vessel … Such an uncommon occurrence brought together one of the most representative assemblies that ever in those days met. His Excellency the Governor General, His Lady and suite were all present, and occupied seats on the platform; close to the vessel, merchants and ministers, priests and laymen, the wealth and beauty of Montreal were all there … And now arrives that sublime moment, that eventful time, when Her Excellency breaks the traditional bottle of wine across the bow of the vessel, and baptizes her by the name of Swift-Sure, at the same moment her stays are cut away, and amidst the thunders of the salute of 19 guns, amidst the huzzas and cheers and the waving of hats and handkerchiefs of the privileged spectators and of the thousands of utilizers who congregated every inch of ground, where one could see, on St. Helen's Island, Isle Ronde, Longeuil shore and the Gale Farm seabeach, the Swift-Sure slid gracefully from her moorings on, into the waters of the mighty St. Lawrence, her future home.*

Even though John Molson Senior's name was in every conversation in Montreal, he was established thirty miles away with his battalion at Coteau du Lac. John Junior, installed as a cornet in the Royal Montreal Troop of Cavalry, cut out and saved an article from the Montreal *Herald* about the *Swiftsure*:

> *Good praise is due to Mr. Molson for his exertions in preparing a cheap, safe, expeditious and commodious conveyance between the Metropolis of Lower Canada and Montreal, and we heartily wish him all the success his public spirited undertaking merits.*

By the time of her successful trial run up to Quebec in November, the *Swiftsure* was not the biggest steamship in the world, as her builders had set out to make her, but she was the biggest in North America. It fell to William, now nineteen years old, to captain her for the first season, a post in which he, as a young ensign in the infantry, considered himself to be serving both his father and his country. Molson Senior had written a letter to the military secretary, offering to modify the vessel for "the Transport of Troops and conveyance of light Stores" and to lease her to the government in the spring. Initially, the military chose to charter the steamship on a voyage basis, and over twenty trips conveyed an estimated eight thousand men (sergeants, officers and privates, as well as escorted prisoners of war and deserters) and many loads of light stores (including clothing, food and camp equipage) on their way to Upper Canada. Later, John Junior managed the lease of the *Swiftsure* to the British Army, which netted the healthy sum of £5,000 per month. Though Colonel Joseph Morrison and his British troops had won the battle at Crysler's farm near today's Morrisburg, Ontario, the Americans' position had enabled them to continue their advance east. When troops heard that the enemy's boats had passed Prescott, all battalions in the district mobilized to Montreal. The sight of burning torches at night and the tolling of church bells during the day kept everyone alert for danger. Montreal spent the first half of the summer engaged in preparations for defence.

Near the end of 1815, as Molson approached his fifty-second birthday, he pondered, once again, taking his sons into partnership. It was time, he felt, for the older two to be married and begin families of their own.

CHAPTER NINE

PROSPERITY AND POWER

February 12, 1813

JOHN MOLSON springs from his sleep at the sound of musket fire. He blinks into the darkness for a moment; he can't remember where he is.

Another voice in the room startles him. "It's the signal, Captain. No need for alarm. Supplies have arrived."

"Major Shaw."

Molson lies down again on his lumpy mattress, aware now of the other mattresses and sleeping men around him. He is exhausted and sore after the two-day ride from Montreal. The fire has gone out and the room is bitterly cold. He turns on his side to face the wall and tries to sleep.

"Haul her up!" The sounds of men shouting and the heavy crunching of boots over snow carry loudly across the compound.

The company Molson has joined is the 5th Battalion Select Embodied Militia, which had been financed by the North West Company of Montreal. He has purchased a captain's commission. Now under the command of General Murray, this battalion has just joined several other detachments that are converging at Coteau du Lac. The fort's defences need reinforcing, larger barracks have to be built and the warehouse must be converted to a hospital.

Molson takes in his surroundings at daylight. Montreal is thirty miles east; Cornwall, thirty miles west. Rapids dash over rocks stretching between shore and a deserted island. The rampart that skirts the river's edge is dissected by a narrow canal, the first of its kind built in Canada. The Union Jack snaps on a tall pole standing by a log palisade at the north end of the site.

He takes part in military drills, carried out three or four times daily, "for discipline and control."

While in Coteau du Lac, Molson's diet consists of rations of bully beef, pea soup, hard tack and salt pork. When they have time, the men net fish and shoot wildfowl, rabbits and an occasional deer. They barter with local Indians, exchanging army biscuits for dried eels. There is never enough wood or candles, never enough fresh straw to stuff the soldiers' cotton sacks that serve as mattresses. The barracks are cramped and conditions are unsanitary. The winter is bitterly cold.

Convoys of *batteaux* in summer and sleighs in winter need military escort, and Molson's instructions are to help protect the stream of provisions transported from Quebec to the Upper Country.

Word reached the company shortly after Molson's arrival that the American army had begun to break camp at French Mills and Four Corners (near present-day St-Anicet). Hercules Scott, commander of the garrison at Coteau du Lac, assembled 600 men and set out across the ice. Molson was among the troops who arrived at the American encampments and began releasing prisoners and seizing sleighloads of provisions before burning barracks, blockhouses and boats. They followed the retreating Americans as far as south as Malone "for safe measure," before turning back to Coteau du Lac.

In November 1813, Molson's regiment was one of several withdrawn from Coteau du Lac and other forts to defend Montreal. As the soldiers set up their artillery lines, "filled with the spirit of resistance," the morale of the inhabitants was lifted. More British reinforcements arrived. Then Governor-in-Chief Prevost (who had moved his headquarters to Montreal in anticipation of invasion) was told that Wilkinson had turned away. The city heaved a sigh of relief. Some of the militiamen were sent home, while other troops, including Molson's, returned to their original stations.

Molson had left John Junior in charge in Montreal, although the twenty-five-year-old had wished to take up arms alongside his father. John Junior had written to Sir George Prevost, hoping to raise his own company of cavalry. Molson Senior had endorsed the letter, agreeing to finance a troop "to consist of forty men, or more if required." But, as explained in a letter to John Molson Senior from the military secretary's office, although Prevost was grateful, the offer "cannot be considered until the present levies are completed."

It wasn't that the enthusiastic young man didn't have enough to do. Sales were brisk, since the brewery was purveyor to the troops. John Junior spent every day at St. Mary's Current. With help from his brother Thomas, the young man directed another major brewery expansion and supervised the building of a third steamship. The new vessel, launched in the fall of 1814, was christened *Malsham*, a sixteenth-century variant of the spelling of Molson.

The war was over; the Americans had been driven back. John Junior took over again as captain of the *Swiftsure,* and soon both steamships were making trips between Quebec and Montreal in opposite directions, providing weekly or twice-weekly service to each city.

October 29, 1814

John Molson Junior is sitting at a table with two first-class passengers: Charles Ogden, a solicitor, and Abner Bagg, a manufacturer of hats. They are in the dining salon aboard the Swiftsure.

"We run twenty-eight return trips each season," Molson tells Bagg.

"Some say it is not inspiration, but foolhardiness, to run your steamship at night. What have you to say to them, Mr. Molson?" asks Bagg.

"I have nothing to say to them."

"I rather question the safety of a steamship maintaining the same speed at night ... most particularly on this protean river," Ogden intones.

"You are a capital solicitor, Mr. Ogden," comments Bagg, with a laugh. He has known Ogden long enough not to take him seriously now.

John Junior's face darkens. "Quite right, sir, a solicitor, not a sailor, nor, evidently, a pilot."

Ogden leans forward. "Do you mean to deny that should you strike a shoal and cause injury, there is no question of liability?" John Junior remains silent as others join the conversation, commenting on recent disasters. Finally, he has listened enough. "I believe I shall leave you foolhardy fellows to your spirits." He rises stiffly. "Good evening, gentlemen."

In the uneasy silence that followed, Ogden devised a mischievous plan to lighten Molson's mood. The solicitor was the last to retire to the gentlemen's cabin, which accommodated forty-four passengers. We can presume there was much to drink that night. Taking advantage of the passengers' deep sleep, Ogden, using a piece of burnt cork, lightly rubbed "black moustaches of every shape and size" onto each man's face, leaving John Molson Junior's "guiltless of any decoration." He embellished his own face with a moustache more preposterous than all the rest and then placed the cork in John Junior's hand.

A "general uproar" ensued in the morning. Molson, who apparently woke last, was furious. In the end Ogden confessed, but Molson did not yield. "Strained relations" existed between the two men from that day after.

War had been effectively over since August, but it wasn't until December 1, 1814, a few days before the Treaty of Ghent would formally seal the end of hostilities, that Molson Senior was on his way home. Of his time spent at the barracks he left only one record, a note on the page where he'd left off in his ledger book. Under "General Expenses Accounts" appears a notation dated September 10, 1812. The next entry, dated January 1815, reads: "I joined the 5th Battalion Incorporated Militia the 20th Sept. 1812, went up to Coteau du Lac the 9th Feb 1813, and returned home the 2nd December 1814."

Montreal in the aftermath of the war was enjoying a new sense of security. For the Molsons, profits had been steadily accumulating, not only from the brewery but from the steamship operations too, in spite of competition from the first steamship to rival Molson's–the *Car of Commerce*, owned by Thomas and John Torrance, entrepreneurial brothers who had emigrated from Scotland. John Senior bought several more properties. In April 1816 a newspaper notice caught his eye. It was a description of a "trading establishment" for sale, a property known as Près de Ville, just west of Quebec City, at the foot of the Citadel. The property included every accommodation Molson would need to establish his business presence in Quebec City:

> *...a convenient house, good yard, stable, coach houses and other buildings, also a large store, suitable for grain or goods of any description, with a large cellar under it; two wharves extending into deep water ... [and] a very powerful crane ... [that] extends about 17 feet beyond the edge of the wharf.*

The purchase of Près de Ville anchored Molson's steamboat business at Quebec City and at the same time drew attention to the need for permanent wharves in Montreal. *Batteaux* and small craft still unloaded their passengers and stores by gangways and carts at the landing place near the market. Rafts that were tethered to posts on shore frequently went adrift, and stray logs were a frequent nuisance.

In 1815 Sir John Johnson made it known that he wanted to sell his stone mansion by the waterfront, an impressive structure on St. Paul Street that dominated the east end of the landing place. Molson saw opportunity at once. He knew that the mansion, whose property offered access to the river, was ideally suited not only for a hotel, but also for a permanent commercial wharf. If he bought it and turned it into such a worthwhile enterprise, surely the legislators would be convinced, this time, that the city was ready for a wharf. Molson already owned two wharves in Quebec City. One in Montreal would give him a huge advantage, with business that would spill over from hotel to steamboats and back again, and at the same time hamper the Torrances' ability to compete. A wharf would be an obvious asset to everyone in Montreal. All the same, to maximize his influence, he offered his candidacy in an upcoming election and was promptly chosen to represent Montreal East in the House of Assembly.

Near the end of 1815, as Molson approached his fifty-second birthday, he pondered, once again, taking his sons into partnership. It was time, he felt, for the older two to be married and begin families of their own.

John's brother Thomas had died in 1803, leaving two daughters and a son. The son and heir, Thomas Molson Junior, had signed away his right to his entailed estates a year earlier, on his twenty-first birthday, "the Jews having advanced him money, and he having run through the 20,000 pounds of his wife's … dowry."

The two daughters, Mary Anne and Martha, inherited their father's estate. At the time of their mother's death they were of marriageable age, which suddenly made them popular prospects to suitors. The daughters had contacted their uncle, John Molson of Montreal, with whom their parents had an "understanding." All had agreed that it would be desirable for them to encourage matches between John's sons and Thomas's daughters. They would benefit from the merged inheritance, and the prosperity and power they enjoyed could be passed to the next generation of Molsons in Canada.

December 11, 1815

John Molson has summoned his two eldest sons to the parlour. They sit uncomfortably while their father clears his throat. Finally he begins.

"Young ladies will soon be considering you as eligible prizes," Molson begins, "and I would not like to see hasty or unwise matches being made.

"It is out of the question for either of you to marry someone from here. We can know nothing of their background, who their people are. Two perfectly suitable young ladies from Lincolnshire, your cousins the Misses Mary Anne and Martha Molson, are willing to come to Montreal. They are my charges now. I have made it clear that they would be welcome here."

Thomas can think of no objections to his father's plan; it seems a perfectly practical idea to him. In fact, he is even more inclined to support the idea when he notices his older brother so intent on opposing it. The rivalry between them is long established. They are both ambitious and determined men, aware of the advantages they share. When

John turns analytical, Thomas becomes vigilantly alert.

"We have a business to maintain," Molson continues. "It is my wish to take you into partnership with me, and I'd like to be assured that the brewery will carry on in the family."

"I'm in favour, Father," Thomas says evenly.

"Very well. As I have many pressing obligations, I shall need one of you here. Only one shall go to Lincolnshire to escort the young ladies to this country. Thomas … "

John Junior glowers. He has learned long ago that when his father's tone sounds the way it does tonight, he is not to be opposed.

Molson is unperturbed. He believes his sons will thank him in the end.

Thomas Molson was a self-assured and earnest young man, who, bordering on vain, paid more attention to dress and demeanour than his older brother did. As long as he could remember, he had observed others deferring to his father, and while the father would treat deference modestly, this son would not. Both Thomas and his brother, though rarely agreeing on personal or business matters, harboured convictions of their own superiority.

Molson sent John Junior to travel as far as New York with Thomas, where they spent a fortnight seeing sights and visiting breweries and steamboat companies. This trip was the first either of them had taken south of Quebec, so it's not hard to imagine the excitement with which they toured New York. The day before he boarded the *Everetta,* Thomas bought a clothbound notebook to record his voyage to England. "Thomas Molson," the young man wrote in a grandiose, embellished script on the inside of the cover. Under his name, he added, "Ever sincere. *Toujours sincère.*"

Everywhere Thomas went, he recorded what he did and whom he met. He filled pages with details, descriptions, drawings, recipes. He recorded the names of all his fellow passengers on board the *Everetta.* He copied out "scientific tricks" that were popular entertainments of the day. He tucked a letter from his father in the notebook, which included instruction and advice:

Mr. Grayhurst [of Grayhurst and Harvey, agents for the Molsons] is

> *the person to show or get somebody to show you everything about London. The Brewhouses and machinery are well worth seeing there and every town and place endeavour to get some person to introduce you to such places in the manufacturing towns. Neglect not to see such manufacturies as that you can get at.*
>
> *The Steam Boats in England or Scotland be particular in seeing and sailing; on some occasions it may be necessary to let know that you are from Canada to strangers; it will ease their minds from any fear of your stealing anything to their prejudice, and when necessary let know that I have built three Steam Boats, two of which are running that will draw questions from them, your answers will convince them of your knowledge & at least some of them will be more communicative. These items nicely worked will procure what you want. You will perhaps be jaded with my repeated requisitions; however be perfectly persuaded 'tis only for your good, I cannot have any other motive.*

In London, Thomas had gone immediately to look at steam engines "at the coal pits" and contacted Michael Grayhurst, as his father had directed. He wrote to Ann (Nancy) Elsdale, conveying his father's good wishes. Thomas stayed with James Watt in London, and later travelled with the elderly gentleman from Birmingham to Bristol, for a tour of the Boulton & Watt manufactury. He brought a recent purchase with him called a "Quarto Copying Machine," a device that Watt had invented which used ink and copying paper.

But it was a visit to Guy's Hospital in London that really seemed to inspire Thomas. He was taken there by a friend of his father's, Dr. Charles Loedel. In 1816 each patient at Guy's Hospital was daily allotted one pint of water, gruel porridge, eight ounces of meat or six ounces of cheese, a bowl of broth, twelve ounces of bread, and two to three pints of beer. Wards of thirty patients were common, wood floors were rubbed with sand to clean them, and mattresses made of hair or straw were often infested with bugs.

Thomas was invited to the dissecting room. Any squeamishness the young man might have suffered was overcome by his eagerness to see new things. He described his experiences in sentences that didn't stop to take a breath: "[I] saw the operations on the several dead bodies performed there and after that had the pleasure to take Tea with [Dr. Loedel] and he mentioned that he sees more in one month here than the whole of his life in Canada and cannot get away before 18 months, and his brother Henry is in France and very well."

Engrossed as he was in his enjoyment of London, Thomas must have been hurt to receive the following letter from his father, clearly a reflection of his brother's ill-will:

> *Dear Thomas,*
> *I am very much surprized at not having recd a Letter from you on your sailing from New York. We received a short epistle to John dated on the 18th Dec 1815. If I can judge from that Letter, you had seen or heard nothing during the time you remained at New York–the loss of your doubloons I hope will be a lesson to you to take better care in the future–John tells me it was with the greatest difficulty that he could get you to see & sail in the Steam Boats; I should have thought you would not have lost a moment in seeing everything that was worth seeing & hearing–manners & knowledge are to be acquired most particularly by travelling on that principle to let you take so long and expensive a Journey, & can assure you shall have no objection to any reasonable expense; so as you profit by all the circumstances that present themselves; on the contrary, shall be much disappointed & angry if it is not the case–you must be aware that my anxiety is only for your welfare, & that all & every advice from me is as perhaps I am nearly the only friend you have–with the exception of your Mother & Brothers–by all means lose not an opportunity of seeing all kinds of machinery that you can get to see, even should it cost a trifle for in seeing nothing, it will cost you a great deal; & all your time and money is lost for a few dollars & pounds spent on proper objects will repay the whole expense ...*

While Thomas was in England, John Junior managed the steamboats and William took charge of the brewery. Molson Senior was preoccupied with planning his hotel and forming his application to the Assembly for the right to build a wharf adjoining it. For John Molson to argue on his own behalf for an Act from which he'd benefit as a businessman was not considered a conflict of interest. In spite of public support in the form of a petition, and newspaper endorsements about the "perseverance of Mr. Molson in all his pursuits, mark[ing] him as one of the most valuable members of the community," he was to encounter more opposition than anyone had expected.

John Junior, who stayed in Quebec City for the winter, kept his father informed by letter of their bill's progress from the Assembly to Council:

February 26, 1816

I presented the petition to his Excellency [Sir George Prevost, the Governor General] myself and had the satisfaction of meeting with a favourable reception, his Excellency seemed to approve of the plan … His Excellency referred it to a committee of the whole Council, and from what I can learn there is every appearance of its meeting with success.

February 27, 1816

Robert Armour [a member of the Assembly] will oppose it if they can even upon the most trivial circumstances … I do not expect to leave this week, the Chief Justice tells me not to leave sight of the business I am on unless I care nothing about it [and] that I should call upon him frequently–

… I think that you had better not lose one moment in getting the Steam Boat fitted up as it is impossible to depend on me; you aught to engage as many work men as you can possibly give employ to.

The wharf motion had been opposed by Assembly members Jacques Viger, Robert Armour and some Torrance allies. According to John Junior, the Assembly members "had a great parley amongst themselves ... They seem very willing to give all the trouble that they can."

February 29, 1816

I have just come from the Committee Room … (having been called upon by a letter from Mr. Lindsey); the trinity [Harbour Commissioners] have been called to make their report, on the subject of your petition. They seem inclined to hang upon some beach regulations that were made in consequence of a representation made to them by Mr. McGill and some other principal citizens of the city of Montreal some years ago, also that if the present should be granted every body else would ask for the same privilege all along the river front–I explained to them the peculiarity of the situation, and that particular kind of wharf could not be made all along the beach opposite the town, and that the advantages of that wharf would tend to a public convenience, in unloading heavy stores for government or others out of bateaux or small craft will [cause] much less expence and risk that rafts going adrift … would … not ground on the shoals just below ... that the whole of the beach would be for the use of the public with the exception of the communication to be left for carts and other carriages to pass ...

... the only objection which they seem to have is that every body else has the same right to get the front as you have ... I am to meet them tomorrow again, and shall write to you the results as far as I shall know.

It seemed to John that a positive answer from the Legislative Council would never come. He wrote letter after letter to his father, the exasperation mounting as the weeks went by. The letters took on a weary and increasingly frustrated tone. He wanted more and more to be back in Montreal, where, he worried, "William must be at a loss in the malt house, not being used to take charge there":

March 7, 1816

My presence is still required here to await His Excellency's answer, now when that answer may be God knows ... I think that you had better come down here yourself as soon as possible, that I may return to get the Boats fitted up–it is absolutely necessary to make the boats more commodious especially the Swiftsure, otherwise we will be cut out altogether. The time is getting very limited ... I never was more uneasy in my life, doing literally nothing when there is so much work to do–I am like a person awaiting for a fair wind to sail.

Ice still covered the river late in April. The steamboats needed to be moved from their wintering ground (a sheltered channel in the St. Lawrence's Boucherville Islands) to be made serviceable for the new season, and the day the ice broke Molson had his boats out of their moorings. It perhaps was too soon, however. Untended logs, loosened by travelling ice floes, damaged the paddles on both the *Swiftsure* and the *Malsham.* Departures would be delayed until the repairs were completed.

John Junior hired a captain for the *Swiftsure,* but was soon finding fault with him. "I am almost decided in sending him away and taking charge myself," he wrote angrily. Meanwhile, Thomas seemed to be in no hurry to return from England. Because letters often went astray, Thomas sent several letters to different recipients with the same news.

John Junior received letters asking him to ask John Senior to send more money. John passed on his brother's requests in letters to their father, summarizing in one some news he had had from Thomas: that Thomas was "engaged to Miss Martha Molson, that he had all matters arranged, that he had just come up to London with her sister Mary [Anne] to buy furniture, and that he was to be married in about three weeks after the date of his letter, which was the 22nd of March last." By the time the letter arrived (late in May), Thomas had been married for five weeks.

Whatever Mary Anne's feelings were, she kept them to herself. Her own choices were limited now; returning to England was unthinkable, partly because she didn't want to leave Martha, and partly because of the scandalous talk that

Chapter Ten

Duel in Montreal

In 1816 the city of Montreal experienced a host of post-war improvements and innovations. Steel pipes replaced wooden conduits for the main water supply, now drawn from the river by steam-powered pumps whose throb could be heard all over the city. In November and December, whale oil lamps were installed all along St. Paul Street. No one seemed to mind either the sound of the steam pumps or the nauseating smell of burning whale oil. After all, these were considered marks of progress.

Thomas returned to Montreal with his cousins, the younger now his wife. Unfortunately, the young ladies' first summer was not typical for Montreal. There was still ice in the river in May, and frost was common throughout July and August. Potatoes did not sprout; entire crops, including barley and hops, were ruined. The price of flour rose from 14 to 100 shillings per barrel in a week. Even the grass was thin and short; pastures did not yield enough hay for horses and cattle.

Notwithstanding the cold weather and occasional mishaps, the *Malsham* left Montreal every Tuesday morning and returned from Quebec every Thursday evening or Friday morning, depending on the tide. The competing *Car of Commerce* kept the same schedule.

According to advertisements in the *Gazette* and the *Herald*, the *Malsham* typically quartered more military officers and dignitaries, while the *Car* carried more freight. The steamboat captains maintained a gentlemanly rivalry. Inevitably the *Car* would arrive in port "half a cable length ahead" of the *Malsham*.

Although merchants and others had continually petitioned the Legislative Council for permission to dredge the channel in the river, they were put off for many years. Teams of up to forty-two oxen still had to be harnessed to steamships to bring them past St. Mary's Current to Molson's private wharf. Thomas talked about the machine he'd seen at New York that used buckets attached to a revolving belt to dredge the harbour.

Thomas and Martha had moved into the log house in which the brothers had grown up, and Mary Anne became a guest of her uncle John and aunt Sarah. The sisters tried to come to terms with their new surroundings. In the city one day they stood aside to allow a gaily decorated series of horse-drawn cabriolets pass by. A bride rode first, calling out to people in the street and waving her handkerchief, a surprising departure from the reserved and modest behaviour of Englishwomen. Another day they went to see the wondrous clock at the establishment of "Thomas l'Italien" on Capital Street, on which small figures came out and struck the hours. They were shocked to be confronted and elbowed by a melée of crude tavern patrons. On St. Paul Street where colourful displays of wares were mounted outside open doors, salesmen accosted them and one nearly dragged Mary Anne inside. They saw a convicted thief, his hands tied to the back of a cart, being led through the streets and given lashings at designated corners.

There was little to mollify them. The weather was far too cold to make use of the new bathing machine on Windmill Point that they'd heard about. There was almost nothing in the way of general diversions–no concerts at the garrison, no opera house, no picture gallery, not even a theatre. Thomas and John Junior, men of business first and foremost, did not miss these putative delights. John Junior avoided Mary Anne rather than engage in any rites of courtship.

Thomas had justified to his father and brother his marrying Martha in England. She was, after all, the younger of the sisters, and he, the younger of the brothers. Moreover, he reasoned, it was wiser and more discreet for the three of them to travel back to Canada together if he were already married to one of them. Another possibility is that Thomas had been smitten with Martha upon their meeting, and had intended that his choice of the two sisters be irrevocable. John Junior, who now faced two imperatives–when and whom to marry–simply resisted being put in such a position. These circumstances may or may not have predisposed him to dislike Mary Anne, but are likely to have contributed in some measure to the future couple's constant friction and eventual separation. From the beginning, the situation made John Junior deeply resentful.

Whatever Mary Anne's feelings were, she kept them to herself. Her own choices were limited now: returning to England was unthinkable, partly because she didn't want to leave Martha, and partly because of the scandalous talk that would come of it. Once spurned, she would almost certainly remain a spinster. Love matches were the exception, and not necessarily to be envied. Justifications for this pairing were financial and seemed perfectly sound to her. She knew her uncle John would never allow an unpleasant situation to develop when family honour was at stake. Mary Anne judged that the situation with her fiancé would resolve itself in due time.

Molson made it clear to John Junior that if he didn't marry Mary Anne, there would be consequences regarding the partnership. The father assured the son that he only had the son's well-being in mind. Who else could he trust to have no other motive? John capitulated.

A marriage contract was drawn up for John Junior and Mary Anne. The grave couple were married in Quebec on October 12, 1816, by the Reverend G.J. Mountain, the Anglican priest in Quebec whose father, Jacob Mountain, had married John and Sarah in 1801. Mary Anne was happier to live in the house in Quebec than in Montreal, where she felt confined under the watchful supervision of her husband's parents and brothers. Quebec provided a better social milieu; its entertainments were more refined, its dinners more elegantly prepared, its shopkeepers more civil. John Junior was able to attend to the steamship business and his other duties by travelling frequently between the two cities.

The Molsons' first partnership agreement, signed eight weeks after John Junior's marriage, was worded much like John Senior's wills and marriage contract, in unusually demonstrative language: "In consideration of his affection for his sons and good opinion and trust and confidence he has in them and therefore rests on them ..." It outlined the terms of the four Molson men's joint ownership of most of John's assets, including the brewery, steamships, wharf and trading establishment at Quebec. Their agreement was to remain in effect for seven years, and the earnings were subject to an interest charge of 6 percent on the valuation of the brewery and the Quebec property.

No doubt they all felt significantly richer and on fairer terms with each other. The revenue generated from the *Malsham* would remain in Molson Senior's hands, and the revenue from the *Swiftsure* in John Junior's. Profits and losses were to be shared equally. Thomas would manage the brewery and continue to live in his house without rent. John Junior would maintain his house at Quebec and keep a close eye on the other properties there. William would stay in Montreal (where he still lived with his parents) and work wherever he was needed at his family's enterprises.

The newest of these enterprises was the Mansion House Hotel, the two-storey stone mansion that John Senior had bought from Sir John Johnson. Lady Selkirk had rented the house from Molson and had occupied it since February, Lord Selkirk having left to help defend his settlers from attack at the Red River. After his return, the couple continued to occupy the house, apparently unperturbed by ongoing renovations that began on the first of May, 1816. The Selkirks continued to occupy rooms after its transformation, and thus became the first guests at the grandest hotel the city had ever seen.

On May 4, Molson signed a two-year lease with John Dyde and Peter Martinant, entrepreneurs from New Hampshire, who agreed to pay 420 pounds per year to operate the hotel. Dyde and Martinant also agreed to "take all such Malt Liquor as [they] shall require for the use of the said House from the Brewery of the said John Molson."

The Molsons' dogged efforts to win the Assembly's approval for a permanent public wharf finally paid off, and both the Mansion House Hotel and its wharf were completed the same week in July. The main floor of the hotel accommodated the town's first library and a "newsroom" (a reading room where newspapers were provided and news was exchanged), and soon made space for the post office. The hotel's new, 144-foot-long terrace afforded a magnificent view of the river. One traveller's diary praised the hotel's "large and well-furnished" rooms, the quiet attentiveness of its staff, and the "fine scenes of twilight and evening upon the St. Lawrence."

Boats for hire lined up along the river on summer afternoons and evenings. Dances, private and public parties, balls, and Masonic and Bachelor Club meetings were all held at the Mansion House Hotel. It was rumoured that the chandelier in the grand ballroom had cost more than a thousand pounds. The dinners became legendary. One six-course Masonic banquet served three kinds of duck, ham boiled in champagne, vol-au-vent, bar fish stewed in port, veal ragout, snipe and partridge. Beaver Club meetings were notorious for excesses of alcohol. Forty-two gentleman guests one evening consumed forty-three bottles of wine and twenty bottles of champagne in addition to unrecorded amounts of whisky and beer.

Molson's hotel became a favourite rendezvous of the elegant and the affluent. On July 30, 1817, the governor-in-chief of British North America, Sir John Sherbrooke, "and his Lady and suite" arrived in Montreal from Quebec aboard the *Malsham* and ensconced themselves at the Mansion House Hotel. The couple's first duty, the day after they arrived, was to break a bottle of champagne over the keel of the Molsons' fourth and newest steamship and christen her the *Lady Sherbrooke.*

Three years in the planning and building at Logan's shipyard in Montreal, the *Lady Sherbrooke* was the ultimate in luxury steamships. "Her magnitude and symmetry of construction is such as to exceed any vessel of the kind that has yet been seen on the waters of the St. Lawrence," reported the Montreal *Herald.*

Built of white oak and spruce, and installed with a Boulton & Watt engine of sixty-three horsepower (compared to the *Malsham's* and the *Car's* forty-five horsepower), *Lady* was 170 feet long with a thirty-four-foot beam. She sported two masts, a square sail, square topsail, and jib sail. Her flat bottom would enable her to navigate over the sand banks, reefs and rapids that thwarted other steamships. Twenty-five single-passenger cabins were built into the stern, the ladies' cabins installed below the gentlemen's. An onboard orchestra entertained passengers. The *Lady Sherbrooke* could steam from Montreal to Quebec in merely twenty-three hours.

All employees on board–crew members, waiters, cooks, cooks' mates, ship mates, engineers, stewards, pilots, pursers, and ladies' maids–operated under strict regulations. One of the steward's duties was to give each of the crew three glasses of whisky during the day: one at 6 a.m., one at 11 a.m., and one at 4 p.m. A fireman, at the direction of the engineer, was expected to carry all the coals on board, "and no assistance to be given to them by the Crews." A boot boy cleaned all the gentlemen's boots and shoes and placed them back in their cabins before 6 a.m. Washerwomen collected the linen upon the arrival of the ships at port.

Drinking in excess of three glasses of whisky a day was frowned upon by the Molsons. Within two weeks of the *Lady Sherbrooke's* launching, John Junior wrote in a letter to his father, "I am afraid that Lee [an engineer] is beginning to go wrong; he has been in liquor yesterday and today tho' he has been at work." Problems with alcoholic employees continued to plague them. "Pierre Papin told me in the Brewhouse in the presence of Antoine Grignon, Carpenter, that John Ley [sic] Engineer of *Lady Sherbrooke* was drunk at Grondines when he stopped the Engine short … which made something crack …" wrote Thomas some months later. John Junior and Thomas both suspected that alcohol was involved when an unidentified passenger slipped off the *Malsham's* gangway as he was disembarking, to be swept away and never seen again.

Le Père Molson (as he was sometimes called, to distinguish him from John Junior) must have felt he was a lucky man. A popular host at the Mansion House and a brewer of increasingly wide repute, now, less than a year into a successful partnership with his sons, his first grandchild was born. Thomas and Martha named their son John, after him.

Whether welcoming guests to the Mansion House or greeting passengers on board the *Lady Sherbrooke*, Molson was a vision of elegance in his black suit, white waistcoat and fashionable lorgnon attached with a long ribbon. After Molson was addressed in a letter one day as "Le Bourgeois des Steamboats," the name stuck. (In the heyday of the fur trade, the company agent in charge of a canoe brigade was called the "bourgeois"; when the brigade reached the trading post, he would be recognized by his top hat.)

For a while, the new steamship seemed cursed. The *Lady* accidentally rammed into and sank another vessel at William Henry (later called Sorel), but thankfully no lives were lost. When an elephant, en route to a circus in Quebec City, refused to board, onlookers wondered if the creature had a premonition of danger. On another journey, several steerage passengers (most likely emigrant settlers), who had been sleeping on the ship's paddlewheel box, slipped off and drowned.

The summer of 1818 was not an easy one. On June 25, Mary Anne and John Junior's newborn daughter, Sarah Anne, died of unknown causes on board the *Malsham*, presumably on the way to a doctor in Montreal. Two weeks later, on July 9, Thomas and Martha's infant son died. A solemn entry appeared in Thomas's diary: "Died this day at 10 minutes before 12 o'clock John Molson son of Thomas Molson Aged 9 months 22 days."

Molson was deeply affected by the deaths of his two grandchildren. The state of health in Montreal was, he believed, deplorable. The only medical hospital was the Hôtel Dieu on St. Paul Street, which had just thirty beds. The Grey Nunnery, an institution known to offer "general asylum" to women, girls and foundlings, had even fewer beds. In response to the suffering of many of Montreal's poor, a number of concerned Englishwomen had even formed an association called the Female Benevolent Society of Montreal:

> *A number of Ladies, deeply distressed with the destitute situation of the poor in this place, and solicitous if possible to mitigate their sufferings, have formed a society for relieving Indigent Women with small children, the sick, the aged, and the infirm … [to] visit the poor, enquire*

> *into their circumstances, administer necessary and appropriated relief, and endeavour to stir them up to industry, order, neatness, and economy–to make them useful to their families and better members of society ... [to] promote the grand object of the Society ... Surplus of donations or contributions ... shall be appropriated ... until it become sufficient to establish and support a school ... where the children may be taught that fear of God which is the beginning of wisdom and those habits of industry, order and economy which will best form them to become useful members of the community.*

Benevolent Society ladies met on the first Monday of every month. Some were appointed each week to visit those in need and administer donated medicines, clothing and blankets. They rented a four-bedroom house in (present-day) Chaboillez Square, called it the House of Recovery, and in one year treated and released thirty-seven patients. It was obvious to all that a lay hospital was needed. Molson, Dr. Loedel, and former army surgeon William Caldwell soon formed a delegation to establish the Montreal General Hospital, which they wanted to supply with 200 beds. On the committee's behalf, in January 1819 Molson presented to the Assembly "eloquent advocacy" to their petition for a grant for hospital funds.

January 15, 1819

"On Mr. Molson's motion, to resolve that it is necessary to establish a Public Hospital in Montreal ... the Speaker recognizes the honourable member for Huntingdon."

Michael O'Sullivan, an Irish Catholic lawyer who mistrusts the medical profession, rises to his feet and raises his fist in the air. "It's rubbish!" he thunders.

All heads snap around with surprise. No one has anticipated the vehemence with which O'Sullivan opposes the delegation's petition for a grant.

"However much we admire English institutions, gentlemen, it can never be enough to overlook our means! As a war veteran, a lawyer, and a thinking man, I contend that we have a perfectly good hospital, the Hôtel Dieu, which has served this city for more than a hundred and fifty years!"

Murmurings of assent and dissent ripple around the room. O'Sullivan leans forward and thumps his fist on the table.

"What good is a hospital to the incurable? I ask you, if it were God's will that you were to die, would you choose the arrogant fumbling of some greedy heathen over the tender ministration of a good sister? Patients should be nursed by women devoted to the service of God, not by mercenary hirelings!"

The room grows quieter as he continues.

"What are men like Molson and Richardson, or doctors like Caldwell and Bender, to do with a grant, except buy new carriages and coats? It's indecent for this delegation to be masquerading such mercenary intentions as altruistic. Ill immigrants, they say? Soon immigrants will stop coming. I, gentlemen, will be casting my vote against this motion."

An anonymous letter is published in the *Canadian Courant* some weeks later. The writer names O'Sullivan a coward, one of the most insulting things a man can call another. O'Sullivan demands and is given the letter-writer's name: William Caldwell. He promptly challenges the Scottish surgeon to a duel.

Most duels these days are formalities only. The majority of those involved consider the mere presence of their opponent to be a worthy and honourable response, and simply fire their shots into the air. In this case, however, O'Sullivan's rage runs deep and will not be assuaged. The men meet at Windmill Point in March. When Caldwell's first bullet strikes O'Sullivan in the leg, horrified witnesses think O'Sullivan will concede defeat. He insists on a second face-off. Caldwell shoots him in his other leg. Still, O'Sullivan will not give in. Five times they exchange fire. Dr. Caldwell's arm is shattered and bloody, his neck grazed. There is a look of shock on his face. O'Sullivan has been shot thrice. The third bullet has entered his chest and lodged in his spine, but he survives.

Governor Sherbrooke supported Molson's hospital lobbying, sympathizing with the group from more than an altruistic point of view. He didn't enjoy the best of health himself. Sherbrooke, who was an albino, had a malformation of one eye, which gave him the appearance of almost always having his eyes closed, and he suffered from a paralysis of his left side. During the time that the Sherbrookes stayed in Montreal, the Molsons frequently sent them gifts of apricots, plums and "sweetwater grapes" that their gardener, Mr. Mackenzie, had grown. Sir John gave Sarah a prize-winning pig, which was looked after in a pen near the brewery.

In the wake of the Assembly's disappointing lack of response to the hospital bill, private donations accumulated, most from the petitioners themselves: Molson, Richardson, Peter McGill, Sir John Johnson, the Torrance brothers and Benaiah Gibb. Dr. Xavier Bender, so delighted with the progress of the hospital plans, "promenaded" in front of his house on Nôtre Dame Street, in his old-fashioned ruffled shirt and silk stockings, tossing his powdered hair over his snuff-coloured coat.

By May of 1819, a twenty-four-bed institution was opened on Craig Street (now St-Antoine), and the official Montreal General Hospital admitted its first patient. The first "committee of management" included Alexander Skakel, Thomas McCord, Abner Bagg, Horatio Gates, Dr. Blackwood and John Torrance. Bread, butter, meat, soup and beer were provided for the hospital's five hired staff. Richardson donated £4,000 to the building fund, while Molson gave £1,000.

It is difficult to imagine how Molson might have found time to go fishing, yet his account book lists several purchases of fishing tackle during this time. In addition to steamship duties and Masonic, hospital and Council meetings, he hosted fancy dinners at the Mansion House, including one for the Duke of Richmond and another as a farewell for Sherbrooke, when his ill health finally forced him to return to England.

In June 1821, the cornerstone for the new Montreal General Hospital on Dorchester Street was laid by Sir John Johnson, with solemn Masonic rites; corn, wine and oils were poured over the stone. To show support, ships in the harbour were festooned with flags, and the 60th Regiment band played "God Save the King" under arches of flowers near the Nelson monument. A dedication service for the hospital was held at St. Gabriel's. Afterward, the Masons hosted a dinner for Sir John Johnson, which Molson attended both as a mason and as a hospital patron. John Richardson sat as chairman and first president when the hospital's charter was granted in 1823. All four Molsons were named to its board of directors.

The bank's stability depended entirely upon the morals and reputations of the owners. It wasn't money Richardson, Moffat, Gates and the others needed from Molson.

CHAPTER ELEVEN

MOLSON'S "MADNESS"

AT THE time the Molson partnership was drawn up in 1816, John Molson Senior was worth about £70,000, making him, at fifty-three, though not so wealthy as some, a functional millionaire by today's terms. According to the Lincolnshire *Boston & Spalding Free Press*, he had by then become "the most wealthy and munificent of Montreal's citizens." This was probably an exaggeration, for Simon McTavish, "the Marquis," in his lifetime known as the richest man in Canada, had accumulated a fortune estimated at £160,000 at the time of his death in 1804. Another fur-trading Scot who had courted prosperity was James McGill, who died in 1813 leaving more than £100,000.

While the economic peak of the fur trade had passed, there were other sources of profits in Montreal, and the areas now growing rapidly were brewing, lumber, shipping and real estate. Three more breweries had been established since Molson's: James Goddard's Black Horse Brewery on St. Mary Street, Miles Williams's brewery on College Street, and James Dunn's brewery (to become Dow & Dunn's) at Chabiollez Square. Soon there would be other competitors in the St. Lawrence steamship business.

Brewing, banking, hotelkeeping and shipping shared one important advantage: almost every item or service bought was on account, while almost every sale made was for cash. Hotel staff and steamship captains, engineers and crew were paid at season's end. Brewery equipment, hotel furniture, butchers' bills, steamship supplies and maintenance costs were invoiced.

The Molsons invested conservatively and were able to keep every account up to date so diligently that credit was never denied them. In fact, by the eve of the Lower Canadian Rebellions, when government money was considered worthless, newly printed "Molsons Bank" bills would be readily accepted. With their attention riveted on maintaining a scrupulous reputation, the Molsons' profits multiplied.

Molson had numerous advantages over his competition. He owned coffeehouses and inns where lessees agreed to patronize only his product. Steamships' saloonkeepers were obliged to buy all their malt liquor from him, the only exception being imports from Europe. No taxes, fees or licences were required of brewers or landlords. But Molson's most powerful economic advantage may have been his shipping business. Along with passengers and freight, all his boats shipped beer up and down the river.

According to business historian Merrill Denison, the *Swiftsure* grossed £40,000 in her accident-free, six-season career. She retired in 1817; the next Molson steamboat to be built after the *Lady Sherbrooke* was, for luck, named *New Swiftsure.* The Molson boat's accident-free record was exceptional, for casualties on the river were not infrequent. The Torrances' *Car of Commerce* ran aground one day, and no sooner was repaired and steaming her way into Montreal than merchant Thomas Webster fell overboard and was drowned. The horrors were nowhere near the scale of those in England and the United States, however. Some accidents were described with more relish than others. "The ... spectacle of eight mangled carcasses is yet before our eyes," wrote a *Gazette* reporter about one accident.

The Molsons' and the Torrances' steamships continued to winter in the westernmost channel of the Boucherville Islands. In January 1818, an unusual rise in water caused the ice to shift dramatically, tearing the steamships from their moorings. The *Lady Sherbrooke, Malsham,* and *Caledonia,* a Torrance vessel, were carried on moving plates of ice across thirty acres of land, coming to rest farther down the river, an acre away from the high-water mark. Fortunately, they sustained little damage. The *Swiftsure*, although not lifted as far as the others, was damaged beyond repair. But the loss was inconsequential, since her engines and other salvageable equipment had already been removed the previous season; Molson had not intended to run her any longer.

Of the six steamships that plied the St. Lawrence in 1818, the Molsons owned two (the *Malsham* and *Lady Sherbrooke*, and were part-owners of the tow boats *Quebec* and *Telegraph*). The Torrance brothers owned the *Car of Commerce* and *Caledonia*. The Torrances also ran a successful grocery business, importing liquor and other goods, including raisins, figs, soap, orange and lemon peel, fish sauces and butter.

As a sign of his success, John Torrance began that year constructing a fine residence on Sherbrooke Street. The cut-stone house, occupying the corner of Sherbrooke and St. Lawrence, was considered so far from the city that it was dubbed "Torrance's Folly." The epithet was, in retrospect, appropriate: seven years later, he sold it to John Molson in order to cover debts.

John Richardson, George Moffat (a fur and grain trader), and Horatio Gates (a merchant importer) were among John Molson's business allies who urged him to join them in the formation of the "Montreal Bank" in 1817. Although it seemed natural that a man of Molson's wealth and influence would want to have a stake in the banking community, the brewer was initially hesitant to commit himself.

The founders of the Montreal Bank (later to be known as the Bank of Montreal) had applied several times for a charter from Britain, but had been turned down each time, for reasons that are unclear. Choosing to open without a charter meant the bank could not claim bankruptcy protection. The bank's stability depended entirely upon the morals and reputations of the owners. It wasn't money Richardson, Moffat, Gates and the others needed from Molson; they had amassed a more-than-adequate £25,000 in capital stock. But they all knew that Molson had the soundest reputation among them as a financier. His not joining the others would undoubtedly be perceived as a vote of non-confidence.

Molson's reasons for hesitating were many. A depression had followed the initial boost in the economy in the years after the War of 1812. Uncertain trade conditions and high British tariffs had caused many shareholder-owned banks in the United States to fail. In 1817, many of the investors in the Montreal bank were the same men from Massachusetts who had already backed another private institution, the Bank of Upper Canada. That bank was now reputed to be in a precarious position. (It would fold five years later.)

"Articles of association" were signed in June 1817 by fourteen men including Richardson, Gates and Moffat, who thereafter appointed themselves "directors." Molson was not among them. Instead, as a show of involvement, he offered in October to build premises to the bank's specifications on land he owned in the centre of the city, and lease it on a favourable, twenty-one-year term. The founders may have felt offended by this offer; they promptly and unanimously rejected it.

In March 1818, a bill incorporating the Montreal Bank was passed in the Lower Canadian legislature. By then, the friction between Molson and the bank's owners had been resolved, and John had even joined them as a shareholder and director. That summer the Montreal Bank invested thousands of pounds sterling in government bills of exchange. The cargo was transported aboard Molson's *Lady Sherbrooke* to Quebec, carried in beer kegs to keep it inconspicuous.

The young bank's initial stability was followed by a U.S. financial crisis in the fall of 1818. Boston shareholders sold their stock back to the bank's Montreal promoters, and the bank became exclusively Canadian-owned. The bank issued paper money conservatively, maintaining a slow but significant growth. Late in 1818 a second branch was opened, in Kingston.

When the Montreal Bank received its charter in 1822, its name became Bank of Montreal. In July 1822, editor L.L. MacCulloch, of Montreal's *The Scribbler*, wrote that he, for one, would be happier to see someone like John Molson open a private bank, to give the Bank of Montreal some needed competition:

> *A report that was afloat in the beginning of this year, that the senior partner of an eminent house of trade here, who has more than once been president of our senior bank, intended retiring from mercantile business, and establish a private bank. Such an undertaking, would, I think, be both praiseworthy and profitable. There is another individual in town (and why should I hesitate to name him? I mean Mr.*

John Molson) who, if he would devote part of his capital, time, and exertion, to such an object, would no doubt, succeed in establishing a private bank, that would soon out-rival both the illegal unincorporated banks here, in credit and in custom. All he has to do is to pay the numerous trades-people and work-men he employs in his various undertakings with his own promissory notes, payable to bearer on demand, and they would soon be in extensive circulation, and enjoy the highest credit. A private bank set up by that gentleman, would not only be one of perfect solidity and respect, but would not be liable to the objection of rivalship, urged against the directors of our banks, for his concerns are not of a nature to interfere with the mercantile interests of our general traders."

Montreal was still a small community, especially for men and women of marrying age. No doubt John Senior was as anxious for his third son, now twenty-six, to marry as he had been for his two eldest. By 1819, William Molson had begun to call on Elizabeth Badgley, called Betsey, the nineteen-year-old only daughter of Francis Badgley, a prosperous Montreal merchant. At one time an Assembly member and a former accountant at Molson's, Francis Badgley and his family also attended Christ Church Cathedral. Betsey's brother, William Badgley, was a solicitor who counted the Bank of Montreal among his clients.

Betsey's protective brother had always discouraged suitors, but he tolerated William Molson. He let him take her out on walks from time to time. The couple may have strolled down "Flirtation Lane" between Bleury and Dorchester, a favourite promenade for romantic rendezvous during twilit summer evenings. They may have driven in a carriage up to Mount Royal to walk among the ruins of Simon McTavish's abandoned, unfinished house, which some believed was now haunted by the fur trader's ghost.

All who knew the Molsons and the Badgleys agreed it was a good match: William and Betsey's brief courtship was followed by a simple marriage ceremony.

Also in 1819, Martha gave birth to a daughter, Sarah Anne. Thomas duly recorded in his diary, "Mrs. Thos. Molson confined this date at ½ past four o'clock PM Tuesday of a Daughter named on 17th August at my home by the Rev. Bethune Sarah Anne Molson but not ent'd in his Register book."

The parents' hopes were raised again. Over the next several days Thomas's diary entries were filled with advice gleaned from Mrs. Henry, the nurse:

> *The first thing given to a child after it is Born and for a Day Muscavado sugar and water to purge it, and Womans Milk does not come much before the 3rd day ... when Womens nipples are sore Borax mixed with a little honey and water dissolved to harden them ... first a sweet oil rag put round the nipple with a hole and then a piece of cloth in this Ingredient put over the nipple ... scorched linen Rags to cover Childrens navel after they are born with a bandage ...*

Unfortunately, Thomas and Martha–in common with everyone in those days–did not know about the importance of sterilizing things such as sucking-cloths on babies' bottles, to prevent the growth of bacteria. Many children died of unchecked infections; others died from being given medicines that, instead of helping, did them harm. The infant Sarah Anne died in February 1820.

That spring John Junior and Mary Anne had their second child, a boy named John, and William and Betsey welcomed a little girl, Elizabeth Sarah. John Molson doted on his grandchildren and insisted on seeing them often.

Fire was a constant threat in old Montreal. Churches, homes, businesses and warehouses were frequently gutted. People covered their roofs with sheet iron or tin to avoid using the easily combustible boards and shingles. They kept ladders on their roofs; buckets were filled and ready. But the quantities of water transported to quench a blaze were never sufficient. Unchecked fires frequently left whole sections of suburbs in charred ruins. Even the Molsons would not be spared the devastation of fire.

On March 15, 1821, a steward dropped a candle among some scattered straw in a narrow basement corridor in the Mansion House Hotel. Flames quickly rushed along the floor as the terrified steward fled upstairs. Guests were alerted and were able to make their way out before anyone was injured. Molson joined the frantic efforts to check the fire's spread; but soon it was obvious that there was nothing anyone could do to save the hotel, and the men lined up in relay teams to heave buckets of water at the nearby buildings. Timbers collapsed among showers of brilliant sparks, and the terrible colours were reflected on the surface of the river. By morning the hotel was a gaunt, smouldering shell of stone.

Peter Martinat, the innkeeper, had insured the contents, including furniture, and Molson owned £15,000 of insurance on the building itself. Thanks to the nimble actions of a librarian, the books in the Montreal library were saved, but the Beaver Club's furniture and silver plate were all destroyed.

Three weeks after the fire, an estimate of £13,707 was submitted for rebuilding the hotel. Molson seemed undaunted by the disaster, and in fact was busy making the most of the hand dealt him. Already he was incorporating plans for improvements in the design and operation of the hotel. He had no reason to be discouraged: he was at the peak of his health and vigour, and the brewery was about to surpass 100,000 gallons annually for the first time. But this business genius also had recorded moments of eccentricity.

Lord Dalhousie, who succeeded Richmond as Governor of Lower Canada, found that Molson was anxious to form good relations with him. When he and Lady Dalhousie took their first trip on the *Lady Sherbrooke,* in June 1819, Lord Dalhousie wrote:

> *Mr. Molson, the Proprietor, thinks it his duty to attend the Governor whenever he embarks, and accordingly is now with us. He is a great treat, a speculative enterprising enthusiast, with a great share of quick & drole conversation and repartee.*

Lord Dalhousie wrote about John Molson again on July 6, 1819:

> *Our hotel is altogether magnificent, a splendid house furnished from London, & the Proprietor, Mr. Molson, quite a character. Hearing that he was a curiosity I sent for him today to thank him for his attentions last night. He came to me in a light bed gown as is worn in the East or West Indies, told me his whole history & all his speculations & intentions with prodigious volubility of tongue, & at once breaking off in his harangue, he bolted away laughing in a most eccentric manner. He is quite mad in my opinion, but his madness fortunately runs towards public improvements. He is very rich & very liberal, sole proprietor of several steam boats, of an extensive Brewery of Beer & Porter, of large works in the blacksmith trade–a variety of others, & this Hotel, which he has let for £800 a year, but touches nothing, & saying that he broke away from me.*

Martha's labour pains started for her third child at midnight on the first of December 1821, and she delivered another boy at 3:15 the following afternoon. Again, Dr. Robinson and Mrs. Henry attended the birth. The infant, named Thomas, was christened four weeks later by John Bethune Junior, rector of Christ Church.

A few months later, another grandchild arrived. William wrote to his brothers and his father from Quebec on the first of July 1822:

> *Gentlemen*
>
> *I received yours per* Lady Sherbrooke *as also my Beer per* Caledonia, *my Buckets and Hams by last Car for which I am much obliged to you for your trouble ... I have the satisfaction of being able to inform you that Betsey was put to Bed on Sunday afternoon of a Boy / not a very large one but fatter than Elizabeth was, and she has been able to eat a slice of toste for her tea this evening, I shall say no more in her*

favour; the Boy is also quite well and has taken his bottle like a young soldier.

William seems to have been quite an attentive parent both to his daughter Elizabeth and his son, William Junior. This time, however, Thomas Senior couldn't give as much attention to the doings of his family. He was busier than ever, for in November 1821 he had started a distilling business next to the brewery. Twenty years had passed since Molson's earlier attempt had been abandoned, but Thomas, who had never lost interest in the idea, remembered that distilling could be far more profitable than brewing. He filled his diary with scrupulous notes and details on the distilling process–the time involved, the expenses and the potential production. Because there were no published books on the subject, he wrote down everything that others told him:

29 Nov 1821

Gin is made from Whisky. Thos White our Cooper tells me that Juniper Berries are put with the Whisky to give it the Gin flavour, and the Liquid Roman Vitriol is mixed with it to take away the coarse flavour from it and Doctor Robinson tells me that Juniper Berries are put into the Still with the Wash, and up the Country the people make one Gallon Whisky from a Bushel of Potatoes.

In November 1822, Thomas sent 237 gallons of whisky on board the *Lady Sherbrooke* to Quebec, to be shipped from there to Greyhurst & Hewatt (formerly Greyhurst & Harvey), the Molsons' agent in London. The response was extremely encouraging. The following spring, Thomas shipped them another 1,385 gallons of whisky. Whether the second shipment was lost, met with some accident, or was stolen is not known, but the whisky never arrived at its destination.

Chapter Twelve

Ten Years in Kingston

June 3, 1824

Martha Molson's back aches. The coach road that links steamship service to Upper Canada is muddy and uneven between Cornwall and Prescott. The air is unbearably humid. Just when Martha thinks she can put the baby, three-week-old Martha Junior, in her basket, the coach lurches again. Innumerable blackflies buzz around them. Two-and-a-half-year-old Tommy, or "Master Thomas" as his grandfather calls him, has become irritable; he keeps kicking at the lid of the picnic basket at their feet. The servant maid has run out of ideas to amuse him. It is their third day of travelling. It seems as though they will never get there.

"Madame," says Ducette, the servant maid, sympathetically, *"vous savez qu'ici c'est plus comfortable que dans un batteau, n'est ce pas?"*

"One traveller called this a road that should have been included by Dante as the highway to Pandemonium, for none can be more decidedly infernal," Martha replies.

Ducette smiles. Martha tries hard to think how fortunate they are, particularly to be sitting here in a coach and not, like the majority of steerage passengers who were on board the steamer, herded into the *batteaux* at Dickinson's Landing. She knows that the servant maid, whose wages are a gift from John Senior, is trying to be kind. She manages a weak smile.

"Undoubtedly you are right," Martha continues, "but what I have heard of the barbarism of Upper Canada–the woods, the bears, the Indians, the log-huts–has caused my nerves to receive quite a shock."

Martha and her children were on their way to Kingston, where Thomas was waiting for them. The Molsons' seven-year brewery partnership had expired, and Thomas had decided–after much serious thought–to break out on his own.

"Balance, apparently in his favour, subject to his share of loss by bad Debts and other Contingencies winding up the Concern ... £4022/4/0," his father had written in the account book. Four thousand pounds was no sum to scoff at, particularly for a brewer-distiller with experience and determination. Thomas wanted to settle in Upper Canada's fastest-growing garrison town, Kingston, and had bought from Captain Henry Murney a house, stables, and a brewery on two acres of Kingston waterfront. With a population of 2,336 in 1824, the town was surrounded by farms that produced an abundance of barley and wheat.

Martha had not been able to make this journey to Upper Canada earlier because she had been advised not to travel very far during her pregnancy, especially in the springless stagecoaches. The previous November, when she and Thomas had left on a trip to England to purchase brewing equipment in London, she hadn't known she was pregnant. They had taken Ducette with them, leaving–for the first time–their adored Tommy Junior, who was to stay in Montreal with his grandparents. But Martha had taken their leather-bound bible with them, tucking inside it mementoes such as a lock of Tommy's blond hair, which she had snipped when he was four months old.

In London, they had stayed in a modest but respectable west-end hotel and busied themselves with practical as well as business matters. Thomas took their pocket watches to the clockmaker to be repaired; Martha purchased brooches and a pearl necklace, ordered some dresses, and consulted Doctor Bousfield about a sore foot. It was he who had confirmed her pregnancy. Perhaps to celebrate this news, Martha had her hair done up in French curls. Thomas purchased equipment he would need for his new brewery. Because of her delicate condition, she did not accompany Thomas when he took a coach to Lincolnshire to visit relatives, including Ann Gibbins, and call on tenants in the county to collect old rents owed to his father.

After a quiet winter back in Montreal, the new baby, Martha, was born. Two weeks later, Thomas was packing up their furniture in preparation for their move to Kingston. Together the couple emptied wardrobes and filled trunks with broadcloth, cotton, beddings, tableware, seal slippers, boots, drapery, cloths, cambric handkerchiefs, calico, silk hose, shawls, parasols, a "riding habit of ladies, extra bronze green cloth elegantly braided," silk corsets, silver thimbles, fine steel scissors, combs, toothbrushes, Martha's embroidered, lined silk pelisse, Thomas's brewing books, and their leather-bound bible.

Martha had confessed none of her trepidation about living in Upper Canada to Thomas, who had left two days ahead of them to prepare for their arrival. Thomas's stories of orderliness and finery certainly contradicted the wild tales about bears and Indians that she had read in the travel books. The changing of the guard in Kingston, he had told her, was an event as eagerly anticipated as Sunday afternoon church parades. Assemblies, promenade concerts, dances, charity fêtes and balls adorned the town's social scene, and citizens came to the waterfront to hear the bands play.

June 3, 1824

As the coach continues along the "infernal" highway, Martha tries to think of all there is to look forward to, but it is an effort. Right now she wants only a comfortable place to rest and a chance to wash off the mud caking the bottom of her travelling skirts.

Tommy finally settles on the floor next to Ducette's feet, absorbed in one of the picture books that his grandfather has given him. Martha sets the baby into the basket. She closes her eyes and says a prayer. Her eyes are shut for what seems a short time. When she opens them, the forest has given way to swamp and meadows. To her surprise, she can see for miles.

Martha hands the basket to Ducette, and lifts little Tommy up to the seat next to her. Tommy clamps his chubby hands on the sill and cranes his neck to get a better view. He stretches an arm out to point at oxen dragging ploughs through even furrows. Settlers raise their hats in greeting as the convoy of coaches passes by. Split-rail fences define the edges of fields. Martha's spirits lift as the river comes into view again, and along its shore the town of Prescott materializes. Supper and lodging have been arranged for them here.

Even before the Molson partnership agreement had run its course, Thomas had decided to leave Montreal and start his own brewery. First, there had been fifteen months of frustration working with Thomas Purcell, a brewer whom John Senior had hired but with whom Thomas never saw eye to eye. There was also the matter of the lost shipment of spirits. John Junior blamed his brother Thomas for the £200 loss (which, under the terms of the partnership agreement, was shared equally). John Senior extended Thomas his blessing: "Our friends think it wrong we should have separated. I know that but had it not been for your reasons I should not have listened to it … To me you are all alike; I shall Act as nearly equal to you all as I can–whatever you decide on, whatever you do, may it turn out for the best ..."

One very clear advantage of Thomas's move to Upper Canada was that there, the prevailing British law meant that both he and Martha could will their assets to whomever they wished. Molson Senior's advice to Thomas before he left Lower Canada was typically empirical: "James Stuart observed yesterday that … Martha's making her will in your favour would be drawing [away] all the danger … [I] told him I was fully aware of that but that wills could be altered or destroyed every day–and that nothing human was perfectly certain–but of that judge for yourself."

June 4, 1824

The steamship they take the next day is festooned with flags and bunting on this last leg of their journey. Martha has forgotten it is King George's birthday, still faithfully celebrated in Upper Canada five years after his death. By early evening, the calm expanse of Lake Ontario comes into view, and a gentle momentary silence falls. The scene is mesmerizing. For a moment, fully rigged sailing vessels seem motionless in the distance. Clouds of smoke from steamers cease streaming in the sky. As they draw nearer to the town wharf, they can see that bands are already assembled at the park, and people, all gaily dressed, surround a platform. They can hear the peal of church bells across the water. Martha and Ducette can see Wolfe Island and the limestone ramparts of Fort Henry on the hill. The last of the sun's rays seem suddenly to melt and the town of Kingston is awash in a buttery light, illuminating cream-coloured limestone walls and clusters of pale blossoms on fruit trees. The bustle of Montreal seems a world away.

At the steamship wharf Thomas is waiting with a carriage to meet his family when they disembark. With a characteristic gruffness that conceals his pride, he escorts them along King Street to their new home on the waterfront, pointing out George Herchmer Markland's house on the lot next to theirs. And then, Martha's heart suddenly swells at the sight of a picturesque homestead, its garden springing to life, and beyond, its own wharf, brewery, stables, coach-house, wood house, ice house, and more gardens.

Thomas has spent half of his capital–two thousand pounds–to buy this waterfront lot from Captain Murney outright. He has already installed his equipment and begun improvements on the brewery building. In the fading light, Martha can see scaffolding strapped to the tower. Long shadows bloom from a grove of trees behind Church Street, a tiny woods that separates their property from open fields. Farther up King Street is a cluster of frame houses, their squared lots lined with whitewashed fences. A cow lifts her head, and chickens scatter as Thomas slows the horses and their carriage pulls into the yard.

Some weeks after the Molsons took up residence in Kingston, a series of anonymous letters to the editor appeared in the Kingston *Chronicle*. Similarly panegyric in tone, each praised "Molson's Brown Ale" and expressed the writer's appreciation that this superior brew was soon to be available in Kingston. The last of these thinly disguised advertisements appeared in the early fall of 1824, just before the first hogsheads of Thomas's ale and porter were ready:

> *Mr Editor:*
> *I some time since took occasion to draw your attention to Mr. Molson's new Brewing establishment–I then observed, that of all the improvements going on about town, not one of them interested me half so much as the new Brewery. I lately visited the premises and was certainly much gratified–and without waiting at present to give a minute description of the building, I may say generally, that there is something so substantially English about it as at once to insure to the public both beer and porter, not only at a much cheaper price, but of a quality far superior to any thing of the kind hitherto known in this Province. Mr. Molson is just the kind of character we wanted here–he has capital, and he has also industry, energy and enterprise, to apply that capital to useful purposes. Indeed the community are already beginning to feel the advantages arising from his exertions–they are now supplied with excellent beer at the very moderate rate of 6d per gallon ... Malt liquor ... as is well known, affords a cheap, healthy and invigorating beverage, especially to the working classes. That my anticipations in this respect are already in some measure verified, will appear from the following circumstance–A few evenings since as I was sauntering along the streets, I heard a noise proceeding from a house near me, where as it afterwards appeared, a few tradesmen met to spend a merry evening together. That they were merry and happy was very evident, but there was a mellow softness in their voices that plainly told they were indulging in neither rum nor brandy–there was no fierce brawling or ill-humour there–the very essence of harmony prevailed. They sung something like the following catch with great glee. "Drain the jug, draughtily, Tipple boy, tipple boy: Lay to it mouthily, Swigging boy, swigging boy; Warm it now nosily, Rosy boy, rosy boy, And be not outfaced by Molson's brown ale."*
>
> *An Inhabitant*

Once he had the brewery in order and running to his satisfaction, Thomas hired a sixteen-year-old Irish Protestant apprentice named James Morton. When warm weather brought brewery production to a standstill, Thomas and Morton set about building a distillery on the Molson property. (Morton worked with Molson for seven years, then established his own brewery on premises leased from Thomas.)

Martha and Thomas quietly made themselves at home in Kingston. They attended St. George's Cathedral, known as the "Kingston Garrison Church," with their neighbours and had their next babies baptized there: John Henry Robinson, born in 1826; Mary Anne Elizabeth, in 1828; and Harriet Bousfield in 1830.

Invitations came and went between Martha and her neighbours Mrs. Markland (George's elderly mother) and Miss Clark, who were members of the Ladies' Benevolent Society. The women piously stitched bookmarks (one proclaimed, "Righteousness exalteth a nation") and embroidered household ornaments to be sold for Christian missions. When Thomas was away, which was frequent, Martha wrote him long letters.

When the children weren't doing chores for their mother, they found time to play games of marbles, tag, and make-believe. They built a makeshift shelter within the grove of trees, which would be a play house one day and a garrison fort the next. Mary Anne, who loved animals, tended pigeons and rabbits in outside coops and pens. When a rabbit litter was born, she briefly cuddled the newborns, not realizing that the mother would reject them. The cow on whom the family relied for all their household milk was never fenced in and repeatedly wandered off. The neighbour's poultry occasionally helped themselves to the Molsons' garden.

In September there was tomato ketchup to make, melons to preserve. Martha had her hands full with five children under ten years old. With Ducette's help she tried to manage the often unruly household. While Ducette cooked, brought in kindling, and fed the horses, Martha did the mending, scrubbed and wrung out the washing, and with practised fingers pegged wet clothes to the line in the wind–carefully, since it was against the law to hang her undergarments next to Thomas's.

During the summers Martha and the children would go on weekly boating parties, where a favourite destination was Garden Island, three miles away. Thomas would note in his diary when the first basket-bearers of each fruit would appear at the door, so the family could go to the island to gather their own wild grapes, cherries, chokecherries, plums, gooseberries, currants, strawberries, raspberries, bilberries, mulberries, butternuts and filberts.

When they tired of picking berries, they climbed the fifty-foot tower erected in the middle of the island to enjoy the panoramic view. One day, from the lofty platform the wind carried to their ears a single harmonious musical note that sounded like a dignified Franciscan choir. They could see the tin roofs of the city, the surrounding green-checkered countryside, and the widening whiteness of the lake. Closer and clearer were Navy Bay and Fort Henry, where traces of the footpaths that curved down the glacis to the water's edge were marked by a scattering of goats placidly munching on the grass, weeds and clover.

Martha found her place in the quasi-aristocracy of United Empire Loyalists and British immigrants who dominated the social strata. She joined the Female Benevolent Society, the "little band of capable and large-hearted ladies," staying on as a "manageress" for them for five years. She became a member of the Kingston Auxiliary Bible Society, supported local charities, and organized bazaars. Thomas, too busy with his successful brewery and distillery to do so much as attend a single society dinner, was nominated and appointed Town Collector in June 1827. In the conflict between the administrators (or "nobs," as they were known) and the wealthy businessmen (the "snobs"), Thomas fitted somewhere in the middle.

Pomp and pageantry in Kingston were generated by the military presence. Ceremonies marked the arrival of each garrison relief. Patriotic societies hosted dinners. In 1830 an invitation from the Honourable Captain and Lady Byng arrived at the Molson household requesting their attendance at a fancy dress ball, a new fashion from Europe. Some of the 103 guests, dressed as royalty, three as "free and independent niggers," one as a "Highland Shepherdess," another a "French Cavalier," and another a "Greek Chieftain." Most women saw in this event an opportunity to wear their "most beautiful and fancy dresses." Martha, who went without her husband, dressed as "Sister Ruth, a very pretty, formal, stiff Quakeress," perhaps better to conceal her latest pregnancy. Such a grand success was the ball that "every individual saw daylight."

On May 10, 1832, Kingston residents were warned that Asiatic cholera was making its way up the river. Men were hired to remove "filth" from the town's streets. May 16 was proclaimed a Public Fast Day, and nervous murmurs of humility and prayer could be heard in every hall and home. All along the waterfront, including Thomas's property, ramshackle sheds were set up to isolate immigrants and treat the sick among them. People smoked tar through pipe-length sticks as a preventive.

On May 20, the first case of cholera was confirmed. The Female Benevolent Society, which ran a primitive hospital, held an emergency meeting. Volunteer efforts were coordinated to administer brandy and water to the patients in the hospital and the tents. Lemons, lemon juice, and peppermint were stockpiled. The beds began to fill up. Patients died. Doctors came and went, giving their patients opium, laudanum, cordials, sulphate of quinine, or emetics.

By June, dozens of people were succumbing to the epidemic daily. From their home, Thomas, Martha and their children could hear the constant groans, prayers and curses emanating from the waterfront shelters. Hammers tapped incessantly as rough coffins were assembled. There were not enough coffins for the numbers of people dying. By late July, corpses could be seen piled on the "dead cart" that passed along King Street in the mornings and the afternoons. The burying ground was five or six bodies deep, with layers of lime between.

Church bells pealed in widening circles across the water; Martha prayed and watched helplessly as smoke rose next to the shelters where clothing and belongings were burned in an attempt to halt the disease. She saw the pyres being fed with rich velvet and silk gowns, costly bonnets and shawls, children's frocks, the rags of the poor curling next to resplendent uniforms, boots with spurs attached, and the pieces of charred lacy handkerchiefs fluttering and dancing wildly away from the infernos, whose flames rose higher than houses.

In 1833 another son was born to Thomas and Martha; they named him Markland in honour of their neighbour and friend George Markland, who had just been named Attorney General. The new baby was, fortunately, unaffected by a scarlet fever epidemic that swept through Kingston in October of that year. The epidemic would, however, claim many lives over the next several weeks, including, sadly, that of eleven-year-old Master Thomas Molson.

A fire in the brewery in December 1833 was quickly contained, though not before many livestock and articles were destroyed. Thomas was unable to persuade his father that insurance still held by him in Montreal was valid and could be applied to the replacement of his lost equipment. "It is supposed," reported the Kingston *Chronicle,* "no part of the property was insured." In addition to the brewery, 30 hogsheads of ale were destroyed, along with 5,000 bushels of grain, and 50 puncheons of high-wines.

The grief and losses felt by the family at this time were acute. It is not surprising that a few months later, early in 1834, Martha wrote Thomas that nine-year-old Martha's behaviour had become "more ungovernable than ever":

> *I am sorry to say she appears to have lost all sense of Religion, Duty, Modesty, and propriety of conduct altogether. I know not what she will turn out to if you do not find some place for her. I am doing all I can to bring her to a sense of her duty. I cannot even send her to a closet but she will take something and hide it and then declare she has not got any thing and in the course of the day I shall perhaps find it hid. I am seriously unhappy about her. I try what indulgence will do and I try what severity and it is all the same. I can neither make her sew, learn her lessons, or practice, as soon as I turn my back away she goes to Ducette and behaves in a most improper manner. Do pray seriously consider what to do with her as she is now at an age that if put under proper restraint may still turn out a comfort to us.*

Thomas had refused to consider sending the children away to school. Both his brothers in Montreal had sent their first sons to the Cornwall Grammar School, where the Reverend Hugh Urquhart was now the head master. Thomas didn't agree with Urquhart's Presbyterian principles, so young Tommy, Martha and John Henry had been kept at home while their father sought acceptable schools for them. Their mother worried about John HR's health ("my dear little John I am most truly concerned for") and that Martha was growing up immodest and unchecked.

Kingston too was changing. A penitentiary was being built in 1834, the first section of which was to have 144 cells. A petition in January 1835 claimed that "experience has shown, that if a Penitentiary should go into operation ... it will bring the labour of convicts in competition with the interest of your Petitioners ... and will ultimately ... drive from this town a large, valuable and industrious portion of its population." Reformers won a second majority in the Assembly. Another cholera epidemic broke out. After nearly eleven years in Kingston, Thomas didn't hesitate when he received his father's letter asking him to come home to Montreal.

Chapter Thirteen

Rumours in the Boardroom

In 1824, the first Molson partnership agreement had ended, and the second one, excluding Thomas, had begun. For five years, William had been acquiring and managing properties in Quebec, as well as overseeing the eastern end of the steamship business. He and Betsey had lived right by the Molson Wharf at the foot of the Citadel. Here William had coordinated ticket sales, monitored freighting, and hired stevedores, engineers and steamship crews. He was known as "Monsieur William" to all, even the ship chandlers from whom he purchased the *cornets de brume*, the *hublots*, the *portes-voix* and the marlinespikes that he needed.

Quebec was a dramatic and lively port in summer. Ceremonial processions led past the Mariners' Chapel toward Près de Ville, where church bells and ships' bells would peal together in joyous clamour. The waterfront teemed with life: lumberjacks; the *gaffes* who ran among the log booms; groups of sailors; carpenters; priests blessing ships while anxious masters looked on. Along immaculate narrow streets and steep *ruelles* leading to the upper town, flowers seemed to dance in windowsills of the three- and four-storey houses. Laundry lines criss-crossing the uppermost storeys were hung with linens that rippled like sails in the wind.

In 1824, when Thomas and Martha has departed for Kingston, William and Betsey returned to Montreal and settled their household (including three children and four servants) into the home at St. Mary's Current that Thomas's family had vacated. The three children were four-year-old Elizabeth, two-year-old William, and newborn Annie. While Betsey was grateful to be among her close-knit family again, both she and William missed Quebec City.

Mary Anne and John Junior, who lived nearby, had two sons now: four-year-old John, and two-year-old Elsdale. Their household included a nurse/cook and three male servants. William and John Junior worked long hours away from home. But Betsey and Mary Anne were not comfortable with each other, so the two families rarely socialized.

After Thomas and Martha had left for Kingston, John Senior, John Junior, and William found themselves busier than before. The brewing season was coming to a close, the shipping season was upon them again, and reconstruction had begun on the Mansion House Hotel. By now John Senior was hoping to retire from the brewery and enjoy the role of steamship proprietor. He also wanted to be able to consult daily with the planners, carpenters, joiners, masons, and painters involved in the rebuilding of the Mansion House Hotel (soon to be renamed Masonic Hall Hotel). Mostly, he looked forward to spending more time on his experimental farming.

Farming appealed to the elder Molson on many levels. It was in his family background; and he knew good soil when he saw it, and how to coax crops to grow. He had installed tenants on the farms and often joined them on summer afternoons, discussing weather or weeds and sharing the satisfaction of seeing the fields come to fruition. Molson grew wheat, oats, barley and potatoes. The barley was sent to the brewery to be malted, and the spent grains would then be fed to the delivery horses. In turn, all the horse manure (collected even en route) was carted to the Molson farms and used as fertilizer. Molson's patience and success caught the eye of the editor of an agricultural report in July 1824:

> *Two farms belonging to J. Molson, Esq. which but a few years back were completely over run with weeds, and almost incapable of producing any*

crop, but which by a summer fallow and drill crops, that gentleman has now brought into a state of the highest cultivation, and where he has this season crops ... which may outvie with any in the District for cleanness, quality and quantity, on the same extent of ground. Such examples cannot fail to be beneficial in the country. They afford to the Canadian husbandman, occular proof of what may be done by well directed exertions, and it is only to be regretted they are not more numerous in the Seigniories.

In 1824 John Molson Junior took his father's place on the Bank of Montreal's board of directors. At thirty-seven, John Junior was the youngest board member. When the effects of an economic depression in England hit Montreal, John Senior once again became uneasy about the future of the Bank of Montreal. His fears were well founded. Simon McGillivray, one of the institution's largest clients, became insolvent–the largest in a series of business collapses. Rumours flew; Montreal's confidence in the bank plummeted; stock dropped to half its previous value; and worried clients lined up to withdraw their money.

Through his son, Molson Senior was aware of what was going on in the boardroom. Some believed the president, Samuel Gerrard, should be held personally responsible for a large portion of the bank's losses. One day in October 1825, Thomas Thain, who was both the bank's vice-president and McGillivray's accountant-partner, vanished–locking the door to his office and apparently taking the key. Months later a letter from Thain arrived from Scotland, where he had gone "to obtain medical advice in the country and visit relatives." In fact, he was in an asylum. For him, returning meant answering some difficult questions, which he was not prepared to do.

When Samuel Gerrard announced his immediate resignation as president of the Bank of Montreal, everyone except John Molson Junior seemed unprepared. Horatio Gates was elected as Gerrard's replacement, on the explicit condition that the position would be temporary, and John Fleming became vice-president. Expectation of Thain's ever returning had faded, and a new resolution was passed permitting the replacement of board members after an absence of three months. On June 2, 1826, Gerrard asked the senior Molson to consider taking on the presidency of the Bank of Montreal.

June 9, 1826

Another directors' meeting is under way. It is apparent that neither Horatio Gates nor George Moffat, another senior member, is interested in the presidency. Gates wishes to pursue politics, Moffat to expand his large and successful business into Upper Canada. Bank policies would not allow either venture.

When Gerrard mentions the Molson name, Moffat stutters. "Molson? Why, he's not even two score. He has no experience!"

"John Molson Senior, Moffat. Senior," Gerrard corrects sharply.

"Molson? But he's only a shareholder," Fleming objects.

"Then we'll put him back on the board."

"Who would like to step forward, to tender his resignation, to make way for him?"

No one is surprised to see John Junior rise instantly to his feet–as if rehearsed to do so. But suddenly Frederick Ermatinger, former sheriff of Montreal, is waving him down and loudly composing his own resignation.

"Is Mr. Molson agreeable to this plan?" asks Gates.

"Yes, he has given his assent," Gerrard answers.

"Very well then, I would like to resign immediately," Ermatinger repeats. "Who will make a motion for his nomination as president?"

"I will," replies John Molson Junior.

"John Molson Senior, to the position of president of the Bank of Montreal. Any opposed? All in favour? It is unanimous. The motion is carried."

Long respected for his "unswerving honesty, creative imagination and bold achievement," Molson was a diplomatic choice for this weighty position. Two weeks later, on June 20, 1826, Ermatinger was persuaded to rejoin the board, and John Junior stepped down. One of Molson Senior's first memos as president made his priorities clear:

> *The Board, having had under its consideration the evil tendency of disagreement among the officers of the Bank, deem it necessary to declare that it is their bounden duty individually and collectively to uphold the character and respectability of the Institution by the performance of their daily avocations with temper and forbearance thereby conciliating the confidence of the public and the respect and esteem of each other. And the Directors are fully determined to mark any instance of neglect of such duty or breach of decorum in the Bank with the severest displeasure of the Board.*

Molson cast the deciding vote not to prosecute Simon McGillivray for his unpaid loan, an action that might have landed the debtor in prison. Eventually, McGillivray recovered financially and repaid the bank. For a time under Molson's leadership, directors and staff saw their salaries reduced while dividend payments were suspended as capital reserves were replenished. But before long, employees were earning more than they had been, and when payments to shareholders resumed they were calculated at a higher rate. Public confidence in the institution was restored.

By the end of the summer of 1825 Molson's hotel was completely rebuilt. The new sign read "Masonic Hall Hotel." (It was subsequently renamed the British American Hotel to correct the misconception that accommodations were exclusive to Masons.) The new premises were even more spacious and opulent than the old. Another cellar had been excavated, and a billiard room added. Windows were double-glazed. Peter Martinat was rehired to manage the hotel.

While the new hotel was nearing completion, Molson commissioned a design for a theatre and undertook its construction next door. He managed to raise £5,000 (two-thirds of the cost of construction) by selling 200 shares in Montreal's first permanent theatre at £25 each; he paid for the rest of the construction himself and retained forty-four shares.

November 21, 1825

Everything is in readiness for the opening night performance at the Theatre Royale. The senior and junior John Molsons, along with William and Betsey, enter their reserved box with the white and gilt arches and red-plush railings. John Senior and William escort Sarah and Betsey. Mary Anne is not with the family. The men, looking well turned-out in black suits and cravats, carry their top hats and greatcoats to the cloakroom. Betsey, in a gown of pale blue organdy, with the empire waistline that is the fashion of the day, and Sarah, in tweed lined with silk that rustles and makes sparks in the darkness against the plush seats, survey the theatre.

Molson's Theatre Royale is the first theatre to be built in Montreal. It is designed to resemble its namesake in Drury Lane, London. The interior's domed ceiling supports a great crystal chandelier that matches the one at the Masonic Hall Hotel next door. An orchestra pit wraps around the front of the wedge-shaped stage. Red curtains hang throughout. Heat is provided by wood stoves, and the footlights are straight candles in glass vases that line the edge of the stage. Two tiers of boxes grace the sides of the orchestra pit. Two balconies overlook the stage, and beyond them are the ladies' and gentlemen's cloakrooms and the saloon.

The first half of the evening's entertainment is an interpretation of the popular comedy *The Dramatist,* or *Stop Him Who Can.* Betsey claps enthusiastically; Sarah waves her lace handkerchief over the railing.

Just before intermission, everyone rises while the orchestra plays the British national anthem. Then a quartet of ladies and gentlemen sing some popular songs, the company of actors behind them providing the chorus. After a break for refreshment, there is a second play, a farce called *The Spoil'd Child.* At the end of the evening the entire company joins in a rendition of "Rule Britannia."

While fortune was smiling on the Molsons, John Torrance was reconsidering his involvement in the steamship business. Competition was cutting into his profits. The *Car of Commerce* had run aground and had to be scrapped. The company's newest steamship, the tow-vessel *Hercules,* rammed into the *New Swiftsure,* "injuring her most materially [and] rendering her thereby unnavigable." Torrance's defence of his Captain Brush was not helped by the testimony of Joseph Frignon, a twenty-year-old clerk, who, at the inquiry which followed, insisted that "from the moment the *Hercules* began to prepare to leave the dock, the people aboard of her had a settled determination to run foul of the *New Swiftsure.*"

Repairs took four weeks and cost the Molsons £2,000. John Junior brought a suit against John Torrance and his partners for damages and was awarded £6,000. Torrance's partners, John Brown and William Martlane, then offered either to sell the *Caledonia* outright to the Molsons for £3,500 or to lease her to them for three years at £500 annually. Molson and his sons negotiated, knowing they had little to lose, and finally agreed to lease the *Caledonia* for one year at £225.

Shortly afterward, John Torrance sold his cut-stone house on Sherbrooke Street to Molson, at a loss. It was a well-built and beautiful structure: every joist had been morticed and fastened with hardwood pegs, and the interior woodwork was all of yellow pine. Molson renamed it Belmont Hall. The site–at the northwest corner of Sherbrooke and St. Lawrence–was considered so far out of town that for many subsequent decades tradesmen refused to make deliveries there.

When William McGillivray died in 1826, John Molson was invited to take McGillivray's place in the Masonic Hall as provincial grand master of the District of Montreal and William Henry. William's brother, Simon McGillivray, wished Molson well:

> *Although I have been much occupied and harassed with other matters ... I have not been unmindful of the Masonic Arrangements of your District, and I have the satisfaction to inform you that ... you are ... appointed to succeed my late brother as Provincial GM ... I have the pleasure to enclose under this cover your Patent as Provincial Grand Master, and a very elegant gold jewel befitting your office, which I have taken the liberty of causing to be prepared for you ... I beg leave to congratulate yourself and our Brethren of the District of Montreal.*

By the end of 1826 Molson had acquired several new steamships, tow boats and barges. He formed the St. Lawrence Steamboat Company (known as the "Molson Line") which, in its lifetime, would control thirty-six vessels. Each vessel was faster and more luxurious than the one before it. Competition-conscious, John was careful always to take advantage of the best and newest equipment, and to offer service that exceeded expectations. As each old or damaged ship became unserviceable, it was duly stripped and sunk.

The fastest, most powerful steamship to date, the *John Molson,* broke the Montreal-to-Quebec record on August 15, 1827, when the vessel docked in Quebec after only twenty-one hours, including two stops of forty-five minutes each. Yet by far the crowning achievement of Molson's steamship line was the palatial *John Bull,* launched in September 1831. Her gun streak was painted "so as to represent the upper deck port holes" of a seventy-four-gun ship. John *had* succeeded in building the largest steamship in the world. Nearly 200 feet long, the *John Bull* was so lavishly furnished and finely fitted up that when Governor General Lord Aylmer and his entourage came to Montreal, he would often contact Molson and have the ship anchored in the river to use as his floating residence.

Seasonal accounts reveal that sums between £100 and £300 per vessel were paid annually to the brewery for beer. Steamship company profits rose to exceed £30,000 per year. The Molson family was in control of the most efficient vessels on the St. Lawrence, with a fleet of steamships that outnumbered those operating in the entire United States.

The entire Molson family emerged unscathed from the epidemic. Meanwhile, support for the railway had lost its momentum. Two more years would pass before events would bring the railway closer to becoming a reality.

Chapter Fourteen

A Toast, Your Excellency

Lord Dalhousie described Lower Canada in 1824 as "a country most sadly distressed by party spirit, national jealousies, political speculators and general poverty in all classes and conditions of people." Racio-political feelings were more divided than ever by 1827, when Molson Senior decided to run against Louis-Joseph Papineau, son of Joseph Papineau, in the east ward for the upcoming Lower Canada election. The English Party was publishing tracts, organizing rallies and redefining constitutional issues. When the poll station opened in August, each side tried to prevent its opponents from voting by controlling the approaches to the square. Molson, who had underestimated Papineau's overwhelming support among the French and Irish electorate, withdrew after the first two days of balloting. The poll stayed open for twenty-four days from dawn until dusk, forbidden by law to close until an hour had passed without a vote being registered.

Louis-Joseph Papineau, who had formed the anti-British Patriote Party in 1826, was re-elected Speaker of the Assembly in 1827. Lord Dalhousie, refusing to recognize Papineau as Speaker, prorogued Parliament. In response, Papineau successfully petitioned London the following year to have Dalhousie removed from office. A passionate advocate for a more democratic approach to colonial government, Papineau believed there were too many British-appointed representatives controlling revenue and wielding power in Lower Canada. After the 1827 election, as ransom for his demands, he exercised his right to withhold certain supply bills, including funds consigned to the militia. The announcement that no money would be released to pay the army and public officials was immediately followed by the dissolution of the House. Administration was paralyzed. Watchmen stopped patrolling St. Paul Street; lamps stayed unlit; garbage collectors left refuse to accumulate in rat-infested ditches.

Distrust spread. When La Banque du Peuple began business, rumours circulated among the English that it was run by Patriotes who were using its profits to purchase weapons. The St-Jean Baptiste Society and then Les Fils de la Liberté were created to bring about the end of British rule. Militant anglophones retaliated by establishing the Doric Club. The British Loyalist members called for taxation of land and a union of the two Canadas.

Other passionate Patriote leaders began to emerge, not all from the French community. Thomas Storrow Brown and brothers Wolfred and Robert Nelson raised their voices against their colonial rulers. Dalhousie resisted all their demands. When Britain announced that Dalhousie would be recalled, Sir James Kempt was appointed as interim administrator, with the hope that he would be a more effective conciliator and mediator. As a farewell gesture, Molson Senior organized a lavish six-course dinner for Dalhousie at the British American Hotel.

September 30, 1828

Lord Dalhousie ends his speech by professing that he has no regrets about his term as Governor General.

There is applause, some sincere and some polite.

"A toast, your Excellency! May God grant you speed and a safe voyage home."

"Hear, hear."

It has been a most splendid dinner. A bevy of chefs had prepared a trio of soups–mock turtle, mulligatawny and *potage à la reine.* Next came a second course of fish stewed in port, boiled doré, roasted maskinonge, hams boiled in champagne, legs of mutton, turkeys, chickens, tongues, *bouillé* and corned beef. The third course, laid out around two centrepiece saddles of mutton, consisted of roasts of beef, pork, turkey, lamb and chicken, and *ragout* de veal. Then appeared vol-au-vents browned to perfection, and an arrangement of fancy-dressed partridge, duck, teal, snipe, woodcock, brandt and blue wing. The abundant variety of meat dishes was a supreme compliment to the guest of honour. Finally, the sweets: plum and rice puddings, mince and apple pies, calf's foot jelly, blancmange. Molson's reputation as a host *extraordinare* was confirmed.

By the time the Molsons moved to Belmont Hall in 1826, Sarah's health was failing. Her life had evolved from one extreme to the other, from her privileged birth to her years of financial hardship in the middle of her life. It was a sad irony that although she'd worked hard alongside her husband to gain and save, and was living in relative opulence again, she was, at seventy-three, so affected by rheumatism that she was largely unable to enjoy a life of ease.

Once all their belongings had been safely conveyed to the new residence, Molson had their former home at St. Mary's Current converted into a dwelling-house for brewery staff. The commodious Georgian three-storey house suited Molson perfectly; its distance from the city was not an inconvenience to one who loved space and solitude, as he did. Moreover, the house and its surrounding gardens bore a resemblance to Snake Hall, his boyhood home. Here the servants could have their own quarters, as they had in Lincolnshire. But Molson lived at Belmont Hall for only three years.

In January 1829 the worst snowstorm in its history fell on Montreal. In hours, between three and four feet of snow muffled the city and stranded many people in the country, including the Molsons, for ten days. City dwellers shovelled snow into banks that stood ten to twelve feet high. Sarah's rheumatism worsened, and she was in almost constant pain. Laudanum was the only known remedy at the time, and she began to take more and more of it in an attempt to control the pain.

On March 18, 1829, Sarah died. In keeping with the rest of her life, her quiet passing was unmarked but for a short service at the English Church and burial in the old grounds on Dorchester Street. At seventy-six, she had succumbed quickly to a weakened constitution and the effects of too much laudanum. After living at Belmont Hall for only three years, John Senior saw no point in staying on with servants in such a large house. He moved to his smaller home and farm on St. Marguerite Island, allowing John Junior to establish himself and his family, as well as their cook, nanny and three male servants, in the Sherbrooke Street mansion.

Not long after his mother's death, John Junior sold his share of the brewery back to his father and entered into a partnership with George Carew Davies, a Quebec City merchant. The business was a specialized one, trading in spirits, hardware, cables, anchors, and canvas for sails. Molson, Davies & Co. would operate for nearly ten years.

The partnership of John Molson & Sons (John Senior, John Junior and William) was dissolved, and a new agreement was immediately drawn up between John Senior and William. It seemed, then, to the elder Molson, that William was the only one of his sons who had not deserted him. He made up his mind that he would will the brewery to his youngest son.

Molson's four-year term as president of the Bank of Montreal ended in 1830; he did not run for a second. He was sixty-seven years old. When his colleagues wished him well, one ventured a question: With two of his three fine sons in Montreal whom he could call upon to help him, would Mr. Molson now be retiring from public life?

In fact, retirement was far from Molson's mind. Since 1825 he'd followed with interest the newspaper stories about the progress of a twelve-mile railway that had been constructed in England. Local railway promoter Jason C. Pierce had been to see him, and they had discussed the feasibility of a similar venture in Lower Canada. Although the Bank of Montreal board would not consider putting up the money for a railway, Molson let Pierce know that as a businessman he had a strong personal interest in supporting the venture.

Pierce didn't forget Molson's interest. He returned to Montreal to speak to him again. The railway Pierce had in mind, covering the fourteen miles from La Prairie to St. John's on the Richelieu River, would require an investment of £150,000. Once there was sufficient start-up cash, other investors and government approval would soon follow. Molson quickly invested £36,000, making him the largest single shareholder of the first railway company in Canada.

Since the end of the first decade of the nineteenth century in Canada, haphazard and poorly maintained transportation links between the east and the west had gradually improved with the building of canals. But accelerated trade between Upper Canada and the United States was putting pressure on the inadequate early routes to the south, and in 1830 travellers still took several days to get to New York from Montreal. The longest portion of the journey was made by steamer, which had to cover 100 miles to reach a place only 20 miles away: St. John's. To replace the troublesome, much-avoided portage road, some had proposed building a canal, but the idea was promptly rejected by the Legislative Assembly. A canal would make Montreal too vulnerable in the event of another war with the United States. On the other hand, as the *Gazette* pointed out, a railway could be broken up "on the shortest notice."

Among those businessmen coaxed into enlisting support for the proposed Champlain and Saint Lawrence railway were Horatio Gates, Samuel Gerrard and Peter McGill. But despite the influence these men wielded, other investors held back until August 1831, when news came of the success of the Mohawk and Hudson Railroad connecting Albany with Schenectady. Within weeks, a bill for "Making a Rail-Road from Lake Champlain to the River St. Lawrence" was introduced in the Legislature of Lower Canada. It was passed in December and received Royal Assent by February.

In January 1832, John Senior was appointed to the Legislative Council of Lower Canada. Daniel Tracey, the Irish editor of the pro-Patriote weekly, the *Vindicator*, described the appointments as "eight or ten men with scarcely common talent." Tracey was running in a new by-election himself, pitted against Stanley Bagg Junior (nephew of Abner).

In spring, as the by-election approached, gangs began prowling the night streets. Newspapers vied with each other in harsh opinions and accusations. Polling began on April 24, and the English immediately complained that supporters of the French party were milling about the square–the one voting place in the riding–carrying clubs and knives and intimidating people from voting for Bagg, the Loyalist candidate. When the poll was moved to a house on St. James Street near the Bank of Montreal, unruly mobs followed.

On May 21, a rainy afternoon, Daniel Tracey was declared the winner by a margin of four votes. Many Loyalists suspected fraud. A victory procession soon turned into a riot and magistrates summoned the troops. Rioters hurled stones that had been piled for street paving, and soldiers received orders to advance and open fire. In the panic that followed, three men were killed: a printer named Casimir Chauvin, and two labourers who had helped rebuild Molson's hotel, Pierre Billet and François Languedoc.

These upheavals did not daunt the would-be railroaders. That very month, Jason Pierce, John Molson and the other partners met several times at the Molson's British American Hotel to draw up a prospectus for a railway company, which they eventually published in the Montreal *Gazette.* As Pierce had promised, progress after that was rapid. Experts were called in to the Legislative Council to answer questions about the effect of climate on the "iron roads." How did the company propose to deal with the thirty or forty farms and seigneuries the railway would intersect? Members of the Assembly were brought in to vouch for the "character and responsibility" of the original petitioners.

The partners used the address of the Molson's Exchange Coffee House to collect subscriptions for the railway. Their timing in soliciting public support could not have been worse.

June 1832

The words are first whispered, then shouted.

"God forbid, it's ship fever!"

When the first cases of cholera are diagnosed, no one wants to believe it. The disease creeps insidiously through the town, brought in by immigrants arriving in the *Carrick*, a ship from Dublin in which 59 of 133 passengers and crew have died during the voyage. Newspapers publish grave warnings against putting bare feet on cold floors, drinking on empty stomachs, eating oysters, and sleeping with the windows open. Tar bonfires are lit in the streets at night for fumigation. Camphor and medicinal solutions made with lavender or brandy are routinely recommended.

"Ship fever" is indiscriminate. The newly elected Daniel Tracey is one of the first to die, followed by John Fleming, Molson's successor as president of the Bank of Montreal. Less than a month following the election, a pall of disease hangs over the city. The Montreal General Hospital and the Hôtel Dieu are filled, and hundreds of patients are housed in makeshift tent-clinics. Throughout the scorching heat of summer, more and more people come down with the symptoms: a white, furred tongue, followed by nausea, spasms, cramps, a bluish pallor, then rapid deterioration. Miracle cures and preventatives are sworn by their manufacturers to be effective, yet every hour church bells sound the slow knell of another funeral. Signs appear advertising coffins at lower and lower prices, and funeral services are provided "on short notice, at the lowest prices." The poorest are buried in mass graves as clergy and undertakers become overwhelmed. Troops from St. Helen's Island are called upon to dig more burial pits.

Those who bore the brunt of the cholera epidemic were the Irish immigrants, the general poor and the agricultural workers. The stricken and their families inhabited a different world than those who remained healthy, whose lives continued as they had before. Ladies and gentlemen accustomed to attending dances, dinner parties, balls and ballet performances carried on doing so even in the midst of the surrounding crisis. Merchant families like the Shaws, the Baggs, the Frothinghams and the Molsons not only carried on, but also prospered. Molson's Brewery showed no appreciable change in production or sales; the fourteen steamboats and barges of the St. Lawrence Steamboat Company kept to their schedules. Molson's 1832 account books reveal that the brewery made as much beer, paid as many wages, and bought as many bushels of coal and barrels of meat as usual. On July 5, William Molson invited thirty-two guests to a dance. On July 26, John Junior had twelve guests to dinner at Belmont Hall, and in August both brothers attended "the ballet" at the Theatre Royale.

Writer Susanna Moodie arrived in Montreal in September, on her way to Upper Canada. The streets were still squalid, gloomy and, to her horror, filled with miserable and dejected sufferers of all ages. In her diary she described "darkened dwellings and mourning habilements," "expressions of anxiety" and people's "haggard, care-worn appearance."

Moodie's sister, Catharine Parr Traill, felt "overpowered by the noisome vapour rising from a deep open fosse that ran along the street behind the wharf":

> *This ditch seemed a receptacle for every abomination, sufficient in itself to infect a whole town with malignant fevers ... The opening of all sewers, in order to purify the place, and stop the pestilence, rendered the public thoroughfares almost impassable, and loaded the air with intolerable effluvia, more likely to produce, than stay the course of the plague.*

By October the epidemic had abated; the death toll dropped, and people dared to think the worst was over. Normal daily life appeared to resume. Bills were sanctioned incorporating the cities of Montreal and Quebec; Jacques Viger was appointed Montreal's first mayor. A proposal to annex the Island of Montreal to the Upper Province in order to give the latter a seaport (after all, it was reasoned by anxious English Montrealers, Lower Canada had two and Upper Canada, none) prompted a highly emotional public meeting where the proposal was soundly defended, but equally soundly denounced.

The entire Molson family emerged unscathed from the epidemic. Meanwhile, support for the railway had lost its momentum. Two more years would pass before events would bring the railway closer to becoming a reality.

April 26, 1833

Dr. Robertson is on his way to call upon a sick patient this evening, when, turning on to St. Paul Street, his horse is frightened and rears, upsetting the carriage. It happens so suddenly that Robertson has no time to see what has alarmed the horse. As the doctor staggers to his feet, he immediately understands what has caused the horse's dismay.

The British American Hotel is on fire. Near the entrance, well-dressed ladies and gentlemen are hurrying out, some clutching bundles wrapped in sheets. Others are coughing and crying, handkerchiefs pressed to their faces. A man in a smudged satin uniform, his face badly burned, is half carried, half dragged away from the pandemonium by his fellow musicians, still in their performance suits. Forgetting his own plight for a moment, Robertson turns to reach for his black medical bag. But his horse and carriage are nowhere to be seen.

Robertson can't remember when the fire bells first started to ring, but now the noise is deafening. Then the urgent shouts of *"Marche! Donc! Marche!"* become sharp under the approaching tremor of horses' hooves. The fire engines (wheeled carts with water reservoirs, pumps and hoses attached) have arrived.

"*Ici!* Over here!"

"Attention, messieurs!"

"Sir! Can you spare some water, sir?"

"Au secours!"

"This man is hurt!"

"Out of the way!"

Horses are cut free and bolt when their hind quarters are whacked. People dodge out of their way. French and English brigades of volunteer firemen rhythmically crank the pumps. When nearby houses catch fire, the blazes are quickly contained. The adjoining Theatre Royale is saved.

Dr. Robertson sees the burned musician into a carriage bound for the General Hospital. The others tell him that the concert in the grand ballroom had been about to commence when the fire broke out. The fury with which it spread was spectacular. Lidel Hermann, the injured man, had lunged in an abortive attempt to save his prized violoncello. His face was badly burned.

One of the last people to be taken to hospital is Robertson, who has suffered a contusion on his head. He hears later that the ballroom and reception rooms on the hotel's ground floor had been still festooned with the evergreen boughs used for the Bachelors' Ball eleven weeks earlier. A flame had darted from a suspended lamp, and branches were ablaze in seconds. Nothing was saved from the hotel. Not only the priceless violoncello but every other instrument in the band, including a borrowed piano, was consumed. All the furniture was gone too, as were the original records of St. Paul's and the Grand Lodge of the District, whose charter was the oldest in the country. But no lives had been lost.

That summer, British actors Charles Kemble and his daughter Fanny performed in a series of recitals at the Theatre Royale. "The heat, while we were in Montreal," wrote Fanny dismissively, "was intolerable–the filth intolerable–the bugs intolerable–the people intolerable–the jargon they speak intolerable ... The only inn in existence at Montreal was burned down ... and everything you ask for was burned down in it."

John Molson Senior decided not to rebuild the hotel this time. Not only did he think two fires were bad omens, but he'd never be able to justify more insurance. He seemed to have lost heart in the hotel business. He found it ironic that only the hotel had burned, while the theatre, which had "not been sufficiently patronized even to pay the necessary disbursements," had been spared. A "solitary ruin" was how one historian six years later described the blackened parts of the building still standing.

Molson had faithfully attended Legislative Council meetings in Quebec, and Masonic and railway shareholder meetings in Montreal. Another cholera epidemic made its way through the region in the spring of 1834; for its duration he tried not to stray too often from his farm on the island, having supplies brought to him by boat. He noticed that labour was becoming scarce. On April 11, 1834, Molson wrote to Alexander Buchanan, an officer of St. Paul's Masonic Lodge:

> *Will you be so obliging as to inform the Master of St. Paul's Lodge that I had fully intended being at Lodge tomorrow. But the situation of the health of the people at Boucherville making us short of labourers (though not a single instance of cholera at this place to this period) has obliged me to call in the aid of my tradesmen for the harvest work, the which could not have been so well done by my Foreman. I therefore purpose being at Lodge the next regular Lodge night when I shall settle all dues up to that period.*
>
> *Fraternally yours,*
>
> *John Molson*

At the end of the summer John Junior and William began spending more time at St. Mary's Current, where malting was once more under way, and they made arrangements for the St. Lawrence Steamboat Company to close its operations for the season. Father and sons communicated by letter. From William:

> *Montreal*
> *Nov 16, 1834*
>
> *Hon'd Father,*
>
> *I received your note last evening by the Carpenters and was surprised to find that you had not gotten the oat meal and other things sent by the Car on Friday last ... the Captain of the Varennes refusing the day before to put your things on the St. Lawrence giving for reason that he only did so when you were on board yourself. The election for the West Ward still remains unsettled, but am sorry to say every night there are disturbances in the streets, people beaten, and Glass or Windows of Houses broken, Mr. English's House was almost made a wreck of on Friday night and had it not been for Captn. Tydy and Mr. Macmeder [?] (as I am informed) a party were on their way to Papineau's house for retaliation. In haste for church I remain Hon'd*
>
> *Father your dutiful son*
>
> *William Molson*

As a new election approached, fresh hostilities were stirred in the city, and, as a result of mob violence, the 1834 election was declared closed before all the votes were taken. The returning officer declared Louis-Joseph Papineau and Robert Nelson elected in their local ridings. This time the Patriotes had taken nearly every seat in the province.

Under the law in the 1830s, fathers were the unquestioned guardians of their children. Legally, Mrs. Molson was powerless... "John, I did not willingly leave you," she wrote later to her eldest son.

Chapter Fifteen

The Patriarch Passes On

Mary Anne had at first resigned herself to an unhappy alliance with her brusque husband, whose views were opposite to her own. Brought up resolutely to do her duty, she'd determined at first to weather the domestic storms. Indeed, as Reverend Mountain had reminded her, she suffered no lack of material comfort. Moreover, hers was a respectable position in society. Every other spring a new baby arrived. She had no reason to be discontent.

While not an unkind man, John Junior could be impatient, arrogant and intolerant in business and rigid and overbearing at home. His children would remember their father as a diligent but morose man; his grandchildren and great-grandchildren would repeat tales of his formidable temper. There is some evidence, both in letters sent to John Senior from John Junior's first schoolmaster, and incidents as an adult, that he was quick to use his fists. We do not know if he ever struck his wife.

Mary Anne may have been a solicitous mother, as she seems in her letters to her sons, but she was also remembered for being critical, snobbish and controlling. She could be harsh in her opinions of others. About her father-in-law she wrote, "Gratitude is not a prominent trait in his character." She expressed herself in sentimental terms to her children, yet was as earnest as her husband about keeping their private troubles private. In fourteen years Mary Anne and John had had seven children; five (all boys) survived. As the years passed, their mutual unhappiness and disillusionment only deepened.

After the birth of their last baby in the spring of 1830, a British niece joined the household to help out, but she soon "met with the displeasure of her aunt." The girl, whose name was also Mary Anne Elizabeth Molson, was caught in a compromising position with a servant, revealing what her aunt saw as her "early promise of depravity which ... seems ... matured to perfection." John Junior believed the young woman's protests of innocence, but Mary Anne did not. The issue with the younger Mary Anne brought friction in the already strained household to an unbearable peak. It was with a mixture of relief and anxiety that Mary Anne, John's wife, finally left Belmont Hall.

Mary Anne wrote terse notes to her husband on scraps of paper:

> *We each have sensible and cleaver friends to advise with and it cannot be made better by Mr. Tom's interference. Your Opinion of him I know to be the same as my one. Will you request him to have nothing to do with either party. Your father and brother William have said nothing to me and I am sure that when out of passion would wish to do what was right.*

Eventually the separating couple signed an agreement in which Mary Anne said she'd return to England and would release John Junior from all her future debts. A wife's debts were, under the law, a responsibility of her husband. In return, he would provide her an annual allowance for life. John Junior agreed to send their niece Mary Anne back to England also, at the first opportunity.

John and Mary Anne Molson's five children, John, Elsdale, George, Dinham and baby Alexander, stayed in Montreal with their father. Under the law in the 1830s, fathers were the unquestioned guardians of their children. Legally, Mrs. Molson was powerless; she'd had to choose between staying with her husband and the boys, their niece and servants, or leaving them all. It must have been a very painful decision. "John, I did not willingly leave you," she wrote later to her eldest son. She described the morning she said good-bye to the boys, in particular the heart-rending moment when "dear little Dinham ...

said he would get his hat and coat and go with his own Mamma." She thought of that moment day and night. "George would not remain in the room," she remembered, "he told me he should get not any good things if he loved me." The two oldest boys, John and Elsdale, were sent to Bishop Strachan's boarding school in Cornwall, Upper Canada.

When she reached England, Mary Anne first took rooms in Liverpool. "I never quit the house and speak to no one," she wrote in February 1832. She continued to fret about their niece. "John will be twelve on the 20. Think what mischief she might do him in four years were you to break your Word," she wrote to her husband in a letter without a salutation. Even more, the thought that her boys might forget her or turn from her made Mary Anne's heart break. "Think, Els," she implored her second son, "the sleepless nights your poor Mother has had with you all and what her feelings now ..." To her eldest, John, she wrote, "You cannot have forgotten my care and love for you all, the unhappy life your poor Father and I led for some years, you were in part witness ... that strengthened my love for you ..." At the end of January 1833, having been "so very unwell from anxiety of mind that I could neither eat nor sleep," she wrote again to her eldest son:

> *My dear Child, speak to your papa and get some arrangement made that I may hear from Montreal ... tell your papa that you hope he will keep to the promise he made me, prior to my signing the papers. I fear my dear John it will be a distressing business to us all should he deviate in the least. I am certain every act will be tried by the person [Mary Anne Junior] to remain in Montreal, and in that case your papa's house would always be considered the Home but I think he will on no account break his Word.*

Mary Anne received her first letter from her estranged husband in March 1833, more than two years after their separation. She replied angrily:

> *Your account of my dear children was most interesting, but it was not a faithful one. You did not say my youngest child had fallen out of a window or that my dear George had been severely ill: I receiv'd this information from a gentleman who lately left Montreal ... I sincerely hope that the accident may not be the cause of future suffering to my dearest boy. I had hoped that time and absence had in some degree quieted those irritable feelings towards a person too far off to give you*

> *any annoyance with respect to the amiable qualities of your Niece. Your letter was one of accusation from the beginning to the end–of course afforded me no pleasure otherwise than it informed me my children were well, the promise I do say you made to send her to England you have not kept. When you take her home I shall return.*

Mary Anne wrote many letters to her children, but for a long time she received no replies. She suspected her boys were being "persuaded or advised to slight and wound the parent that gave [them] life." She agonized, "It is surely enough to be parted from all I love on earth without that sharpest Sting, a thankless Child ... Believe me," she added, "the day will come when you will think my fate a very hard one." She swung between abject depression and grim determination. "I have lived quite secluded, having devoted myself to study. I am surprised what application and inclination will do in a little time."

She wrote to her eldest son again in March 1834:

> *John you have now entered your fourteenth year, time is fast carrying you from childhood to youth and manhood. Improve then your time usefully and diligently. And it is my earnest desire that the religious instruction you receive may at all times influence your conduct and teach you to love and Honour your absent parent, and to be kind and affectionate to each other. Read carefully the books I have sent you, they are both amusing and instructing ... I am afraid you are not so good a french scholar as Mama ... Be kind to your dear little brothers, it will be the greatest proof of regard you can show for me ... Dinham and Alexander can have no recollections of their poor Mother but you have my picture. Do you oft look at it and show it to them.* It is my wish *that you should.*

Between the spring of 1833 and the fall of 1839, Mary Anne lived in Kensington, sustaining herself on a small allowance that her husband forwarded to her. She bought her children toys, puzzles and books, and wrote them letters. She spent most of her money on books, and most of her time reading. She filled shelves with volume after volume of *Byron's Life and Works,* edited by Moore; Kirke White's *Life and Remains,* collections of poetry and letters; the complete works of Alexander Pope; biographies, including Lockhart's *Sir Walter Scott's Life;* tomes of theology and philosophy; printed lectures; and French dialogues. "I shall be most happy my love to give you any of my books if you are a reader," Mary Anne wrote to her eldest son.

On Saturdays Mary Anne could hear the pop-pop-pop of rifle shots in Hyde Park, where gamesmen hunted partridge and quail. From her flat in fashionable Kensington she seemed unaware of the presence of an infamous slum sprawled just at the north end of the village, which Dickens called "the plague spot." She did not attend the coronation ceremonies for Queen Victoria. "Yesterday was the coronation," she wrote on June 29, 1837. "I find my head very stupid from the noise and light. I did as little as possible, and did not stir from home during the illumination."

She was grateful that she never had to go into London, for the miles of fields that lay between Kensington and the city were known to be rife with highwaymen. She was invited (but never went) to the new racecourse called The Hippodrome. The regular outing in her otherwise seemingly antisocial life was attending St. Mary Abbott's Church every Sunday.

Seventy-four subscribers had bought shares in the railway company in Montreal by November 1834, when the company was formally chartered. The first stockholders' meeting was held on January 12, 1835. By the following December all the fencing, grading, masonry work, bridges, large wharves and frames of station houses had been completed.

Many of the subscribers to the Champlain and Saint Lawrence Railroad, including William Badgley, George Moffatt, Peter McGill, Dr. Robertson and John Molson Junior, were taking active roles in politics as well. They and a handful of other men formed the Constitutional Association the same month the railway was chartered. They believed they were "on the eve of great political changes," and wanted to make sure "that the best talents and energies of Britain's sons be arrayed" in order that "Canada not be surrendered or given away." On November 30, 1835, the Montreal *Courier* reported:

> *Constitutionalists acquitted themselves yesterday right nobly. They met and in such numbers as showed that they were alive to the preservation of their rights, and the promotion of their interests. It was a soul-stirring spectacle to witness so great a crowd assembled, animated by a*

> *spirit of zealous and ardent attachment to their liberties. The business of yesterday will not soon be forgotten by friend or foe, but will, we hope, be widely taken as an indication of what may result from any rash tampering with the rights of free men.*

John Junior often hosted the Constitutional Association's meetings at Belmont Hall, though neither of his brothers ever joined the organization. John went on to become president of the association, to which he delivered an address that was then published as a tract, entitled "To Men of British or Irish Descent in British North America." Molson's address included a list of carefully worded grievances against the Patriotes, one of them being "the want of education among the French majority, and their consequent inability to form a correct judgement of the acts of their political leaders."

In 1835, John Junior was managing the steamships and helping to establish the railway. He was spending increasingly less time at the brewery, which had not expanded in ten years.

"I have sent for Thomas," said Molson Senior. "It's time he came home."

Thomas was back in Montreal within two weeks of receiving his father's letter.

That fall *le Père Molson* continued to attend railway and freemason meetings, while taking the *John Bull* to Quebec when Council was sitting. Every day the country slipped a little closer to rebellion.

In December 1835, Molson returned to Montreal from Quebec with a high fever. Dr. Robertson came to see him, prescribing rest and a regimen of pills. Betsey alternated days at his home, where she nursed and comforted and read to her agitated father-in-law. Suddenly at midnight on the tenth of January, 1836, Molson demanded a notary to whom he could dictate a new will; at eight the next morning, he summoned the man back to make a correction. John Junior, Thomas, William, George Moffat, and Peter McGill were named executors. Molson died later that day.

Three days later the Quebec City newspaper *Le Canadien*, printed this item: "We hasten to associate ourselves with the regrets which have been expressed by our Montreal contemporaries, on the occasion of the loss experienced by Canadian industry through the death of the Hon. John Molson, to whom Lower Canada owes the introduction of steam in inland navigation, and who was at all times a zealous supporter of every important commercial and industrial enterprise. Few men have rendered better service to their country in connection with its material development."

Thomas's wife, Martha, who had given birth to a daughter named Anna on December 31, did not attend John Senior's funeral. Anna was the youngest of fourteen grandchildren at the time of Molson's death, the eldest of whom, John Molson III, was fifteen years old.

In four prior versions of his will, John Molson had settled the brewery on his youngest son, William. He changed his mind, however, before dictating and signing his final version, in which the "brewery, and all its appurtenances thereof," he left to "John Molson, son of Thomas Molson." John Henry Robinson (John HR), only ten years old when his grandfather's last will was written, was too young to appreciate Molson's motivation. By leaving the brewery to John HR, the elder Molson was doing more than tactfully avoiding a choice between his sons or bequeathing it to all of them, whom he rightfully feared would always be at odds with one another.

Up to the very end of his life, John Molson's gaze was fixed on the future, and he saw hope in the youngest generation. The brewery had not increased its output in ten years, yet Molson had known its profitability was sound and would stand the test of time. He believed it would be his children's only enduring link to him, and therefore considered the brewery separately from the rest of his estate. This was revealed not only by the careful way in which he bequeathed it, but in another respect as well. The will contained instructions that his portrait painted in oils in London in 1826 would hang in the boardroom for as long as his descendants continued to own the brewery. "If it should pass into the hands of strangers," he dictated, the portrait would be passed down to his son William or his descendants.

To his eldest son, John Junior, Molson left the property on which the hotel had stood; the theatre next to it; the foundry establishment next to the brewery; St. Jean and St. Marguerite islands (in the Bouchervilles), including farms, houses, barns, tools, stock and cattle; and his shares in the railway. To Thomas he left all his Montreal real estate, including the farm at Long Point. To William he left the Près de Ville wharf and property near Quebec City, including twenty-three houses on the property that were drawing rent. To Thomas and William, their father left the "enjoyment" of the brewery until 1847, the date that John HR would become twenty-one. The rest of Molson's estate, to be divided among the three sons, included shares in the Bank of Montreal, the Ottawa Forwarding Company, the Montreal Library, the British American Land Company, the St. Lawrence Steamboat Company, the Quebec Fire Insurance Company and the steamship *Varennes*–and his pew in Christ Church.

John Junior had more reason than his brothers to be taken aback at the contents of the revised will. The fact that Thomas and William were appointed to act as joint managers until John HR's twenty-first birthday was small consolation to either of them. Tension ran high among the brothers in the weeks that followed their father's death. When the existing partnership had to be dissolved, Thomas and William didn't act as expediently as John Junior would have liked. Two weeks after the elder Molson's death, on January 28, 1836, John brought a suit against his brothers for "the termination of the question as to copartnership."

Thomas considered the possibility that John HR would not live to see adulthood. He was a sickly child, more so than his first son, Tommy Junior, had been, who had died before he was twelve. If John HR died before coming of age, the brewery would pass to his brother John's eldest son. There was only one solution: God willing, Martha would have another boy who could be named John also. After all, the will didn't specify which "John Molson, son of Thomas Molson … "

Thomas left for England in the spring. The Champlain and Saint Lawrence Railroad–managed by John Junior now–was still two months away from opening, so he took a *calèche* from Montreal to St. John's. Captain Benson, of the steamship *Erie* that went to New York, refused to take Thomas's fare when he heard that his father had died.

In New York, Thomas stayed at the National Hotel on Broadway for two weeks. He visited distilleries, attended lectures, shopped at his leisure, and visited tailors and a barber. The packet for England sailed on June 8; his ship, the *Sheffield,* commanded by Captain Allen, arrived in Liverpool on July 25. A fortnight later Thomas was in London, where he spent the following three weeks shopping. He recorded in his notebook every item he bought: a London map, a pencil case with pen and pencil, a ladies' box, two children's parasols, best satin brocade, tortoiseshell and pearl handles for toiletries, a pearl ring and hook, other jewellery, parasols, grease paint "to take grease from silk," a "sand glass to boil eggs by," pocket books, pens, a small pen knife, two children's black silk hats, a young lady's blue satin bonnet adorned with feathers, a pair of garters, a portmanteau, a medical spoon for children, small forceps for splinters in the fingers, a "probong to put down the throat for fish bones," a nipple shield, tooth forceps, shirt front, suspenders, linen cuffs, black trousers, black waistcoats, cotton socks, a ready reckoner, a camera obscura, a skittle board, silk hats, white threshers, black kid gloves, satin garters, white satin shoes, gold ink with a small gold seal, a 202-piece china dinner set, a dessert set to match, a 120-piece dinner set for common use, a gold hair-ring set with pearls and garnets, a gilt neck chain, a pink topaz ring, amethyst bracelets, mosaic gold chains, cotton nightcaps, a silk purse, whips, an imitation diamond brooch, gold earrings, and a grand piano forte and a packing case for the instrument to be shipped to Montreal. He also ordered an elaborate headstone from a London firm for placement on his father's grave. He did not go into Lincolnshire or attempt to visit Mary Anne.

Thomas was back in Montreal by the autumn, where no doubt his wife and children were delighted to receive such fine presents.

July 21, 1836

Mrs. Peter McGill swings the traditional bottle of champagne against the ship's bow and christens her *Princess Victoria.*

"Hip, hip hurrah!" leads Peter McGill, followed by a chorus of echoes.

"Champagne for the *Champlain,*" observes Stanley Bagg.

"How do you do, sir," says McGill. " I believe we met at Mr. Shaw's ball ten days ago."

"Ah yes, Mr. McGill. How do you do? I hear you will be addressing the gathering anon."

Three hundred guests are assembled at Molson's wharf in Montreal to board a new steamship belonging to the Champlain and Saint Lawrence Railroad. They have been invited to witness the ceremonial opening of the railway in La Prairie. Aboard the pristine steamship, the band plays without a pause from Montreal to La Prairie.

In less than an hour they have docked where the train is waiting. The gleaming black locomotive called the *Dorchester* is thirteen and a half feet long, with a smokestack that rises eleven feet from the ground. Four passenger coaches are arranged behind it. The disembarking guests–only some of whom are going to be lucky enough to board the train–listen to speeches of thanks and praise, and more music.

The locomotive parts, which had arrived from England just a month before, had been assembled by Ziba Pangborn at the Molson foundry. An experienced British engineer was contracted to be the engine's operator for its first season. After arriving in Canada he had inexplicably deserted, necessitating a hasty replacement by a mechanic from Molson's foundry. To spare the inexperienced engineer undue embarrassment, trial runs of the Dorchester were made at night.

"Why do you call her a kitten?" ventures young Elsdale Molson, John Junior's boy, who is following the proceedings intently.

"Because she's exactly like a kitten," jokes the assistant engineer, Mr. Livingston, "playful, unpredictable, and none too gentle!"

John Molson Junior gazes at the crowd that surrounds the gaily decorated platform. He is standing with the Governor General (the Earl of Gosford) and suite: Lady Gosford, Sir George and Lady Gipps, Sir Charles Grey, and Mr. Eliot, the secretary of the Commissioners.

Peter McGill is addressing the gathering, the sweep of his arms seeming to draw everyone together in the celebration. Among the invitees, Molson recognizes Louis-Joseph Papineau, the Speaker of the House, and Thomas Storrow Brown, the outspoken Patriote who had written the manifesto for the Fils de la Liberté.

"What a pleasant change it is to have speechmakers who are not shouting about oppression and war," says Lady Gipps.

"Give them enough time, and enough to drink, they will," counters Molson.

"I disagree," interrupts Sir Charles. "It is surely to their credit that

Mr. Brown and Monsieur Papineau are here today. I am sure they have no intention–"

Molson stiffens. "They are already plotting trouble. Dr. Nelson pointed out that Dr. O'Callaghan and Mr. DeWitt are not here. He asked, 'Did they not receive invitations?' Of course they did!"

"Perhaps their invitations were misaddressed," says Mr. Eliot.

"We cannot make an honest mistake without being accused of malicious intent," John Junior replies.

"Perhaps they chose not to come," suggests Lord Gosford.

"That," mutters Molson, "would certainly be their prerogative." He swiftly changes the subject. "Have you seen the two first-class coaches, Your Excellency? They have recently arrived from the United States."

After the speeches, the railway coaches are examined and admired. Elegantly painted in green and gold, the first-class coaches have cut-out openings for windows and doors, and can seat eight passengers each. The two second-class cars are decidedly less comfortable. One must climb aboard, stepping over the wooden coupling mechanism to enter the coach, which seats twelve. Other passengers will have to stand. Because of a minor accident on a trial run that had slightly damaged the locomotive, the second-class coaches will be drawn along the track by horses this time, while only the first two are pulled by "the *Kitten*."

Everyone at first marvels at the gentle rocking motion, how much more comfortable a railway is overland than the infamously tedious seven-hour stagecoach journey. Then the engine picks up speed and men jocularly hang on to their hats when they round a curve. Thick clouds of smoke pump into the air, and the passengers are showered from time to time with fiery sparks. Ladies open their parasols to shield themselves from flying cinders, discarding them with shrieks of surprise when the parasols catch fire.

The train arrives at the Station House at St. John's within an hour. The station, decorated with green branches, is pleasantly cool. A buffet lunch is served for the inaugural guests, with plenty of champagne and Madeira, and more speeches and toasts are made. On the return trip all four coaches are attached to the locomotive, and the train reaches the extraordinary speed of twenty miles an hour. For many of the passengers, it is the fastest they have ever travelled.

Five days later, Thomas Storrow Brown writes about the event: "We are in Canada so accustomed to see things done ill, that a work well done is a miracle."

For the next two weeks the train was crowded with overzealous passengers. The promoters were delighted with its popularity and profitability, but soon found they had to restrict the number of tickets sold for each trip and post regulations at each station house:

> *No dogs allowed in the first-class compartments; no seats to be occupied unless tickets are presented; no walking on top of the carriages when train is in motion; no foul language and no fighting permitted.*

By the end of July, the Dorchester was reaching the speed of thirty miles an hour. The Champlain and Saint Lawrence's first season was a memorable experience for its owners. The train continued running even after the first heavy snowfalls began. In December, section men kept the track cleared of snow near the station houses. On the miles between, the locomotive had to rely on two large birch brooms fastened on the buffer beam to sweep the wooden rails. On certain uneven sections and inclines, passengers had to disembark and push.

When winter trips became too treacherous, the locomotive was taken on board the *Princess Victoria* back to the foundry at Molsons, where Ziba Pangborn took it apart, cleaned and checked the mechanisms, then replaced parts and reassembled the engine to be ready for spring. A second locomotive, *La Prairie*, was ordered that winter from Philadelphia and shipped to St. John's that spring.

The first level-crossing accident occurred in early 1837 at Côte St. Raphael, when a team of oxen collided with the new locomotive, throwing it off the track. All the double-swing gates that had been placed at level crossings were then removed, and watchmen were put on duty.

During one trip, the *Kitten* left the track along a curve. Although no one was hurt, the locomotive sustained enough damage for service to be discontinued while repairs were made. Ten days later, the coaches were again crowded with eager travellers. The day was marred, however, with the line's first fatality: an employee tried to jump up on a coach at the last minute and missed his grasp. He was caught under the wheels, suffered a broken leg, and died of complications the next day.

Although John Senior didn't live long enough to see the railway completed, like most everything else he'd dreamed of, he'd made it happen and it was prospering.

As many as a third of Montreal's men – including William Molson – volunteered to administer martial law. Each fresh disturbance would be followed by a few days of "sullen, fearful quiet."

Chapter Sixteen

Rebellion

September 25, 1837

"The best way to fight England is to continue to buy nothing from her!" Papineau rages, addressing a crowd of five thousand. "My friends, we must attack her in her dearest parts–her pockets!"

To his consternation, he is shouted down. The Patriote tricoloured flags and cloth banners agitate above the crowd: "Death to the Legislative Council!" "For liberty I will conquer or die!"

"We expect them to govern by reason and justice, not by passion! And so must we behave, my friends, with reason! With justice!"

His words are lost, engulfed in a cacophony of impatient jeers and challenging shouts.

Papineau waits for the crowd to settle down. Those who hear him speak are usually moved by his eloquence. But at this Patriote rally they don't seem to want to hear what he is saying. The mood of the party had become increasingly turbulent since the beginning of the year, when nine British sympathizers were appointed to the Legislative Council. England had refused to listen to any talk of reform or compromise; the king had responded finally to Papineau's "92 Resolutions" with "10 Resolutions" drawn up by the Earl of Gosford, which essentially denied the Patriotes everything they asked for. By June he was dead, and the young Queen Victoria succeeded to the British throne.

The crowd has gone quiet now; Wolfred Nelson is suddenly standing beside Papineau. He has none of Papineau's sartorial elegance, but he says what they want to hear. His words fall like thunderclaps among them.

"We must arm ourselves!"

Papineau's protestations are lost in the uproar of the crowd.

"The time has come," Nelson cries, "to melt our spoons and make bullets of them!"

The crowd erupts in even louder cheers.

"We will extract everything we need from our oppressors–beginning with John Molson of Belmont Hall! From him we will demand–we will *seize*–eighty thousand pounds!"

John Molson Junior, is not a random target. To the Patriotes he represents English control. He is a high-profile member of the community as harbour commissioner, banker, landlord and steamship company owner. He has just become a major investor in the newly formed City Gas Light Company. Soon he would be appointed to the Special Council of Lower Canada, receiving more honours in one year than had his father in his lifetime. He is president of the Constitutional Association, is known as "a staunch Tory of the purest water," and is believed to be the wealthiest man in Montreal.

In what must have been an extraordinary undertaking, in anticipation of trouble Molson hired labourers to dig secret escape-tunnels under Belmont Hall. Workmen brought tools and supplies in at night and carted dirt away by wheelbarrow before daylight. When completed, the tunnels had thick walls that were built from a mix of stone, mortar and broken glass (an additive intended to kill rats gnawing through). The tunnels were not discovered until the house was demolished a hundred years later. One tunnel–though its length cannot be verified–led to the brewery, and the other toward the corner of Clarke and Ontario streets.

Molson was confident enough of his family's safety to host a wedding at Belmont Hall. His niece, Mary Anne Molson, now twenty-three, wed twenty-five-year-old John Crawford in early October 1837.

The economy was in a state of collapse in the fall of 1837. Between 1832 and 1837, a series of disasters, including insect invasions, floods and droughts, had spoiled crop after crop. The harvest of 1836 was the worst ever recorded. Businesses were failing, imports were overpriced, and Britain was refusing to extend any more credit. Even the Bank of Montreal had stopped lending money; it sent all its specie to the Citadel in Quebec City for safekeeping.

"In my day, such times have never been experienced," Peter McGill commented at a Bank of Montreal board meeting.

John Molson Junior, who had been elected back on the board following his father's death, concurred. He knew his brothers, Thomas and William, now partners in business at St. Mary's Current, were already acting upon an opportunity to make a profit from their cash-rich position as brewers. They had engaged an engraver/printer in New York City to print paper currency with the words "Molsons Bank," and would begin to circulate the notes by using them to pay their accounts. The name "Molsons Bank" did not refer to a legal entity, but was an assurance of the good credit of both the brewery firm and the family who ran it. (Many inhabitants had long been familiar with the reliability of the Molsons' brewery tokens and demand notes).

No legislation governed the issue of notes payable on demand. The scarcity of gold and silver currency prompted many firms and individuals to issue paper currency, which offered varying degrees of reliability. William had returned from New York to Montreal on September 1, 1837, with 12,000 "bank" notes in denominations of between five pence and five pounds. They were in circulation so quickly that within a fortnight a second order had to be placed.

The Champlain and Saint Lawrence Railroad also issued its own bills in denominations of twelve-and-a-half-, twenty-five- and fifty-cent notes.

For seven weeks, anarchy ruled in and around Montreal. At night gangs, whose members' faces were blackened with charcoal, led a reign of terrifying intimidation. On the evening of October 30, when Martha went into labour, the midwife would not come; Martha delivered a son–John Thomas–early the next morning with only her husband and a maid there to help her.

All along the upper Richelieu, homes were pillaged or burned. Skirmishes left both British soldiers and rebels dead. On November 6, members of the Fils de la Liberté and the Doric Club clashed in Montreal. Many Patriotes brandished pitchforks or axe handles; others wielded muskets rammed with lead balls. When the Catholic Bishop of Montreal took the view that revolt was against church doctrine, parishioners who sided with him found their barns burned and their animals mutilated.

Armed Patriotes controlled many parts of the countryside. Barricades were built in Montreal's suburbs and armed by guards who admitted only Loyalist refugees. The sound of the tocsin seemed to peal continuously from all quarters.

Warrants were issued in the city for the insurgent leaders' arrests. Newspapers accused each other of printing lies; the office of the *Vindicator* was gutted one night, its presses and type paper strewn all over Fortification Lane. Doric Club members collided in skirmishes with the Fils and the St-Jean Baptiste Society. Thomas Storrow Brown lost an eye. Loyalists marched to Papineau's house intent on breaking his windows, and had to be forcibly restrained by magistrate's deputies. As many as a third of Montreal's English-speaking men–including William Molson–volunteered to administer martial law. Each fresh disturbance would be followed by a few days of "sullen, fearful quiet." Warrants for the arrests of Papineau, Robert and Wolfred Nelson, Brown and other leaders prompted them to flee to the United States.

On November 23, the rebels defeated Colonel Charles Gore at St. Denis. The same day in Montreal, John Molson Junior, as chairman of the City Gas Light Company's Management Committee, presided over the installation of the first gas lighting in some commercial establishments on St. Paul Street. Two days later, while controversial arrests were being carried out in Montreal, Molson Junior was despatched to St. John's with seventeen other members of the Volunteer Cavalry, under Lieutenant Ermatinger.

November 26, 1837

John Molson Junior and the seventeen others who make up a volunteer militia are returning from St. John's where they had been directed to seize two inhabitants charged with treason. They have made the arrests without incident, shackled their prisoners into a wagon, and are now headed back to Montreal on the road through Chambly to Longueuil. The moon is up and the air is still; they decide to press on, and not stop for the night. Not far from Chambly they see about thirty Patriotes, variously armed. The men disperse as they approach. They are outside Longueuil at about half past two in the morning when a habitant woman comes out to warn them that a large party of men is waiting for them a little farther on.

Ermatinger thanks the woman, and she hastens off. He considers her words, and turns to Molson and Joshua Woodhouse.

"The first group of men we saw was headed away from Longueuil," he says flatly.

"True," Molson growls, "it's likely a trick."

They ride in alert, suspicious silence for about a mile, then suddenly Woodhouse gives a sharp shout. To the right of the road, Patriotes materialize, a body of about three hundred, protected by a high fence and armed with rifles and muskets. They pick up their pace in the vain hope that they can pass by. Some Patriotes immediately start firing while others head toward the volunteer cavalry that surround the prisoners' wagon. Ermatinger, Molson and the others are vastly outnumbered and have only pistols with which to defend themselves; their swords are useless as long as they are separated by the fence. A bullet passes through John Junior's cap and grazes his forehead. Ermatinger falls, wounded with duck-shot in the face and below the shoulder. Woodhouse takes a direct hit in the chest. The wagon is overturned and the prisoners make their escape; the Patriotes disperse across the field. The ground trembles from the retreating horses' hooves; the moonlit, frost-tinged darkness is punctuated with celebratory whoops and howls.

The men gather their wounded and make their way for a mile across fields into Longueuil. There, they find two companies from the 32nd Regiment (under Major Reid) are waiting for them, having come from Montreal under orders to support the Volunteer Cavalry. They had arrived on time, but because of orders not to proceed beyond Longueuil had been a mile away when the ambush occurred. The wounded are tended to in Longueuil; the others return to Montreal for further orders.

Luckily, Molson's wound is not serious. Ermatinger will also survive his injuries, but Woodhouse's fate is uncertain.

In England, Mary Anne knew nothing about any of this. In November of 1837, she was even unaware that there were armed conflicts in and around Montreal. She wrote wistfully to her son:

> *I wish you were fond of reading. The last few years of my life have been spent in reading the best authors say, Scott, Byron, Cowper, Hannah More etc etc. This is the only expense I indulge in and as I have five sons I hope one at least will not think the money ill spent.*

And in Canada, Thomas seemed curiously indifferent to the tension that was all around him. In the same month, November 1837, showing a selective parsimony that characterized him all his life, he carefully copied a recipe for eau de cologne in his notebook:

> *Ladies, who may be disposed to practice a little domestic economy, will find the following preparation a cheap substitute for Eau de Cologne; its cost being from three to four hundred per cent below what they can purchase from the shops.*
>
> *To one quart of alcohol add 60 drops of lavender–60 drops of Bergamot–60 of essence of lemon–60 of orange water. If wishing to mix on a large scale, put 240 drops of each to one gallon of alcohol.*

The news that her husband was a member of the Legislative Council, and, therefore, the second Honourable John Molson, came to Mary Anne in a letter from George Davies, her husband's business partner. This prompted Mary Anne to address her son John as "Esquire" for the first time, in a letter written from Spalding. She had also learned from Davies that the young Mary Anne was married. These two items of news seem to have caused some warmth to kindle toward her estranged husband. She wrote to her eldest son, John:

> *Mr. D[avies] mentions your Father as being very busily engaged in affairs of State. He being one of new council, so my dear John I shall for the future designate you Esqr by way of distinction ... in expectation of a letter either from you or (The Honourable John Molson) present my congratulations and say I hope he will write me every particular all that concerns the children and as much of his own affairs as he thinks proper … I am convinced nothing ennobles the mind more than Books my dear Son well chosen, at the same time a proper attention to business and care of what is entrusted to you ... Did you know the pleasure and happiness your letters give me? I hope you would write more frequently, pray fill the paper, all things interest me that come from you ... Adieu my very dear John may you be good and then you will not be unhappy is the onstant wish of Your*
> *Affectionate Mother*
>
> *M.A.E. Molson*

By the first snowfall in Montreal the fighting had come to an end. In mere weeks, hundreds of men had been killed and many more wounded. Papineau and Robert Nelson were still in the United States. Some believed the leaders were merely escaping arrest; others thought they would return with more men. The Au Pied du Courant Prison (also called "The New Jail") held more than five hundred captured rebels. Those seventy-two classed as "principal offenders" were shackled to wall rings of wrought iron. One of the seventy-two was Dr. Wolfred Nelson. Patriote newspapers had been silenced. Loyalist papers, emboldened, were raging for ropes and scaffolds.

That winter, 108 Patriotes were convicted of treason by courts-martial; of these, ninety-nine were condemned to hang, but only twelve were actually executed. The rest were transported to Australia. Several, including Papineau and Robert Nelson, remained at large.

Social life resumed, and at least some of the participants enjoyed themselves at various engagements. Order seemed to have been restored; the Molsons and other English families slipped back into the comfortable annexes of the colonial establishment. During the summer months of 1838, Lord and Lady Durham were frequent luncheon guests at Belmont Hall, usually accompanied by Lord Durham's private secretary, Edward Ellice, and Edward's wife Jane, who kept a diary. Jane Ellice was a shrewd observer of others, and habitually wrote in a matter-of-fact style. She saved her most honest–and vicious–words for describing John Molson Junior:

> *Saturday, 7 July 1838. Went with the D's to luncheon at that horrid little Mr. Moleson's, who would hold Lady Durham tight under his arm all the time we were walking thro' his garden, to her great annoyance.*
>
> *Friday 27 July, 1838. Edward returned, & did not bring the wretch Mr. Moleson as he threatened. He saw the Durhams start in the Bull for Quebec.*
>
> *Thursday 2 August 1838 ... Mr. Moleson came with his little bow legs & ugly red face. Tina & Charlie did the honours of the Pointe du Buisson [catching fish at night by means of shining lights into the water] to him by torch light. As he has neither romance nor Poetry in his composition I should think he must have been extremely bored.*

Lord Durham's tenure in Canada ended two months later. He had blundered when–in an inexpert gesture to restore harmony after a second, unsuccessful uprising that fall–he issued an amnesty to Patriote leaders. His action met with instant outrage from the British government and he was subjected to intense criticism for making decisions outside the bounds of his authority. Durham resigned on November 1.

During the cold, dry days of the new year, accidental fires broke out in and around the city. Dried evergreen decorations were susceptible to errant flames, as stoves were heaped up with wood to ward off the chill. In the early hours of January 5, 1838, someone smelled smoke in Molsons' distillery, and an alarm was raised. As the blaze spread, fire brigades arrived from different parts of the city. The Royal Artillery came out and volunteer militia members pitched in as well. In all, more than a hundred people fought the fire.

In spite of the river's proximity and the use of all the city's fire pumps, the only buildings that were saved were the dwelling house and stables. The brewery, the foundry and much of the equipment were lost. Insurance didn't cover all the Molsons' losses.

December 1838

It is a bitterly cold Christmas morning in 1838 when Montrealers make their way to their various churches. The Molson brothers and their families attend Christ Church, though John Molson Junior wants to become a Unitarian. To the English, Scots and French Canadians, Christmas is not a time for an exchange of gifts (which they will do on New Year's Day), but it is a time for celebration, decoration and tradition. Sleighs, heaped with evergreens, whisk along the roads. Families gather at their dining tables where fattened geese, browned vegetables, plum puddings, pies and blancmange grace the china. In some households dancing will complete Christmas evening, to the music of gaily dressed fiddlers.

At Belmont Hall, all five boys are home from school. The older two tell the younger three what life is like at Upper Canada College, a private boarding school in Toronto. They tell them about the battles between city boys and country boys, the cricket games and the foot races, the pillow fights in the dormitories. The younger boys are now enrolled at Bishop Strachan's School in Cornwall.

"I am Molson Major," John tells his younger brothers, "Elsdale is Molson Minor, and you, George, will be Molson *Minimus.*"

"No, I *shan't,"* says George.

"You will be given sour bread," Elsdale adds.

"All the boys get sour bread," corrected John. "And treacle, twice a week."

"John can't even swim across the bay yet," Elsdale says, "can you, John. Molson Major. Ha."

"I have a letter from Mother, and if you all mind me, I shall read it to you."

"Go straight away to the part about the presents," urges George, who's heard it already.

"Very well. … '[A] circassion puzzle ... representing plans of fortifications, bridges, towers, churches, houses, monuments, altars, etcetera ... to which are added twenty-eight geometrical problems ... curious little saws and ... toy watches.'"

As the turmoil of the past few years settled, citizens were able to turn back to their businesses and other interests. In the Molson family, Thomas and William initiated a new partnership agreement as brewers and distillers. William began investing in real estate and sent commissioned brokers into Upper Canada to buy grain, since Lower Canada's crops continued to be lean. In 1839, the government passed a law restricting the issuing of currency to chartered banks. Molsons Bank notes, among others, had to be withdrawn from circulation.

Mary Anne did not read about the "war in Canada" until two months after the fighting broke out. She was suddenly beside herself with worry, fearing for her children. She wrote her son John:

> *My distress of mind has been beyond description since the accounts reached England ... Mr Davies sent me all the newspapers he received … had the Rebels gained the ascendency we should have been reduced to beggary ... I made myself almost certain your Father would be killed and knowing he had not any property in England or the States*

> *I did not know what would become of us. I came to the determination to sell my plate and furniture and keep [the younger children] at school with the Bishop and if possible get a situation myself.*

In another letter (in which she seems desperate not to offend and thus be refused), Mary Anne tried to persuade her husband that it would be best for the boys to be with her in England:

> *I think it would be (mark what I say* only think*) advisable to send of the Cleverest home to England for education particularly as ... [we could] ... do our utmost to place them eligibly. The War in Canada I consider very detrimental to youth but of course you will use your own better judgement. I hope and trust God will direct you ... Thomas and Wm are not sparing in expense upon their Children. Martha Anne is at a first rate establishment the last six months, she will be introduced ... What I was thinking for our boys was to send Dinham to the High School of Edinburgh; many of our first rate scholars have been educated there ... Elsdale I fear is too old for school [he was sixteen by now] but why not send him to Cambridge or Oxford if not sufficiently qualified let him be with a Clergyman for a year or two. Mr. Doncaster has sent some clever young men to Cam[bridge]. My own dear little George Mr. D[avies] says is quick at everything but his Book, so we need not think of making a scholar of him.*

In a postscript she added:

> *King's College in the Strand is very highly spoken of but I felt afraid you might think that I wished to get some of my Children near me which God knows is a secondary consideration ... The Bishop considers the two Boys to have very good abilities and you could place them both there. Mrs. Thomas has got a very excellent introduction for her children–a Mr. Foggo and Mrs. I think young Foggo is at King's College. You need not fear me I have too much Love and Pride to retard their progress.*

John Junior was not so opposed to Mary Anne as to reject her ideas out of spite. Beginning with John Molson III, their father sent each of his sons to England to complete their education.

As many as a third of Montreal's men – including William Molson – volunteered to administer martial law.

Each fresh disturbance would be followed by a few days of "sullen, fearful quiet."

Chapter Seventeen

Thomas Builds a Church

In June of 1839, Mrs. Thomas Molson took fifteen-year-old Martha to England to consult specialist Dr. Thomas Cammack about her daughter's irregular menstrual periods and symptoms of anemia. Saltwater bathing was considered particularly restorative to health and often prescribed for those subject to "general debility and lassitude." Dr. Cammack recommended a change of air, suggesting that Martha be taken to some "watering place" in the summer:

> *Spalding*
>
> *July 16, 1839*
>
> *Thomas Molson, Esquire*
>
> *Sir,*
> *At Mrs. Molson's request I have visited Miss Martha Molson. Though unwell she is not more disordered than young ladies at her age frequently are; and will I trust soon rally. Still it is necessary for her to take exercise, and it will be right during the summer to go to some watering place, where she can make use of proper baths ... This too*

will render some degree of caution necessary in avoiding too close an application to her studies, which when very rigid so often brings on or increases afflictions of this nature.
I am, Sir,
Your very obedient servant,

Thomas Cammack

A popular bathing place among wealthy Canadian families at that time was Cacouna, a village near Rivière du Loup, a two- or three-day journey from Montreal by steamer. Dr. Campbell, the Molsons' local doctor, Canada's leading physician, and regular summer visitor to Cacouna, insisted that Cacouna was "immeasurably superior" to all other watering places in North America.

That summer Thomas took his wife, servants (including a nurse named "Pierce"), and eight children (Martha, John HR, Mary Anne, Harriet, Mark, Anna, the toddler John Thomas, and the new baby, Frances) by steamer down the lower St. Lawrence. Little did they realize that this trip was the first of what would become an annual highlight in their lives.

There were no hotels in the village at that time, so local residents rented out their homes to health-seekers for the summer and moved into their bake houses, which were often original settlers' cabins. The Molsons stayed in Cacouna for four weeks that summer, in a house along the sea on the main boulevard of the village.

A beautiful evergreen slope led from the village to the river's edge which at low tide was calm and flat, revealing clusters of boulders and rocks. At high tide, the clear salty water rimmed a series of small bays separated from each other by rocky outcrops. Thomas and Martha felt at ease among the other English summer visitors, most of whom were also from Montreal. Many, including Dr. Campbell and the Frothingham family, came to "the great natural sanitarium" on the St. Lawrence.

Martha and the children welcomed Thomas's announcement, at the end of that summer, that he had decided to make arrangements to rent the house the following year. Days of bathing, boating and fishing suited him very well. Moreover, Thomas could not deny Cacouna's salubrious effects. Appetites increased, moods were improved, sleep was sounder. Before long, Thomas obtained permission to build two wooden stills on the property. Their presence would serve several purposes: they would keep him from becoming idle; they would allow him to conduct experiments that were not practical at home; and, most significantly, they would allow as long a stay as possible.

June 10, 1839

The *John Bull* is en route from Quebec to Montreal. Most of the passengers are asleep at 3 a.m. as the steamship leaves Sorel (formerly William Henry), having stopped there to tow the *Queen* into the city. By the time the passengers begin to stir, they will be safely docked at their destination. The purser, Mr. Thomas, asleep in his berth near the foot of the main stair, is roused from sleep by the crackling noise of fire. Thomas leaps from his bed and takes the stairs to the deck two at a time. To his horror, almost the whole of the boat amidships is ablaze, "the flames ... making such rapid progress to the stern that it would be difficult to rouse the passengers from sleep, and get them on the main deck in time to save them from the raging element."

Thomas immediately sprints back down to the captain's door, which he pummels with his fists. "Fire! Captain Vaughan! Fire!" On his way back to the deck he grasps an armload of firewood billets and begins throwing them through the skylights of the gentlemen's cabin. Panes of glass smash, and Thomas shouts through the stifling smoke and heat that rages between him and the passengers, "Danger! Fire! *Get out!*"

No one has time to dress or find any of their luggage, and some are compelled to escape by windows. Captain Vaughan has ordered the engines to run in full operation and the ship to be steered directly to shore. A passenger identified only as Miss Ross throws herself into the river to escape "so dreadful a death" in the flames, and drowns. At 3 a.m. the *John Bull* grounds in about eight feet of water, her engines still running, her hull still burning and smouldering.

Most of the passengers have been rescued and put into lifeboats, thanks to Vaughan, his crew, and the masters and crew of the *Queen,* which the *John Bull* had in tow. About twenty are still unaccounted for. Among those who are missing are the second engineer of the *John*

Bull, a fireman, and a third crew member. Mr. Thomas delivers the news of the disaster to John Molson Junior.

"Their zeal and activity," the *Gazette* will report afterward, of Vaughan and his crew, "was truly worthy of British sailors." The newspaper called the event "one of the most disastrous calamities that has ever occurred during the navigation of the river St. Lawrence by steam." Moreover, the John Bull is insured only for £5,000 while she had cost £20,000 to build. The article goes on to describe some "disgraceful" conduct of local *habitants*:

> *It is more in sorrow than in anger that we are compelled to state, that the conduct of the Canadian habitants to the unfortunate passengers on board the John Bull, was of a description which reflect the utmost disgrace upon their ancient character for good feeling, humanity, and hospitality. They could not be prevailed upon to lend the smallest aid, unless assured of payment of an amount beyond all reasonable compensation, and when they did launch their canoes, it was, evidently, more for the purpose of plunder than with the view of saving life and property. As an instance of their misconduct, one gentleman, who was clinging to the stern of the John Bull, cried to some habitants in a canoe for assistance, but they cruelly refused to comply with his request unless he would promise to give them ten dollars. Another of the passengers asked for a glass of water, but was horribly told that there was plenty in the river. And, shocking to state, it is said that such was their avidity for plunder that the earrings of Miss Ross were torn away. A considerable quantity of baggage, and articles which floated from the wreck were found secreted.*

On June 13, the *Gazette* reported that a rumour had been circulating about the cause of the fire. Someone had sworn he had seen all three of the missing (and presumed drowned) second engineer, fireman and sailor, who were "on duty at the time she caught fire," at Sorel, making their escape. Later the three were reported as being seen again on "the frontier of the Province, while attempting to escape into the United States," and having been arrested at the border on suspicion of having set fire to the boat. The *Gazette* inquired at the Police Office "with respect to the truth of these various reports" and found "nothing is there known of such occurrences."

In April 1840, Thomas and Martha's seven-month-old baby, Frances, died. All the children were ill by Christmas. Six-year-old Anna succumbed in January 1841 to "water on the brain after measles." Martha's world was shaken again.

Soon after Anna's death Thomas decided to build a private chapel. By spring he had chosen a lot he owned in the brewery vicinity and had accepted a tender of £2,300 for the construction. He would be sole proprietor of the chapel, but at the same time it would be fully recognized as a parish of the Church of England. Family services, baptisms, weddings and burials could all be performed here, and he would name it St. Thomas's Church, possibly in honour of St. Thomas, the patron saint of brewing. Built just west of the brewery, on the south side of St. Mary's, the front of the neat brick building would have two towers in which numerous bells would chime. Upon its completion in 1841, Reverend Charles Bancroft would lead Sunday services for family members and any friends who cared to join them.

The same spring the church was being constructed, Thomas took two of his children to England. John HR, known to his family and friends as Jackey, was fourteen, and Mary Anne was twelve. In early May, snow still sat in muddy patches in the streets, in contrast to the buildings decorated lavishly in preparation for the celebration of Queen Victoria's twenty-first birthday.

When the three Molsons left on the steamship *Queen* for Quebec and Halifax on May 12, 1841, a thick lining of ice encrusted both sides of the river. At the wharf, Martha made all three promise to write to her and send their letters back by the *Unicorn.*

Travelling from Pictou to Halifax in their lurching open wagon, the passengers became drenched with rain and splashed with mud. They stopped to take refuge in a farm house to dry their clothes, but as soon as the journey commenced again, so did the rain. Jackey, who usually endured discomforts with good humour, found the frustration immense.

Continuing the habit into a new generation of Molsons, Jackey carried notebooks with him in which he wrote all his experiences and observations, exhibiting a prodigious memory for detail, a self-conscious wit, and a degree of understanding of one much older.

When they reached Halifax, Jackey was intrigued to visit a brewery belonging to a Scotsman called John Oal:

> *[He] very kindly invited us to see his establishment. He makes 60 bushels and works it by hand; his kiln is of an oval form and it can dry 40 bushels. He manufactures rum and whisky, for the molasses (for making the rum) he gives from 1 shilling to 1 shilling and sixpence per gallon but has to pay 1 shilling duty on every gallon ... he also manufactures porter, ale, peppermint shrub and ginger beer. He does not grind his malt but bruises it between two rollers which are set in motion by an overshot water-wheel.*

Jackey also visited a museum, noting the displays of various stuffed animals, assorted statues, and a collection of Indian spears and hatchets. The family visited a church that had been built in 1750. "The curate is Rev. Mr. Pike," wrote Jackey attentively, "son of Chief Justice Pike of Montreal." On the Queen's birthday, the twenty-fourth of May, the Molsons observed the "grand review of all the troops of the garrison at 12 o'clock in the rear of the city, and ... a brilliant display of flags of all kinds." Later they boarded the *Britannia,* "a noble vessel about 1,200 tons burthen and furnished with two low pressure engines each 220 horse power, for to supply those engines there are four boilers ..." Jackey noted all the dimensions of the ship, noted where her engines were made, and by whom, and described her three masts, seven sails, and stud-sails. "There is a cow on board," he added, "which supplies us with an abundance of milk."

He listed the names of passengers he could remember having been introduced to. After filling three pages with first and last names and titles of gentlemen, ladies and officers, with their respective ranks and companies, he concluded, "and some other passengers whose names I have forgotten who with the crew, stewards, etc., make upwards of two hundred souls on board."

During the voyage Jackey spent some time each day sitting by the funnel, writing in his notebook. "It is warmer here than any other place on deck," he commented. On the first Sunday morning, the

Reverend Mr. William Potts, a Presbyterian minister from St. Louis, gave a sermon in the forecabin. Jackey saw "several whales spouting." He wondered from time to time if the ship was still on course, for whenever the sky clouded over, the captain and the navigators could not "take an exact observation." The *Britannia* passed close to an iceberg, which so intrigued Jackey that he sketched four different views of it in his notebook. "Beautiful," he wrote, with the simple wonder that marks a thing seen for the first time.

When they neared the Welsh coast and the ship slowly nosed through the fog, Jackey wrote, "Mount Snowdon in his lofty majesty raised his head above the clouds." Aboard the *Grand Junction* to London, where "all the land was clothed in the richest verdure," the same view after nightfall revealed an inky horizon "frequently lit up with the flames from the pottery furnaces and other manufacturies." In London they stayed at the Angel Hotel near St. Clement's Church, Strand, and left for Lincolnshire the next day to see the children's great-aunt Martha Rayment (John Molson Senior's sister), who was in her mid-seventies. They visited their aunt Mary Anne, who was now living in Spalding, and observed the ancestral tombs in Moulton. Outside Moulton, they spent a few minutes at Snake Hall, "a place," Jackey explained briefly, "that belonged to my grandfather." Jackey found Glasgow "smoky and bustling," like London. After touring more castles and visiting a distillery, they returned to London, where they made the round of museums, galleries and glassworks and toured the zoological gardens, the wax works, the Thames Tunnel "built of brick under the river bottom," and the "Politechnical Institution." Afterward they went to Greenwich to tour the Royal Observatory. On their last day in London they attended *Romeo and Juliet* at the Haymarket Theatre, to see Charles Kean and Miss Ellen Tree in the lead roles. They left straight from the play to tour the National Gallery.

About Lewes in the very south, Jackey wrote:

> *We went to Lewes, a very old place which existed from the time of William the Conqueror. Its venerable old castle is in ruins, it stood for many ages all the changes of political power and held out for a long time against the Parliamentary forces under Cromwell until despairing of ever being relieved it was forced to capitulate.*
>
> *Cromwell levelled the fort to the ground with the exception of one*

> *part which was situated on the top of a hill which yet remains and is called the Keep. We went to the top of the castle and had a very extensive prospect of all the surrounding country and I had the satisfaction of sitting in the chair in which King John sat when asked to sign the Magna Charta.*

One of their last stops was Brighton, just outside of Lewes. Jackey described it as "a very fashionable watering place and a very handsome town and in my humble opinion is the prettiest town in England." Riding the *Grand Junction* again, this time to return to Liverpool, was most uncomfortable, for the rail car "creaks most stressingly and rocks to and fro like a ship at sea with a swell-a-beam."

July 30, 1841

By the end of July the three Molsons are crossing the Atlantic to return to Canada. They meet squalls and rough seas from time to time, but most days are calm.

"Watch me have a little sport with the sailors," Jackey says to Mary Anne, and sprints off to mid-deck. She doesn't have time to respond, but follows him and crouches behind a lashed barrel to watch what he will do. Their father is talking to the captain in his cabin; the sailors are otherwise engaged. No one notices the children.

Jackey swiftly begins climbing into the rigging among the main shrouds, and when he reaches the main-top mast head, he is suddenly spotted by a sailor in the forecastle.

"Oi!"

In Jackey's words, "an active pursuit commenced." As soon as Jackey sees that the sailors are heading after him, he laughs and begins to descend the shrouds. But two sailors start up after him, to block his way past. When they've almost gained on him, the boy quickly swings round the shrouds, takes hold of one of the braces "from the fore top yard," and slips down all the way to the deck like an arrow.

"Mr. Molson! Your son!" the captain cries, recognizing Jackey.

Thomas has only a moment to be alarmed. The captain can now see the boy is safe.

It is certain that Jackey is chastised by his father, the captain, and the sailors as well. Yet in Jackey's version of the event, he is a hero:

The Captain was watching the whole fun and when he saw me descending so quickly he thought I was falling but as soon as I was safely landed on deck he went into the saloon and informed them of the noble manner in which little Jackey Molson had got clear of the sailors.

John HR didn't stop writing in his journal when he returned home. Enrolled at Upper Canada College in Toronto, he travelled to the school in February 1842. By this time the boy, who was thoroughly enjoying putting his pen to paper, retold in his journal an account of an accident that occurred outside Cobourg. The driver "was singing songs with a couple of passengers on the box beside him and not attending to his horses" when the coach wheels left the road. This caused

a most thundering upset in this old stage, and the passengers inside 9 in number lay piled on top of one another like so many bags of salt, the under ones of course sustaining all the weight of the upper ones unfortunately I happened to be one of the under bags and no mistake but I got a good weight on my old timbers but being a stout built vessel I managed to hold out against it all until some of the upper bags managed to get out of the window for the door would not open, however my old head came with such a crash against the side of the coach that it made my brains dance about like a hasty-pudding although they did not come through the bony walls by which they were surrounded, we got out of the coach without any accident to any one worth mentioning and we found the old concern lying on her beam-ends in a most muddy situation and it raining all the time, the passengers had all to assist in unloading the coach and then to raise it up and bring it to the road.

"If I were going to take the upset," Jackey wrote later, contemplating the accident and his near-perishing, "I should like to make my will before-hand to prevent any trouble among my family, but as I have no family at present, and no property to leave, I think it is as well to say no more about it."

By the time he arrived at school Jackey realized he had forgotten his bible, prayer book, slippers and two slates, "all of which I absolutely require." John HR wrote regularly to his mother from Upper Canada College. He asked about the distillery, the state of the *Montreal,* and the *Queen,* "for I take a great deal of interest in the boats." He also told Martha to give his "love to Papa and Martha, also to Harriet, Mark, and Thomas, give my love to Anne and Elizabeth [his cousins, daughters of William and Betsey], and also the Miss Halls [daughters of Samuel Hall of the Legislative Council]." He learned dancing, hoping that when he returned home at the end of his last school term, he might be able to "mix with Society and join small parties of friends if required."

In February 1841, an Act of the British Parliament had formally united the old upper and lower colonies and created the Province of Canada, a move long advocated by the Constitutional Association.

That spring Thomas had begun construction of Molson Terrace, eleven luxury attached dwellings adjacent to the brewery, with gardens that looked out onto the river. He would let the smaller units for £30 a year, and the more spacious ones on either end for £35. He also bought some property in Port Hope, including another distillery and a flour mill. In 1842 William moved to Kingston, the newly appointed capital, where he lobbied the government on behalf of the brewers and distillers in Montreal who were concerned that the growing temperance movement would prompt hasty or disadvantageous legislation.

Temperance became a more volatile issue in Canada East once the subject was raised by Father Chiniquy, a Roman Catholic priest who had made it his personal mission to curtail the consumption of spirits; he had vowed to end the "Godless debauchery that liquor engenders."

While overall consumption in Canada East fell, Molsons' sales of spirits were healthier than ever.

September 1843

Robert Orr, whom Thomas had hired to manage his distillery and mill in Port Hope, is peering at an account book opened on the table. He pulls off his spectacles and gestures to the bottom of the last column.

"We are at a loss to explain it, Mr Molson," Orr remarks. "It seems our sales have been increasing at an unhoped for rate."

"It's Father Chiniquy's bewildered converts, no doubt," submits Thomas. "They are, it is said, collectively drinking more, due to misguided ardour!"

Orr looks puzzled.

"When Chiniquy said, 'I recommend no more than three drinks a day,' apparently those who never drank before understood that they must quaff three every day without fail, to be in God's good graces," Thomas explains, with some amusement.

An image of Father Chiniquy retracing his steps across the countryside, his black soutane flapping in the wind, makes Orr smile. "The good Father must have difficulty convincing them of their error now."

"Aye, who are we to interfere?" agrees Thomas.

If there are sides to take in the temperance debate (for, after all, who could disagree with exhortations against any excesses?), Thomas is certain that God is on *his*. Even through the Rebellion years, when so many others had suffered financially, God saw to it that his fortune was spared. Moreover, God had saved Thomas's life many times. No doubt, God would be there for him again.

> *In 1842 William moved to Kingston, the newly appointed capital, where he lobbied the government on behalf of the brewers and distillers in Montreal who were concerned that the growing temperance movement would prompt hasty or ill-considered legislation.*

Chapter Eighteen

Saltwater Summers

A small crowd of admirers gathered outside Rasco's Hotel on St. Paul Street on May 25, 1842, in the hopes of catching a glimpse of Charles Dickens, who arrived in Montreal that day. The *Pickwick Papers* and *Nicholas Nickleby* had made Dickens a celebrity. Mr. and Mrs. Dickens were hoping to enjoy some rest during this, the last portion of their tour of North America, where, especially in Boston, New York and Cleveland, they were besieged by eager fans and written about ceaselessly in the press.

To the Dickenses' relief, the curious crowd who approached their carriage at Bonaventure Station were not nearly as numerous or as persistent as they had been south of the border. Dickens's friend in Montreal, the Earl of Mulgrave, was at the station to lead the couple to Rasco's. They took the long way so Mulgrave could show the Dickenses the flower gardens that extended all the way from the Château Ramezay to the hotel. Before they arrived at Rosco's, Mulgrave had found the opportunity to ask his friend to consider participating in a theatrical performance with the city's Garrison Amateurs. (Dickens had some reservations, but he did not refuse.)

Mulgrave called upon John Molson Junior later that evening to ask about using the Theatre Royale as a venue. Molson hesitated: at first it didn't seem possible. The theatre hadn't been used in a year, and the building was already destined to be sold to the city and demolished. But he agreed to meet Mulgrave and Dickens to discuss it the next day.

Thursday, May 26, 1842

"Why should I court more attention, Mulgrave? I am tired of giving myself up as a spectacle. Mrs. Dickens and I have had neither rest nor privacy in the last four months."

"You must be heartily tired of all the fêtes and calls with which you were greeted by our neighbours, Mr. Dickens," says Molson.

"Balls, dinners and assemblies without end." Dickens nods and sighs.

"Is it really that bad? Surely your genius has gained you many friends," ventures Mulgrave.

"The wretched barber who cut my hair," Dickens exclaims, "sold strands of it to admirers! Why, I cannot drink a glass of water without having a hundred people looking down my throat when I open my mouth to swallow!"

"We hope repose will be afforded you in Montreal. Although my father's hotel," Molson goes on, "was unfortunately never rebuilt, you must be comfortable enough at Rasco's. As you do enjoy the stage, however, may I suggest a series of private theatricals?"

"We might endeavour to keep your presence a secret from everyone but the players ..." Mulgrave suggests.

"What a grand idea!" Dickens agrees.

And so they begin to plot.

Keeping Catherine and Charles Dickens's participation in local plays a secret from all but fellow participants and organizers, and the contents of the event a secret from even the guests, necessitates a masterpiece of planning. Dickens chooses three plays: *A Roland for an Oliver, Past Two O'Clock in the Morning,* and *Deaf as a Post.* A rigorous rehearsal schedule is arranged. Molson has (in Dickens's words) "that very dark and dusty theatre" cleaned up, and hires Henry Tuthill to manage it for the short time that it will be active.

Speculation buzzes in the press about the Dickenses' plans in the city. Meanwhile, Molson issues invitations to five hundred guests, including Governor General Sir Charles Bagot, Lady Bagot, and Sir

Richard Jackson, the commander-in-chief for Her Majesty's forces in British North America.

Molson had asked Dickens to usher His Excellency and Lady Bagot to their box seats. This he did, walking backward before them with lighted candles.

The curtain opened and the first play began. To the surprise of many, Dickens himself suddenly strode on stage in a light flaxen wig, flannel house coat, tights and slippers, "so well made up," he would write later, "that Sir Charles Bagot, who sat in the stage box, had no idea who played Mr. Snobbington until the piece was over." Dickens also played Alfred Highflyer in *A Roland for an Oliver*, and Catherine Dickens appeared as Amy Templeton in *Deaf as a Post.*

The following morning, May 27, 1842, he wrote:

> *The play came off last night. The audience, between 500 and 600 strong, were invited as to a party; a regular table with refreshments being spread in the lobby and saloon. We had the band of the 23rd (one of the best in the service) in the orchestra, the theatre was lighted with gas, the scenery was excellent, and the properties were all brought from private homes. Sir Charles Bagot, Sir Richard Jackson, and their staffs, were present; and as the military portion of the audience were all in full uniform, it was really a splendid scene.*

A second performance of the same three plays was then given for the public, also at the Theatre Royale, wherein Dickens appeared on stage again, but Mrs. Dickens did not. This time the plays were advertised in the *Gazette;* the proceeds were given to charity.

By now all five of John and Mary Anne Molson's boys were living in England with their mother. John Molson III, who had enrolled at Cambridge, wrote to his father regularly, letting him know how he and his brothers were faring. In 1842, the boys and their mother spent two weeks in Paris. The younger boys were placed at boarding schools; John III, age twenty-two, informed his father that Mary Anne would need £600 for their expenses. Twenty-year-old Willie Molson, William's only son, travelled to England in the summer of 1842. Neither the purpose of his trip, nor whether he stayed with or visited his aunt Mary Anne and his cousins, was recorded. Returning to North America, he contracted an illness on the ship, and in January 1843, shortly after arriving in Montreal, he died.

In May 1842, John HR was nearing the end of term at Upper Canada College. In a letter to his mother he recounted a memorable dinner he had attended on April 21, during which a fellow schoolmate had read a poem dedicated to the Governor General:

> *His Excellency the governor General Sir Charles Bagot arrived at the Commercial wharf in the steamer Traveller from Kingston ... We heartily cheered his excellency who was on deck when she arrived at the wharf. I had a most beautiful view of his person, he is a fine noble-looking man and a prime picture of a "fine old gentleman." He is without the least spark of personal pride and is very obliging and civil ... His Excellency and suite together with the pupils and masters of the Upper Canada College, the members of the learning professions, the mayor, sheriff, aldermen and magistrates of Toronto ... marched in procession ... [For the] dinner a Greek poem was rehearsed by Norman Bethune, son of Angus Bethune of the Hudson's Bay Company, of his own composition in compliment to His Excellency, which did him great credit and made him worthy of the name of an Upper Canada College student.*

John HR completed his third term at Upper Canada College, then returned to Montreal in June 1843 to spend time with his parents. He was also readying for his apprenticeship at the brewery, eager for experience that could be gained at his father's side. David Rea, who had worked at the brewery for twenty years, also spent time counselling Jackey. Then Thomas took him to his next station–into the stillhouse.

Rea had noted on October 28, 1843 that too much pressure had built up in the shut copper still. A ten-inch crack had formed on one of the side plates on the flue, causing a leak. Rea assured Thomas that the problem had been alleviated, but later that evening, after everyone else had gone home, Thomas and his son returned to examine the still for themselves. As soon as they neared the still, it exploded. Jackey's hand and face were badly burned. As a shaken David Rea wrote later, to William:

> *I ... have ... to communicate very unpleasant intelligence. We have all however great reason for thankfulness that lives are spared and comparatively little damage done ... on [John HR's] reaching it an immediate explosion took place, his hand is burned, and his face cut ... but not otherwise injured. Mr. Thos. escaped unhurt. The still house is lifted off, the bottom sprung out, and the connection with the reservoir severed. The second fire was put out with no further damage than related. The Windows in still house is all smashed and thirteen frames in office window upstairs, part of the brick in end of boiler house out. How Mr. Thos. and John escaped is next to a miracle. I imagine the manhole being open saved them and all from being blown up ... Should anything further turn up respecting it I will advise you.*

The true extent of Jackey's injuries was revealed in subsequent letters from Mr. Rea to William; his jaw was injured, and the boy's face "became much swelled." Weeks later Rea described him as "getting better but slowly ... very weak from lying in bed and want of food, having been obliged to drink milk from a quill for sustenance." Eventually, Jackey made an almost complete recovery and was able to return to work. It's possible that recurring problems with his eyes in later years were connected to the accident. If he had scars from his jaw injury, they were well hidden behind a generous beard that he maintained all his life.

July 1844

Without a doubt Thomas and Martha enjoy their summers down the St. Lawrence, but their children are most unreservedly enchanted with Cacouna. Every spring they find themselves anticipating the day they will escape the stifling heat of the city, the tedium of lessons, scrupulous etiquette, and those dark, formal drawing-rooms where they'd wriggle and scratch under their layers of wool and worsted.

When their steamer docks at Rivière du Loup, the children's exhilaration makes it hard for them to be attentive. Their parents have to remind them of their promise to help carry the baggage. Buckled leather rolls and brass-studded pigskin trunks loaded with every imaginable item must be lined up and counted at the wharf before being hoisted onto a waiting horse-drawn wagon. Thomas, Martha and Pierce lift the youngest children in, and everyone else climbs aboard. Seven miles of lawns, playgrounds and promenades go by until they finally arrive at their spacious wooden beach house. They know, because arrangements are always made in advance, that the larder will be full of provisions, the rooms swept of cobwebs, the rugs beaten, the beds all freshly made. If the evening is cool enough, a fire will have been lit in the hearth.

From the steep granite escarpment that marks the upper end of Cacouna, they can see the far shore on all but the foggiest of days; its craggy peaks rise into the sky beyond. When the tide is low, the fisheries are exposed–a dozen parallel structures with branches woven between posts. Wet clusters of seaweed sag on the rocks dotting the flood plain.

The children are awed by the daily transformations of the river, the way the tide creeps up imperceptibly in the bay, the sharp cries of the herring gulls. Even the youngest are mesmerized by the spindled rhythm of bleached fish bones, the wooden ribs of an overturned *chaloupe,* the scudded clouds strewn above the pine-prickled horizon.

The family dines on fresh salmon, which Thomas catches, as well as lobster, crab and oysters brought to them by local fishermen. They hire a cook, who varies their seafood suppers with tourtières and packed picnic baskets. Their vegetables and bread are purchased from itinerant basket bearers. While the adults play languorous games, the children make their way to the beach, fill buckets and pockets with stones, and clamber up the hill to watch the harbour porpoises gambol and the distant ships pass.

On clear nights Thomas sets up his thirty-inch-diameter leather-covered Cichromatic telescope to observe the moon and the planets. On calm days the Molsons cram crude fishing gear, jugs of water, cold sausages, and seed cakes into a skiff, and row to their favourite destinations along the coast. They build driftwood fires. Other days there are shipwrecks to explore, castles to build, berries to pick, and ghost stories to listen to. Thomas and Martha's children–and their children, in turn–will for the rest of their lives associate happiness with the sound of a fog horn, the smell of oilskins, and the remembrance of chinoiserie parasols being chased along the sand.

Almost from the moment of its foundation, Thomas's private church had conflicts with Church of England Bishop G.C. Mountain. Reverend Mountain's son, described by one as "high bred ... and courteous" and by another as "formidable and melancholy," had been appointed Lord Bishop of Montreal in 1837. He believed in the sanctity of traditional procedure, which interfered–or so Thomas felt–with his authority over the church. Thomas objected to the necessity of the consecration ceremony. His argument was that, with the city expanding and changing at such a pace, a consecration would one day need to be followed by the much more complicated, and difficult to obtain ceremony of deconsecration if he wanted to convert the building to secular use. Both Thomas and the bishop knew a consecration would diminish Thomas's control and devalue the property. Moreover, the grim bishop regarded Molson's religious convictions as a corruption of his own "high church" standards. Animosity between the bishop and the brewer/distiller roiled under a thin veil of decorum.

Late in 1843, William returned from Kingston and joined his brother John Junior as a Bank of Montreal director. By 1844 the seat of government was moved to Montreal, and Parliament House was established in Youville Square in old Montreal. William was asked by John Young if he would run for election for a seat in Montreal West, against Lewis T. Drummond. Young and Molson had many powerful allies, including Bartholomew Gugy, who was delivering a panegyric for Molson one evening, addressing a large crowd in Tattersall's Yard. A cheer was heard from a crowd of Drummond's supporters outside McCann's Hotel in Haymarket Square (later named Victoria Square). Gugy ceased speaking, assumed a theatrical pose and said pointedly, "Gentlemen, but the yells of savages." This, as one participant recorded afterward, "was electrical, and the cheers that followed were tremendous." Nevertheless, William eventually lost the seat to Drummond.

Both of William's daughters were married in 1844. The youngest, Ann, married her cousin John Molson III, eldest son of John Molson Junior. Elizabeth married D.L. MacPherson, who would later become a railway contractor. This same year Jackey, having recovered from his injuries, began his formal apprenticeship at Thomas and William Molson and Company, "to faithfully serve and obey his masters, keep their secrets, and do no damage to them or see it done by others without giving them instant information thereof." His father and his uncle agreed "to instruct the said apprentice in the science and business of brewing, allow him access to such books from their library as they might see proper and necessary ... and pay him Fifteen pounds currency for each and every year of the said term."

Even without a seat in Parliament, William Molson had taken on an active public role. Recognizable from a distance in the full-dress satin waistcoat, black cloth frockcoat and coloured trousers that he wore regardless of the weather, he was a city councillor as well as a director of the Bank of Montreal. In addition to his interest in the brewery, he continued to apply for a bank charter and submitted and supported charters for various railways.

Railways seemed to be all the rage in Montreal in 1845. One capitalist engineer, James Ferrier, sought a charter for a railway from Kingston to Prescott. Another hopeful, John MacDonald, sought one from Montreal to Kingston, and John Molson Junior, who had sold his remaining interest in the steamship line, was planning to build a railway from St. John's to the International Boundary. Heavy "T-Rails"–made of iron, replacing the old wooden rails–were placed upon the eleven-year-old Champlain and Saint Lawrence line, greatly improving its capabilities. John Young was advocating building a bridge across the St. Lawrence.

For his part, Thomas bought Handyside's Distillery in 1844. The old Theatre Royale was torn down, after Molson had sold it to the city for the value of the land it stood on–together with the site next to it, where still stood the ruins of the British American Hotel. The Bonsecours Market, which still exists, was built on this site.

By the time he met young Martha Molson in 1845, William Prosperous Spragge had been working in the Land Survey Department for twenty years. A government position, otherwise known as "an official appointment," was considered a stable one. William, like his brothers, had been groomed for his career; their father, Joseph, the superintendent of education in Upper Canada, had lofty ambitions for his sons.

Spragge was in his early forties and Martha twenty-two, when he asked her father permission for her hand in marriage. Thomas was agreeable; however, he expected tradition to be followed and asked Spragge to provide a statement of his financial affairs and, to seal his good faith, to settle some property upon Martha:

February 15, 1846

Mr. Thomas Molson

My Dear Sir,
In compliance with the wish which you expressed during our conversation for a memo concerning my affairs, I now enclose one in which are specified the principal items of my property. With reference to your suggestion that I should settle property of a certain extent upon Miss Molson I now repeat the satisfaction it will afford me to do so, and accordingly name Forty, twenty-five pound shares of the Commercial Bank Stock.

The generous intention you have evinced of providing liberally for her entitles you as an instance of your confidence and good will toward us both; to our sincere acknowledgements: But permit me my Dear Sir to assure [you] that so far from anticipating your coming forward in the manner you had alluded to, all my plans have been

> *formed independently of any such aid, for I neither counted upon nor looked for anything of the kind. I have proceeded with my arrangements with no other impression than that my own resources were to be made to suffice, and you may probably recollect, upon my applying for your consent immediately before Miss Molson's departure for England, my expressly stating that I should not have felt justified in taking that step, had just believed that with prudent management my own means would prove quite adequate. I am fully convinced of the kind intentions which have dictated the course you have decided upon, and I trust that I shall never for a moment be without the confidence and regard of those with whom my union with your admirable Daughter will connect me. And believe me my Dear Sir always faithfully yours,*
>
> *William Spragge*

Spragge and Martha were married at St. Thomas's Church on November 3, 1846, the marriage presided over by Reverend Bancroft.

In 1847 on his twenty-first birthday, John HR became sole owner of the brewery. This event was marked by no change in his circumstances, habits or activities; his father and uncle continued to operate Thomas and William Molson and Company as a partnership, and began paying John HR rent–worth £500 a year. The young heir continued to devote "his entire time and attention to the business of the concern" and was paid a higher wage–somewhat higher than the £15 per year he had earned during his apprenticeship, but not quite in keeping with the wages of the other employees. Thomas and William also agreed to pay him £3,872, an amount they had been awarded ten years ago from an insurance company, after the 1838 brewery fire. They offered John HR no interest, nor did they offer him a place in their partnership. John HR walked a wary line around his elders, feeling emotions he couldn't express.

That same year, seventy thousand Irishmen, fleeing the potato famine, emigrated to Canada. Typhus raged through the ships. Arriving on dry land, the sick were confined to 150- by 50-foot sheds built for them on Point St. Charles, where half the passengers and crew members perished. Many Montrealers became victims also, and deaths rose to more than sixty per day. Mayor John E. Mills as well as dozens of the physicians, nurses, clergy and nuns who attended to the sick succumbed. Hundreds of children were orphaned. Even at St. Thomas's Church, some of the dead had to be buried without witnesses, for there were none to be found.

May 1848

When Martha begins to feel ill, at first she thinks it is only "rheumatism, as usual." She develops a cold and cough, feels pain in her chest. One day she coughs into a handkerchief and discovers it tinged with blood. These are the undeniable indications of consumption. She knows she doesn't have much time left to put something right that she has been troubled about for ten years. Her husband, a person who tends to dominate her and their children, has been growing exceedingly parsimonious. Moreover, after John Senior's death, and the revelation that John HR was to inherit the brewery, Thomas had changed his own will, giving his eldest son only a token £5, justifying this by explaining that the boy had received "from ... his Grandfather, a considerable amount over and above the shares of my said children."

Martha does not feel that her husband is being fair to their children, and acts while she still can. She directs a final will and testament in which she commits her own estate to Thomas on condition that he, in turn, assigns *his* more equally among their children. The omission of an alternative distribution is evidence of her certainty that he will comply.

One day in early May, Martha carefully lifts a heavy package from the bottom of the steamer trunk and places it on her bed. The book's wrappings and ribbon fall against the quilt as her fingers work at the knot and unfold the cloth that encloses it.

Martha's bible falls open at passages she and Thomas most often read; its pages contain clippings saved from newspapers, cross-stitched sampler bookmarks, notes in margins, loose recipes, pressed flowers. Seeing the fragile petals that mark the beginning of the Book of Psalms,

Martha remembers the hot July afternoon at Cacouna when she stooped in a field to pick them, sniffed the blooms' vanilla scent, then held them at arm's length to admire their colour. She had never seen red swallowwort growing anywhere before. She remembers waving her hat to ward off the mosquitos with one hand, while cradling the flowers gently with the other, as she walked back to the cottage.

Now she lifts the treasured volume and holds it against her chest for a moment. No object as reassuringly familiar as this has better eased her transition into new surroundings, and surely she is once more destined for new surroundings. She sets the bible carefully on the bed, runs her fingers over its tooled leather markings, then opens its cover once more. Beginning at the top of the first page are the names and birth dates of each of her children, the deaths of the first two infants, Tommy's death in 1833, and the deaths of her youngest two daughters. Her own birth date is recorded near the bottom of the page, followed by her marriage date, which has a space left blank under it. She will leave the book near the bed, so that Thomas can fill it in later.

The year 1850 would be remembered by some in Montreal as the year the dredging of the St. Lawrence was completed, the rails of the Champlain and Saint Lawrence were extended from La Prairie to St. Lambert, and Christ Church became a cathedral. Thomas Molson would remember it as the calm before the storm...

CHAPTER NINETEEN

SILK HATS, SATIN GARTERS

IN 1848 at St. Thomas's Church there was a burial in May, followed by a baptism in June: Martha had died just thirteen days before the birth of her first grandchild, Arthur G.M. Spragge, whose parents were William and Martha (Molson) Spragge.

Thomas Molson, at age 57, was now a widower, with four minor children at home: Mary Anne (20), Harriet (18), Markland (14) and John Thomas (10). In addition to working at the brewery, Thomas kept close watch over his distilleries and mills and travelled often between Montreal, Kingston and Port Hope. An agreement between Thomas and his eldest son, John HR, was reached in July 1848 that made John HR a partner in the brewery with his father and uncle William. Of twelve equal shares, now Thomas and William each owned five, and John HR, two. A clause limited John HR to a maximum annual withdrawal of £500 from the company, while allowing the elders to withdraw unlimited funds.

As a father, Thomas was more demanding of John HR than any of his other children. At the brewery, his son was under his intense scrutiny most of the time, and Thomas was particularly scrupulous about the extent and quality of John HR's work. It was in his nature to become most autocratic when family honour was at stake.

John HR lived, according to Lovell's Montreal directory, "in a house at the brewery." Martha had left the income from £1,000 to each of her children. John HR (who had long known about his father's intention to will him the token £5) sided with his younger siblings later that year when Thomas claimed he was entitled to encroach upon his children's inherited income in order to pay for their upkeep. A lawyer, John Rose, advised him otherwise:

4th December, 1848

Dear Sir,

I have carefully examined the marriage contract between Miss Molson and Mr. Spragge, together with the will of the late Mrs. Molson with reference to the question submitted for my opinion of Saturday. By the marriage contract Mrs. Spragge renounces all claim to dower and other successive rights, and agrees to make no claim to any further provision "unless as he the said Thomas Molson or she the said Martha Molson shall by their or either of their last Will and Testament direct." Now Mrs. Molson having by her last will which bears a subsequent date bequeathed the Interest of £1000 to each of her children I am of opinion that Mrs. Spragge is entitled to claim it in addition to the other amount mentioned in the marriage contract. The interest of the £1000 need only be payable yearly.
I remain Dear Sir
Yours truly

John Rose

27 May, 1849

Dear Sir,

I have maturely considered the question whether you as Tutor to your minor children have the right to appropriate so much of the interest of the £1000 left to them by their mother as may be necessary to defray what you pay for their education and maintenance.

I am of the opinion that you have the legal right to apply such reasonable part of the interest as may be necessary to defray the charges in question but that you have no right to encroach on the principal sum.

You ought to open an account with each child crediting on one side the annual interest and debiting on the other what sums you necessarily disburse for the objects in question.

John Rose

In October 1849, Thomas wrote to John HR, "I sent Mark and Thomas to McGill College last Wednesday ... and keep Johnson the Master from 6 to 9 p.m. to prepare their lessons, etc." Markland was then sixteen, and John Thomas just twelve years old, and both were attending McGill College, a high school that was using the university buildings. The boys dressed like McGill University students, who were required to wear black gowns to all the lectures.

The site used by the fledgling university and college–Burnside, James McGill's old house and grounds–wore a look of neglect, the residue of decades of legal wrangling that had followed James McGill's bequeathment of it to the Royal Institution of Learning. The fence that separated the property from the neighbour's was so dilapidated that its various openings allowed cattle to file through onto college grounds. By mid-mornings it wasn't unusual for the Molson students to look out the window and see several cows browsing under the large elm tree said to have been planted by James McGill himself. This sight would inevitably be followed by that of the principal, Edmund Meredith, striding purposefully across the field toward the imperturbable animals, shouting words that were lost in the distance and randomly jabbing his walking-stick into the air like a series of exclamation marks.

December 1849

At a meeting on a Thursday night in the Temperance Hall on St. Maurice Street, the Annexation Association is born. Its founder-members include John Redpath (a wealthy merchant who later opened a sugar refinery), Alfred Savage (a partner of the jewellers that became Birks Jewellers), John Torrance, Cornelius Krieghoff (the painter of Quebec landscapes and rural scenes), George Moffat, William Dow (a brewer), John Converse (a merchant), J.J.C. Abbott (a lawyer, and partner of William Badgley), John Frothingham, Alexander Galt (minister of finance in the first federal cabinet after Confederation), William Molson, and John Molson Junior and his twenty-three-year-old son, George. Six weeks ago, all the members of the meeting and more–more than a thousand men–signed and published a document advocating Lower Canada's peaceful separation from Britain and annexation to the United States.

John Redpath agrees to take the chair.

"The purpose of this meeting," he begins, "is to form an association, composed of the persons who have signed the Address to the People of Canada.

"The Parliament of Great Britain has thought fit to change the commercial policy of the empire from a protective to a free trade system. Consequently, our agriculturalists are obliged to sell their grain at ruinous prices. Our artisans are obliged to leave the city ..."

The grievances these men have against England centre on market protection. As Redpath sees it, and as his listeners agree, only an imaginary line divides them from a country that seems more prosperous in every way. Wages, land values and prices of agricultural produce are all higher south of the border.

William Dow seconds a resolution made by Moffat that the new association "adopt the sentiments of the Address to the People of Canada."

"I beg leave to say a few words," William Molson begins. "Numerous evils afflict Lower Canada–I feel that we are called upon to come forward and propose some remedy for her suffering–I agree that annexation to the United States is the answer, and I trust that when this province separates from the parent state, the children may retain their affection and respect for the parent."

The resolution is unanimously carried.

At the end of the meeting, when William Molson is asked to be the organization's chairman, he accepts. Before they disperse, the members join in a rendition of a song:

On Loyalty we cannot live,
One ounce of Bread it will not give,
Clear the way for Annexation,
Or we shall meet with Starvation!

⸻

The Annexation Association's vitriol subsided in time. The economy took a sudden turn for the better, and the association's former faith in the wisdom of the mother county began to be restored. But the British government continued to view the publication of the manifesto with outrage. Letters were despatched to every citizen whose name had appeared on the document, and, upon confirmation of their involvement, those who had ranks, offices or titles were stripped of them. Now solicitor general for Canada East, Lewis T. Drummond personally informed John and William Molson that their ranks in the militia, their commissions as justices of the peace, and in John's case, his office as a warden of Trinity House, had all been withdrawn by the Crown. (Both Molsons were offered their ranks and offices back a year later; both, still offended, refused.)

⸻

The year 1850 would be remembered by some in Montreal as the year the dredging of the St. Lawrence was completed, the rails of the Champlain and Saint Lawrence were extended from La Prairie to St. Lambert, and Christ Church became a cathedral. Thomas Molson would remember it as the calm before the storm, the year everything seemed to be going for him. The temperance movement had relaxed. His commercial and social position was strong in Canada East and Canada West; he felt respect from the public and his family.

Thomas now owned over a hundred properties in Montreal, in addition to those he maintained in Kingston. In 1852, Thomas and William opened a distillery in Toronto, but closed it after one season. They had wanted to establish a brewery in Toronto, an undertaking that held much possibility, but their application was turned down by the city council. Thomas decided then to expand his establishment at Port Hope. He had some years earlier bought Crawford's Distillery on the Ganaraska River, and had let the premises. In subsequent years, to solidify his holdings, he bought a property in town and a warehouse on Lake Ontario. In 1851, he bought 110 acres of land along the

Ganaraska River, including a stave factory, a flour mill, a saw mill and a second distillery. Thomas's manager, Robert Orr, ran the mills, factory and distillery for him. Thomas, who requested that Orr write every other day, communicated buy-sell instructions in code (using a telegraphic dictionary) and visited Port Hope more frequently than Orr thought necessary. At its peak, the stave factory put out 7,000 flour barrel staves, the flour mill 300 barrels of flour, and the sawmill, 6,000 feet of lumber per day.

Thomas gave his attire, personal habits and interests the same scrupulous attention to detail that he gave to his businesses. On his left pinky he wore a ruby signet ring; a Maltese cross was pinned to his lapel, and three strands of gold watch chain looped across his middle. At sixty-one, in 1852, he still cut a dashing figure whether sitting upright in his carriage, striding about the distillery or attending his church. Thomas wore suspenders, silk hats, black kid gloves, satin garters, white satin shoes and black trousers with linen cuffs. He sat for artists to have his portrait painted, and visited Doane's daguerrotype studio in Place d'Armes. He cultivated an air of taste and elegance.

"I pay no waiters," Thomas wrote in one of his many notebooks, "as I believe they expect nothing." He spent much time committing meticulous notes to various leather pocket-notebooks, recording births and deaths, details on distilling, the weather, arrivals and departures of steamships, accounts for wood consumed, and lists of properties and stock he owned. Always, the penmanship was perfect: straight, tight lines of figures and script.

Thomas was intensely curious about all things scientific. He loved gadgets, instruments and inventions, collecting the "remains of an electric battery," a "Quarto copying machine," a camera obscura (a pinhole camera, one of the first ever developed), a "Cichromatic telescope," a hand organ and pianos.

Thomas Molson had always prided himself on his strength and agility. When he was only fourteen he'd amused his friends by standing inside an empty hogshead and leaping from it directly into a second one. He didn't mind all the lumps and bruises he'd endured as he'd practised the feat; his mother had admonished him, but in lighter moments would joke that she should send him to a circus. Thomas's energy was unabated as he aged. In 1852, he still travelled at a pace that would have exhausted many, and he seemed constantly determined to make the most instructive use of each minute of every day.

It is possible that Thomas's spectacular act during a brewery fire in 1852–saving the family papers by "leaping" on the shoulders of a fireman–is a tale that has grown in the telling. It is also conceivable that it was carried out precisely as told from generation to generation.

July 6, 1852

Thomas has heard that a fire has broken out at the brewery and arrives at the scene as quickly as he can. One of his first thoughts is of the many decades of family papers and brewing records still in the office strongbox on the brewery's second floor.

Fearing it might be too late, Thomas dashes into the smoky doorway and climbs the stairs two at a time. At the same moment, firemen begin ascending a ladder to the office window. When the first fireman nears the top and reaches up with his axe to smash the glass, Thomas is above him, charging at the window from the inside with the corner of the strongbox. Thomas realizes he will have to climb out the window. There are flames behind him, and the stairs are already engulfed.

Thomas lowers the heavy box out the window and into the fireman's arms. The fireman grasps it and passes it down, then reaches back up again to help Thomas. But Thomas, realizing he has no time to climb out easefully, scrambles over the jagged edge and swings his feet for the rungs of the ladder, finding instead the sturdy shoulders of the fireman.

The two men make it safely to the ground, the documents intact. Later, Thomas tersely describes the extent of the damage:

> *6 of my houses burnt down in the block with my church; dwelling house and 10 houses on the Molson Terrace saved. My household furniture was all taken out and put back again. Son's brewery all burnt down. Distillery [formerly Handyside's] near the jail was saved; the whole of the Quebec Suburb on St. Mary Street was lost.*

The fire had broken out in St. Mary's Suburb from the east side of St. Lawrence-Main and had taken a day and a night to make its way to Molson's Brewery before it was brought under control. "The flames fanned by a very strong westerly wind," wrote Alfred Sandham, "rushed from street to street and from house to house like water pouring down a rapid." The following day, the Gazette described the extensive ruins as "a smoking wilderness, covered with chimneys, like a burned pine forest with its scathed and scarred trees." In all, twelve hundred buildings had been destroyed; more than nine thousand people were homeless.

The mayor put out a call the next day for citizens to help fund and coordinate the needs of the destitute. Almost immediately, the Montreal Relief Committee was formed; the group included George Moffat, Dr. Wolfred Nelson, John Molson and William Molson.

John HR looked over the ruins of his brewery and determined that they would rebuild almost immediately. Insurance covered most of the losses this time. As his predecessors had done–more than once–before him, he decided to take advantage of the opportunity to improve and expand the premises and install the newest brewing equipment.

In the aftermath of the fire, Thomas's problems seemed to multiply. St. Thomas's Church had also been razed, and Bishop Mountain, now Lord Bishop of Quebec, proposed immediately that it be rebuilt and consecrated. Thomas refused. Mountain's replacement, Bishop Fulford, then proposed building a new church in the same parish not far from its predecessor (on the corner of Dorchester and Champlain,) to be called St. Luke's. Fulford offered former St. Thomas's minister Reverend Irwin chaplaincy of St. Luke's, and Irwin didn't hesitate to accept. By the time Thomas had rebuilt his church, he had lost his original congregation to St. Luke's.

William served his brother notice not long after the fire that he wanted to quit the partnership and asked Thomas to buy him out for £8,000. Thomas, afraid a temperance law "something similar to the Maine Liquor Law, having been sanctioned by the Queen, in New Brunswick" would soon be enforced in Canada East, wrote his brother, "I cannot at present think of it." However, he then offered William £7,000 for his half. William refused to consider it.

Thomas had ongoing conflicts with John HR as well. He was in a black rage when he wrote to Markland in October 1852:

> *I shall carry on the Brewing & Distilling, making Brandy, Gin &c on the Distillery Premises, & John H.R. may do as he pleases as I can not agree with him ... The Bible tells us that a son that calls his Father an Old Fool and a Damned Liar, & that he would not take my Oath (as Mr. Wm. Molson told him he would) … ought to be stoned to Death, & if it had been my brother John or my Brother Wm [who] had received such language from any of their children I believe they would have shot them if they had a Pistol in their hands at the time, & Scripture would justify them in so doing ... I have made up my mind that if any of my children do not please me I shall please myself as thank God I am not depending on my children and should give my property as I please ... I have also made up my mind that any of my children that do not show me respect as due to a Father, then I shall treat them not otherwise, I am sure that I spared no expense in all my children's education &c as the Public know it well.*
> *I remain Dear Wm Markland your kind Father,*
>
> *Thomas Molson*

Production in the Molson distillery would begin every December and continue until the middle of May, during which time sales often climbed to well over three million gallons. Thomas agreed to give William his final decision about the distillery property by November 15, 1852. But that date came and went, with no word from Thomas. William finally heard from his brother five days later, and replied:

> *Nov 20/52*
>
> *My Dear Thomas,*
>
> *When I went up stairs into the Upper Office this evening, I found a letter directed to me by Mr. Rea, on opening it found it to be an answer from you to my note concerning the Distillery Property which I had requested an answer by the 15th. Inst as I now know your decision, do not blame me if I sell it, I mean my half of Distillery, to some other person, as I have no intention of continuing in the business and I have given you the first offer, and certainly you had the first right.*
> *From yours sincerely*
>
> *William Molson*

But Thomas became alarmed at the idea of having a partner other than his brother. At one time he had considered offering his son-in-law William Spragge a management position at £300 a year, a rent-free house and travelling expenses. Yet Spragge, living in Quebec City with his family, had his own career in mind, working his way up in the federal government, within the Crown Lands Department. Thomas drafted another letter to William:

> *If you sell your half to any one else, it must lie idle for me, as I shall not allow another person to ruin me, or to give him a chance to do so (suppose you sold it to Wm. Paine or David Handyside or any other person I could not agree with? If by myself I have no one to blame but myself...)... I would have no objection of taking stock with you in a bank ...*

Eventually, Thomas agreed to give William £8,000 for his half of the distillery premises. "Dear Thomas," he wrote in early December 1852. "Your having accepted my verbal offer of the Distillery premises and requesting my committing it to writing ... " It was a momentous turning point for the family: at the close of the dea, the ownership of the brewery and distillery would rest solely in Thomas's family.

Thomas bought other lots of land from William at the same time, including the late Sir John Johnson's country house, which he had inherited from their father. Thomas's distillery would thrive for another eight years. Meanwhile, William had some very grand plans for his money.

In 1853, when legislation was passed enabling him to apply for a licence to run a private bank, William was ready. He had resigned his position on the board of the Bank of Montreal and liquidated his assets; he was no longer a brewer or distiller. His application was accepted, and after a year of operating as a private bank Molsons Bank was granted a charter. William became its president. He retained his vice-presidency of the Champlain and Saint Lawrence Railroad, and his directorship of the St. Lawrence and Atlantic Railroad. John Junior, still president of the older railway, now became vice-president of the Molson Bank.

The Montreal *Gazette* reported on October 4, 1853:

The first Bank organized under the recent law, was opened on Saturday by Messrs. John and William Molson. In addition to the high standing of the name of Molson, and the extensive credit which it has always commanded in Canada, the public have the farther security, that for every dollar issued, public securities have been deposited with the Government.

The Honourable John Molson Junior, by now in his sixties, continued to provoke (or his manner, to emit) malevolence and animosity. In May 1856, Sheriff of Toronto W.B. Jarvis found himself in "old Molson's" company on board the North America. In a letter to his daughter, Fanny, Jarvis singled out Molson Junior as one of only two persons on board whom he had met before. "[He] is as very an old Put as I ever met with," wrote Jarvis. ("Put" is archaic for a "stupid man, silly fellow, blockhead, lout, or a bumpkin.")

Markland had completed his schooling in 1851, then was sent to Boston to be an apprentice to a distiller. In 1853, at twenty-two years of age, he joined his brother John HR. to work in the brewery. At this time, Molson's was mashing 2,500 bushels of grain a day, six days a week, working with between 175 and 200 brewings per season.

Markland was made a partner under the same terms of apprenticeship upon which John HR had joined the company. However, the brothers were not on the best of terms, and their first disagreement reached litigation within months of their association. Less than a year had passed before their father suggested not only that John HR and Markland part, but also that it was time for father and son–Thomas and John HR–to go their separate ways:

Montreal, 15th February 1854
To Mr. John H.R.Molson

My son,

I beg to inform you from words passed from your Lips regarding your Brother Markland, and yourself, that it would be better for both parties

> *to dissolve Partnership by mutual consent, to prevent further litigation.*
>
> *And you also say that I always keep my children down, which is not the case, but I will not be governed by my Children as long as I live. Now I will say I have done more for my Children (particularly Markland) than my Father did for me before the age of 26 years, or my two brothers, John, and William (which you can ask them the same question). Thank God I have never been under any obligations to my Children and hope I never shall be.*
>
> *And I suppose the best way [for] settling the affairs, would be for I to take my Distillery from last June, and you to take your Brewery, with the profits, and losses, and expenses of each respectively. When I purchased Mr. Wm's half share of the concern, I fully made up my mind to be alone, as I was afraid there might be still some disagreement, but was persuaded by Mr. Wm it would be better to keep together.*
>
> *I remain my Son your well wisher*
>
> *Thomas Molson*

In spite of their father's advice, the brothers' partnership was not dissolved.

Molson collection

Illustration of Molson's Brewery, c. 1880. At the upper right, St. Thomas's Church and the original Molson College can be seen. The insert at lower right depicts the old (pre-1865) Molson distillery and malthouse, premises which would be converted into a sugar refinery and later used as a warehouse.

National Archives Canada

Photograph of the Molson brewery, facing Nôtre Dame Street, 1885, showing the view in the illustration above. The figures standing on the wooden sidewalk are unidentified.

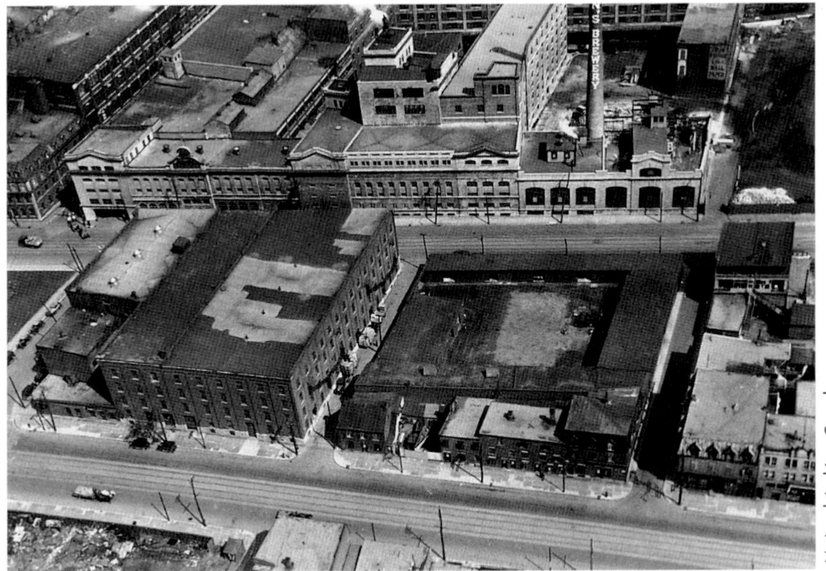

National Archives Canada

Aerial shot over Nôtre Dame Street, showing Molson's Brewery in 1921. Prohibition restrictions had been lifted in 1919, and sales had climbed to 5 million gallons in 1920. Molsons was about to undertake another significant expansion, this time to accommodate a larger brew kettle and new bottling facilities.

National Archives Canada

Modernization transformed Molson's Brewery facility at the turn of the nineteenth century. The brewery's first delivery truck made its appearance in 1910. Horses and wagons were still used for many more years, and the brewery stables were not dismantled until the last horse retired to pasture in the 1940s.

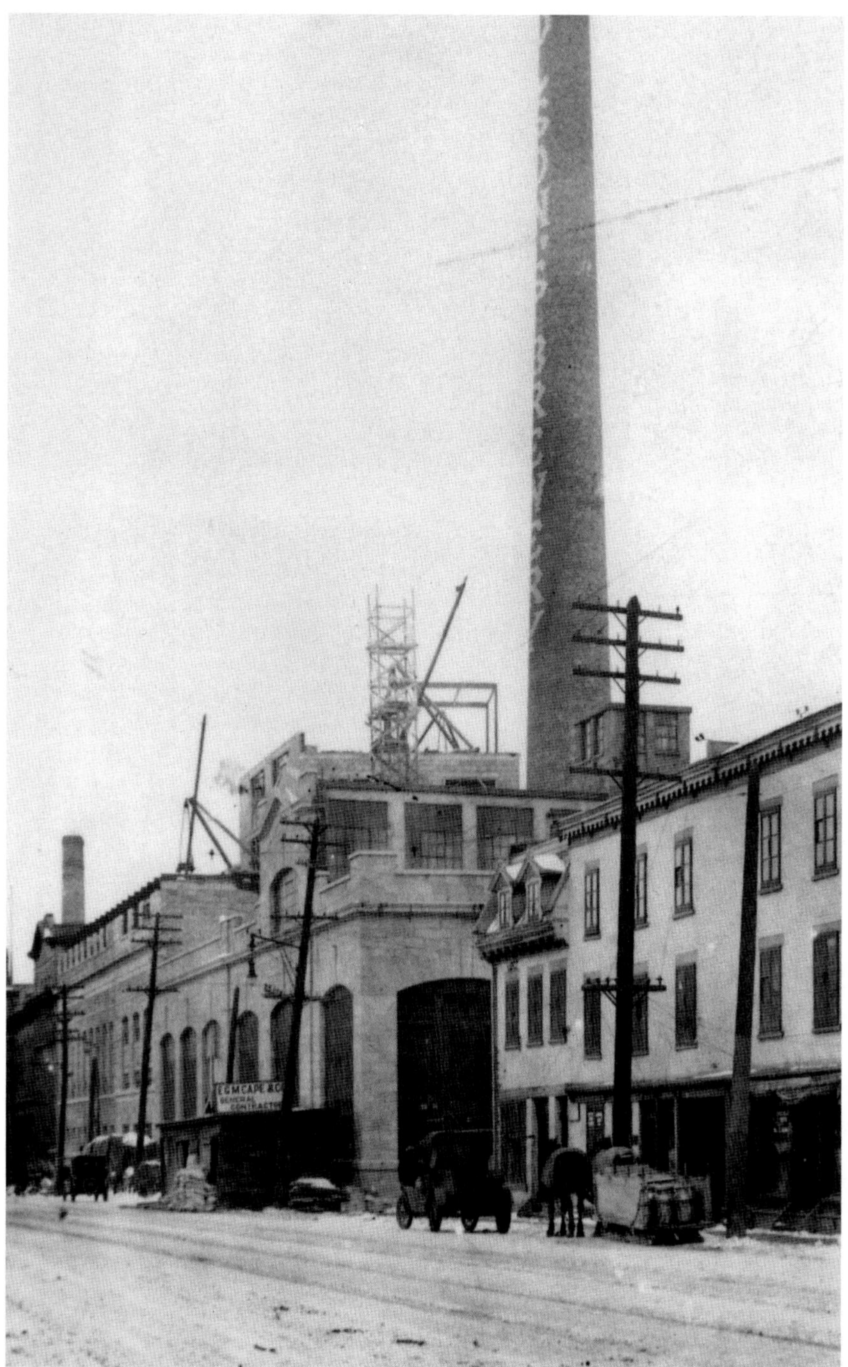

National Archives Canada

Molson's Brewery, 1920. Note the horse-drawn delivery wagon with barrels aboard.

Notman Photographic Archives, McCord Museum

Molsons Bank, St. James Street, Montreal, Quebec, 1905.

Notman Photographic Archives, McCord Museum

Molsons Bank, Pierreville, Quebec, c. 1910.

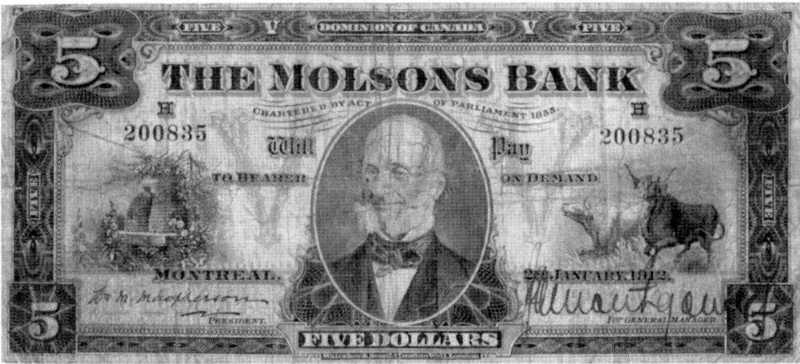

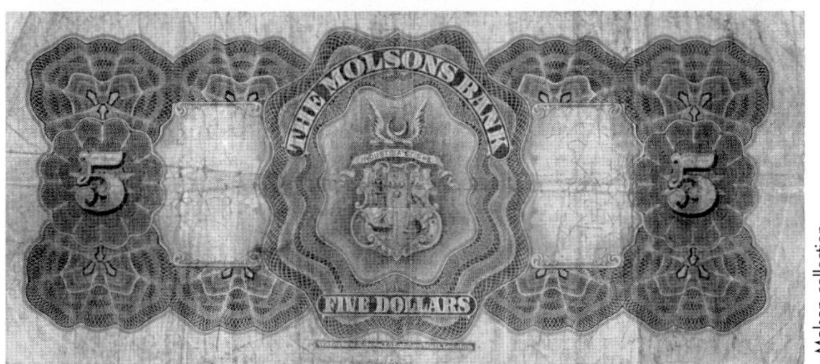

Molson collection

Like other Molsons' Bank notes, the front of this five-dollar bill depicted an image of the bank's founder, William Molson. The signature in the lower-left corner is that of William Molson MacPherson, president of the bank when this note was printed in 1912. The Molson family crest is depicted on the reverse of the note, with the motto "industria et spe" (industry and hope) at the top. By the time Molsons Bank merged with the Bank of Montreal in 1925, it was operating 177 branches across Canada. (This particular note was part of the only series of Molsons' notes printed by Waterlow and Son, London, England. All others before and after this series were printed in Canada or the United States).

Molson collection

Built in 1825, John Molson's Theatre Royale, like his luxury hotel next door, faced the St. Lawrence River. For fifteen years, the theatre offered audiences a variety of plays in French and English (including those of Shakespeare, Molière and Goldsmith) and hosted some of the greatest British actors and actresses of the time (including Charles Kean and Fanny Kemble). Charles Dickens appeared here in 1842. Today the Bonsecours Market building occupies this space.

Molson collection

St. Thomas's Church, built by Thomas Molson in 1841 a block west of the brewery, was destroyed by fire in 1852 and rebuilt in 1855. In 1906 the bells and clock were removed, to be installed in a new St. Thomas's Church on Sherbrooke Street. Today's St. Thomas's is in Nôtre Dame de Grace and remains the only church in the Montreal diocese that is maintained "in the gift" of one particular family. Accordingly, the head of the Molson family must approve the bishop's and the parish's nomination for rector.

Molson collection

Between 1809 and 1855, Molsons built and controlled over thirty steamships and barges that travelled between Montreal and Quebec City. *The Steamship Quebec* (above, painted in 1853 by Cornelius Krieghoff), like other Molson passenger boats, provided first-class accommodations, elegant dining facilities, an orchestra and a chapel.

Hilbert Buist

The Molson Mill at Port Hope, Ontario. Purchased by Thomas Molson in 1851, the extensive property along the Ganaraska River included a stone dwelling house, a brewery, a saw mill, and this flour mill (photographed in 1999). At its peak in production, the mill turned out 300 barrels of flour per day.

Molson collection

The Champlain & St. Lawrence Railroad, financed by John Molson Senior and later headed by John Molson Junior, printed a series of one-sided notes in 1837. Banks in Lower Canada had suspended specie at the time, prompting some merchants to issue their own scrip, by which they simultaneously met a need in the community, made a profit, and circulated advertising for their business. The Champlain & St. Lawrence notes, printed in three different denominations, were illustrated with drawings of contemporary steam locomotives. Each note identified several units of currency with which Montrealers were familiar.

Molson collection

Detail of 15 pence note.

Karen Molson

Snake Hall, Moulton, Lincolnshire, in 1998. From 1699 until 1789 this manor house belonged to the Molson family, during which time it included a brewhouse and stables and was surrounded by hundreds of acres of rich farmland. John Molson Senior, born here in 1763, became sole heir to Snake Hall when orphaned at age 8. He sold it in 1789, to finance his new venture in Canada.

Molson collection

Belmont Hall, Sherbrooke Street, Montreal, c. 1870. Built by John Torrance, the original house (centre portion) that John Molson bought in 1825 bore a striking resemblance to Snake Hall. The east and west wings were added in the 1850s. John Molson Junior lived at Belmont Hall until his death in 1860; his eldest son, also called John, became known as "John of Belmont Hall." The people in this photo have not been identified.

Molson collection

Molson Terrace, c. 1875, was built in 1841 between St. Thomas's Church and the St. Lawrence River. Owner/landlord Thomas Molson lived at Number One (in foreground) until his death in 1863. His sons John HR, Markland and John Thomas lived in middle units at different times. Molson Terrace was demolished in 1925 to accommodate a brewery expansion.

Molson collection

Rosebank was for many years the home of William Molson (1793-1875), his wife Betsey Badgley (1799-1887), and their children. John HR Molson (1826-1897) also lived here for a time. This dignified dwelling, situated east of the brewery, was torn down in the late 1870s. The people in this photo have not been identified.

Château Ramezay Museum

Piedmont, on a summer afternoon, c. 1869. John Frothingham and his daughter Louisa are standing outside. Louisa and John HR Molson lived in this spacious home after they were married. She willed the house to McGill University, and it was later torn down to accommodate the Percival Molson Memorial Stadium.

Notman Photographic Archives, McCord Museum

John Thomas Molson (1837-1910) lived on Prince of Wales Terrace on Sherbrooke Street, until he moved to this house on University Avenue in 1884. At that time his household included his 18-year-old daughter Lillias (from his first marriage), his wife Jennie Butler, six younger children, and a staff of seven live-in servants.

Karen Molson

Above: The Pines (photographed in 1999) was the summer home of Markland Molson (1833-1913), the son of Thomas and Martha Molson and father of Fred (1860-1913) and Harry Molson (1856-1912). Markland, who had this villa designed by architect John J. Browne, erected it first in Montreal in the spring of 1863, then dismantled and transported it by barge to Cacouna, Quebec, to be reconstructed.

Top right: Fred Molson's house on Drummond Street was one of many Molson houses in the "Square Mile" on the southern slope of Mount Royal, a fashionable neighbourhood that featured wide, tree-shaded streets. Fred's house, designed by Robert Findlay, was built in 1901 and was faced entirely in brick. The house was demolished in 1957 to accommodate the extension of McGregor Avenue (now Docteur Penfield).

Bottom right: Fred Molson's summer home near Nantel, Quebec. Known as Father's Rest, this cottage is situated on 1,100 acres that included three small islands. Fred expanded the original cottage and adorned it with perennial flowers and climbing vines. Father's Rest became Fred's haven for fishing and playing croquet with his friends.

Canadian Architecture Collection, McGill University

Molson collection

Doreen Lindsay

Dr. Wm. Alexander Molson's house, built for him in 1906 on Sherbrooke Street in Montreal, was one of many Molson homes designed by architect Robert Findlay. The original entrance portal included segmented pediments decorated with sculpted masks and fruit. The side walls are rock-faced greystone.

The dining room **(top right)** in 1912 displays a Hamel painting on the right wall, "Mrs. Molson and Her Children, 1850." The portraits of John Molson Senior and William Molson hang on the left wall.

This photo of the drawing room **(bottom right)**, also taken in 1912, reveals much about the style in which the Molsons lived. Note the Caen stone fireplace on the far left, the oval painting of William Molson on the left wall, and the piano and gramophone on the right.

Today the building faces the McGill University campus and houses the Italian Commercial Bank. It is dwarfed by the surrounding modern office towers.

Notman Photographic Archives, McCord Museum

Notman Photographic Archives, McCord Museum

Notman Photographic Archives, McCord Museum

Herbert (1875-1938) and Bessie Molson's spacious house at 3617 du Musée (formerly Ontario Street), as it appeared in 1915. Behind the façade of red bricks and buff-coloured sandstone was a grand entry hall and central staircase (see below), drawing room, library, dining room and solarium. The upper floors included Bessie's bedroom, her boudoir, Herbert's master bedroom suite, a guest room, and the children's rooms. The servants' quarters were in the attic. The house is now the Russian Consulate in Montreal.

National Archives Canada

I was one of those persons who entirely refused and would not sign the memorial to the Governor General as to the question of annexation with America.

Chapter Twenty

From Beerage to Peerage

Montreal in the 1850s was evolving from a city "having a dismal aspect"–the city had suffered a drop in population owing to the removal of government, and many premises stood empty–to one that bore considerable signs of optimism and expansion. Public buildings became larger, while cast iron and brick were added to the cut stone and wood frameworks. Old Montreal was beginning to be taken over by commerce, industry, religious institutions and hospitals; well-to-do residents moved northward and westward into new urban areas. Improvements to the city included expansions to the Montreal General Hospital (for which the Molsons continued to be active members of the board), and the construction of Victoria Bridge, the train bridge for the Grand Trunk Railway, a six-year undertaking begun in 1854.

McGill University was undergoing transformations. In 1855, new principal William Dawson and his board introduced more modern and practical subjects such as science, medicine and law, and Dawson even volunteered to live off his savings and donate his administrative earnings to the improvement of the grounds. By the end of the decade walkways would be laid out, all the fences would be repaired, trees planted, and renovations under way. Though there were only sixty-four students enrolled at McGill in 1855, the first drive for endowment funds was initiated the following year, and the Molson brothers –John, Thomas and William–donated one-third of the university's financial objective. Their gift, £5,000, was directed toward the endowment of McGill's first academic chair: English Language and Literature. All three brothers were named to the board when the university's charter was amended.

Dawson and the university board discussed moving arts students to the campus and accepted an offer from William to cover the cost of repairs to the out-building they would occupy. Molson proposed also that he build a west wing to provide a convocation hall and library and connect the sections with hallways lined with classrooms.

William Molson, sixty-two years old in 1855, had an aura of ease about him. His marriage remained an affectionate one. He could see that his two daughters' prospects were happy; Anne (Mrs. John Molson III) and Elizabeth (Mrs. D.L. MacPherson), whose husbands' careers were well established by the mid-1850s, had, between them, ten healthy children. Both his sons-in-law had chosen careers he actively supported: John III at Molsons Bank, and MacPherson in railway contracting.

As president of Molsons Bank, William was well regarded within the financial community. His influence and involvement in railways was also wide-reaching. He was a generous benefactor of various public causes and faithfully supported McGill University.

Molsons Bank was situated on Great St. James Street. William would not have had to walk far from his office to run into family members, friends and even one-time enemies. The financial and legal district, bounding the greater part of Great St. James Street, was a tight-knit but competitive community. John Junior's youngest son, Alexander, who was one of the first law students at McGill and had studied under William Badgley, had a law partnership with Christopher Abbott on nearby Little St. James Street. Across the road William Badgley and his partner J.J.C. Abbott (Christopher's brother), who would become Canada's third prime minister, had their practice. A stone's throw away, on the corner of St. Lawrence Hill, Dr. Wolfred Nelson's shingle announced his position as provincial inspector of prisons. L.J. Papineau, also practising law, had his offices on the same street, just east of the Place d'Armes.

Although John Molson Junior's youngest son, Alexander, had been called to the bar, he never actually practised law. Instead, once the government passed the *Free Banking Act,* he applied for a charter and opened the Mechanics Bank. (The Mechanics Bank was described as "one of the most badly managed of Canadian Banks." It opened other branches and issued notes before ceasing business for good in 1879, at a substantial loss to its creditors and shareholders.) In 1855 Alexander met and married Eliza Holmes, daughter of the general manager of the Bank of Montreal. Their permanent home was in Montreal, but they built a summer home, Fern Hill, on a 200-acre property along the south bank of Lake Memphremagog in the Eastern Townships, where they kept horses and farmed the land.

In 1857 Alexander became one of the dozen founding members of Montreal's St. James Club. This gentlemen's club, the first of its kind in Montreal, was established on St. James Street and provided for its members an elegant setting for various pursuits. Rooms were available for billiards, smoking, coffee, cards, reading, writing and meetings. There was a dining room for members and another for guests. Early members included Peter McGill, John Young, George Frothingham, the Workman brothers, John Torrance, George Moffat, John Redpath, William Logan and John Ogilvy. The diminutive inspector general of military hospitals in Canada, Dr. James Barry, became a member later that year.

The Spragge family had lived in Toronto, moved to Quebec City, and then returned to Toronto. William Spragge had been promoted to chief clerk in the Survey Department. Variously described as choleric, procrastinating, brilliant but haphazard, and, in one opinion, "really dangerous," Spragge appeared blustery and seemed always to be in a rush. His administrative work involved land transactions within the older settlements of Upper Canada. He dealt with settlers, prospectors and lumbermen who had bought and sold properties that were poorly surveyed and who now faced legal complications and lawsuits.

The Spragge and the Molson families did not see much of each other in fall, winter or spring, but in summer, members of the extended family continued to travel to Cacouna. Martha Spragge and her children, Markland (with his wife Helen), Mary Anne, and John Thomas returned year after year to spend time at the seaside. New wharves in Rivière du Loup drew crowds of tourists to the Point Promenade in summer. Many came to watch the glitterati of Europe and America disembark from the steamers, waiting while their luggage was transferred to the smaller craft that would take them the rest of the way to Cacouna, St. Patrick, Tadoussac or Murray Bay. Sea-bathing had become unprecedentedly popular. Luxury hotels began to spring up to accommodate growing numbers of people who were convinced of the salutary effects of fresh air and saltwater at these sites.

Thomas Molson was rarely found in one place. Since his church had burned down, he spent even more of his time travelling. In 1854 he took his daughters Mary Anne and Harriet to England, and while there bought a book about a new aristocratic, evangelical sect of the Church of England that had caught his interest, known as the Countess of Huntingdon Connexion. Founded under the influence of evangelist George Whitefield by the Countess of Huntingdon, this mission church was known for its earnest style; its services were bare of the trappings of ceremony and its ministers preached a straight message of saving souls. Back in Montreal in 1855, Thomas rebuilt St. Thomas's, but soon had another disagreement with the bishop of Montreal, Francis Fulford. Thomas wanted to retain the right to appoint the priest of his church.

Every spring Thomas travelled to London, staying either at Pall Mall or Cecil Street Strand and often attending lectures with such titles as "Apostolical and Primitive Church," "The Apology of the Church of England," "Is the Bible True?" and "Free Discussion Versus Intolerance."

In 1857 on his trip to England he looked for a clergyman to bring back with him. He ordered 250 copies of the Countess of Huntingdon Connexion hymn-books and returned to Montreal with Reverend and Mrs. Alfred Stone. Once home, he began to lay out plans for a college and school near the riverbank behind his church. The rebuilt church (known simply as Molson's Church) was "a neat brick building … comfortably fitted up to seat 500 persons. In the north east tower is a superior chime of bells; in the north west tower is a service bell; and in the front is an illuminated clock."

The new college was to "be devoted to the education of the poorer classes," as well as to train clergymen in the Countess of Huntingdon denomination. Reverend Stone and his wife would be live-in teacher-professors.

Thomas's faith was profound. One night during his stay in England in 1858 he awoke at the touch of something brushing across his foot:

October 1858

On Wednesday Night at 3:30 After Midnight the Lord must have touched me on the sole of the Right Foot. In bed in No. 8 House Cecil Street Strand London. And I got up immediately and examined the Room. And found nothing, or no one in the Room after I lighted my candle. And prayed to the Lord, I said Is it Thee Lord and went to Bed again. London, England, 20th October 1858 3:30 minutes after midnight

---

In 1859, on August 25, over the tacit disapproval of his grown children, sixty-eight-year-old widower Thomas Molson married thirty-eight-year-old Sophia Stevenson. The daughter of a Protestant Irish mother and an English architect father, Sophia had emigrated with her family to Canada in 1836, when she was fourteen. The eldest of ten children, she was the last of the siblings to marry, having stayed at the family's Bexley Township homestead, north of Lindsay, Ontario, to help care for her parents. She most likely met Thomas at her sister Charlotte's wedding to Robert Orr, who was managing Molson's Mills in Port Hope.

Rector Jonathan Shortt, an ardent Port Hope temperance man and a fellow summer resident of Cacouna, officiated at the Anglican parish. In keeping with second weddings, it was a small, dignified affair. Thomas was looking forward to a quiet life with his young bride. Neither of his brothers, nor any of his children (all distinctly uncomfortable with the union), attended the wedding.

During their honeymoon in England the Molsons stayed at 14 Pall Mall, a dignified street in the heart of London known for its exclusive gentlemen's clubs. Thomas and Sophia moved in exalted circles in London. They felt comfortable staying there and taking their place among others who shared their drive for power, recognition and prestige.

In December 1859 from London, Thomas wrote a friendly letter to John HR, asking about repairs on his rented homes and how business was faring. "I hope my Houses are all done on the Terrace, & give satisfaction." He alluded to Sophia obliquely, using the word "we" in a postscript:

"Thank God we are quite well, and hope you are all quite well & happy."

Thomas did not tell his son that he was campaigning to be granted a title from the British crown. Both Thomas's father and brother had received the right to call themselves "Honourable," and Thomas now wanted to join the titular aristocracy. Earlier in the century, peerages had been sold to raise money for the crown; indeed, Thomas was familiar with the expression "From beerage to peerage." Sir Samuel Cunard, founder of a steamship company that became the Cunard Line, had been created a baronet the previous spring. Sir John Beverly Robinson, a lawyer, politician and judge, had been knighted and then given a baronetcy in 1854.

Thomas had started his campaign in December 1858, when he wrote to Upper Canada's Solicitor General John Rose, to whom he had spoken in Toronto the week before:

Port Hope, 18th Dec., 1858

Dear Sir,

Since I had the pleasure of seeing you on Thursday last I called on His Excellency the Governor General at the Government House and was showed in his Room, he asked me what was his wish, and I said if His Excellency would recommend to the Secretary of State for the Colonies for a Baronetcy as it would descent to my family. And I also mentioned that my Father was the first that commenced Steam Boats in Canada in the year 1808 [sic]. And I also volunteered my Services at the Rebellion of Canadians at Lachine, etc.

He answered me and said there was nothing done by me in the Official Capacity to merit such a Title, but he gave me a letter to the Secretary of State for the Colonies stating that I was a Gentleman well known through all Canada.

His Canadian efforts not yielding the desired response, Thomas renewed his missives from London, England. Molson dispatched a letter to the Duke of Newcastle, a senior member of the House of Lords, in December 1859. He prepared five rough copies and covered a page with multiple elegant scripts of "Dear Sirs" and "My Lord Dukes" before sending this version:

21 Cecil Street Strand
December 1859

My Lord Duke,

I venture to enclose a letter to your Grace from the Governor General of Canada and also from Messrs. Glyn Mills & Co, Bankers, Lombard Street, as an introduction for the honor of an interview with your Grace, during my limited sojurn in England.

As a son of the late Honorable John Molson, and as having held a commission in the Canadian Militia and as now occupying the position of one of the chief proprietors of the Molson Bank (first established in Montreal, in 1837), I venture to ask that your Grace will do me the favor to present to Her Majesty at the next Levee.

It does not become me to make any statements regarding myself personally, and I would simply ask your Grace to be so obliging as to peruse the enclosed documents to which the following signatures are attached.

There then follows a list of twenty names, including Peter McGill, former mayor of Montreal; C.S. Rodier, then mayor of Montreal; and several MPPs and judges. Thomas's first request was ignored, but Sophia encouraged her husband not to give up. Remembering that he had been introduced to the Earl of Elgin by Sir George Simpson while Elgin was Governor General, Thomas wrote to him next:

14 Pall Mall
18th February, 1860

Dear Sir,

May I venture to ask your Lordship to peruse the accompanying papers and further if you would kindly give me a Note to the Duke of Newcastle, stating your Lordship's knowledge of myself and my family …

I have the honour to remain your Lordship's humble servant,

Thomas Molson

Although the Earl of Elgin declined to see Thomas, he agreed to speak to the Duke of Newcastle on his behalf. Thomas drafted another letter and showed it to Sophia:

14 Pall Mall,
February 22, 1860

My Lord,

I have to thank your Lordship for the message sent to me on my call in Eaton Square that you would speak to the Duke of Newcastle on the subject of the papers enclosed you.

I shall feel greatly indebted if your Lordship will mention my name to the Duke and I believe it cannot be done unfavourably: but I am not the person to speak on that point …

I may venture to remind your Lordship that though my Brothers signed the Memorial to the Governor General as to the question of Annexation with America, I entirely refused and would not sign such document.

May I ask your Lordship to kindly favour me with a reply after you have spoken to the Duke.

Sophia carefully crossed out Thomas's reference to his brothers and the Annexation manifesto, and replaced the entire sentence with one much more diplomatic:

I was one of those persons who entirely refused and would not sign the memorial to the Governor General as to the question of annexation with America.

Thomas was eventually invited to have an audience at Windsor Castle with an equerry on August 28, 1862. His dream of acquiring a title, however, would not be realized.

The members of the first Canadian-born generation of Molsons were growing older, and at least one of the three brothers, John, had begun thinking about his life, health and funeral arrangements. John had been diagnosed with dropsy and was told he had approximately a year of life left. He considered the newly established Mount Royal Cemetery as a good place to build a permanent family mausoleum. He spoke to Thomas, who was also in favour of the idea. The subject of the afterlife wasn't far from Thomas's mind either: he kept a copy of a temperance lecture delivered at "the Tanneries" in 1860, in which he wrote in the margin: "Can a distiller enter the Kingdom of Heaven?" Thomas began closing and selling his various distilleries that year.

By the spring of 1860, the three Molson brothers had pooled $15,000 to purchase a large plot on "the highest summit" in the 165-acre cemetery and commissioned the architect George Browne to design three octagonal vaults. These domed units–to be built of cut stone and cast iron–would have turfed roofs and surround a sixty-foot-high column, a commemoration to their parents. William and Thomas met with Browne and discussed the various symbolic decorations such as helmeted urns, winged female creatures, crossed arrows, the stylized pine cone (an ancient symbol of immortality) and the Molson coat of arms. The completed units were the largest and costliest private vaults in North America.

John Junior died on July 12 that year, at the age of seventy-three. A grand funeral was held at Christ Church Cathedral, which his widow, Mary Anne (who had returned to Canada), and three of his five grown children were able to attend. John Junior's remains were the first to be interred in the new vault. John Senior's and Sarah's remains were "removed from the Old Burial Ground" (on Dorchester Street) the following year, and over the next three years other family members who had been buried at St. Thomas's Church, including Martha, Mary Anne, and their dead children, were re-interred in the family vaults at Mount Royal.

Six weeks after John Junior's death, eighteen-year-old heir apparent Prince Edward Albert made a much-celebrated visit to British North America. It was his first official visit on behalf of his mother, Queen Victoria. The youthful prince, who had been asked to open Montreal's Victoria Bridge, attended a ceremony where he drove in the last gold spike in front of a cheering crowd that immediately burst into an enthusiastic rendition of "God Save the Queen."

Thomas and Sophia witnessed the bridge ceremony and later attended the Prince of Wales Ball, the most inspiring social event in Montreal in decades. The vast circular ballroom built just for this occasion was a stunning sight. Artificial waterfalls and groups of full-grown trees adorned the interior, and the twenty-four support columns were numbered so that guests could rendezvous without losing one another among the hundreds of feet of refreshment tables. The orchestra was settled in the middle of the 30,000-square-foot dance floor, around which two thousand gas lamps were strung in concentric circles.

Between five and six thousand guests, showing off their finest attire and most splendid jewellery, spent the evening with the young prince; a select few ladies had the honour of dancing a set of quadrilles, a waltz or a polka with him.

After their honeymoon, Thomas and Sophia had moved into No. 1 Molson Terrace. They had this six-bedroom, three-storey home with attic, cellar and private stables all to themselves. The last of Thomas's adult children to remain at home, Mary Anne and Harriet, had left when they each were married in 1858.

For two and a half years, Reverend Stone, Thomas and a handful of English Montrealers faithfully attended services at Molson's Church. The congregation did not grow but rather dwindled. Many of the 250 hymn books were still unopened by 1861, the year Civil War broke out in the United States and British troops arrived in Montreal. The shortage of barrack accommodation for the soldiers led them to inquire of Thomas about leasing Molson College and his chapel to the troops. It was an easy decision.

In July, 1862, Mr. & Mrs. Thomas Molson travelled to England again, this time with Sophia's sister, Mrs. Isabel Vansittart. Thomas kept a diary in which he recorded that he gave Sophia a few pounds every other day, bought her a bonnet, paid her cab fare, bought her gifts including a silver chain, locket, a plated ink stand with silver edges, and several dresses. On one page is an entry which reads, "Am I to pay Mrs. Vansittart's Lodging bill? [Sophia] says yes."

Adam Skaife, a brewery employee since 1852, wrote a letter to John HR Molson on February 16, 1863. The letter, which did not reach him until mid-March, reported that Thomas, who was seventy-one years old, was "alarmingly ill." He had been suffering some ailment since the previous Thursday "to such an extent as to induce him to take some medicine and keep [to] the house." Friday morning Sophia sent for their doctor, Dr. Campbell. When Campbell arrived, he found Thomas up and washing in cold water, to all appearances perfectly well. Thomas ate a hearty breakfast and "departed the house," determined that he would do his banking on "discount day."

The next morning, Sophia found Thomas weak and partly conscious. She sent to the brewery for Markland and John Thomas, who went to fetch Dr. Campbell again. By then Thomas was lying on the bedroom sofa, weakly but steadfastly denying his debility. He refused to return to bed as the doctor requested. Dr. Campbell explained to Sophia that Thomas had experienced "a rush of blood to the head, or apoplexy." Another doctor was sent for, but he agreed that the case was hopeless. Paralysis had set in on Thomas's left side. He died before the day was over.

Chapter Twenty-One

Confederation

How little did I expect a fortnight ago that I should be writing on black-edged paper on your father's account. Martha often said she felt certain he would outlive her …

(*William Spragge*)

IN THEIR marriage contract Thomas had assigned Sophia, upon his death, an annuity of £300 ($1,200). This amount may have been fair but was not particularly generous, considering that the wage of an employee at the Molsons' sugar refinery in 1866 was more than twice that. However, he also left her the use of No. 1 Molson Terrace. If Sophia moved out of the house, an additional allowance of £200 a year was to be added to her annuity for rent. If she remarried, she forfeited both house and annuity.

Thomas died on February 22, his will was "proved" five days later, and the next day John Thomas and his brother-in-law, William Spragge, as well as two notaries public and two appraisers, stood on the step of No. 1 Molson Terrace.

February 28, 1863

John Thomas raises the knocker and strikes it sharply against the brass plate.

When the men are admitted into the house, Sophia is dismayed to see John Thomas and five hirsute men she does not know enter the hall and remove their hats.

"Excuse us, Mrs. Molson," one is saying, but he is not looking at her.

Sophia's stepson pulls off his gloves and lays them on the front hall table, next to the plated salver with its scatter of calling cards. He introduces Sophia to William Spragge, who explains to her they are there to take an inventory. The four others stoop to unbuckle their boots.

The men begin on the third storey, shuffling and murmuring as they move from room to room with their pads and rulers. They summarize five bedrooms while Sophia waits anxiously in the carpeted hall. They must unanimously agree about the description of something before it gets written down. One dictates it to the next, while the others discuss and estimate the value. One room at a time, each wardrobe, washstand, mattress is noted. Each silk blind, even a matchbox and pincushion found on a small table in the servants' bedroom, is itemized. Each chamber pot and coal scuttle is counted, as are 681 books, and seven cakes of soap in the spare room. The men come across maps, charts, microscopes, telescopes and even a case of butterflies. The notaries question Sophia about the origin of some trunks, a basket and a bonnet box, "in all, 9 pieces" which, Sophia objects, belong to her. The inventory will take days to complete.

On Monday the men enter the courtyard again, but this time Sophia won't allow them inside the house. They stamp their feet as much with frustration as with the bitter cold on the snow-packed stone, and they breathe snorts of vapour into the crisp air. John Thomas persuades Sophia to let him lead one of the notaries inside to a chair and table so that he may write an official statement, a document that they all can sign:

> *And afterwards on this Second day of March one thousand eight hundred and sixty three, We the same notaries at the request aforesaid repaired to the last residence of the said late Thomas Molson with the view and in the intention of continuing the said Inventory in accordance with the said Adjournment, but the said Dame Sophia*

Stevenson deeming it expedient and desiring to take legal advice in the premises refused to permit the continuation of said Inventory, whereupon the continuation hereof was in consequence indefinitely postponed and the said parties hereto have signed.

What had probably attracted Sophia to Thomas was that he was devout, highly respected, and owned his own church. It's true his material wealth was nothing to be scoffed at; Thomas was one of the richest men in Montreal. Living at No. 1 Molson Terrace, with servants, rosewood and mahogany furniture, busts of Byron and Scott on pedestals in the entrance hall, a Broadwood piano, Brussels carpets, two carriages, a cab, a phaeton, a "very fine (covered) double sleigh," and no fewer than five horses in the stable, was luxurious. But Thomas was always a difficult man to live with, and had become even more so as he aged. Their marriage had had its stormy moments. In a rare emotional diary entry, in early August 1862, Thomas wrote, "I told Sophia that she solemnly disavows her marriage ceremony by *acting the way* she does, first to obey her husband which she has not done." Nevertheless, in spite of any marital difficulties, Thomas had ensured that Sophia would have a house to live in and a small income. Unfortunately, he hadn't considered that his widow might be left in the embarrassing situation of being without cash within weeks of his passing. (Sophia's income from Thomas Molson's estate was payable semi-annually.) Sophia wrote short, pointed notes to John Thomas, and slipped them in his letter-box next door:

I would be much obliged if you could lend me $100.00. Please let me have it this evening as I have several accounts to pay tonight.

Sophia Molson

The house was painfully quiet. Thomas's man-servant had expressed his condolences and taken his leave. The four servants had left. Sophia made an appointment to see Judge Aylwin, an ex-Patriote lawyer known as an excellent criminal jurist. "Mrs. Molson's sleigh is continually going & returning from Judge Aylwin's house," John Thomas wrote portentously to Spragge. But Aylwin must have advised Sophia to cooperate:

> *Dear Sir,*
>
> *You would oblige me by supplying the horses with provender. You can take the inventory as soon as you like.*
>
> *Yours truly*
>
> *S. Molson .*

On March 4, 1863, John Thomas had written to William Spragge:

> *Enclosed you have a certified copy of my father's will which I got this afternoon I have just returned from seeing Strachan Bethune at his house as Mrs. Molson sent for Uncle William this afternoon & demanded the key of the room that I have, he told her I had it as executor. She was very ugly with him, Bethune told me he thought I had better see her tomorrow morning after ten o'clock and by tact to find out what she wanted with it, in fact to gain time while he manoeuvred with Judge Aylwin. [He] says that the things given to her, are given outright ... Things look very warlike at present. Bethune says you should immediately send me a full notarial power of attorney so as to act while you are in Quebec as things may require it to be in the right.*

It is difficult to question the motives of someone who came into a marriage with no money of her own, yet signed a contract that made it clear she would not be a primary beneficiary of her husband's will. Sophia's annuity would make for a respectable living, but it could not be considered extravagant. Was she the devoted, devout second wife or the scheming, would-be wealthy widow? Did she consider her alienation from the family a just, or unjust, cross to bear? John HR expressed his criticism of Sophia and his ambivalence about his father this way: "When in his right mind and with no evil disposed persons to prejudice him there was no kinder or more obliging man alive, and had our poor mother only lived until now to have comforted and counselled him how happy it would have been for us all."

Thomas's grown children either allowed or encouraged disparaging stories about Sophia to circulate. Ignored entirely by family members during the three years that she had been married to Thomas, Sophia Molson, in the weeks that followed Thomas's death, was referred to (in correspondence between her adult step-children) once because she was "troublesome," and once when she "got very ugly with [Uncle William]." "All is now over," wrote John HR a year later, "and all we have to do is our duty, what we ought to do, and tho' misfortune & disappointment should be our portion … what we did we did because we thought it right."

Later generations repeated stories that Sophia was illiterate, had a poverty-stricken backwoods upbringing, and even that she had stolen Molson family silverware. In 1933 a biographer commissioned by the family was asked not to mention her in his book. The Stevenson family was, in fact, highly gifted and particularly literate. Sophia's cousin John Frederick Stevenson, "the best speaker of his day in Montreal," was a man of "wide literary culture [and] refinement." Her brother F.W. Stevenson, a politician, was remembered as being "highly articulate and intelligent." Her sister Katie married Charles F. Wood-Leigh, a scholar of medieval social history.

The "stolen" silverware–eventually returned to the Molson family by a member of the Stevenson family in 1959, nearly a hundred years later–had been left to Sophia in Thomas's will.

From a financial point of view, it was better for the young widow to accept the extra £200 and live in rented premises than to stay where she was. Before spring was over, Sophia Molson moved to No. 3 Montmorency Terrace on St. Catherine Street, an exclusive residential terrace where her neighbours included prominent businesspeople, a judge and Thomas D'Arcy McGee. A year later she left Montreal, first moving to Port Hope and then Mount Forest, always to be near Stevenson family members. She had kept her wardrobe, her baskets, her bible and the silverware that Thomas had left her. But the grandeur of the life she had led with her husband was left behind. Apart from acknowledgments of annuity payments which were administered by John Thomas, she had no further contact with members of the Molson family. Every day she read verses and marked the date in the bible's margin. In the tone set by Queen Victoria after the death of Prince Albert, she continued to wear mourning clothes for the nearly fifty years she remained Thomas's widow.

When his father became ill and died, John HR was travelling in England to pursue some business matters as well as to see a specialist about his eyes. His brother John Thomas wrote him with the sad news. John HR replied on March 18, from Pembroke Dock:

> *I was much surprised and shocked as I had not known that he was even unwell. I have since your letter one from Mr. Skaife but none from either you or Mark which much disappointed me. I have seen Mr. [Alexander] Clerk's [Harriet Molson's husband] letters to Mrs. Barrett [Mary Anne] giving considerable information. I hope however to receive one today from one of you as by what you write or recommend I shall regulate my time of departure from here for Canada. I had intended to return home by the Great Eastern which sails from Liverpool on 4th April but whether I shall leave as proposed or not will depend on the nature of your next letters …*
>
> *The mail has arrived but no letters for me which I much wonder at as I fully expected one with full particulars of the will and some remarks as what the family expects or wishes me to do as to returning immediately or not. However as nobody tells me anything I suppose there is no hurry about anything in reference to the estate …*
>
> *John H.R. Molson*

John Thomas was quick to reassure him that their intentions had been for the best. On April 10, 1863, he replied:

> *Dear John,*
>
> *I received yours of March 18th and we all thought you would have been in the Asia so we telegraphed to you per Cunard steamer. Mrs. Molson has been very troublesome but is now a little less so, she sells the furniture by auction on Tuesday week and leaves the house on 1st May. We have put off doing any more than actually necessary till your arrival here but I am afraid we shall have to do several things as Alex. Clerk leaves for England about the tenth of May and would like as he is acting for Barrett and Mary Anne. Spragge has been in a great hurry for some of the money and I have put him off and off. The mill at Port Hope has twenty thousand of wheat in it and something must be done*

> *immediately with it. We would have written since, but expected you could come as soon as you arranged what you had to do in London. I hope your eyes are improved you did not refer to them in your last ... The Spring is long and tedious, Skaife writes by this mail I told you in my last the particulars of the will. I think if you could come as soon as you can the better it will be but we did not want to hurry you. I am placed in an awkward position here as only executor in Montreal and nothing thoroughly decided which if once done would be easy.*

The "long and tedious" spring dragged on for John Thomas. There was a continuing crisis at Molson's. The brewery (since 1859, a partnership between the three brothers, John HR, Markland and John Thomas) was trying to recover from its first "foxed" batch of beer. The term was applied to beer that had become exposed to a strain of wild yeast or other infectious matter, as a result of "neglect, uncleanliness, or bad heats" and gave off an unpleasant smell. The entire batch had to be poured into the St. Lawrence; all their equipment had to be scoured and they had to begin again. Customers were hesitant to taste the new, untainted brew. As late as April 1863, manager Adam Skaife was writing, "It is very difficult to re-establish our beer in the public favour ..."

Since John Thomas was the only one of his father's appointed trustees in Montreal, as he pointed out in his letter to John HR, all the work involved in disbursing his father's estate fell to him. When he expressed his frustration about this to William Spragge on May 28, he had been up nearly all night:

> *There is one thing I would like to remark which is this, that all the work has to be done at Montreal & it takes my time away from our business, as at present I am doing little else. I have all the leases & property & repairs to look after which is the disagreeable part of the work; now you should either give full power to me & be satisfied with what I do, or else to come & live in Montreal and do your half because you cannot do it elsewhere & trips up & down could not be borne by the estate any more than for me to charge my time against it. If you reflect that I am more interested than the others (excepting Mark) you cannot fail to see that the best possible care will be used in everything connected with the estate, but things cannot be done rashly & it adds greatly to the work to keep writing "by return of mail or by telegraph." Everything will be done as quickly on my part as is consistent but one must look ahead of them to see where they are going ...*

John Thomas and his brothers considered converting the distillery–and its equipment–into a sugar refinery. John Redpath's sugar business, begun in 1854, seemed to be doing well. Did the market have room for another sugar refinery and starch works in Montreal? A new art of producing and manufacturing crystallized sugar and syrup "from Indian corn and other cereal grains or roots" had been patented by Montrealer Narcisse Pigeon, who was willing not only to sell his patent to the Molsons, but to also advise them in the business. John Thomas spoke to his eldest brother shortly after the latter's return from England. At first John HR was hesitant about the idea, but Markland was enthusiastic. George Drummond spoke for Redpath, and seemed to settle the matter when he wrote to John HR: "We are ourselves only half employed ... There is no reasonable opening for further employment of capital in this business in Canada."

Markland was also a beneficiary of their father's will, inheriting the mills and property in Port Hope, and some stocks. At this point in his life he had undertaken a series of financial commitments and made some bad investments, including a land transaction described by his younger brother as "the possession of some real estate in Montreal for which he has not paid." He seems to have been flightier, less responsible, and more gullible than the other brothers. He was willing to take the most risks, and he would pay dearly for some of his mistakes.

In March 1863, a month after his father's death, Markland commissioned architect John J. Browne to build him a cottage, which was assembled in Montreal in the spring. There Mark inspected it, pronounced it suitable, then had it dismantled and shipped by steamer to Cacouna, to be reassembled there. It was the first summer cottage in the village. Built in a medieval style called Rural Gothic, it has a turret and pointed, arched windows. Named Pine Cottage after the wide pine boards that cover the house's interior and exterior, it was referred to as the Gingerbread House by family members–on account of its "twirly-go-wiggles" of Victorian trim.

Markland and his family–wife Helen, and two small sons, Frederick William (Fred) and Harry Markland (two daughters had died in infancy)–enjoyed their house in Cacouna. Mark would drive his horses and carriage directly onto the steamer, and drive them off again at his destination, the wharf being only three miles from his cottage. None of his siblings built a house in the village, preferring to rent accommodations. A few, including John Thomas, were even considering leaving for nearby Métis Beach, for Cacouna was getting more and more crowded with tourists every summer and beginning to lose some of its charm.

In the fall of 1864, after spending his first summer in Pine Cottage, Markland took Helen and the boys home to Montreal (where the boys were enrolled at Dr. Carpenter's School for Gentlemen) and left for an extensive tour of Europe. It was clear he had not entirely dismissed the idea of a sugar refinery, in spite of the negative reaction from Redpaths, for when he returned from Europe the following spring, via New York, he made a point of visiting sugar refineries and starch houses. He wrote a letter to John HR from New York in April 1865, trying to persuade him to change his mind about the feasibility of converting the old distillery premises into a sugar refinery:

> *There is not much outlay, say about ten to twelve thousand dollars, and in addition we might be ready to start in about four months. It is the greatest pity that we have thought so long about it, for we have every facility, and no obstacles ... 1. there is an opening for a refinery [in Montreal], 2. we possess a large share of the kind of knowledge requisite for a business, 3. we have the means (although you rather quake at the idea), 4. the premises are well-located as water is needed, 5. we have the most expensive part of refinery [equipment] now, all of which will be comparatively worthless if we do not work them up, and lastly but not least, we will find Mr. Pigeon of great assistance.*

The decision whether to convert the distillery must have been a difficult one for John HR. Would sugar refining be any more stable an industry than distilling? In 1859 his father had described whisky sales reflecting "a demand ... being greater than ever anticipated," and, from December until May, monthly production of proof gallons of spirits often totalled more than 500,000. But by 1864, sales of even their last stored puncheons of whisky were "languishing," and John HR noted later that year that business was "as dull as ever–of whisky we sell scarcely anything but an occasional puncheon." The brothers had stopped production of whisky entirely, endeavouring instead to sell their old stock. Stored whisky, John HR knew, grew more valuable: "What we have on hand being old is worth at least one penny per Gal more than new, both as to flavour and strength."

John HR ordered several books on sugar refining so he could learn as much as possible about the business. In eight weeks, he offered to purchase Pigeon's manufacturing patent for $4,000 and agreed not to disclose his method of refining sugar. Pigeon accepted the offer.

Thomas's youngest child, John Thomas, twenty-seven years old, married Lillias Savage on June 22, 1865. The red-headed Lily was the eldest daughter of a retired jeweller and lived with her family and servants in a house called The Elms. Lily's father, Alfred Savage of Savage & Lyman, which had been taken over by Henry Birks in 1854, was now a successful commission merchant (an agent in trade). Savage was in the habit of giving his daughter a piece of jewellery every year on her birthday. Many of the wedding guests gave her gifts of jewellery as well, including a gold bracelet with carbuncle and diamonds from Markland and Helen, and an opal ring from John HR.

The young couple's honeymoon trip lasted six months. They left Quebec on Saturday July 1 at 10 a.m. When they passed Cacouna, Lily watched from the port deck of the *SS Hibernian* in the hope of seeing her friend Maggie Drummond's white sheet, held up as a greeting to the couple. (The ship was too far offshore.)

During her trip, Lily kept a diary. She recognized "in Switzerland the same blue-bell and nearly the same ferns, as are to be found in Cacouna." In Dresden by the end of October, she wrote, "I have fallen in love with this place at first sight." There she and Thomas attended "English service in Reformed church in the Afternoon," where she noted that "Thomas [was] very indignant at the Yankee clergyman." In getting to Paris from Cologne, they "travelled all day with two Russian Ladies in fur cloaks–one [who] took snuff the whole time." "T. as x as x," she wrote one day, "Thomas as cross as cross," but did not elaborate.

Another day, she wrote, "John Thomas & Lily Savage have had a small fight this afternoon. He wants to make me write a little miserable scribble such as will make ones eyes ache to read–is he that cruel to me and the community at large–However tho' these are the pleasures of giving away your liberty …"

By the time the young couple returned from their honeymoon, Lily was pregnant. They moved into No. 1 Prince of Wales Terrace, on the north side of Sherbrooke Street, between McTavish and Peel streets.

On July 22, 1866, thirteen months after her wedding day, Lily delivered a healthy daughter. Some hours later, Lily was dead.

Death in childbirth is common in these times, but grief is manifest when a woman has died after her first confinement. In such cases the deceased is given a maiden's funeral

Chapter Twenty-Two

Childbed Fever

July 22, 1866

THE BLINDS of No. 1 Prince of Wales Terrace are drawn. The physician closes his bag and steps out to his carriage, his head bowed. Childbed fever has claimed another young woman's life.

A hush falls over the household. The baby sleeps in a nurse's arms in a stilled rocking chair in the nursery. From Lily's room the silence spreads like a heavy cloak, enveloping the upstairs hall, quieting the maids' footsteps, muffling visitors' voices on the stairs. Annie Savage, Lily's younger sister, begins to sob next to the bed. John Thomas turns to Lily's mother, proffering his handkerchief to pass on to the girl. The young father is stricken; he can't speak. Nothing will console him over his loss: even the red-faced, healthy baby seems to bewilder him.

"If you wish, I will–take care of the arrangements," Mrs. Savage murmurs to him after a while.

John Thomas nods.

"And of course Baby will have the best of care with us, as Lillias would have wanted."

John Thomas nods again.

It seems that others have accepted his wife's loss before John

Thomas has even begun to believe she is gone. Hired assistants arrive to wash her body in the afternoon, then dress it in white, before carrying it to the parlour, dusting her face with powder, and placing a small pillow under her head. People come to view the young mother's lifeless body and whisper as if she were merely sleeping. Cakes and pies and meats arrive in the kitchen. The male servants reappear in mourning livery; the maids in black, with white aprons, cuffs and collars. Even the nurse has black ribbons sewn into her cap. A mourning-scarf, with a white rosette and ribbon, covers the knocker on the front door. John Thomas doesn't know how it got there.

Death in childbirth is common in these times, but grief is manifest when a woman has died after her first confinement. In such cases the deceased is given a maiden's funeral, with girl attendants dressed in white and wearing floral chaplets. The long service, held at No. 1 Prince of Wales Terrace, is delivered in tones of religious awe, hope and gloom. John Thomas won't later remember the words of the opening prayer, or which psalms or verses from Revelations were read, but he will remember the clergyman's remarks on the mystery of life and death, and the way he spoke about Lily's suffering on earth as a prelude to a more glorious life to come. "Abide with me," the mourners sing, before taking their places in the long queue of coaches and professional mourners assembled behind the hearse.

Lily's funeral is almost as elaborate and extravagant as Thomas Molson's had been three years earlier, conducted with all the formality, pomp, and show that is proper. Lily's flower carriage is laden with white wreaths. The pallbearers walk with wands of black ostrich plumes; long black scarves are draped over their left shoulders. More ostrich plumes adorn each of the black horses pulling the hearse, where urns grace each side.

It is a hot and dusty day. Mourning coaches convey the women, who might otherwise have fainted from exerting themselves in the heat. Mrs. Savage and Lily's sisters wear black bombazine and crepe, black mourning bonnets, and jet jewellery. Mrs. Savage dabs at her eyes behind a veil. John Thomas wears a suit entirely of black cloth with a plain white linen shirt. His shoes, gloves, cuff-links and hat are all a dull black. He feels hollow inside. He doesn't know yet what he will do with the rest of his life, but already he is starting to feel a need to go somewhere far away.

The Molson Sugar Refinery had been in operation since the end of 1865 under the direction of Narcisse Pigeon and John HR Molson, with John Thomas and Markland as absent partners. The company processed – melted, crushed or ground – 1.3 million pounds of raw sugar each month. The cash and credit sales of sugar, syrup, and molasses grossed $58,000 in the month of May 1867. The Grand Trunk Railway shipped the refinery's goods by the barrel to most destinations east and west. Yet, in spite of seemingly healthy sales, the refinery was actually operating at a loss. Each brother tried to advise the other on the best way to cut costs and increase sales. Markland was the first to suggest they close the business:

> *Montreal April 8, 1867*
> *John HR Molson*
>
> *Dear Sir,*
>
> *I find you are ordering more utensils both for the Refinery and Starch Works, and that you are still keeping up an immense staff, which is quite unnecessary for the repairs of a new establishment. Charging their wages to running expenses, whereas two thirds of their time is at new work but the wages are small compared with the enormous bills from Frothingham and Workman and all the others with whom we have bills … and I would much prefer that the Refinery were closed at once … you are [losing] per day … $350 to $500 … I would like an answer at an early date whether you intend to continue business on this basis, as I am some what reluctant to lose any more money.*
>
> *William Markland Molson*

On April 10, 1867, John HR drafted a reply to Markland, and seemed to get angrier as it continued:

> *Your note dated 8th arrived this morning 10th. Your assertion that I am still keeping up an immense staff is incorrect. We have not one third of the mechanics about us that you had when you pretended to look after things and a great deal of the mechanics work done since we began is owing to your bad arrangement and mismanagement of*

almost every part of any work you had any hand in erecting and things are now in a much better state than they ever were when you were here. However we (that is Thomas and myself) are and intend to do all we can to make the business profitable and carry it on as economically as we are able and make it as profitable as possible … [I]f you are not satisfied to carry on the business you have the option of returning, and as to making any new utensils or machines I consider that as I make them at my own expense and for the benefit of the business you have no right to give your opinion, particularly as only three months [passed] since you wanted me to lay out a large additional sum of money and when I objected as having laid out so much already you became very excited and violent.

John Thomas helped his brother write a second, far more composed and authoritative letter, which they sent:

Montreal April 11, 1867

Dear Sir,

I have submitted your letter of the 8th Inst received yesterday to my brother Thomas and we have given its contents our most careful consideration quite irrespective of its tone and the manner in which it was transmitted to me though on these subjects we both think we have reasonable cause to complain of your course and we do not agree with you either as to the correctness of the assertions contained in your letter, or as to the course which ought to be pursued in the business. It is therefore our intention as the majority of the firm to continue to carry on the refinery as we are now doing until circumstances occur which satisfy us that it would be for the interest of the firm to change it. But on this or any other subject connected with the affairs of the concern we shall be happy to have your advice and assistance as contemplated by our articles of copartnership, though we think you would be more competent to afford both if you paid some attention to the actual business we are carrying on as well as to American Statistics and New York Refineries.

John Thomas withdrew from the sugar refinery and brewery partnership when the contract with his brothers expired in 1868. He put his intentions in writing to his brother John HR in April, although he had "several times verbally" let him know of his intention to retire from the business:

I always wish to be on the best of terms with the several members of our family and if at any time I have done any of them any injury, it has not been from any intention on my part I feel myself in a comparative independency which I consider is only jeopardized by remaining in business and when an older man I may have to begin to work for subsistence, whereas by carefulness and caution I hope to be able to keep what I at present possess.

In 1869 fewer sales than ever were recorded at the sugar refinery. By November, though the plant was still operating, morale was grim. The manager and superintendent of the refinery, Mr. Bennett, quit in November, submitting an angry letter of resignation:

JHR Molson Esq.

Dear Sir,

On reflection you will, I am sure, not be surprised at [the] contents of this communication.

You have engaged me as manager and superintendent of your Refinery. I have never been neither one nor the other, nor is there the slightest likelihood that I shall ever act in either of these capacities.

The facts on which I base this assertion are too glaring to require elucidation – suffice it to say that my ideas about propriety as well as the very terms of my engagement will not allow me to continue in your employ.

Things went downhill from there. Redpath's refinery competed successfully by lowering its prices. John HR tried many ways to save the business. He travelled to Cuba in late 1869 to inspect a new source for quality raw sugar. He installed a new kiln in January 1870, a new melting pan in June, a new centrifuge in August, and a new boiler in December. He experimented with manufacturing beet-root sugar but discontinued when he found it had "a strong, rank flavour." He developed a "pure white syrup" for druggists, in addition to his other syrups, which he sorted by colour: amber, golden and standard. He even began to process honey. Sales rose, but not sufficiently to defray expenses. John HR made a notation at the end of the refinery's record book that the centrifuge was stopped on April 11, 1871.

Only two days after his young wife's death, John Thomas received a letter from William Spragge, saying, "I am sorry to … trouble you while you are still in distress of heart from your sad loss, on any business, but you will see that a reply to the enclosed cannot ... be delayed." We know not whether the matter was important or unimportant. Nevertheless, the insensitivity and irony must have been evident to John Thomas, who believed Spragge delayed matters whenever it suited him.

Spragge and John Thomas had been on strained terms for some time. Conflicts between the two centred on Thomas Molson's estate. At the beginning, they had seemed to be in polite agreement about the best course of action to take, but things soon reached at an impasse. In April 1867, when John Thomas wrote the following to Spragge, matters were still not resolved:

> *I should like very much to have a conversation with you about the affairs of the estate as I really think we as Executors ought really to invest at present instead of dividing – you & I of course hold the double position of legatees & executors & in the former position both us wish for a division, but as executors with their responsibilities of trust, we must act in that capacity for the best. There are various reasons I could give you too long for a letter in support of my view & I hope you will think with me when I say I wish to perform all my duties of executorship with justice, ability & honour.*

After some months had passed, John Thomas continued to express his exasperation to Spragge:

> *There is one thing I would like to remark which is this, that all the work has to be done at Montreal and it takes my time away from our business, as at present I am doing little else. I have all the leases and property and repairs to look after which is the disagreeable part of the work; now you should either give full power to me and be satisfied with what I do, or else to come and live in Montreal and do your half because you cannot do it elsewhere and trips up and down could not be borne by the estate any more than for me to charge my time against*

it. If you reflect that I am more interested than the others (excepting Mark) you cannot fail to see that the best possible care will be used in everything connected with the estate, but things cannot be done rashly and it adds greatly to the work to keep writing "by return of mail or by telegraph." Everything will be done as quickly on my part as is consistent but one must look ahead.

Spragge's objection to liquidating much of Thomas's estate rested in his belief that the properties and stocks to be divided would increase in value if left alone for a time. John HR (who was not an executor of his father's estate) wrote to John Thomas:

Spragge will do nothing. I have had no communication with him but Clerk is very angry and has had some correspondence with him. He was quite anxious to apply to the courts to compel him, but [J.J.C.] Abbott said nothing could be done as there were only two executors. Had there been three, two of them could have done it being a majority ... Abbott told Clerk that it was desirable for the estate to get rid of the responsibility instead of retaining it.

John Thomas continued to write to Spragge:

The purchaser of the Sherrington farm ... calls continually to see when he can get his deed as he wants to register it – I am at a loss to account for your apparent objection to fulfil your obligations and to place me in the position I am in after promising the man that you would sign the deed in two or three days as you wrote to me you would do.

Another letter to Spragge from John Thomas begins:

Mr. Shay writes tonight with reference to the Kingston Property which I promised an answer to and got Mr. Shay to write to you some seven weeks ago but he has had no reply and the enquirer calls on me and reminds me of my *(I should say* your*) neglect in the matter.*

Estate affairs and delays were affecting everyone in the family. Spragge's procrastination meant that much of the estate's holdings remained in the form of stocks and properties. For nearly ten years, the majority of Thomas's estate remained unconverted and undistributed.

Letters between the brother-in-law executors argued over the wisdom of selling Bank of British North America stock against that of buying Molsons Bank stock, and disagreed about where to draw a balance between financial prudence and familial generosity. John HR wanted to buy some property from the estate, but withdrew his offer when Spragge allowed the cut-off date to pass. When confronted by John Thomas, Spragge blamed the solicitor, J.J.C. Abbott. Martha, Mary Anne and Harriet, all married with families, were also anxious to appropriate some means for themselves. Martha and William Spragge managed to "pay a fair premium for the advantage" of setting up their son Arthur in a law partnership in 1872, but a year later Martha complained of "no end of expense" when their daughter Annie was preparing to marry a gentleman in England. Markland, in financial straits, owed more money than that which was due to him. The sugar refinery venture had been a disaster for him. When his grist mill at Port Hope burned in November 1871, insurance was immediately claimed by his creditors.

While the tedious and long-drawn-out negotiations of the settlement of the will were occupying the older Molsons, young Lily (called "Baby") was being raised by Jane and Alfred Savage and their daughter Annie. The Savages kept in regular touch with John Thomas, who was away more months than he was home. Extended yachting, hunting and fishing trips took him all over the world. In the spring of 1867, while Canada was experiencing the birth pangs of Confederation, an epidemic of infantile sickness – today known as polio – kept the Savages anxious for Baby's health. Although Baby's grandparents doted on her, it was young Annie (whom Baby called "AniAni") who became a second mother to the little girl. Annie wrote to John Thomas regularly from The Elms:

> *You will know why I am writing worse than usual when I tell you it is 11 a.m., and I have been "on the go" since I got up, having bathed and dressed Baby, made our two beds, dusted, etc ... Baby is looking very well indeed, and looking lovely in a hew hat ... J.H.R. came to*

tea on the 24th of May and Baby was very friendly, evidently feeling the relationship ... It is too warm to try and hold Baby on my knee and hold her little fat hand to write you a letter as I would try and catch her–she is racing about so.

"Ganpapa" Savage so adored his granddaughter that he wrote her letters in "baby-talk" when he couldn't be with her, to be read out loud by Annie. One began:

My own dear Sugar Plum, I want to see you very very very mupt ... I am very lonesome when I go home at night–there is nobody to say how de doo Ganpapa & give me a kiss, and no body to say good ni, and make me a pretty bow, so I feel at times so sad that I could sit down and cry.

During the summer months the Savages stayed in Cacouna, where other Molsons–including Mark and Helen and their two boys, and Martha Spragge and her children–kept constant company. Occasionally Thomas would return from a fishing trip down the lower St. Lawrence on one of his chartered yachts and meet them all there.

Jane Savage wrote to John Thomas:

When we told Baby you were soon coming she was taking her tea and I wish you could have heard the gusto with which she said, Oh, I am so glad! Baby is as well as she can be and is getting to be a regular little girl; [she] plays all kinds of practical jokes on Grandpapa. The Doll fever is strong upon her again, only this time the doll goes to bed with her and is regularly dressed in her own old clothes. First thing in the morning, she looks to see where the thing is.

John Thomas had accepted a $50,000 payment for his share in the business partnership in 1868. The separation was amicable. At thirty-one, still suffering over the death of his wife, John Thomas was not yet ready to settle down and take on new commitments. He discovered he had inherited his grandfather's interest in boats; now, he was infected with wanderlust and had even more ambitious travel plans.

John Thomas decided to travel the world. On his first journey to Liverpool, England, he took a course in navigation, the study of which had long intrigued him. He was invited aboard locally crafted steam and sailing vessels and met others who shared his passion. He began following news about races and joined the Royal Mersey Yacht Club. Back in Canada, he joined the Quebec and the Royal Montreal yacht clubs. After being awarded a master's certificate in navigation, he continued to work on improving his knowledge. In both summer and winter he chartered steam yachts and invited friends to join him on fishing and hunting parties.

After three years of chartering steam craft, John Thomas began to consider purchasing his own, and in the fall of 1869 he sent inquiries to Liverpool to find a screw-driven steam yacht that would stand up to a trip across the Atlantic.

The first yacht that came to his attention, the *Meteor,* was "one of the finest screw steam yachts of her tonnage afloat," but the owner refused John Thomas's offer. St. Claire Byrne, a ship designer in England, advised him that he would be better off having one built, for "there is really nothing whatever in this country in the shape of a steam yacht equal to all your requirements." The designer recommended it be built by Laird Brothers, "which in this country means a faithfully built vessel," and added that it would cost about £5,300.

Byrne's next letter was more specific:

> *I have got them to offer to build her for £5200 which includes three expensive engines (compound engine) and everything of the best from beginning to end ... Bye the bye I have made her exceedingly strong rather more so than usual ... I forgot to mention that the engines are being allowed for as more powerful to gain the extra speed.*

In early February 1870, John Thomas sent a telegram to Byrne, bearing the words "Commence yacht." Byrne was delighted and wrote that construction would soon be under way.

In a letter showing attention to detail worthy of his father, John Thomas wrote back in March:

> *I observe Laird Bros. speak of having her completed in June whereas in my letter I spoke of her being here June 1st. I would like her ready as soon as possible, although the work must be well done. You make no*

> *reference to my remark about the funnel this I should like to come down some way so as not to be seen at all and that when under canvas she may appear a sailing yacht.*

John Thomas spent a lot of time studying drawings and plans, intent on considering every contingency and scrutinizing every detail. On April 1, 1870, he wrote to Byrne:

> *The arrangements forward seem very good, [and] the room on starboard side [shall] be fitted as officer's mess, as I do not see how it can be done without. The stateroom opposite captain's, I wd. want to have two berths in, for mate and engineer. Aft, I wd. have the drawing room divided in two, making the room on starboard my room fitted with table, and place for charts (not rolled up), chronometer, and other things. The other half to be a ladies room, and arranged to be able to make a state room of it if necessary for an emergency ... I feel sorry I cannot have the full sized drawing room as I think it wd. be very good, but gained at too much sacrifice ... I want to have a piano on board and I suppose it will have to go in dining room somewhere.*

Wanting to name his steamship after a bird, John Thomas considered native words, including Tellegoo, an "Esquimo" word meaning plover, and Napisse, a Cree word meaning swan. By the middle of April he had decided to call her *Nooya,* or silver gull. An enthusiastic Byrne wrote to John Thomas on April 28, 1870:

> *I note your wish to name her* Nooya*–I will arrange to have a pretty and well carved seagull for a figure head–nothing could come in better.*

John Thomas wrote anxiously to Byrne in April:

> *I shall feel very much disappointed if the yacht be not completed in time for crossing with the other yachts on 4th July, as my season will be broken into & partly on a/c of the companions I am likely to have across; in addition the sooner I cross the smoother passage I will have.*

In spite of Byrne's optimism, the *Nooya* was not completed by the date John Thomas had requested. The *Nooya's* maiden trip from Liverpool to Quebec did not begin until Wednesday, August 10, 1870. Under the command of Captain William Christall, it got under way that day at 7:55 a.m. The captain kept a log book to compare the ship's mileage with the number of bags of coal being used and recorded changes in the weather and other occasional events.

On August 21, the "fog dense to hazy, then clear," Captain Christall eased the engines to "dead slow," but still managed to log 117 miles. The following day they rounded the Strait of Belle Isle and sighted eight icebergs. On August 23, they sighted the *SS Scandinavian,* sporting a "strange sail." In the early morning hours of August 25 they came abreast of Anticosti Island, and a few hours later passed Cacouna, "steaming under bare poles ... bound up to Quebec." The historic trip had taken them sixteen days. John Thomas's *Nooya,* though he made no mention of it, was the first pleasure steam yacht to cross the Atlantic.

John Thomas's trip from Liverpool to Quebec in the *Nooya* was a triumphant beginning to his and his crew's first season together. In early September 1870, they moored alongside the Victoria Wharf in Montreal. Over the next three weeks crew members were occupied caulking, painting, clearing up the decks and restocking provisions. John Thomas took the opportunity to visit four-year-old Lily at the Savages', meet with his brothers, and attend to some business and banking matters, but he stayed in Montreal for barely four weeks. At the end of September, he and his crew left once more in the *Nooya* for the Gulf of St. Lawrence. He returned at the end of October and ordered the *Nooya's* engine taken apart, cleaned and reinstalled. Next year, John Thomas determined, he would sail around the world.

From San Francisco, John Thomas steamed to Japan.
He didn't stay there longer than a few days;
for he was in Shanghai by Christmas.
By February 1872, he reached Bombay.

Chapter Twenty-Three

Yachting Days

Since its formal inception in 1855, Molsons Bank had been steadily growing. Total assets had risen from $1 million to $3.5 million in the bank's first fifteen years of operation. William Molson, who continued to be president, saw it through a liquidity crisis in 1868 (contracted circulation, caused by the market's abundance of American silver) by decreasing dividends and issuing a million dollars' worth of new shares. In 1870 in London, Ontario, Molsons Bank opened its first branch. The following year the bank opened more branches in Ontario and a branch in Sorel, Quebec.

The majority of shareholders and the core of the board of directors continued to be members of the Molson family. John HR and John Thomas, directors since 1855 and 1863, respectively, kept in touch while the latter was at sea. On October 4, 1870, John HR wrote John Thomas:

> *Alexander [Walker] Ogilvy was not at the Bank meeting this morning and Mr. [F. Wolferstan] Thomas [general manager at Molsons Bank head office] read a letter from him resigning his office of director assigning as a reason that he might be away in Europe a considerable*

> *time this winter. I objected to his resignation being accepted and recommended that Mr. Thomas should see him and induce him to consent to be re-elected which Mr. Thomas consented as all the other directors agreed with me, but I was hardly out of the bank before Mr. William Molson came into Mr. Thomas's room and told him not to see Mr. Ogilvy as the family wished to put Mr. John Molson on the Board – so it seems that the reports out of doors were correct. I have not had time to think what I shall do in the matter but as the annual meeting takes place next Monday there is not much time.*

Ogilvy's resignation was accepted, and John Molson III (son of John Junior) replaced him. It seemed that William Molson was the only member of the board who supported this change. John HR may have been protesting this appointment when he resigned as a director. In any event, John HR was later re-elected, but, as John Thomas predicted to William Spragge, John HR would resign again. On October 25, 1872, John Thomas wrote from on board the *Nooya:*

> *With reference to the Molsons Bank I hardly know how things are, John Henry having been elected since his resignation, so he is actually a director until he sends in another letter of resignation. I wish you not to say anything about it, but Annie Molson is at the bottom of the whole thing and has got her father [William, president] whose mind is weak to put John (Rufus) as vice instead of John Henry – I should like Martha's proxy for next year's election if anything could be done which is very unlikely as Wm Molson & John Molson have the majority especially if they get the support of Alex Molson, Dinham, & Elsdale … Say nothing of this if you wish John not to be Vice or Pres.*

In the 1870s, the family's alliances were clearly defined. Thomas's descendants, John HR and John Thomas, were in direct opposition to John Junior's and William's descendants, John III and Annie. The uneasy rivalry that existed between the siblings of the first-born Molson generation in Canada had burgeoned into a power struggle between the siblings and cousins of the second. Was the "banking side" of the family separating itself from the "brewing side"?

William, eighty years old in 1873, president and majority shareholder of Molsons Bank, had two daughters but no son. But his son-in-law, John Molson III, had not only the ambition and the ability to manage the institution, but also sons with his surname to succeed him. John HR, too, had valid claim and qualifications as a successor–though still unmarried, and childless. Moreover, John HR had been a member of the board since the bank's inception and its vice-president since 1860, following the death of his uncle John Molson II. When John Molson III was, by the end of 1872, installed as the new vice-president, John HR resigned from the board for the second time and was replaced by R.W. Shepherd, who owned a steamship line, the Ottawa Navigation Company.

It is unclear whether his uncle William's "weak mind" was exaggerated by John Thomas, or whether William's mental state did indeed concern the other family members or fellow directors. John III turned out to be a more than competent vice-president. It was his initiative that steered the institution through the Jay Cooke banking failure. The financial empire of Jay Cooke, a Philadelphian "railroad king" and capitalist, collapsed in September 1873, bankrupting five thousand businesses, including brokers, banks and small U.S. railroads (including the Northern Pacific). Molsons Bank's New York agent was also one of those affected. For the first time in its history, the Molsons Bank announced a loss.

One of Markland Molson's most ambitious endeavours was his investment in Moisie Iron Works, a venture he leapt into very soon after he and his brothers had established the sugar refinery. Located on the lower north shore of the St. Lawrence River, this ironworks developed a method for extracting iron from the rich deposits in the sand along the shoreline. That others didn't share Markland's faith in the enterprise was evident from a letter from J.J.C. Abbott to John Thomas:

> *[Mark] will manage it. I said, then of course he will leave the old firm in order to devote himself to it. He said no, he will not dissolve but will retire from the administration of the old firm. The sums he speaks of are large, as he says they calculate it will take $200,000 to $300,000 to set the concern in operation. And he proposes to clear the modest sum of $3,000,000 by the manufacture of 15,000 tons of iron. This profit he says can be proved to a demonstration by those who understand chiffres! Imagine any man of common sense joining in an enterprise that professes so largely!*

On December 29, 1871, John HR wrote to his brother John Thomas:

> *Mr Mark has just returned from Syracuse but we have not yet seen him. He has not yet paid the $5,000, and is about to leave for England. Expects to be away about 2 months. His affairs seem to be in about the same state. No improvement financially.*

The final stroke in Markland Molson's financial downfall appears to have been the collapse of the Moisie Iron Works in the wake of the Jay Cooke disaster. Just as John HR weathered the losses from the sugar refinery before he finally closed it, so William Molson could afford to lose his own relatively small investment in Moisie. But Markland had invested in both, and he now found himself facing bankruptcy.

A North American depression started that would last for five years. Creditors now became intensely interested in Markland's share of the undistributed portion of his father Thomas's estate. How he managed to keep his house in Cacouna, The Pines, is not known, but it may have been partly because it was worth considerably less than when it had been built ten years earlier. Markland, once the most enthusiastic of the brothers over the operation of Molson's sugar refinery, was among the first to recognize that their business was a permanent liability. In 1869, George Drummond, the manager of Redpath Refinery, wrote: "Before the Messrs. Molson went into the business I pointed out exactly as I have now done the expected results, and one of them [Markland] told me ... he repented not taking my advice having lost $150,000. A business dies hard."

John HR finally closed the sugar refinery in 1872, and the equipment was sold to Redpath's. He decided to transform the old refinery space into the "Molson Stores," a warehouse offering "first class" storage and fire- and frost-proof vaults "above all floods." Wines and apples were among the goods that people stored at the facility.

Numerous investments in property and shares had made John HR, the selected grandson of the brewery's founder, a very wealthy man. He still lived near the brewery in a house on St. Mary's Street. Nearing fifty, with more to do than ever and with worsening eyesight, John HR acknowledged that he needed a partner. Yet his brothers John Thomas and Markland had each left the partnership in 1868 and were now leading lives incompatible with the brewing business. John Thomas was now almost always at sea, and Mark was insolvent.

In 1872 John HR turned to his former chief clerk and bookkeeper, now manager, who had been an employee for twenty years. In their agreement, which spanned three years and stipulated that the name of the company would remain the same ("John H.R. Molson and Bros."), John HR would retain five-sixths of the value and profits of the business and Adam Skaife would own the other one-sixth. Adam Skaife thus became the first non-family member to join a partnership at Molson's brewery.

Meanwhile, problems had been developing at The Elms. The settled and familiar world of Miss Lily Molson, now nearly five years old, was shaken up. In April 1871, John Thomas wrote to William Spragge:

> *Miss [Annie] Savage is to be married to the Rev. Geo. D. Redpath [a son of John Redpath] ... The wedding will take place about the end of this month, so my child will only have its grandmother to take care of it.*

In May, Annie left Montreal with her husband to live in England. John Thomas's sister Martha wrote him, "Your little daughter will miss her Aunt's care very much."

Lily's grandmother, Jane Savage, found caring for the daily needs of a small child a heavy burden in her advancing years. She hired a nurse named Charlotte to join their household staff and look after the little girl, but Charlotte was to stay with the Savages for only four months. On November 10, 1871, John HR wrote to John Thomas:

> *Baby is very well, but Mrs. Savage has had to get a new nurse. Charlotte appears to have gone to ruin. Her beau the painter was a married man and appears to have systematically intended the girl's ruin. She has left and gone to a sister in New Glasgow. The other girl –Mary Anne I think is her name–[is] in the same position. She has been getting drunk and her beau was also a married man–a painter and companion of the other fellow whose name is Thomson (both old soldiers). Mr. and Mrs. Savage have been much distressed. They found it out by Mrs. S. going to Craig [a more senior servant] to enquire whether the man was a respectable man when he told her he was married three years. Charlotte must have known it all the time.*

John Thomas continued to enjoy his time on the *Nooya.* His expeditions to fly-fish for salmon had not taken him far afield, but by late summer of 1871 he was on his way to California, on the first leg of a trip around the world. No records have survived about this part of the journey, but he would have had to head south once reaching the Atlantic, continue to the southernmost tip of South America, and loop north along the Pacific coast to reach San Francisco, where he arrived by November 1, 1871.

John Thomas loved everything about being at sea. He thrived on the challenge, the discipline and the danger. He loved how the bow sliced into the surface of the water, how the tiny, silvery fragments flew, and how the splinters of liquid leapt up from the *Nooya's* bow like sparks caught in the sunlight.

Everyone on board the *Nooya* (including guests, ten crew members and four firemen) was allowed the same daily rations: one pound of pork; eight ounces each of flour and biscuits; two ounces each of oatmeal, pea meal, beans and onions; four ounces of sugar; and half an ounce each of sugar maple, tea and salt. John Thomas's private, "indispensable" provisions included special peppers, curry powder, cocoa, dried ("portable") soup and compressed vegetables. His personal kit included two flannel shirts, two pairs of pantaloons, knickerbockers, worsted socks, a mackintosh, a Norfolk jacket and a thick sailor's jersey.

From San Francisco, John Thomas steamed to Japan, a country that had been closed to foreigners until 1867. He was in Shanghai by Christmas. By February 1872, he reached Bombay. Refuelling stops gave him a glimpse of China and of British India. From Bombay he travelled to Europe through the Suez Canal. He stayed in Rome for a few days, stopped again in Spain for refuelling, and headed back across the Atlantic. The entire journey had spanned nine months. John Thomas Molson without making note of it, had succeeded in being the first man to circumnavigate the globe by steam yacht.

John Thomas was back in Montreal in May 1872, to see his daughter and attend to correspondence and business. He was anxious to leave again in June, but everything from delayed telegrams to the necessity of arranging fishing licences and dealing with the continuing and seemingly endless estate matters frustrated his plans; he was unable to get away again until July.

During the summers of 1872 and 1873, John Thomas travelled the

St. Lawrence River to the gulf. Abreast of Cacouna, he saluted the Savage family; if they were there, sometimes he would go ashore. Farther east, opposite Crane Island, he would often anchor and row to the dock at his cousins'–the MacPhersons'–and visit at their house.

John Thomas ran a tight ship. Occasional troubles with the firemen and crew were summarily resolved. One day an angry mate, refusing to wash the decks, brandished an axe, defying anyone to force him. He was put ashore at the next port.

Equipment always carried on board the *Nooya* included extensive fishing tackle and gear, a gun collection, tools, medicines, surgeons' needles, threads, mosquito oil, quinine, tape, ink and papers. All of these practical but minimal provisions were counterbalanced by the luxurious accommodations on board. The decks and walls were fashioned of oak, and the piano in the dining room emitted the clearest of tones. All china, brass and silverware had been ordered specially for the *Nooya* and were the finest quality. The silver set included sugar tongs, tea spoons, egg spoons, dessert spoons and forks, and separate glassware for sherbet, port, claret and soda.

In the winter, John Thomas hunted caribou. He had both a caribou coat and *capuchon* made for him. An English hunting coat and "Eskimo" snowshoes completed his ensemble. He liked to think of himself as someone who was equipped not only for any weather, but for any eventuality. His life had become a search for adventures and challenges.

A serious and intensely private person, John Thomas enjoyed pitting himself against the sea and the wilderness, navigating his own course, being rootless and self-reliant. There was, he might have admitted, a bit of a poet in him, for he kept copies of his favourite poetry in his pocketbook. He would not have admitted to any weaknesses. He was fiercely loyal to his principles; some would say he was simply fierce.

Anne, who had wanted to pursue physics and mathematics, was bitterly disappointed that she could not attend McGill. She was determined that her own daughter Edith, seventeen years old in 1870, would have the opportunity to do so. Wealth will not take care of itself if not vigilantly cared for.

Chapter Twenty-Four

McGill Welcomes Women

Sunday April 27, 1873

The old chestnut mare trots in front of her master's carriage, headed west along St. Mary's Street. Every Sunday afternoon since 1844, John HR Molson has left his house, Rosebank, for Piedmont, home of Louisa Frothingham. Today, as usual, he continues along the road parallel to the river, occasionally passing other carriages; many are neighbours out for afternoon visits, their calling cards tucked in clutches and waistcoat pockets. The drivers steer the horses to avoid the potholes in the road, the muddy ruts and *cahots* caused by freezing and thawing. Those here in the suburbs are more fortunate than residents in lowertown, who have had to contend with flooded streets again this spring.

On St. James Street John passes Molsons Bank, where on Sundays, a watchman armed with a nickel revolver patrols the premises. Molson is happy that this is the last time he will make this trip. He turns on Craig Street and passes Victoria Square, making his way northwest to Sherbrooke Street. There, at the corner of the McGill campus, the carriage turns right and heads toward Durocher Street. In three days, John Henry Robinson Molson, age forty-nine, will marry Miss Frothingham, age forty-five, whom he has courted for twenty-seven years. They will live together at Piedmont, the house she has inherited from her father.

He passes the Church of the Messiah, where they will be married. The previous Unitarian church structure burned down in 1869, and the new building stands without a spire. John HR will have a spire built. He joined the congregation at first to see his betrothed more often, and now is among the church's most dedicated members, along with the Frothinghams and the Workmans.

At the head of Durocher Street, the Frothingham estate is fringed by pine trees and replete with plum and apple orchards. The grounds are entered by a circular driveway flanked by rising flower beds where crocuses and muscari are in bloom. Piedmont, which overlooks the McGill grounds, had at one time been the Governor General's official residence. Louisa's father bought the estate in 1841, hoping the house and its grounds would inspire his chronically ill wife and encourage her recovery. But Mrs. Frothingham would die a year and a half later.

John Frothingham's business, which he ran in Montreal, was Frothingham and Workman, Canada's largest hardware company. His association with the City Bank was also a long one; he had joined Stanley Bagg and John Molson Senior to establish it in 1831, and he was president of that bank for fifteen years. Retiring in 1859, he joined John HR's uncle, William Molson, as a governor of McGill.

The Frothingham family, originally from Maine, had been Presbyterians in earlier generations, but soon became strong Unitarians. When her mother died in 1843, both Louisa – then fifteen years old – and her father had been devastated. Frothingham wrote in his journal, "Almost everything around us reminds us of her, as many things were planted, and all directed by herself … but it is folly for me to attempt to describe the treasure I have lost." Louisa, named after her mother, had vowed that she would stay with her father and look after him as long as he needed her.

Three years have now passed since John Frothingham's death in May 1870. John HR had proposed marriage to Louisa that spring and she had accepted him; they'd agreed then that a mourning period of three years would be seemly. Louisa and John HR's marriage contract stipulates that Piedmont, all its furniture, silver, musical instruments, books, paintings, statues, jewellery, carriages, horses and cattle will remain, after their marriage, Louisa's sole possessions. John HR's house is slated to be torn down for another brewery expansion.

Louisa and John HR are eminently well suited. Plain in looks but elegant in manner, Louisa is gracious, humble and generous, while John is respectful, demanding and very much a perfectionist. She provides the ideal balance for a husband so conservative, idealistic, independent and ambitious.

John HR's diary, which he continues to keep fastidiously, has long ago lost all its florid affectations, all its adjectives, all its self-deprecating humour. In 1874, brief, twice-weekly entries such as "Jan. 19 – moved bottling into new office building," and "Feb. 21 – Mrs. Gardham house-keeper 8 years and 3 months left this afternoon," are typical. He took to writing about himself in the third person: "J.H.R.M. returned from Lake Superior this evening." One day he wrote, "J.H.R.M. not in brewery today," for a bee sting on his eyebrow the day before had caused his face to swell.

John leaves Piedmont in time to join the Savages for tea. Because Piedmont is not far from the Elms, the Savage home, John HR has for the last several years visited both households on Sunday afternoons. Alfred and Jane Savage share news about John HR's brother John Thomas, and they talk about John HR's upcoming wedding to Louisa. Lily Molson, now six, looks forward to her uncle's visits.

"Uncle Crusoe, you are not very well, you are winking," she says this afternoon, frowning up at him.

"It is true," he replies with an exaggerated sigh and an indulgent smile for his niece. "My eyes are very weak this spring."

Montreal in the 1870s, was the scene of vice-regal costume balls, fancy dress balls, skating carnivals, pageants, and private theatricals. These events crested each social season; guest lists included all the important personages in political, commercial and social life. Prince Arthur, Queen Victoria's third son, who had arrived in Montreal in 1869 to join the Prince Consort's Own Rifles, hosted the decade's first fancy dress ball in January 1870. Among the guests were the three Molson brothers, John HR, Markland and John Thomas; their cousins John III and his wife Anne; and their uncle William and aunt Betsey.

British flags were strung along Sherbrooke Street, leading the way to the prince's residence, Rosemount, to which a new wing had been recently added. The walls within were covered in white and green stripes, the pillars were wreathed in evergreens, and large mirrors reflected the forms of the dancers. The supper room, reported the *Gazette,* "glittered with a profusion of plate and china." Seated at the head of the table and also enjoying the "dazzling spectacle" were titled guests including Sir George Etienne and Lady Cartier.

In March, John William (J.W.) and William Alexander Molson, the two sons of John Molson III and Anne, were guests at a lavish skating masquerade. John William–who dressed as a courtier of George III–had finished his education at Bishop's College in Lennoxville, briefly attended McGill and then joined a Montreal insurance firm. His brother Alexander–who dressed as a Greek–was in his first year of medicine at McGill, the faculty from which twenty-two-year-old Dr. William Osler had just graduated.

The prominent photographer William Notman used the skating carnival as the occasion for his first composite picture. Like many guests, twenty-one-year-old J.W. had his photo taken in his costume and was asked afterwards if he wanted his likeness arranged in the composite with the other guests. Either Notman had been impressed by the elegant George III's courtier costume or J.W. had paid a higher fee and requested that his whole figure be shown, for, although he is one of the smaller, background placements, his costume is not obstructed or hidden by any other skater. Prince Arthur is in the foreground, watching the proceedings.

Notwithstanding such resplendent entertainments, it was an age of prudence and moderation, and particularly an age of temperance. The voices of reform–dominated by women and the clergy–were growing louder. Montreal's Temperance Society erected a cairn in Victoria Square and called it the "Fountain of Health."

The issue of prohibition was never far from any political platform. Arguments abounded over medicinal uses of alcohol and the recognition of wine, beer and cider as excepted from ardent spirits. John HR saved a March 1873 copy of *The Christian World,* across the top of which he wrote, "Can brewers or wine merchants enter the Kingdom of Heaven? Mr. Moody says not." His father, Thomas, had penned a similar question thirteen years earlier–"Can distillers enter the Kingdom of

Heaven?"–within the margin of a temperance lecture transcript.

In 1875 hundreds of prohibition-supporting societies, lodges and church groups convened in Montreal and formed a federation called the Dominion Prohibitory Council. A year later it was renamed the Dominion Alliance for the Total Suppression of the Liquor Traffic. Yet moderate use of beer and wine continued to be the prevailing standard in Quebec. Successive governments carried out referendums on the subject, each remaining reluctant to lose tax revenue, proposing various compromises that would keep all factions happy. In 1878 the *Canada Temperance Act* (or *Scott Act)* extended 1864's *Dunkin Act* to the whole of the Dominion of Canada. Yet the citizens of Montreal and Quebec, though municipally enabled to vote on the issue of prohibition, never came close to doing so.

After seven years as a widower, John Thomas had decided to remarry. He announced his intentions to his family on March 30, 1874. Upon hearing the news of his engagement, Annie Redpath, who had not been in touch with John Thomas since her own marriage, wrote to him from London that she was so glad "our 3 years of silence may be broken today by such a happy cause. My acquaintance with Miss Butler was but slight, but I have very pleasant recollections of her–she seemed genuinely good & kind & I hope we shall renew our acquaintance sometime. I should like your wife, & dear little Lilly's 'Mamma' to be my friend."

John Thomas Molson married Jennie Baker Butler at Christ Church Cathedral in Montreal at 5 a.m. on June 2, 1874. The early hour was chosen so that John HR could attend the wedding and still catch the train for Boston to attend the Congress of American Brewers.

John HR's wedding gift to John Thomas and Jennie, a life membership in the Art Association of Montreal, was a fitting one. John Thomas had been collecting paintings and sculpture from all over the world; Jennie, who had schooled herself in many of the masters, applied her hand to some small watercolours. The association's members regularly organized exhibitions of oil paintings, watercolours and photographs at the Crystal Palace. John HR had been a founding member of the association and a generous contributor to the endowment fund.

On their honeymoon the couple travelled first to Niagara Falls, Ontario, which Notman had photographed and which many from Montreal were curious to see. They took the train to New York, and from there boarded the steamship *Scotia* for Liverpool. On their six-month trip, they visited England, Italy and Russia, travelling from one art gallery to another.

In 1875, the last of John Senior's three sons, old William Molson, succumbed to "debility and old age." His widow Betsey, who had been deaf since 1870, moved from Montreal to Toronto to live with her eldest daughter Elizabeth and son-in-law David Macpherson. (Their son, William Molson Macpherson, was fifteen years old when his grandfather William died; he had been raised in Toronto, but this year he was sent to England to finish his education.) Betsey would live with her daughter until her death in 1887.

A clause in William's will made his nephew/son-in-law, John Molson III, president of Molsons Bank. Macpherson's subsequent election to the board now put William's and John Junior's branches of the family in control of Molsons Bank. But this situation did not last for long. By 1879 the depression had weakened John III's financial position; although his troubles were not as serious as Markland's had been, his credibility as bank president was questioned. His wife, Anne, was aware that some board members believed he should resign. She wrote to her cousin John HR, asking if he could use his influence to ensure that her husband kept his position. Her letters have not survived, but two of his drafted replies have:

Montreal Oct. 6, 1879

Dear Anne,

I have your letter of this morning asking if I received a letter from you while I was in New York and if I had requesting an answer.

The letter came to hand and would have been answered at the time but owing to my long absence from town I knew so little of John's affairs and what was going on that I could not say anything, knowing nothing and I could not be expected to make any promise under such circumstances so I decided as I expected to return every day to wait until I got home.

I know but little yet and cannot make any promise now but will act as I think your father would do if he was still living knowing everything and in the full possession of all his powers. Considering also what is most for the interest of yourself and sons as well as Mrs. Macpherson and her family.

I am sorry I cannot say anything more satisfactory as any wish your excellent mother or of your own would always be gratifying to comply with as far as I am able.

Montreal
October 8, 1879

Dear Anne,

As I suppose you wish to talk about John's affairs and his connection with the bank I would say now that as he is the person concerned I think the matter should be discussed with him and at the bank.

The welfare of the bank should be the first consideration of its shareholders and free from any influence and setting all sentiment aside.

If John's position financially and towards the bank is such as to make him unsuitable for the position he now holds he cannot reasonably expect to retain it and I may add that I am not alone in this opinion as I find it is the general one held by everyone whenever the Molsons Bank is discussed. Nearly all my father's family are largely interested in the institution and are of course keenly sensitive to its prosperity.

In conclusion I would say as I did in my last that as an executor I will act as I believe your father would do were he still among us.

In 1879 John III was, according to Anne, "removed from the bank's presidency," although the records of Molsons Bank state that he resigned. John HR Molson stepped in to replace him.

Lord Dufferin, Canada's Governor General since 1872, was, like his predecessor Baron Lisgar, an accomplished yachtsman. The Molsons and the Dufferins were both sailing on the river the day in 1873 when George Etienne Cartier's body was transported by steamer. John Thomas had ordered the *Nooya's* flag to be lowered to half mast. Lady Dufferin wrote:

> *Looking out, we saw, passing slowly in the darkness, the steamer with the body of Sir Geo. Cartier on board. It was a striking moment–the chapel on board lighted up, the band playing, and bells tolling at sea, answered by bells tolling on shore.*

Molson and the Governor General spent time together in the Gaspé, where John Thomas and his guests had dinner on board the Dufferins' yacht *Druid,* and the Dufferins joined the Molson party afterwards on the *Nooya.* Lord and Lady Dufferin had spent their first Canadian summer in Rivière du Loup. While there, they visited Cacouna, "a fashionable watering-place," wrote Lady Dufferin, with a touch of humour, "where there is a large hotel frequented by Americans, who amuse themselves by dressing four times a day." Two days later the Governor General and his wife crossed the river in a steamer, arriving in Tadoussac, and by July 27, 1872, they had chosen a site for their own cottage there. Their house was built in Quebec City, transferred in barges, and rebuilt in Tadoussac in the spring of 1873.

The *Druid* became a common sight anchored in Tadoussac Bay. Often the *Nooya* would be anchored not far away. The peals of the bell in the wooden chapel that ushered English residents out of the church could be heard across the water and throughout the village. People lingered to speak to one another before they departed, mingling among the trees before the little gate that marks the church's entrance to the road. The Tadoussac Protestant chapel, which was ten years old the summer of 1877, looked as though it had always been there.

Among the congregation that summer were Lord and Lady Dufferin and their seven children, Principal Dawson of McGill and his family, Quebec attorney Charles Pentland with his wife and children, and John Thomas Molson and his wife Jennie, with their two-year-old son Herbert and eight-month-old daughter Naomi.

Jennie Molson never pursued a higher education in art, or in any other subject that might have interested her. Women who excelled at academics were derided, called bluestockings, and considered unfeminine. Jennie found she had no time for reading, anyway. The couple had immediately welcomed young Lily into their home, and Jennie was soon occupied with her own babies. She gave birth to four children in the first four years (Herbert, 1875; Naomi, 1876; Kenneth, 1877; and Mabel, 1878).

Jennie knew other young women who wished they could enroll at McGill. But those who opposed admitting women to the university pointed out the limited space in the classrooms and the absence of separate halls and waiting rooms in the buildings. William Dawson, McGill principal and friend of John Thomas's and Jennie's, looked for ways to overcome these objections. He wholeheartedly supported women's post-secondary education. "Small beginnings of any good thing," said Dawson, "are to be cherished and cultivated."

William Molson had been the university's most generous and consistent supporter since its inception. His most visible contribution was the financing of a convocation hall and library, formally opened in 1862 as the William Molson Hall. By then, McGill had more than two hundred students. Yet he who had declared that his children would be educated "as amply and respectably as the country will afford" had lost his only son in 1843, and his daughters' education ended abruptly after high school. Anne, who had wanted to pursue physics and mathematics, was bitterly disappointed that she could not attend McGill. She was determined that her own daughter Edith, seventeen years old in 1870, would have the opportunity to do so.

Anne Molson's association with McGill had begun six years earlier, when she had arranged to donate an annual medal for honourable achievement in science, physics and mathematics. On one side of the Anne Molson Medal is the relief of Sir Isaac Newton; on the other, the inscription "Anna Molson Donavit 1864" is surrounded by a laurel wreath and the Molson family arms.

In early 1870 William Dawson and his wife Margaret travelled to Britain to collect information on the modern concept of women's education. When they returned, they drafted a detailed proposal for an organization modelled on the Ladies Educational Association of Edinburgh. On May 10, 1870, members of the English-speaking female bourgeoisie, who included Margaret Dawson and Anne Molson, met at Anne's home, Belmont Hall, and formed the Montreal Ladies Educational Association. Like the Edinburgh association, all officers and members were to be women, with the exception of the treasurer. Anne Molson was immediately elected president, and her husband, John, the treasurer.

With the cooperation of McGill professors the association planned the first courses, although there was no question, yet, of women going on to obtain degrees. The group also worked toward the establishment of a separate women's college at McGill. The first classes for women began in 1871; students could choose among French literature, English language and literature, and natural philosophy. In subsequent years astronomy, logic, chemistry, physiology, nutrition, cooking, domestic surgery and nursing were added.

In 1871, a delighted Anne enrolled Edith in the lectures and followed some courses herself, with other members of the executive. But in September 1872, Edith died suddenly, aged just nineteen. Anne resigned as president of the association, given her grief and her own ill health. Upon her resignation, the members agreed that to Anne Molson's energy and discretion were due "almost the existence and much of the prosperity of the association." She was made an honorary life member and vice-patroness, and thereafter attended meetings sporadically.

Anne Molson was entitled to an annual income of £300 from her father's estate. Her husband managed the inheritance and relinquished only £50 of it each year to her. When in 1881 Dawson approached Anne about helping him fund new courses for women at McGill, she replied, "Were it in my power how gladly would I aid ... but I am not my own mistress to use money as I would, so I can at present only give you my most earnest prayers." In 1884, railway financier Donald Alexander Smith (later Lord Strathcona) donated money to the university to accommodate admitting women to McGill on the same terms as men. The Ladies Educational Association met with Anne in the chair once again in 1885, when she steered through a vote of thanks to Smith for his guidance, his advice and his "unvarying interest" in their cause.

Anne Molson's two sons, John William and William Alexander, both attended McGill. John did not finish his degree in arts, abandoning his studies to open an insurance business. Alexander studied medicine and graduated in 1874, after which he established his own medical practice in Montreal.

Another McGill medical graduate setting up a private practice in 1874 was Dr. William Osler. He had returned to Montreal from post-graduate studies in Europe, having accepted a position as a lecturer at the university. A brilliant physician and teacher, Osler was a notorious practical jokester who played many pranks at Molson's expense. When Molson became assistant editor of the *Canada Medical and Surgical Journal,* Osler submitted a parodist manuscript under a pseudonym (Egerton Y. Davis, MD) on a fictionalized subject (the sexual practices of North West Territories Indian tribes) that included invented terms (such as the "genu-pectoral position" in intercourse) and descriptions that were, for the times, shockingly offensive. The article had been typeset and the issue ready to go to print when Osler alerted the editor. On his own hand-written copy of the article, Osler had gleefully scrawled, "Joke on Molson."

Osler encouraged his eight young cousins (who lived in genteel poverty with their mother and often absent father) to pelt Dr. Molson with snowballs whenever he passed by. Once Osler sabotaged a party that Molson was about to host. He spontaneously gathered his young cousin-children in a taxi and took them to Molson's house, where they absconded with all the food, including cakes and ice cream, taking it home for their personal feast.

Only one record has been left us of a Molson retaliation. When a snowball thrown by Osler had knocked off Molson's top hat, Molson charged Osler with assault, which resulted in Osler's having to appear before a magistrate and pay a fine.

One curious fact that might have fuelled some animosity between the two men is that Osler and Molson had each fallen in love with R.W. Shepherd's daughter Esther, whom they had met in 1875 through her brother, Dr. Frank Shepherd. Molson married Esther in 1876.

Markland Molson, trying to navigate this financially turbulent part of his life, had to cope with another personal blow when Helen, his wife of twenty-two years, left him. She had travelled to England in the fall of 1876 with a relative who needed medical treatment, met a man she knew there, and never returned to Montreal. The scandal set the social columns abuzz.

"Elopement in High Life" read one headline, which preceded an article that gave details but no names. It must have been an awkward and difficult time for Markland; in January 1877 he decided to leave Montreal and try to establish a new life in the west. Oregon, he reasoned, was a good place to start over.

Some options were still open to him: he could sell his share in the still undistributed portion of his father's estate to his siblings, and he could sell his summer home in Cacouna and his land in Port Hope. He'd heard that mining opportunities abounded in Oregon; land was cheap there, and a new railway would render it far more valuable. He was determined to start over, to prove to his family that he could succeed at something.

Markland never obtained a divorce from Helen. To do so he would have had to hire a lawyer, gather evidence, pay a fortune in fees, undergo a trial, and ask the Senate of Canada for permission. Divorces in those days were almost never granted. Markland's lack of one, however, did not prevent him from marrying Velina Nesmith, a Democratic senator's daughter, in Oregon; nor did it prevent Helen's own remarriage, to Sir William Morris.

Markland's seventeen-year-old son, Fred, accompanied his father to Portland. In 1881, at twenty-one, Fred married Catherine Stewart, a daughter of one of the "Pioneers of Oregon" who had come to the coast via the Oregon Trail.

Markland's elder son, Harry, was twenty-one the year his father and brother moved west. He had graduated from Bishop's College School and was then attending McGill. He leapt at his uncle John HR's offer to send him to Europe that year to further his education. Harry's decision may have irked Markland, who had permanently broken contact with John HR, but the son had no need of his father's approval. His father's life, Harry reasoned, consisted of one example after another of what *not* to do.

Eventually John HR became both Harry's and Fred's unrivalled mentor. In turn, the childless uncle would welcome the opportunity to be a positive influence on–and fatherlike example for–members of the younger generation.

In August 1880 Jennie gave birth to her fifth child, a premature but healthy son at their summer home in Cacouna. John Thomas loved being a father and having a family around him. After six years of marriage, he and Jennie were parents of six children: Lily, age fourteen; Herbert, five; Naomi, four; Kenneth, three; Mabel, two; and now, baby Percival.

In a profound gesture of personal sacrifice, John Thomas sold the *Nooya* that summer. An incident with Herbert had convinced his parents to keep the children closer to home. The boy had gone missing on board the *Nooya* one afternoon, and after an agonizing search, to their great relief he was found sleeping in one of the main-stays. John Thomas realized that it was time they put their yachting days behind them. The *Nooya's* Captain Bernier, ready to retire, accepted John Thomas's invitation to move in with them to Prince of Wales Terrace; the old seaman remained with the family until his death some years later.

With the sale of the *Nooya* came another decisive change for John Thomas: he rejoined the brewery partnership with his brother John HR. He acquired one-quarter of the business; Skaife had another one-quarter, and John HR maintained one-half. A new brewmaster, John Hyde, was hired.

Character is the real test of manhood. Live within your income, no matter how small it may be. Permanent wealth is maintained and preserved by vigilance and prudence and not by speculation. Be just, and generous when you have the means.

CHAPTER TWENTY-FIVE

QUINTESSENTIAL GENTLEMEN

IN DECEMBER 1880, Sarah Bernhardt arrived at Bonaventure Station in Montreal. The Montreal city band greeted her train and huge crowds pushed forward to see her. Some admirers were even standing on the carriage roofs of an outgoing train. Then when Bernhardt, the Divine Sarah finally emerged, the crowd surged forward. A passageway had to be created for her, but even so the crush was just too much. Crying out, the actress fainted, then recovered herself. She reached her sleigh and was hurried to the Windsor Hotel. The nearest doctor, William Alexander Molson, was called for. He attended to her that evening and then again the following day, and pronounced her well enough to carry out her performances at the Academy of Music, which she did on December 23, 24 and 25.

Alexander Molson, as he was called, had set up his medical practice a few years earlier. He and Esther Shepherd then married in 1876. Their first child, a daughter born in 1877, was named Edith, after

Alexander's sister who had died in 1872. Their second child, not born until 1888, was a son, Hobart.

In 1883 Montreal held its first winter carnival. Honoré Beaugrand, the mayor, declared a half-holiday so that everyone could take part in the parades and races. Members of the Snow Shoe Club, described by the enthusiastic press as "fine specimens of manhood," joined in the nightly torchlight processions. A palace made entirely of ice was erected on Dominion Square, covering an area of 14,000 square feet and illuminated with multicoloured electric lamps. Members of the Montreal Victorias and the Quebec team competed in the first public ice hockey match.

Montreal, a city used to celebrating outdoors in the winter, had never experienced anything like this. All the festivities and celebrations illuminating the streets that winter injected the city with new vitality. But like everyone else, even those club members leading processions avoided certain areas of the old city, particularly those where the poorest families lived among the most crowded and squalid conditions in the country. Most of those who lived in more comfortable circumstances simply avoided districts like Griffintown and Point St-Charles.

Clogged drainage systems and rotting garbage created inescapable noxious odours each spring as the ground grew warm and the snow melted. The flooding in April 1885 was the worst the city had known in twelve years. At Bonaventure Station near the market, the water rose above the seats in the cars, severely damaging eighteen brand-new Pullmans. In Griffintown, more than a hundred houses were submerged. Water broke through the embankment at the point. St. Henri was inundated. Ice shoved abruptly up McGill Street and adjoining streets, doing the most severe damage in lower town where wharves, shops and warehouses were crushed.

Flooding wasn't the only devastation to visit Montreal that spring. The year's first diagnosis of smallpox was that of a Chicago train conductor who had arrived in town on the Grand Trunk. He was promptly installed in isolation at the Hôtel Dieu Hospital. The second case, on February 27, was reported by Alexander Molson, who had diagnosed another conductor arriving from Chicago. The Hôtel Dieu refused to admit the second patient, and since the smallpox hospital had been closed for some years Alexander took the man to a home on Mayor Street. At Molson's request, Dr. Laroque of the city health department appointed a "sanitary policeman" to stand guard at the house. Although Alexander could not prevent two women from leaving the premises before the quarantine order had been instituted he managed to get their names and addresses and then followed up on their health. He spoke to Larocque and insisted that the department also supply a nurse, a washerwoman and disinfectants for the home.

Then a servant at the Hôtel Dieu hospital fell ill with smallpox. Both women who had left the Mayor Street house came down with the symptoms: first fevers, chills, and coughs; then persistent red eruptions beginning on their hands and faces. One of the women was isolated and recovered in a hospital in St. Andrews, Quebec while Dr. Molson continued to monitor the other on St. Catherine Street West in Montreal. When she showed symptoms of the disease he had her moved back to the house on Mayor Street, where she and the train conductor recovered. Afterward the house was disinfected. Dr. Molson and members of the health department were relieved, believing they had "completely stamped out" the eruption of the deadly disease.

They were horribly wrong. Conditions were ideal for the virus to creep into the population. Warmer weather and flooding combined with the discharge of dozens of unknowingly infected patients, who had been sent home so that the hospital could be disinfected. Merchants and tavern keepers who had confirmed cases in their homes continued to serve the public. And la Fête Dieu celebrations brought crowds to the streets. The smallpox hospital was reopened, and a yellow flag, signifying pestilence, was flown from its roof.

Readily accepted by most Protestants, vaccination was widely and sometimes violently resisted by the poorest Catholics. When their children came down with the signs of smallpox, mothers refused to let them be removed to hospital. Black and yellow placards fixed to homes and tenements where cases of the disease were confirmed were promptly torn down. Some people attacked the sanitary police who arrived to remove patients forcibly. The dead-cart made its weary way through the streets twice a day as hundreds of victims succumbed in the summer.

Many doctors didn't want to treat smallpox patients, not from the fear of contracting the disease (for most were vaccinated) but for fear of becoming contagious and scaring away their regular patients. Moreover, the job of disinfecting clothes and instruments, which was necessary after coming in contact with a patient, was tedious, so it was often not carried out. William Osler had accepted a position at an American university a year earlier. The west-end's public vaccinator suddenly left for Toronto in the summer of 1885, when the disease was at its worst. Alexander was one of those who stayed.

Many English Montrealers spent the summer on the shores of the lower St. Lawrence, where residents organized vaccination bees and decided to extend their holidays into September. Most felt secure from danger of infection, knowing that the victims were not only the unvaccinated but also seemed to be from a "different class" one in which, surely, uncleanliness had much to do with the disease being passed on. But in August, when seventy-seven-year-old statesman Sir Francis Hincks died of smallpox in his home on St. Antoine Street West, the English were more alarmed.

Alexander Molson stayed in the city all summer. He revaccinated his wife and daughter as an added precaution. The heat continued to rise and the death toll to climb, with hundreds of reported and unreported fatal cases of smallpox. Citizens throughout the city were urged by the health department to report any suspected cases in their neighbourhood. A frenzied neighbour of Dr. Molson's on Union Street claimed one day in August that Mrs. Molson had died of the disease. When officials arrived at noon to placard the house, Alexander–and his healthy wife–were outraged. A formal apology was later delivered to the Molsons by Dr. Larocque.

Advertisements in the newspapers offered disinfectants, odiferants, pure foods and patent medicines as remedies against contracting smallpox. "Labatt's Ale" was promoted as a "tonic." Unperturbed, Buffalo Bill's Wild West Show starring Annie Oakley opened in Point St-Charles. Unfortunately, many spectators became infected after mingling among those people who carried the virus. On September 28 a riot broke out in Montreal over compulsory vaccination, and angry mobs stormed city council. Members of the army were called out.

In spite of strong public feelings, Osler made no mention of the epidemic when he returned briefly to Montreal on October 22 for the opening of a new medical building at McGill. William Van Horne, gesticulating and puffing on his cigar as he left for the west to attend the railway's last-spike installation, told reporters: "The danger from smallpox in Montreal is enormously exaggerated outside. In the business part and in the English sections there is no excitement about smallpox, and no particular danger. There seems no danger about the hotels. The fuss is all made outside." He was not alone in his view, as life in Montreal continued unchanged for many of its citizens. Indeed, John HR Molson and John Thomas Molson might have agreed with Van Horne. Most of the Molsons, like many others untouched by the smallpox epidemic, were paying more attention to politics, hockey and golf.

In 1884 John Thomas and his family had moved from Prince of Wales Terrace to a home on University Avenue, next door to the Montreal High School. He and Jennie now had two more children, Evelyn and Walter. The new house more comfortably accommodated the couple, their eight children, and seven servants.

The members of the next generation were following the paths laid out for them by their elders. Herbert Molson, John Thomas's eldest son, attended the Montreal High School, played his first game of hockey there, and entered McGill at age fourteen in 1889. Over the next several years, his three brothers joined him at McGill: Kenneth in 1891 (age fourteen), Percy in 1896 (age sixteen), and Walter in 1898 (age sixteen). Herbert went into the sciences, while his three brothers chose arts. John Thomas would not allow his gifted second daughter, Naomi, to attend any courses. In 1900, she married Montreal stockbroker Claude Robin.

Academics and athletics were treated with equal respect at McGill, where Herbert's career was brilliant, and he managed to distinguish himself at rugby football, hockey and yachting. In 1894 Herbert graduated from McGill with an honours degree in Applied Science. The quintessential gentleman, he had been groomed by his father for the business world and knew exactly what his place in it was going to be.

Each of Herbert's brothers played hockey in high school and at McGill as well; these teams frequently played against each other, since there were so few teams in the city. Of the four Molson brothers, it was Percy who most excelled at the sport. In 1896 Percy was the youngest player on the Stanley Cup championship team, the Montreal Victorias. In the spring of 1899, he was at the Championships of Canada where he won gold medals in the 100-yard dash and 880-yard race. He excelled also in track, rugby football, racquets, golf, tennis, cricket, billiards, fishing and aquatic sports.

Percy joined the Montreal Amateur Athletic Association, whose hockey team, the Montreal Victorias, had won the first Stanley Cup, in 1893. By the time he began working at the National Trust upon graduation, the game was beginning to catch on in the business world. Banks, railway companies, hardware companies and other businesses were forming corporate leagues, with each team defending its company's image.

February 25, 1896

Alexander Molson's reputation for acts of kindness has grown by the last decade of the Victorian era. Some of his patients believe that he lives on his wealth and draws no income at all from his practice. On this night, a "deeply anxious" Mrs. Goldbloom, who had lost her first three infants, one after another, to pneumonia, is despairing that her seriously ill fourth child, six-year-old Alton, is "going to go the way of the other three." Dr. Molson, who is sensitive to their limited economic circumstances sits at the cribside in the hovel on St. Antoine Street, waiting.

Mrs. Goldboom tries to sleep in a chair next to the stove. The crib stands about ten feet away, enclosed in shadows, the piteous child within hidden from her by the curve of the doctor's back. She closes her eyes but wakes at the sound of the clasp clicking open or shut on the doctor's bulging medical bag. Every time she opens her eyes, there he is, the tireless physician gently readjusting the little head on the pillow, lifting the child's eyelids, or cooling the small forehead. She can't tell by the man's movements if he is discouraged or optimistic.

"How is he now, doctor?" she asks in a loud, anxious whisper.

"No change, Mrs. Goldbloom, no change."

He doesn't want to give her false hope. The mother looks much older than she is. Her hair is already beginning to grey; her hands clutch at a tattered shawl in her lap as she murmurs Yiddish prayers. As the night wears on Alexander does what he can, which is little more than check the child's temperature from time to time, and wipe the perspiration from his skin with a wrung-out damp cloth. After a while Alexander notes the child's temperature is coming down, and that he is breathing more deeply.

"How is he now, doctor?" comes the familiar whisper.

"There is a great change for the better," he replies.

With the coming of dawn, Alton stirs and opens his eyes, and speaks his first words in three days. Mrs. Goldbloom, weeping with relief, determines then and there that her son will become a doctor, so that he, too, might treat the poor as Dr. Molson has done.*

In May 1897, John HR Molson died. He had been suffering from nephritis, a kidney inflammation. At his death bed, the long-reigning patriarch of his generation requested that his words of wisdom to family members be written down as he dictated them. His nephew Fred, who had returned to Montreal, complied:

> *The Molson family has maintained and preserved its position and influence by steady, patient industry, and every member should be a real worker and not rely on what it has been. All that is good and great of the family should not be underground.*
>
> *Your private life should be pure. Make no compromise with vice; be able to say "no" in a firm, manly manner.*
>
> *Character is the real test of manhood. Live within your income, no matter how small it may be. Permanent wealth is maintained and preserved by vigilance and prudence and not by speculation.*
>
> *Be just, and generous when you have the means. Wealth will not take care of itself if not vigilantly cared for.*

John Thomas inherited his brother's half of the brewery, leaving him with 75 percent ownership. But Parkinson's disease, which he'd

* Alton Goldbloom graduated from McGill in medicine in 1916. He was physician-in-chief of the Montreal Children's Hospital from 1946 to 1953.

had since 1892, had taken its toll. Now, at age sixty, he was wheelchair-bound. He proposed a partnership with his eldest son, Herbert (age twenty-two), and his nephew Fred (age thirty-seven), reassuring Adam Skaife that his quarter interest would not be affected.

Extending the brewery partnership into the fourth generation was a subject which John Thomas had discussed with John HR many times. John HR had seen his nephew Harry well-placed in life and wanted Fred to be "placed in a better position as well." Having managed Consumer's Cordage Company for the last seven years, Fred had proved himself to be more than an able administrator. Herbert, though still quite young, had a graduate background in science and had just completed a course in New York for technical training in brewing.

Thus Thomas Molson's three sons, John HR, Markland and John Thomas, were each involved, at different times, in running the brewery their grandfather had founded. John Senior would have been proud of all six of Thomas's male grandchildren who bore his name: Markland's two sons (Harry and Fred), and John Thomas's four (Herbert, Kenneth, Percy and Walter). It did not occur to anyone to question tradition, to consider, for example, Molson daughters (or their children, who bore surnames other than Molson) for training or succession to the business. The brewery was about to be led into the new century by two of Thomas Molson's most capable grandsons, with the benefit of the wise counsel and experience of John Thomas Molson and Adam Skaife to guide them.

Bessie Pentland's childhood was one of miniature tea sets, little leather boots for her dolls, and dollhouses with handmade furniture. She grew up in Quebec City and summered with her family in Tadoussac. She had witnessed a tragic carriage accident at the age of four, in which her maternal grandmother was killed. The rest of her childhood was an untroubled one. Bessie wrote letters regularly, on lined paper, in a large, childish hand to her aunt Delia Falkenberg in New York, and, when he was away, to her father. On one fishing trip, Charles–who clearly adored his eldest daughter–sent Bessie a letter written on a piece of birch bark, which she saved to the end of her life. The girl grew up attentive, solicitous and sweet. She was exceptionally pretty. She met her future husband when they were still children: from the moment Herbert Molson saw her, he was smitten.

April 11, 1899

Bessie wears a dress of white satin with veil and orange blossoms, and a magnificent diamond star. The newspapers are effusive in their reports:

> *The most fashionable wedding that has for a long time past taken place at Quebec was celebrated at noon today ...*
>
> *For some time past there has been quite a little flutter of excitement in Quebec in anticipation of the event, and when it came off local society turned out en masse, pretty well crowding the noble old cathedral.*

The "noble old cathedral" was the Cathedral of the Holy Trinity, the Anglican cathedral in Quebec City. It was "crowded to the doors with the elite of Quebec society, and was beautifully decorated for the occasion by friends of the bride, who is one of Quebec's favourite belles."

The newspapers agree that Bessie and Herbert seem to inhabit a fairy-tale world. The future is theirs, beginning tomorrow. After breakfast they will spend the afternoon at the Pentlands, then go to the station to catch the train to New York, where they will embark for Europe for a two-month honeymoon.

Kenneth, acting as an usher for his brother this day, is grappling with a dizzying range of emotions. He is to be married only four days later, at a much more sober ceremony.

Kenneth's uneasy secret - everyone knew what had happened, but no one knew the details - set him somewhat apart from his siblings and other members of the family. How

Chapter Twenty-Six

Secrets and Sorrow

The cloistered, Victorian environment in which Mary Snider was raised had taught her that each person harboured two selves: the first, maintained for the sake of propriety; and the other, real but secret self, allowed out very seldom. In Mary's world, servants deemed most "faithful" were those who knew all the household secrets but betrayed nothing to outsiders. Modesty was a most prized virtue–lacquered screens stood in bedrooms for dressing behind; skirts concealed table legs; swimsuits covered ladies' ankles. Hidden compartments in writing desks and locked cabinets handily preserved people's privacy.

Mary's father was the sharp-witted Judge Colin Snider of Hamilton, Ontario, whom his grandchildren remembered as gruff and remote and his contemporaries knew as an excellent arbitrator. Mary's petite, accomplished mother, the former Helen Bligh Grasset, ruled over a large household of servants, liked to host fancy dress balls, and taught each of her daughters to play the piano.

Born in 1880, Mary was the middle child in a family of four daughters and one son. None of them knew what to make of this scornful, high-spirited girl. Judge and Mrs. Snider suspected Mary was wayward with the boys; she was known to have alienated the affections of at least one of her sisters by dating the girl's boyfriend. This spoiled, sparkling, coquettish debutante with a rebellious streak was raised to mimic propriety, but loved to flaunt convention and prove it wrong.

By the time she turned eighteen, in 1898, a seamless facade of nonchalance concealed Mary's restless imagination. The languid confidence worn so casually by her outside self drew men to her like hummingbirds to hibiscus. Her laughter was laced with defiance. In situations where other young ladies would barely raise their eyes, Mary's curious glances would size up her subjects.

This was the summer that Mary met Kenneth Molson.

Kenneth Molson at twenty was tall like his brothers, with thick dark hair and guileless blue eyes. In 1896, when he was only eighteen years old, he had graduated from McGill with a Bachelor of Arts. His first job was with Molsons Bank in Montreal (when John HR was president); after only a year he was transferred to their Simcoe, Ontario, branch. He was working at this branch the summer that Mary came to stay with her maternal grandmother. His vision of his future included working his way up in the bank, marrying and having children, playing the occasional rugby game or tennis match, joining the odd rubber of bridge, perhaps stopping in at the University Club every now and then. An idealistic and sensitive young man, he was insulated in the knowledge that an excellent career was his as long as he gave it his best. While Kenneth never expected his life would be easy, he did think it would be genteel. In love, as in sports, the rules were clear. The lines were sharp between right and wrong, and, in the event of error, gentlemanly behaviour always made the hero.

Kenneth had never met anyone like Mary Letitia Snider. She possessed an uncommon beauty spun of grace and mystery. Her long wrists seemed to float to her sides after she pulled off her gloves. Her eyes flashed with mischief and defiance, challenging his own mild blue gaze. She shocked him and fascinated him at the same time.

They made a striking couple, and Kenneth doubtless felt proud to be escorting her various places in Simcoe. Unfortunately, one of those places was a local hotel corridor. Mary was recognized, Judge Snider was informed that very night, and he insisted that the two be married as soon as it could be arranged. Kenneth agreed, but asked if the marriage could take place after his older brother Herbert's pending nuptials, out of respect.

On April 15, 1899, at St. Matthews Church in Hamilton, Kenneth and Mary were quietly wed. After the ceremony Judge Snider took nineteen-year-old Mary home. He would not allow his daughter to live with her husband until she was twenty-one.

Kenneth's brother Herbert and sister Mabel were the only members of the Molson family who knew about the wedding. Without explaining why, Herbert asked his cousin, William Molson MacPherson, president of Molsons Bank, to transfer Kenneth from Simcoe to St. Thomas. It was by far the most discreet way to handle the situation, agreed those who choreographed it. Judge Snider thought his troubles with his daughter were over. Not only was he wrong, but Kenneth had no inkling that his own troubles were about to begin.

When Mary's twenty-first birthday approached, the bride argued the merits of a second wedding–after all, she pointed out, it would belie the need to explain to relatives and friends why the two were suddenly living together. A scandal being something Mary's parents wanted to avoid at all costs, Judge and Mrs. Snider agreeably arranged an especially lavish second ceremony. There would be no wedding trip, however, and Mary's trousseau would consist of only one evening gown, made of lavender mousseline de soie, falling naturally into small plaits cut into deep points, which cascaded over an underskirt of Brussels lace.

Thursday, April 18, 1901

In the narthex of Christ Church Cathedral, Montreal, on Mary's public wedding day, a black scarf is draped over the portrait of Queen Victoria, who had died on January 22. Mary is wearing a sheer white veiling wedding gown, over a foundation of shimmering yellow taffeta. A delicate scarf of white chiffon is caught at the side in a soft bow with accordion pleated ends. On her feet are snowflake-white kid leather sandals, with pearl-coloured beads on the strap. Kenneth is suddenly shy with her, as well as uncomfortably aware of the hypocrisy of the occasion.

He has given her a string of pearls as a wedding gift; she wears it now.

Mary has prepared a list, written in pencil on a plain white paper, of the wedding guests and the gifts each has given. Among the many names are Lily Molson, Mabel, Percy, Walter (Kenneth's youngest brother), Mrs. J.H.R. (Louisa), Herbert and Bessie, Markland, Mr. and Mrs. C.E. Spragge, Mr. and Mrs. Robin (Naomi and Claude), and Mr. and Mrs. F.W. (Fred and Kate) Molson. The gifts include a sewing machine, a travelling clock and a Davenport clock, a set of books, a mahogany secretary and an armchair, a silver candelabra, a silver tray and tea set, a silver butter knife, and half a dozen silver teaspoons.

Pregnancy made Mrs. Kenneth Molson unwell through the late winter and early spring of 1901–02. On April 26 she delivered a premature boy who weighed only four pounds. He was named Colin, after her father; she and Kenneth agreed he would be called Jack. Mary recovered from the birth with astonishing speed, fitting into her boned bodices and corsets, *crêpe de chine* tucked blouses, walking frocks and dotted mull gowns so easefully, it was as if she'd never been "confined."

Edwardian upper-class mothers were expected to be aloof to the extent that they had nurses and governesses, but those around Mary could tell her curious indifference was something beyond that. Whether her attitude was a result of experiencing sickness during pregnancy and delivering a child she didn't expect would live, whether it was a consequence of her self-absorbedness, or both, Mary was emotionally detached from the little boy.

Kenneth was frequently away on business, and Mary would use his absences as opportunities to entertain and be entertained. Less than a month after Jack was born, and continuing over the next two and a half years, his mother engaged in at least ten indiscretions, each new relationship begun before the previous had ended. During this time they lived first in St. Thomas and later (Kenneth moved first, Mary following eight months after) Quebec City. Her behaviour was quite public: she began by going dancing with a Bank of Toronto clerk, then going riding with a hotel bartender, snowshoeing with an Imperial Bank clerk, driving in the country with a barber, then to the theatre for rendezvous with the manager of the Quebec Auditorium. Her affairs–some conducted concurrently, and most of them with married men–didn't all run smoothly. Emma Larabie, the maid, recalled one evening when Mary had come home from the theatre with George Parent, who was a lawyer, and MPP for Montmorency, and the son of Quebec's premier. After a late dinner, the couple retired to the drawing room, where they stayed until 4:20 a.m. According to Emma, at this late hour they "had a row." Parent never returned. One Monday afternoon, Mary refused Captain Benyon because he was "very drunk." Later she "took a fancy to" physician Dr. C. Smith Parke.

Mary invited her gentlemen guests into her home, sometimes into her bedroom but most often to the drawing room, where one, who had become intoxicated and ill, spent the night on a "lounge" with her. She smoked their cigarettes and drank their whisky and champagne. From at least one of her lovers she accepted cash.

When he wasn't with his nurse, Jack–whose health was reportedly delicate–spent time with Emma, Kenneth's stout Irish maid, who had never warmed to Mary but nevertheless adored the child. Emma and Mary's four sisters, especially Winnifred, lavished Jack with the attention and affection that he never received from his mother.

To dismiss Mary as a sexual addict seems too simplistic a conclusion. Whatever motivated her may have to remain open to interpretation. Suffice it to say that all this time Kenneth did not know what Emma Larabie knew; what the housemaid Edna knew; what even telephone operators in Quebec knew. No one dared tell him.

In March of 1904, Mary met the Honourable Adelard Turgeon, MP for Bellechasse, and provincial minister of agriculture. She asked him to join them for supper. The subject of Kenneth's next business trip came up during the dinner conversation. One week later, when Mary was alone, Turgeon appeared on the doorstep, holding a bouquet of roses.

"Light a fire in the drawing room, Emma," Mary said quietly, tilting her head.

Mary took the flowers while Adelard removed his coat, umbrella and hat, and handed them to Edna to hang on their appropriate hooks. Still holding the flowers, Mary took Turgeon's arm and led him past the curved staircase toward *la chambre de compagnie,* the drawing room.

Emma was kneeling on the wool tapestry carpet next to the fire grate, lighting the gas. She rose with an effort as Mary spoke loudly to her, overcompensating for the maid's slight deafness.

"Thank you. Put these in a crystal vase with some water, and I will fetch them later."

Edna was hovering at the french doors, holding Jack, who had just woken up. Mary turned to the two-year-old.

"Dis *'Mon Oncle Adelard,'* Jack."

As Emma recollected, Mary then told her and Edna to leave the drawing room and close the doors behind them.

What happened then? Did Mary sit demurely at the piano stool, arranging her skirt in folds over her knees? Did she let the tips of her fingers drift gently over the ivory piano keys, preparing to play and sing for her guest, as she had done for others? She was alone with a man who was one of the ablest orators in the Legislature, who had been described as "one of the most courteous and cultured sons of the ancient capital." Moreover, he was devastatingly handsome. It would be easy to fall in love with Adelard Turgeon.

A minute or two later there was an alarming *éclat* of noise in the hallway outside the drawing room. Adelard sprinted for the doors, grasped the handles, flung them open and stared out at the scene in the hall. An empty coal scuttle lay on its side on the floor at the foot of the stairs; a cloud of coal dust was settling around it. He looked up. Emma, one hand clutching her long skirts and the other clapped over her mouth in mute horror, stared down at him from the top of the stairs. The minister of agriculture was in his underclothes. A silent, mutual comprehension passed between them. Turgeon backed into the drawing room and closed the doors again.

Whatever Adelard said next in the drawing room, Emma did not hear. One can only imagine his words, "*Ne t'inquiète pas*–it was just one of the servants."

It wasn't the scene with Adelard in his underclothes that was Mary's undoing. Emma was, after all, the faithful servant through and through. She'd carried Mary's bags to a steamer stateroom next to Turgeon's more than once, knowing that Kenneth believed his wife was going "camping with the Duchess." In the end, which came in January 1906, it was a jealous lover, Dr. Parke, who approached Kenneth in the guise of a concerned friend/witness, claiming to have heard Mary's voice on St. Eustache Street, at her porter's address. Kenneth may at first have refused to believe Dr. Parke. Nevertheless, he asked Emma gently what she knew, and she tearfully told him all. Kenneth's revelation was that learning something could be terrible and beautiful at the same time.

So deep was her shock at finally being confronted, Mary could not speak. All her rationalizations dissolved. A car came for her the following morning to take her back to her father's house.

When a separation agreement was drawn up on January 26, it stipulated that Mary would see her son four times each year for a day, and that if he became dangerously ill she would be called for. Mary objected to only one point in the wording of the document. She wanted to limit her admission of misconduct to the year 1905, arguing that it would unnecessarily tarnish the reputations of the men in the other years who "may have been foolish but not guilty." Judge Snider wrote to his old acquaintance Charles Pentland (Herbert's father-in-law, who had taken up Kenneth's counsel), to present the request to him: "Kindly let me have your answer to the first part of this letter at your earliest convenience so that I may get this very unhappy and trying duty off my mind."

Pentland's answer was no, and the original dates remained.

No one dared ask Kenneth about Mary in the years that followed her departure. No one knew how to offer him either consolation or support. Kenneth had stipulated that he would "keep secret the present agreement ... and the misconduct of the said Mary L. Molson, particularly from their child, so long as she shall live a chaste life."

Confidentiality was not just for the child's sake; some of Mary's lovers were so high-profile that everyone thought it best to protect them, too. As a further incentive for Mary's complete cooperation, John Thomas gave Kenneth $30,000 as a lump sum payment to be given to his estranged wife. John Thomas made it clear to Kenneth that this amount would be deducted directly from the legacy that was due him from his father's final will and testament.

Kenneth's uneasy secret–everyone knew what had happened, but no one knew the details–set him somewhat apart from his siblings and other members of the family. How much of this distance was their discomfort and how much his own withdrawal is impossible to measure.

Kenneth destroyed all photographs of Mary. The documents connected with the separation and later trial were tied with a hand-stitched pink ribbon and laid to rest in a grey-green locked metal box, kept inside another locked cabinet.

At the turn of the century William Molson MacPherson, son of D.L. MacPherson, was a powerful man. Not only had he been president of Molsons Bank since John HR's death, but he also managed major personal investments in transportation and had friends in high places. One of them was Sir Wilfrid Laurier, who, in July 1903, had unveiled plans for the Grand Trunk Pacific Railway. Intended as a competitor for the Canadian Pacific but going far north of its route, it was a popular concept, and the Prime Minister's speech, in which he announced the appointment of Charles Hays as president, was widely acclaimed. MacPherson had ideas of his own, and wrote to Laurier in his effort to pursue them:

> *Quebec*
> *October 31, 1903*
>
> *My dear Sir Wilfrid,*
>
> *Mr. [George] Parent told me that you were expected here the end of*

> *this week or early next week, which was the reason why I wired you as Mrs. MacPherson and myself were in hopes that we might have the pleasure of seeing you, and knowing that Lady Laurier generally accompanies you we were in hopes of seeing her also. Your telegraph disappointed us very much, as in my message to you, I mentioned that Mrs. MacPherson was leaving town on Wednesday, and as I have an urgent business engagement in Toronto on Saturday, we were unavoidably deprived of the pleasure of seeing you. Quebec has lost its charms to some extent evidently to you as we have seen so little of you here, and at the moment when so much is hovering about Quebec calculated to make it a prominent shipping port, I, for one, have earnestly hoped to have seen you here when we could discuss some matters calculated to stimulate the old city. Although I shall not be here next week, I am satisfied that your other friends will represent our requirements.*

In 1901 Molsons Bank was a strong institution. It had expanded to thirty-nine branches and continued to grow. Dividends were at 9 percent, and rising. In 1904, its forty-ninth annual statement revealed that the net profits for the year were nearly half a million dollars, and the reserve fund had risen to three million. By 1911 there were seventy-eight branches, and dividends to shareholders were yielding 11 percent.

The strong position of the bank could also be attributed to another person, Fred's older brother Harry Molson. When Harry had returned from Europe, John HR invited him to work with him at the bank. When John HR died, he left Fred and Harry each $300,000 worth of Molsons Bank stock. Their uncle's instincts proved to be right. Under the presidency of, first, John HR, and then William Molson MacPherson, Harry became a key figure at Molsons Bank, working his way up to become general manager.

Harry was always enthusiastic about public service and had a range of interests. Always nattily dressed, the middle-aged bachelor was a familiar sight at the theatre, where he would arrive in his beaver coat and muffler, gesticulating with one of his cigars or checking his conspicuous pocket watch. He was often seen in the company of his cousin Alexander Morris and Alexander's wife, Florence Nightingale Morris; in fact he shared a house with them in Montreal for at least three years. In the 1898 city directory he jokingly listed his address as the St. James Club. By the end of the century he had a summer house built next to the Morrisses in Dorval. Soon he had a second house built on Mountain Street, in St. Antoine Ward. He joined St. Paul's Lodge, became an alderman for the city, served on many directorates and supported charities. Harry Molson was conventional in many ways, but defiantly unconventional in others. Those closest to him were entirely accepting of his own standard of what was honest, moral and socially conscientious. Harry, they knew, had two enduring passions. The first of these was yachting; between 1890 and 1910 he would buy and sell nine steam yachts, owning several at a time. His second enduring passion was Mrs. Florence Morris.

This part of Fred may have been his way of reacting to the legacy of his father's mistakes ... One might ask: how could Fred's father's circumstances not have affected him in his formative years?

Chapter Twenty-Seven

Mr. Fred

Everybody who knew Percy Molson seemed to revere him. Just over six feet tall, with blue eyes and brown hair, he stood out from the crowd at McGill not only because of his extraordinary sports achievements, but also as the ultimate gentleman-scholar. There was something heroic about him. Once, after a goal in hockey had been attributed to him, he pointed out to the referee that it should be disallowed because the puck had deflected off his arm. He was never penalized in a game. Three years in succession, he was named McGill's best all-round athlete, winning "every athletic honour the university offered," an achievement never matched before or since.

In spite of all the recognition and adulation, Percy remained a modest man. His parents, Jennie and John Thomas, had hoped he would study law, but he chose instead a business career, and after gaining his Bachelor of Arts he took a year of Applied Science (later called Engineering). In the years following his graduation from McGill in 1901, he worked his way from clerk to manager of the Montreal offices of the National Trust Company.

Percy did not give up his physical pursuits, but worked them in around his work schedule. He became a director and auditor of the Montreal Amateur Athletic Association (MAAA), a captain at the Royal Montreal Golf Club, president of the Canadian Rugby Union, trustee of the Grey Football Club, a director of the Montreal Racquet Club, and president of the Park Tobogganing Club. He welcomed as an honour the invitation to join the advisory board for the McGill Gymnasium.

In 1903 Percy travelled to Milwaukee for the Amateur Athletic Union of the United States Championships, where he took first place in the running broad jump, defeating the holder of the world record. There he also won the gold medal in the 100-yard dash, and the bronze in the 880-yard.

Percy returned to Métis Beach every summer, joining members of his family including his sister Mabel, brother Herbert, and cousin Fred. Back in Montreal, he also found time to exercise his memberships in the Royal St. Lawrence Yacht Club, the Montreal Hunt Club, the St. James Club, and the Laurentian Club. He gave his efforts to the city's Carnival Committee, was a director of both the North Montreal Land Syndicate and the Montreal Wrecking Company, and was a member of the Select Vestry at Christ Church Cathedral.

In addition to making stellar achievements as an amateur athlete and moving rapidly up in his banking career, Percy attended MAAA fundraisers, skating parties and soirées. With his brother Walter and sister Mabel, Percy went to summer weekend fêtes at the Papineau home in Montebello.

In 1905 Percy and Talbot Papineau, great-grandson of Louis-Joseph Papineau and sometime beau of Mabel Molson, formed the Canadian Club; Papineau became its president, and Percy its secretary-treasurer. By 1906, everything had changed. Talbot, a Rhodes scholar, had left Montreal and Montebello for Oxford, and Mabel was heading to Quebec City to help her brother Kenneth raise young Jack.

With the ascension of King Edward VII to the British throne in 1901, a new era of fashion and invention had begun. In 1903, the Wright Brothers had successfully flown the first powered plane, and automobiles were about to revolutionize local transportation. Women were graduating from universities and agitating for emancipation. Every so often the papers reported a woman's arrest for smoking a cigarette in public. The gossip of the day was about Governor General

Lord Minto, seen in Ottawa with Lola Powell, who was referred to in discreet whispers as "Minto's Folly." The Liberal government of Sir Wilfrid Laurier was dynamic. Although it had held a referendum in 1898 which came out in favour of prohibition, Laurier was to dismiss the results because only 44 percent of Canadian voters had cast ballots.

With the threat of prohibition over, Molson's brewery began to reflect the country's sense of well-being and prosperity. It had never shown better growth than it did in the century's first decade. Fred Molson's influence and efforts did not go unrecognized; however, when he suggested ways in which the plant could be modernized, the elders balked for some years. It wasn't until 1907, the brewery's first million-dollar year, that John Thomas and Adam Skaife finally agreed it was time to introduce refrigeration. This change meant Molson's could, for the first time, brew beer in overlapping cycles all year long.

Fred Molson was an efficient businessman, an extremely punctual, exacting disciplinarian who insisted upon a first-class performance from everyone around him. From the first day he entered the brewery, Fred wanted to learn everything about all departments of the business. During his early tours of the enterprise, it must have struck him immediately that the brewery badly needed to be modernized. Like other long-functioning and traditional businesses in Montreal, Molson's had retained archaic ways. But Fred had less appreciation for tradition, having entered the business from without, and steam-powered refrigeration was just one idea of many he wanted implemented.

It was Fred who pointed out that the entire premises were still lighted by gas at a time when more than two-thirds of the city had converted to electricity. Introducing electricity in 1908 enabled Molson's to buy and install Montreal's first grain dryer and equip the premises with modern racking and bottling apparatuses. One change led to another; it seemed that no detail was too small to escape Fred's notice. Seeing that old wooden bungs were still being used to plug drain-holes in the casks, Fred soon had all the casks equipped with patent valves.

Fred's character and experience made him an excellent administrator, and his wit made him popular among his fellows. As strict as he was with his employees, most felt sufficiently comfortable in his presence to call him "Mr. Fred." Yet there remained part of his personality that might be described as severe, even malevolent. An aura of discontent seemed to pervade him. His actions and manner were often impatiently purposeful. He had to be in control of circumstances around him, not just through his contribution at the brewery but through his obsessive punctuality, his inflexibility or his austerity.

Fred would not have looked at it that way, of course. He would have argued that every time he came to make a decision, he was simply acting out his burden of duty; he considered a situation and decided what was right. He would have argued that he was obeying a higher order by being punctual; that it was a sign of respect to be on time and of disrespect to be tardy. He would have maintained that compromising in anything made a weaker man.

There was no one with whom Fred Molson was more severe than his own family. His daughter Brenda learned, through humiliating exchanges, not to be late for breakfast. His eldest son, Bert, felt most the difficulty of living up to his father's expectations. "If the snow were not shovelled off the path, it was Bert's fault. If the maintenance man had swept a pile of dirt into one corner and left it there, Bert must see that it did not happen again."

It is more than likely that Fred's difficult, impenetrable side evolved from his troubled upbringing. This part of Fred may have been his way of reacting to the legacy of his father's mistakes, particularly since they were played out in the ever-present shadow of the successes of Markland's two brothers. One might ask, instead, how could Fred's father's circumstances *not* have affected him in his formative years?

Simply called "Father" by both his children and his wife, Fred had a portrait painted by Horne Russell, which hung in the foyer of their Drummond Street house. The painting displayed his "dignified, slightly stiff pose" and showed the "long line of his nose and the level glance of his eyes."

Those who knew him claimed that Fred never relaxed, and that even when at home his mind was occupied with brewery matters. Yet when he was on holiday, and particularly when he was alone fishing, he seemed to be at peace with the world. Fred took his wife and five children to Métis Beach every summer, although he would never stay longer than a day or two, so anxious was he to get to the north shore. There, he could indulge his love of salmon fishing.

Fred could remember fishing the Godbout River with his father in the early 1870s, in the days before Markland's financial and social tailspin. The two were invited to stay with the river's owner, Allan Gilmour, who ran an establishment described as "an oasis of luxury in a desert of wilderness" and whose guests had often included Lord and Lady Dufferin. But by 1898 (Markland's Oregon ventures having failed), Fred had persuaded his father to move back to Montreal and took it upon himself to see that he lived comfortably. He arranged accommodation for Markland on MacKay Street in St. Antoine Ward and set up an income-generating fund for him to live on.

Like others before him in the family, John Thomas's first consideration when preparing his will was the wishes of his ancestors. During the years since his health had begun deteriorating in 1892, John Thomas pondered the future of his father's church, which was in need of major repairs, and he sadly decided it needed to be replaced. As he knew, his father had never permitted the premises to be consecrated, specifically so that if the need arose his descendants could decide to use the building and lot for other purposes. John Thomas decided to build a new St. Thomas's Church on another property.

Herbert went to Canon Renaud (who had been leading services at St. Thomas's for the past fifteen years) and informed him of his father's plan. By 1909 the clock and bells were removed from the old St. Thomas's and erected in the new tower constructed for them. Still, it was difficult to vacate the old church. Canon Renaud wrote to John Thomas:

> *If an association of over fifteen years hallows the old building to me, what must it be to you and yours? ... Thanking you and your son for all your kindness ...*

John Thomas's "kindnesses" continued after the new church was erected. In October 1909 a resolution to convey a message of thanks to John Thomas Molson was passed at the new St. Thomas's Church Hall, in a meeting attended by Bishop Farthing, Canon Renaud, the church wardens, and 300 parishioners. Six months before his death, on February 7, 1910, John Thomas made another "munificent and spontaneous gift … of $10,700, in liquidation of the debt of the new St Thomas Church," the gesture described by the Montreal Diocesan Synod as "a pious wish of a loving son to perpetuate the foundation of St Thomas' Church in 1841, by his father."

Herbert and Bessie lived in a house on Mountain Street in Montreal, next to Bessie's good friends the Cantlies, who had also moved there from Quebec. In the years before 1901 and 1907, Herbert's four children were born in that house; first Tom, then Dorothy and Betty, and then another son, Hartland, completed their family.

The Herbert Molsons spent their summers in Métis, where sometimes Percy would join them. Aunt Mabel would have Jack write and send postcards to his father, addressed to Molsons Bank in Quebec. "We are Most Happy, We Send Love, Jack" was a typical note.

The two cousins, Jack and Tom, played on the beach together, dressed in the sailor suits that were popular at the time. In imitation of the sailing vessels anchored off shore in the bay, their own little toy boats floated in the shallow pools at low tide. As in most families, there were innocent adventures fondly recalled over the years. One day Jack asked the maid at Astley's Hotel if he might have a bit of cloth to make a sail, and she brusquely refused him. Undaunted, Jack procured a pair of scissors, found a tucked-in bed-sheet, cut the piece he needed from the bottom corner, and tucked the sheet back in. To his and Tom's delight the sail worked perfectly; later on, Jack called it a calculated risk that was worth the upbraiding he got when his "crime" was discovered.

Tom was the better at skipping stones and became adept at hitting seagulls on Cow Rock (just out of stone's throw at low tide) with little pebbles shot from slingshots, until his mother told him to stop. The Molsons often rowed out to Bull Rock for picnics, families gathering from several households to join them. From the rock, Lighthouse Point looked closer than it really was. Occasionally someone would spot a whale. The children scrambled over the rocks under

Bessie's protective gaze. On the warmest days they would linger until the sun began to go down. Mabel, long remembered for the shocking boldness of it, liked to row off alone to the far side of Cow Rock and swim with "not a stitch of clothing on."

Mabel took care of Jack in Kenneth's house in Quebec City for three years. In 1909 when Mabel was thirty-one, and Jack, seven, they came to Montreal to live with Jennie and the ailing John Thomas on University Avenue. But another move was imminent. Construction of the new Montreal High School had begun next door to the Molson property. No one noticed–until it was too late–that the excavation next door had weakened the Molson house's foundation, causing irreparable damage. Not long after John Thomas's death in 1910, Jennie and her household (including Lily, Percy and Walter, and now, Mabel and Jack) moved to Pine Avenue. The old house was subsequently demolished.

In her role as surrogate parent, Mabel enrolled Jack at Ashbury College, a boarding school east of Ottawa. During the winter holidays in Montreal, the boy would often be taken by his aunt and his grandmother for tea at Uncle Herbert's house on Ontario Street. Since John Thomas's death, Herbert was the head of their part of the family. It had fallen on him and Bessie to provide a physical centre and strong family leadership, not only for his siblings but, now, for the younger generation.

Like other Molsons before him (including John Senior), Herbert's paternal consciousness extended beyond his family. Adam Skaife's wife had to go to a sanitarium in England when she was diagnosed with elephantiasis, a disfiguring and deadly disease. Queenie, her youngest child, seemed lost and overwhelmed without her mother. Herbert and Bessie stepped in and often took care of her; the little girl often accompanied them to Métis for holidays, and at least once went with them to Europe.

In 1910 Kenneth fell in love again. Isabel Meredith was a dark-eyed beauty he had met in Quebec City; he knew her family well. Her father, E.G. (Ned) Meredith, was a prominent Quebec notary. The Merediths had a summer house, called Rosecliff, built in 1867 by Sir William Meredith in St. Patrick, the other side of Rivière du Loup from Cacouna.

In order for Kenneth to ask Isabel Meredith to marry him, he had some obstacles to overcome. The first of these was obtaining a divorce from Mary. His situation would have to be scrutinized before the courts; his private life would become public. He would have to hire a detective to find his former wife, hire a lawyer to begin drawing up the endless documents, and attend Divorce Committee Hearings in Ottawa. It would also be necessary to petition the Governor General, the Senate, and the House of Commons before a divorce could be granted. Being cross-examined would, in a way, be like going through the whole sordid experience again and would feel like further humiliation. Kenneth prepared himself to do what he had to.

In December 1910 Kenneth resigned from Molsons Bank, both to spare the bank from embarrassment while he was seeking his divorce and to give all his time to the undertaking. In January he hired detectives–one in Canada, and two in Liverpool–to find Mary. By March one of them had traced Mary to Harrogate in Yorkshire, England. There, reported Detective Stockley, she was living with another man, a portly, clean-shaven, forty-five-year-old real estate salesman and part-time auctioneer named Harold Tinker. To confirm her identification Kenneth would have to travel to Yorkshire. He left on an extended trip to Europe two weeks later, trailed by Isabel's letters. In a diary which he kept of the trip, he referred to Isabel as "my little friend."

In Algiers, Kenneth noted that he heard Miserere at a local cathedral, then spent the rest of the evening in "a café, frequented by lower classes where they had singing & dancing." He attended a vaudeville theatre, where he saw "very good dancing, trained dogs & moving pictures." In Spain he saw a cockfight and a bullfight before he took the train from Madrid to Cordova, where "two letters & an Easter card from my little friend" were waiting. In Italy the following month, he visited cathedrals, the Vatican and several art galleries and museums. In June there were "3 more letters from my little friend." Kenneth left for Paris on June 10, where, as planned, he met his sister Mabel, her friend Dora Brockwell, and Jack. They all attended church together, after which Kenneth took Jack to the Louvre and the Champs Elysées. They dined at the Café Voisin ("very good but expensive") and the Hotel Bastille, took a boat trip down the Seine, and went to moving picture shows.

In London, Kenneth bought everyone tickets for George V's Coronation. "On Thursday June 22 Mabel and I walked to Picadilly in the evening to see the illuminations," he wrote. "A dense crowd filled the street from sidewalk to sidewalk."

On Monday June 26 Kenneth began the real business of the trip to England. He met the detective in Harrogate:

> *Mr. Stockley & I spent that evening and next morning trying to see "Mrs Tinker" but without success. Weather cold & unsettled. Returned to London Tuesday p.m.*

They tried again on July 1. This time, Kenneth had bought a pair of field glasses and booked a room at the North Eastern Station Hotel. He and Stockley stationed themselves across the street from the three-storey grey stone house where Mary lived with Harold Tinker, No. 10 Ash Grove. He had to identify her positively and establish that she was not living a "chaste" life:

> *Spent that evening & most of next day watching for "Mrs. Tinker" & finally had a good look at her & then spent some time dodging them but they called at Hotel & found I was staying there …*

It must have been a distressingly difficult experience for Kenneth. He and Mary did not have to meet face to face, nor did he plan to declare himself, but after the encounter at the hotel, Kenneth walked up the steps of No. 10 Ash Grove. Mary answered his knock, but did not react to seeing him there. Kenneth told her why he had come, and she responded that she had been expecting him. There was no sign of Harold Tinker. Kenneth returned to Stockley, waiting across the street, and told him they could go. Mary was, he could see, "pretty well advanced in a state of pregnancy." (On November 23, 1911, Mary gave birth to a baby girl named Helen.)

It was a relief to leave for London on Monday July 3, where they "went straight to Wimbledon for the tennis." For days following his trip to Harrogate Kenneth was often lost in thought. He took Jack to see the Crystal Palace, Kew Gardens and Hampton Court. He wrote very little in his diary, summarizing the entire month of August with one entry: "some weeks in Scotland." They were home again in September.

The months between November 1911 and February 1912 continued to take an emotional toll on Kenneth, but the succession of petitions, evidence and reports finally reached their conclusion. *An Act for the Relief of Kenneth Molson* was passed by the Senate on February 15, 1912.

Kenneth didn't have to think about Mary any more and could now return to a normal life. He formed a partnership as a stockbroker with his brother-in-law Claude B. Robin. He took Isabel to the theatre, and out dancing: the fox-trot had just come into fashion. He went to Henry Birks Jewellers in Montreal, the old store on the corner of St. Catherine and Union streets, and told the proprietor he wanted to buy "the most beautiful and most expensive" diamond ring ever sold in the city. He commissioned a house to be built for them on Pine Avenue near his mother's house and bought an automobile. Kenneth and Isabel were married in March 1913 at the Quebec City Methodist Church. For Kenneth, life was starting all over again.

Molson was the wealthiest Canadian passenger on board the Titanic, and could well have afforded a stateroom. Instead, he paid thirty pounds ten shillings for cabin number C-30, a relatively unpretentious inside cabin on the upper deck – without portholes or private bath.

Chapter Twenty-Eight

For King and Country

Before his death in 1910, John Thomas Molson had prepared a detailed will. To his widow Jennie he left an annuity of $12,000. He listed numerous personal and charitable bequests, and the remainder of his estate, worth approximately four million dollars, was divided into twelve shares–one share to go to each of his four daughters, and two to each of his four sons. This division reflected John Thomas's view of what was seemly and appropriate. The ailing patriarch wished to ensure that his daughters wouldn't be "courted for their money," yet wanted them to be able to live comfortably in case they chose not to marry.

People would remember John Thomas with great respect. He had left a legacy of both generosity and diplomacy, his dignity always intact; he could be counted on to lead in every situation. Yet there was another side of him, autocratic and intolerant, that cowed people. He was known for frequently being "peevish" and telling men to "go to the devil." Lily had often been frightened of him; he had reportedly "made her cry" when she was a girl. She had not dared ask him if she could go to university. When his second daughter, Naomi, asked if she could attend, he had flatly refused. He allowed Evelyn to enroll, however, "for by then he'd grown older and had given up resisting girls and university." (Mabel apparently never asked.)

He must have hated growing older, becoming infirm. During the last ten years of his life John Thomas had never left the house. He had refused even to be photographed in his wheelchair. (A "cripple," the common term in the early 1900s for someone unable to walk, if not tinged with disparagement was nevertheless a word imbued with pity.) It was, to John Thomas, the ultimate indignity to be deprived of mobility while his mind remained clear. He had so prized his physical health most of his life.

Before he died John Thomas saw that his children had achieved or were attaining independence. Herbert was ensconced in the brewery, Kenneth was a stock broker with his own partnership, Walter was establishing himself in real estate, and Percy had embarked upon a banking career. Naomi was married to Claude Robin, Kenneth's partner. Evelyn was married to Dr. Colin Kerr Russel, a neurosurgeon at the Montreal General Hospital. (Neither Lily nor Mabel would marry.)

John Thomas's children inherited another significant legacy from him. It had been their father's idea, the year before he died, to acquire a property north of the city with access to a railway. John Thomas had pointed out that the family could benefit from getting out of Montreal in winter and enjoy cleared slopes for skiing and country roads for hiking. He had suggested that they make a collective purchase: Herbert, Kenneth, Walter, Evelyn, Percy and Mabel became the principals.

The property the family found was near Nantel, and enclosed two lakes: Lac Desjardins and Lac Giroux. They referred to the property as "Ivry," after the nearby town; family and friends came and went all year round. A local farmer was hired as a caretaker, and to pick up groups at the train station and take them up to the house. The siblings built a lodge on the edge of a lake, named it the "Penguin Ski Club," and operated it collectively as a non-profit, or "self-sufficient," as they called it, business. Olympian "Jack Rabbit" Johanssen was one of the ski club's best-known members.

Ivry became a retreat from the bustle of the city, and unlike Métis it was close enough for the Molsons to escape to for a weekend, any time of the year. Water was pumped from a well outside the back door. For refrigeration, they followed young Jack's suggestion that they take a garbage can, fill the bottom with cement, and sink it in a cold stream that fed into the lake. They acquired cows, pigs and horses for the property, grew their own feed for the animals, and planted a prolific vegetable garden. Extra horse manure for garden fertilizer was delivered by train from the brewery stables.

Harry Markland Molson (whose mother, Helen, had remarried Sir Edward Morris, who was to become premier of Newfoundland) was unquestionably destined for presidency of the family bank. He had started as a clerk there and was given incremental promotions during his first twenty years. At age 40 in 1897, when he inherited from his uncle John HR a major stake in the bank, Harry became a director, and by 1900 he was general manager.

Harry had a large heart, supported many charities, and, though he wore a conspicuous beaver coat and muffler in winter, was a particularly generous and outspoken advocate of the SPCA. He accepted invitations to balls; attended concerts and the theatre; smoked cigars and dined out often with his friends in men's clubs. A member of the Thistle Curling Club, the Royal Montreal Golf Club, and the St. James Club in Montreal, Harry was also a founding member of the Forest and Stream Club in Dorval, and also there helped found St. Mark's Church.

Harry never married, but from the time he met her until he died, he loved a woman named Florence Nightingale Morris. Florence was married to Molson's cousin, Alexander Webb Morris (no relation to Sir Edward Morris). The three of them developed an unusual relationship, described as "an open secret" in Dorval, where Florence was seen as often in Harry's company as in her husband's. The paternity of the Morrisses' four sons, the eldest of whom was named Harry, was never questioned. Yet Molson lived with the Morrisses in the 1880s until he bought his own house on Mountain Street in 1892. Later, he moved to Edgehill, also in Westmount. Throughout this time he continued to be a frequent guest of the Morrisses, and made significant purchases in multiples of three. In 1897, for example, he bought three bicycles.

Molson, described by the Montreal *Gazette* as "one of the most influential businessmen in Canada," was a handsome dandy. His broad forehead, greying hair, neatly trimmed beard, and intelligent, steady expression were well known. He was always smartly dressed, in a houndstooth jacket, high collar and watch chain–and a diamond stickpin in the shape of a lucky horseshoe, which Florence had given him.

The Morrisses and Molson owned adjacent summer houses in Dorval, where they would frequently go yachting together. Both men were members of the Royal St. Lawrence Yacht Club there. Molson's yacht *Alycone* was, at forty tons and seventy-five feet, one of the largest in the area. The yacht *Dream* was co-owned by Molson and Morris. Other yachts Harry bought and sold included *Wide Awake, Idle Hour, Lassie, Petrel, Red Coat* and *Noslom,* a palindrome of his name. Molson and Morris entered races together, sometimes competing against each other.

Alexander Morris led a relatively high-profile life as well. Between 1892 and 1896 he was a provincial cabinet minister (under Taillon), and later became provincial treasurer. He was also a Dorval town council member, and commodore of the yacht club. One day during a race in July 1893, when a violent storm burst over Lake St. Louis and capsized and wrecked several yachts, Morris, a participant, "did heroic rescue work at the risk of his own life." He returned to land, calling for volunteers to go back with him and help. Three men went with him into the raging storm. They succeeded, at the risk of their own lives, in hauling many of the yachtsmen struggling in the water over the side of the *Idle Hour.* It was described as "one of the most heroic acts ever witnesses in the Montreal district," and Morris was awarded a medal soon after.

In March 1912, Harry visited England on Molsons Bank business and was booked to return to Canada on the *Titanic.* His friend and fellow yacht club member, Arthur Puechen, had persuaded Harry to return to North America with him aboard the much-lauded ship. Puechen was president of the Standard Chemical Company and a major in the Canadian militia. (He was one of the few men who would survive the disaster, only to suffer the stigma of public accusation of cowardice.)

Molson, whose net worth in December 1911 was calculated to be $699,474 (worth approximately seven million dollars in today's terms), was the wealthiest Canadian passenger on board the *Titanic,* and could well have afforded a stateroom. Instead, he paid thirty pounds ten shillings for cabin number C-30, a relatively unpretentious inside cabin on the upper deck–without portholes or private bath.

According to the "1912 U.S. Senate Hearing on the Titanic Disaster," the night the ship struck the iceberg, Harry had dined with the other first-class passengers including Major Puechen, Charles Hays (president of the Grand Trunk Railway), and Charles's wife, Clara. As Puechen remembered, it was an "exceptionally good dinner." Afterwards he and Molson went to have some coffee, then retired to the smoking room with some of the other men. When the *Titanic* struck the iceberg later that evening, the major immediately went to find Harry, but he wasn't in his room. Puechen never saw him again.

Harry Molson's remains were never recovered. The family erected a memorial grave stone near the Molson Vaults in the Mount Royal Cemetery, bearing the inscription "Psalm 77, Verse 19, Thy way is in the sea, and Thy path is the great waters, and Thy footsteps are not known." He had left his house in Dorval and $30,000 to Florence Morris. His house in Montreal, his mahogany dining room set, his vast collection of clocks and all his fine china were left to his brother Fred.

In early September 1914, recruiting posters were hung over the "Peace Year" banners that still graced the Montreal Exhibition. Suddenly there was khaki everywhere. Red Cross meetings were held in place of moving-picture shows. People began to cluster at bulletin boards to read about the latest developments in the war that was expected to be over by Christmas.

Percy Molson joined a McGill training corps in September 1914, qualifying first as a lieutenant, then as captain six months later. In April 1915, after obtaining authorization from the Canadian Militia Department, Percy and George C. MacDonald raised the second University Company to reinforce the Princess Patricia's Canadian Light Infantry. George was in command, and Percy second in command. In May, Percy, along with George and other friends, attended training camp at Niagara-on-the-Lake. In October Percy went off to France–as lieutenant–to join members of the Princess Pat's, among them his friend Talbot Papineau.

Jennie wrote to her son twice a week, beginning the day he left Montreal. Percy also received regular letters from his sisters Naomi, Evelyn, Mabel and Lily, his nephew Jack, and many friends. He wrote back to them all. Gifts of candy, brandy, coffee, sausages, honey, shortbread and almonds arrived for him. Walter sent him footballs and baseballs; Mabel sent him books; and Jennie, socks. Percy wrote to Jack, who was now thirteen years old:

> *"Somewhere in France"*
>
> *Dec 1st 1915*
>
> *My Dear Jack,*
> *I meant to have written to you some time ago and to have told you how useful the shoes you gave me have been. I wear them frequently and they are fine and comfortable and warm. I have not seen any real fighting yet, but we are within sound of the heavy guns and can hear the firing continually. I went over to see Uncle Herbert the other day, and was within two [illeg.] of the trenches. I saw two German aeroplanes over our lines, and it was quite exciting to hear our anti-aircraft gunfire at them, and then to see the puffs of smoke and the flashes as the shells burst near them. I do not know what happened as we were motoring in one direction and the aeroplanes were going in the other and were soon out of sight.*
>
> *your affectionate uncle Percy*

Percy's trench kit, which he checked every day, included his Colt revolver, map case and maps, prismatic compass, pliers, knives, spoons, spirit flasks, mess tin, water bottle, blanket, shorts, boots, socks and stockings, writing case, raincoat, field message book, toilet holdall, silver folding cup, periscope, wire cutters, puttees and slippers. Most of these items were his life's essentials. His silver folding cup was a gift and had his initials engraved on it. This, and the socks his mother knitted, were his most treasured links to home.

Jack, who had begun his first term at Ashbury College, cherished his uncle Percy's letters, reading them over and over.

> *Belgium*
>
> *March 31st 1916*
>
> *My Dear Jack,*
> *You will be interested to know that I am writing this letter from the front line. I am in a dugout in the trenches quite close to the Germans, and although the shell and rifle fire is continuous, I am just*

as safe as you are, so long as a big fellow does not land on top of the roof. It is not quite so safe when we go outside. Granny has sent me several of your letters and I have seen a copy of your school newspaper. I am very glad to hear that you are getting along so well at the school and that you seem to like it so well. It will be very nice for us all out here to get back to Canada again, and I am looking forward very much to seeing you all again. I have been very interested from time to time to hear news of Nick. He seems to be a great comfort to Granny. You will be glad to know that I wear your slippers continuously and have found them a great comfort & convenience.

Lots of love from Your Uncle Percy

At the end of May 1916, Percy and the other Princess Patricia's were back in France. Under the command of Lieutenant-Colonel Herbert Buller, they had been brought in to defend the 1st and 4th Canadian Montreal Mounted Rifles north of the Ypres-Menin road. Percy's battalion formed a left flank to cover them from imminent attack. On the afternoon of June 2, an unanticipated barrage of fire and shelling began. Moments after 1 p.m., four mines exploded just short of the Canadian Mounted Rifles trenches. The Patricia's saw whole sections of trench disappear while trees and earth hurtled down. Wave after wave of German battalions advanced over Mount Sorrel, the first line with fixed bayonets, grenades and wire cutters, the second line with entrenching tools and sandbags. The Princess Pat's raked the Germans with machine-gun fire, but the enemy kept coming. Someone arrived with the news that five German battalions were supporting the four marching now, and that six more were in reserve. They were marching over the filled-in trenches and into "the cloud of dust and dirt," stepping over the half-buried wounded, and skirting tree trunks and machinery.

As the bombardment increased, Percy's trench became untenable. Buller fell; he had taken a direct hit and died instantly. Percy and another lieutenant withdrew their men to the left trench, from which they continued to try to stall the enemy's advance. The other lieutenant was struck, badly wounded in both legs, and Percy was left to lead the desperate resistance. Then he was struck through the face by a German bullet.

The Princess Patricia's held out successfully for eighteen hours, isolated from the rest of the battalions, all their officers killed or wounded. The battle cost the PPCLI more than 400 casualties, including 150 killed. Arthur Currie and Philip Mackenzie were among those wounded that same day; both of them had been with Percy since the day they signed up.

Fortunately, Percy's wound was not life-threatening. The bullet had entered his left cheek and then came out through his right one, fracturing his jaw. At No. 7 Stationary Hospital in Boulogne, where he was taken, Percy's jaws were wired and he was told they would have to be kept immobile for at least six weeks. He stayed in Boulogne a month. In July between x-rays and minor operations, he started taking driving lessons.

Meanwhile, Herbert took a course at the Royal School of Infantry in Halifax before enlisting in the 5th Royal Highlanders of Canada–also known as the Black Watch Regiment. In early 1915, his company became the 42nd Battalion, Canadian Expeditionary Force. He arrived in Belgium as company commander in November, and wrote to Bessie on the sixteenth:

> *We had quite an experience yesterday. Just after we had received your letters, the Germans opened up on us with their 5.9 howitzers and made things lively here. One shell struck in front of our house about twenty yards away and smashed every pane of glass in the place, blew out my two oil lamps and covered us with dirt. The sense of being shelled is quite extraordinary. There is a hum in the air and everyone says, "Here's another." Then the thing to do is to stand close to some good wall and away from the doors and windows.*

Herbert wrote to his children on November 27:

> *The camp is nearly all little bivouacs or dug-outs holding 3 or 4 men each and it looks like a lot of muskrat or beaver houses. They are dug*

down in the ground and then walls are made of sandbags filled with earth and a canvas roof put over … Uncle Percy walked in to-day and told me that he was only about 6 or 8 miles away from me and from what I hear our regiments are to be put in the same brigade so that we will be close together all winter. Percy looks very well and so did Major Hamilton Gault who is with him. There is a big observation balloon just over us. It goes up every morning and is tied to the ground and the man in it watches the Germans and telephones what he sees. I was told that I can go up in it. Wouldn't Tom like that. I wish he was here to see it. He would enjoy watching the German aeroplanes too.

Just before Christmas, Herbert wrote Bessie:

The mud we are getting accustomed to but it is indescribable. You wade through it from the time you step out of your tent and some places are so deep that you actually get stuck. An officer named Col. McLeod coming home at night a little while ago fell into a hole and was found dead the next day. His feet stuck in the mud and he was drowned close to his billet. We always carry an electric torch at night as to walk without it is very unpleasant and difficult … I think I'll close now with lots of love to the kiddies. I wish I had them all here for a few minutes. I'd hug them to death.

In other letters to Bessie, Herbert described more of his thoughts and feelings:

New Year's Day, 1916

I am so fond of these men that they seem to have become fond of me. I only hope I may continue to deserve their trust and affection as I have really become attached to them as if they were my children. They are like children, to be taught, cared for, and punished and with power such as I have to use or abuse they are so dependent on me & my officers. Even my scapegoats, I'm fond of, and as sometimes happens, I step outside the law a little & say, "Will you take my punishment or go to the Colonel?" of course they will take mine every time.

May 1, 1916

We are in a battalion support just behind the firing line in the middle of what was once a beautiful wood and although badly battered about by shell fire is still in its spring foliage, a fine sight. Trees of course,

> *smashed and knocked down are common but the forest is still lovely and the quantities of song birds would rejoice the heart of Mother and Naomi. In the early morning at daybreak it is like a huge aviary, the little songsters twittering away like mad. Yesterday morning, I heard a cuckoo exactly like its imitator the cuckoo clock. The birds pay no attention to the war and altho at the present moment of writing the Germans are sending in some huge shells, the little birds go on singing merrily. The rats also go about their business in spite of the huge explosions.*

On the first day of the battle of Sanctuary Wood, the 42nd Battalion was ordered forward to Mount Sorrel to reinforce the Patricia's. As Herbert prepared to leave, a shell landed nearby, fracturing his skull. He had his wound dressed at the aid station but "refused to leave the line, and remained with his company throughout the action."

Herbert and Percy were brought back to Canada in July 1916 aboard a crowded hospital ship. Doctors had cautioned Herbert, who had undergone an operation to remove shrapnel from his skull, not to take much exercise. Colonel E.A. Baker, who had been blinded (and who would later become head of the World Council for the Blind), was on the same ship. Every day during that voyage Herbert read to him, while Percy, who could not talk because of his jaw wound, walked the colonel around the crowded deck.

On August 10, 1916, Percy and Herbert arrived in Canada on sick leave. In a letter dated August 27, 1916, from Little Métis Beach, Quebec, Percy wrote to Kenneth:

> *Herbert and I have both spent most of the last two weeks here and are enjoying ourselves thoroughly. We are both getting along well and I have been playing golf in moderation. I find however that my jaws are taking a long time to open up and I am still on soft foods … Métis does not change much and many of the old time faces are still around. Old Jack Astle is the same as twenty years ago although somewhat older and more staid.*

Percy's leave, at first recommended for three months, was extended twice, the second time to April 1, 1917. Both Herbert and Percy were awarded the Military Cross for gallantry at the Ypres Salient, and Percy was promoted from lieutenant to captain.

When war began in Europe, Billy Van Horne was seven years old. The only child of Edith Molson (daughter of Dr. Alexander Molson) and Bennie Van Horne, and the only grandchild of Sir William, Billy basked in the indulgent attention of the adults in his life. He was enrolled at Selwyn House, a private day school for boys. Billy lived with his parents and grandparents in the house in which he was born, the Van Horne mansion on Sherbrooke Street. Every summer he played at a "spacious and harmonious" summer home, Covenhoven, near St. Andrews in New Brunswick. His paternal grandfather enveloped the boy with love.

Billy's every wish was Sir William's command. The summer of 1914 Sir William ordered six model ships from an expert and well-known craftsman in St. Andrews–exclusively for Billy to use as targets for his toy guns. Billy sank them all in the Covenhoven lily pond, and his grandfather ordered six more. When Billy expressed an interest in the Model T Ford, Sir William had a child-sized replica made for the boy.

Billy's Selwyn House classmates remember being invited frequently to the Van Horne mansion. One afternoon, Sir William filled an entire room with a new electric train set–complete with engine, cars, track and landscape–as a surprise for his grandson. His friends were amazed and envious, but Billy announced that train sets bored him. Every day he was away from his grandson, most often attending railway business, Sir William sent a postcard to him. When his grandson was three years old Sir William enlarged Covenhoven, added a nursery in which he installed all Dutch furnishings and (being both an avid art collector and amateur painter himself), painted a frieze on the wall.

Young Billy was kept uninformed of news so that he would not be disturbed by a conflict somewhere outside the perimeter of his world. There was, unfortunately, a great deal of conflict within his own environment, much that he felt but could not articulate at the age of seven.

Billy may have been aware, at some level, of his mother's unhappiness. Mrs. Van Horne had noticed her daughter-in-law looked "worn and sad." Yet public decorum prevailed. At the Sherbrooke Street mansion, Edith and the elder Mrs. Van Horne entertained a stream of guests that included Sir Hamilton and Lady Gault, the Ogilvys, the Morgans, railway financier R.B. Angus, and Miss Edgar and Miss Cramp (spinster teachers who occupied a Victorian mansion from which they ran a girls' school). Before the war, extravagance was in vogue and Van Horne's CPR was pulling in a hundred million dollars a year. Most of their guests would have thought Edith was crazy to be unhappy.

Billy's father, Bennie Van Horne, had been working in New York for a year. Bennie, himself a victim of his parents' "intense, ultimately destructive love," struggled with his addictions to alcohol and gambling. No one spoke about Bennie's problems or overtly acknowledged that there was anything wrong, although Edith's father, Dr. Alexander Molson, and her father-in-law, Sir William, did what they could. Dr. Molson offered Edith holidays in Kennebunk Beach in Maine. Sir William made his son vice-president, then president, of the Cuba Company Railroad, which kept Bennie in New York for sixteen years.

Still in her twenties, she became devout, stern, and seemed to have lost all her joy. Like many women of her age during the Great War, she never married.

Chapter Twenty-Nine

A Knockout Blow

December 25, 1916
556 Pine Avenue, Montreal

Aunt Lily ceases brushing her long red hair in front of the mirror, and Jack watches while she twists it up with a few deft movements of fingers and hairpins. It is one of those things that awes and eludes him, one of those things that women seem effortlessly to absorb from other women, like the not-quite-magic of weaving, needlepoint or knitting. Lily is fifty-two years old, has never married, and treats her young nieces and nephews with a matronly, indulgent affection.

"Master Jack," she says as she notices the fourteen-year-old boy, her eyes glistening as she peers at him from behind her glasses, "you are looking more and more like your uncle Percy every day."

Jack blushes with pleasure. "Merry Christmas, Aunt Lily."

The boy is hoping his favourite uncle will come for dinner tonight, for, between Percy's time overseas and Jack's terms at boarding school in Ottawa, he hasn't seen him for nearly a year and a half. Uncle Herbert and Aunt Bessie will be coming of course, with Tom, Dorothy, Betty and young Hartland. Jack knows that Herbert had been in France with Percy, and although they were in different regiments, they had been injured within days of each other and had been invalided home.

Jack isn't sure if his father will arrive. Isabel doesn't like coming to family dinners. Jack knows it has something to do with alcohol. Her recurring "illness" is one of the things no one likes to speak about, least of all to him.

Grannie has hired extra cook's helpers for the occasion; the most delicious aromas have been emanating from the kitchen all afternoon. The Christmas tree graces the hall where the porcelain umbrella stand used to be. Percy's polished trophies and cups gleam in the study. Pillows are plumped in the sitting room; the dragons on the painted Chinese panels look fierce and fantastical in the dim light.

Delicate Dresden ornaments seem to glow in the dining room cabinet. A maid in a green frock and white apron stands on a dining room chair to dust a brass chandelier; another maid is near the sideboard, polishing the last of the silver. Holly and evergreens twist among the plump cupid-pedestals supporting the banquet lamps at each end of the table.

A housemaid takes the various parcels and presents and places them under the towering Christmas tree in the front hall. The Molsons are all modestly conscious of the finery about them. Like most other Montrealers, they have become accustomed to living plainly and frugally as part of the war effort. They are used to "meatless Fridays" and "fuelless Sundays." This reunion is one to be grateful for, a precious few hours laced with laughter and hope. Sweet things have been hoarded and saved, and Mabel has even found oranges somewhere. Nuts and sweetmeats are assembled in bowls. At either end of the table, cut crystal dishes cradle salt and carved ivory salt-spoons. Twenty-two table settings of white and gold English china are lined up on the monogrammed damask table cloth.

It seems as if the house is suddenly filled with people. Jennie is welcoming Charlotte Spragge, Herbert, Bessie, Walter and his wife Mary, Naomi and her husband Claude Robin, and Evelyn and her husband Colin Russel. The children, some of whom Jack hasn't seen since Métis last summer, are dressed in their best frocks and suits. Looking mildly uncertain at first, the young cousins move into the drawing room and begin to re-establish their familiarity with each other. Neither Jack's father Kenneth nor his uncle Percy is here yet.

Herbert, who smells faintly of pipe tobacco, is leaning over his mother's chair in the drawing room.

"You're right, Mother. It's not fair to the servants to hold dinner off any longer. Don't worry, Percy will be here soon."

The adults, Jack gathers, are not expecting Kenneth. But some of them hadn't seen Percy since he went overseas, and keep anxious eyes on the door.

The ship's bell Grannie uses as a dinner gong is from the old *Nooya,* and it makes a wonderful rich clang when the cook rings it. Jack is aware of a last-minute scurry in the kitchen.

Maids in blue frocks and white aprons bring the bowls of oyster soup to each place; black-uniformed stewards fill the water goblets. Herbert clears his throat and says a blessing. Just after the murmur of amens has travelled around the table, one of the stewards suddenly pulls back the only empty chair and sits in it. A palpable shock settles upon the guests. The table is quiet until the moment the new hand reaches out for the table napkin and the new face lifts to grin. Then there is a shriek, and happy clamour.

"What's wrong? You don't recognize me out of uniform any more?" Percy laughs.

"You may have been in the wrong profession all this time," jokes Walter. "What a capital disguise!"

Mabel pinches him. "How long have you been here? Oh, you rascal! Were you hiding in the kitchen?"

Percy's friend Philip Mackenzie had pulled this joke before; Percy is delighted that he's amused his family now. He bends to kiss his mother's cheek, then shakes Herbert's hand. Before he sits down he raises a glass of sauterne and proposes a toast.

"To the gallant efforts of the ladies, for all their knitting and their nursing–in short, for their devotion–I raise this glass." The men stand to toast the ladies. Percy has lost a lot of weight, and his face looks different. Jack tries not to stare.

Covered platters are placed between the evergreen boughs on the table. Grannie raises the lids, revealing braised turkey and delicate *croustade* of potatoes. Jack longs to ask both his uncles about the war. Voices rise and fall about the table.

Jack reaches under the table and passes bits of food to the dogs, Jerry and Nick. Only his cousin Tom notices. Mabel is telling Walter that Ashbury's headmaster had sent her a favourable report about Jack from school. Jack tells his uncles about the fire at the English master's house. He and the other boys had carried Mr. Philpot's furniture out of his burning house and helped to keep the flames down until the fire brigade arrived, and they had earned a half-day off school for their efforts.

Grannie tells the children about the history of the silverware they are holding. Over a hundred years earlier their grandfather's grandfather had collected silver coins left from the French regime in Montreal, then melted them down into silverware for his sons when they married. The children's eyes follow the portraits of their ancestors on the dining room walls. Herbert stands and proposes another toast.

"To all of those who have fallen in this great war," he says solemnly.

"And to our ancestors … " adds Lily.

"Hear, hear."

The dinner is punctuated by the snap of Christmas crackers that Aunt Lily hands around; each bang makes Jerry bark while Nick takes cover under a chair.

The dessert, a Chantilly pudding, impresses everyone, much to the pleasure of the cook who is hovering near the kitchen door. Crumbled macaroons and candied fruit lashed with sherry fill the hollowed-out vanilla sponge cake, generously glazed with raspberry jam and sprinkled with green pistachio bits. The pudding is topped with a mountain of whipped cream.

"How does this compare to boarding school food, lads?" asks Walter, directing his question with a wink to Tom and Jack.

The ribbons of conversation that rise and fall are presided over by Grannie, who has never looked happier.

The ladies begin to murmur, gathering before they step out to the drawing room. Maids follow them with coffee trays, and the French doors close behind them. The men reach to loosen their ties and pull out their pipes. Jack nibbles politely on the mincemeat pies and sips his tea. The conversation drifts to the minister of munitions Sam Hughes's resignation and whether conscription will be enforced in Quebec. Herbert brings up the topic of the Belgian breweries–how Germany has stolen all their large copper kettles, cast iron mash tuns and lead pipes, which it will melt down and convert into ammunition.

Percy recites part of a comic's monologue: "We had a sarge who stuttered, and it took him so long to say 'Halt' that twenty-seven of us marched overboard. Then they lined us up on the pier, and the captain said 'Fall in,' and I said, 'I have been in, Sir.' "

Jack hears Herbert's chugging "like a train" laughter, the result of his unsuccessful attempts to suppress it, which causes others to laugh the more.

Tom is happy just being there in the company of his father and uncles, enclosed in the velvet and mahogany room, listening to their gravelly voices, matching his wits at a game of chess with his cousin. His father and his uncle are heroes in the family, and soon he will follow in their footsteps by enrolling at the Royal Military College and donning the glamorous uniform of the cadets. He studies the carved ivory rooks and bishops, then looks up at the ancestral portraits, forgets about the game for a moment, and thinks about the people he never knew. Then someone winds the Victrola and a serenade fills the room. The smoke from the pipes disperses into the music. It is dancing music, to be sure, music for light-footed waltzing on a stage lit brightly by hope.

Jack looks at Percy and meets his eyes for a moment. Mixed emotions pass swiftly between them, though neither speaks. So much has changed since the war, thinks Jack, so much has been given, and lost, so much altered, so many lives spent. It is not over yet. Jack ever after will decline mincemeat pies at Christmas, for the taste will bring back the bittersweet memory of this evening's family reunion, the mingling of laughter and horror, music and smoke, courage and loss.

July 4, 1917

Jennie, Lily, Mabel and Jack are in Métis when the news comes. Mabel sees her mother's fingers stiffen over the receiver. They had been dreading the jangle of the telephone, but couldn't be far from it for long. Jennie puts the receiver back; she sits down, and covers her face with her hands. A whole minute passes before she can speak.

"Percy's been killed."

Mabel's greatest fear is hearing this very news. Surely she must be imagining hearing it now. Grief begins to engulf her. She and Lily had both felt something dreadful, both had known. Could she not have stopped her brother from returning to France? She steps backward, moving in slow motion in her stockinged feet on the worn wood floor, her eyes closed in denial and disbelief.

Percy's close friend Talbot Papineau wrote a difficult, moving letter to Walter Molson:

> *July 5, 1917*
>
> *Dear Walter,*
> *I know you will be anxious to hear about poor old Percy. He was killed last night while in the front line but he was mercifully spared all pain and all disfigurement. He with another officer and 2 runners were standing talking together when a trench mortar bomb apparently exploded right between them. Three of them, including Percy were killed instantaneously by the concussion alone. There is not a mark upon him. He will be buried close by and you will be advised of the exact location of the grave. He was killed in Avion [near Vimy Ridge]. I visited Percy in his dug-out yesterday late afternoon. He was in good heart and spirits despite the fact that he had been in rather an unpleasant spot. I need not tell you how deeply we all feel his death and the very serious loss which the regiment has suffered. I don't think we ever had an officer more universally liked and respected. He was truly without fear and without reproach. I have never known him to say or do anything which would not have satisfied the highest standards of thought and conduct. I have often heard Charlie Stewart say that he would gladly serve Percy any time and we all expected that he would be one of the main supports of the Regt. It is not easy to realize he is gone. Always his memory will be very fresh and he will merely seem to be away. With my own deepest sympathy to you and all his loved ones and with the deep sympathy of the others in the battalion,*
>
> *Your affectionate friend*
>
> *Talbot*

The regiment's founder, Hamilton Gault, expressed his sympathy to Herbert:

> *Friday, July 7, 1917*
>
> *My Dear Herbert,*
> *You will have received [the] wire giving you the sad news of dear old Percy's death. He was doing the night rounds of his posts and was*

standing in the street of a suburb (you know where!) with one of his Officers and two runners when a Trench Mortar came out of the night and got the four of them. Percy and his Subaltern were killed instantly and also one of the runners. To-day we buried them in the Military Burial Ground at Villers au Bois Station. The R.C.R. Padre conducted the service with our Padre (McCarthy the R.C.). In attendance, a number of Officers, from the Division and other near by Units, came, and a detachment from our details with those of our Officers left out were on parade. We are all more deeply grieved than words can say. Percy had had his company since his return to France, and needless to say was doing splendidly with it.

I shall ever regret having urged the needs of the Battalion upon him, for had he not returned to the Regiment he would have been spared to the Canada of the future and to his friends to whom he meant so much.

I am enclosing a letter to your Mother.

Would you mind forwarding it to her …

Always sincerely,

Hamilton Gault

At first Mabel thought she would never stop crying. The doctor prescribed her a sleeping draught. Letters came for her, praising her brother, with lines that blurred on the pages. "He was the noblest man I have ever known." "I don't think we ever had an officer more universally liked and respected." "He was truly without fear and without reproach." "I have never known him to say or do anything which would not have satisfied the highest standards of thought and conduct." He was, PPCLI Captain Agar Adamson concluded with undisguised affection, "a great sportsman with the mind of a child with infinite sight. We would probably find a halo constantly over his head."

Herbert wrote to Mabel in August:

I realize very fully that the sad blow has hit you harder than the rest of us as we have our own families who naturally are close to our hearts at the front and even here in England we have become accustomed to

> *news of death and wounds and have become somewhat resigned to whatever bad news may come and we cannot realize fully what it means to you at home and far away to hear of the loss of your best beloved brother ... mother has stood the shock bravely ...*

Lily, who called the news "a knockout blow" in a letter to Mabel, added, "but we've got to carry on like thousands of others." But Mabel would never be the same. It was as though a shadow had passed over her countenance and stayed there. At the age of thirty-nine, she became devout, stern, and seemed to have lost all her joy.

Another close friend of Percy's, and fellow officer in the PPCLI, was Philip Mackenzie, whose wife had just given birth when news came of Percy's death. He had been one of many friends who called Percy "Mole," an abbreviation of his surname and a reference that came of his having been put on command-tunnelling when the Patricia's had first arrived in France. Mackenzie wrote to Kenneth on July 9 from Mille Roches, Pointe au Pic, Quebec:

> *Dear Kenneth,*
>
> *I have just received Creighton's telegram–an hour after our little girl was born–telling me of Percy's death and the whole damned world is upside down. Of course, I could try to express my sympathy to you in a hundred ways, but what is the use and why should I–for I have lost the truest friend a man ever had. It hurts to think of Mrs. Molson. Forgive this, but I cannot realize that our dear old Mole is gone.*
> *Yours,*
>
> *Philip Mackenzie*

Wishing to spare his wife Helen (called Nell) the shock, Philip tried to keep the devastating news from her as long as he could. On July 13, Philip Mackenzie wrote to Mabel:

> *Dear Miss Molson,*
>
> *I have written a very short note to Mrs. Molson and another to Kenneth ... and now I am writing to you. God knows what for, perhaps because I am selfish enough to want to shift some of my burden on to you. I must talk to some one. My heart is sore and with it a*

feeling of rage–that will last until the end of time. The real feeling of loss, I suppose, will come later when I realize fully that I am not again to see the truest man I have ever known and who made up for years practically the whole of my life ... A telegram was handed to me only a half an hour after [our] little girl was born and for a while I could not think ... Poor little Nell would have written to you long ago–but she does not know–we are afraid to tell her, I know it would break her heart; we must keep it from her as long as we can, so please understand why she has not sent you a line ... If it had been a boy, the child was to have been called after Percy–and as it is a girl she will be called after him just the same. I may tell you and I think you will believe, that I would, if possible, express my love for him by changing places with him now so that he might be given back to his family and his friends.

Yours,

Philip Mackenzie

Still ignorant of Percy's death after the birth of her daughter, Nell wrote cheerfully to Mabel: "Philip has decided he would like to christen her Percival [she was given the name Percival Molson Mackenzie*] and call her Percy, what do you think of that? She really is perfectly sweet ... she's not a bit pretty, really, in fact she looks more like the old Queen Victoria than anyone else, but she's very healthy & remarkably good ..."

The well-intentioned lie was impossible to sustain in the face of the grief of their friends. Nell found out, and in due course wrote again to Mabel:

My dear,

Philip only told me last night. I think he felt that we both loved the old Mole so greatly that the shock might upset me and therefore the baby, & the doctor advised him to wait until I was stronger. Mabel dear I can only send you my love & my sympathy & long with all my heart to do some little thing to help you all in your great sorrow. The Mole was so much to us both. So much more I think than most people realized, that I think we can understand in a small measure what you are going through. Philip has been a wonder for he has borne his great sorrow all by himself these last two weeks though sometimes I have wondered why he was so blue.

*Percival Molson (Mackenzie) Ritchie is an acclaimed artist living in British Columbia.

In his will Percy directed that $75,000 be given to McGill University to complete the construction of a stadium. The "Percival Molson Memorial Stadium" was completed in 1919. Percy's uniforms, clothing, and kit bag were distributed to junior officers. On the cross at his grave at the military burial ground, someone scrawled, "A gentleman."

A referendum was scheduled for April 10. "Is it your opinion that the sale of light beer, cider and wine as defined by law, should be allowed?"

CHAPTER THIRTY

TEMPERANCE BREWS

FRED MOLSON's three sons, Bert, Stuart and John Henry Molson, were all ambitious men, each in a different way. Bert, who'd begun his career at the Bank of Montreal, entered the brewery in 1911. He and his brothers each answered the call when war was declared. Bert, age thirty-two in 1914, was turned down because of underdeveloped arches. Bert's younger brothers joined the army when they became eighteen: Stuart in 1914 and John Henry in 1915.

Stuart in particular had long wanted to make the army his career. He had joined the Royal Highlanders in 1912 when he was sixteen, and travelled to Valcartier, Quebec, for training with the Canadian Expeditionary Force in September 1914. Before leaving for overseas, Stuart was commissioned as a lieutenant in the 13th Battalion Royal Scots, known as "The Black Watch."

Stuart Molson exuded confidence. From the time he was a boy he exhibited a fascination with guns, ammunition, target practice, and shooting game such as rabbit and partridge. He took apart a single-shot rifle and converted it into a machine gun. He was, according to his cousin Jack, "a harum-scarum sort of chap."

In February 1915, the first Canadian contingent reached France, and Stuart was among them. Before two months had passed, he was wounded at the beginning of the Battle of Festubert. Stuart was operated on twice for minor injuries. He was promoted to captain and returned to his unit a few weeks later. His record was one of achievements and perseverance. During his three years with the Black Watch, Stuart earned three awards: the Star, the British War Medal and the Victory Medal. By all appearances he felt at ease in the military life and maintained himself in excellent physical shape, but stress that he internalized would manifest itself through stomach ulcers. By 1917 his ulcers had worsened enough to lead him to be declared medically unfit for combat, and he was transferred to transport service. Even so, twice more he attempted to re-enlist (first in Canada, and again in England), but was turned down both times. He then tried to join the air force and was turned down there as well.

John Henry, the youngest of Fred's three sons, was nineteen in the spring of 1915. He joined McGill's training corps, and enlisted with the Black Watch in July 1915. He sailed for England in October 1917; by then Stuart had returned to Canada.

On October 10, 1918, while John Henry's unit was fighting near the front lines at Les Fosses Farm in Sailly (not far from Cambrai), he, another officer and fifty other men found themselves cut off from the rest of their unit. Realizing they would soon be completely overrun, they made a desperate last-minute attempt to inch on their bellies along an old railway embankment, but it was only two feet high and they were discovered. With a quarter mile of "flooded country" behind them and "Huns on all sides of us," as John Henry wrote grimly, one man tried to swim but was shot and drowned. Then a bullet flicked John Henry's temple. Fortunately he was able to apply pressure and a clean dressing to stop the bleeding from his wound; but five others had been seriously wounded, and there was clearly nothing else for the men to do but surrender. He'd never imagined a scenario in which this might happen to him. As he admitted in his diary later, it presented an emotional struggle:

Cannot describe my feelings. Have always looked with admiration on those who are taken prisoner when badly wounded and who are left with a revolver in each hand to face the Hun. Have never thought of being made prisoner this way or any other way so my ideas are all confused.

The Canadians were forced to "march some distance" to the German divisional headquarters to be interrogated, and a "Hun officer" offered John Henry and another wounded officer a drive. They were told "with great decision" that the Germans would make a last stand on the Metz-Namur-Liège line. "I am afraid," concluded John Henry in an ironic understatement, "we were inclined not to believe him."

John Henry noted that he and his comrades were lucky that their captors were "fairly decent" to them, particularly that none of them took any of the prisoners' private things. There existed some measure of mutual respect, and at no time during the weeks of their captivity did John Henry and the other Canadians feel that their well-being was threatened. However, food was a constant problem. At first there was only coffee and "vile Hun bread." Later they would be offered "queer soup," on another day "rotten soup," and finally, "sauerkraut … awful stuff."

John Henry soon became disabused of his "fairly decent" captors. On October 12, he abruptly declined a ride to their second destination twenty kilometres beyond, walking with the enlisted men instead. Arriving "footsore and weary" that night, they slept on the bare floor of a schoolhouse. Members of a French family smuggled food to the prisoners. From there, the men alternately took the train or walked to their other destinations and slept on benches in the station or on cots in a nunnery. Everyone contracted head lice. By October 16, they reached Belgium. There, the local people tried to give the prisoners bread, cheese and meat, but the guards stopped them. John Henry could "hardly walk 100 yards" by the time they joined other prisoners-of-war installed in the upper storey of a one-time leather factory. On November 2, in Nivelles, John Henry was able to sleep in a heap of straw in a hay loft, where he spent his most comfortable night in weeks.

They began to hear rumours of peace and armistice. By November 8, John Henry noticed, the guards were less vigilant, there were "no more sounds of guns, and [the] road [was] crammed with Hun guards and transport" leaving France. On November 14, after a relentless five-day march to get there, they were released at a farmhouse near

Liège. His relief and joy are evident in his enthusiastic descriptions of gustatory pleasures:

> *House just like a paradise to us and we ate loads of bread, butter and jam and drank cups of coffee galore. One hour later we had another huge meal. Most wonderful I have eaten since Canada and home.*

In early December John Henry and other POWs crossed the channel from Calais to Dover. On December 8, eight weeks after his capture, he arrived in London and was reunited with his sister Brenda and brother Stuart.

Another member of the family to join the Black Watch was Walter Molson, John Thomas's youngest son. He went to the front in March 1917, first as a captain and then a major. His unit departed from Halifax on the SS Lapland, which was mined in the Irish Channel but eventually made it safely to Liverpool. Walter asked to be demoted to lieutenant so he could join the lines right away. He was granted leave for Christmas, joined his family in Montreal for five days, and returned to the front in January. Nine months later, the Black Watch was ordered to join other battalions supporting a Canadian Corps attack on the German trenches near Cambrai. The initial attack took the Germans by surprise. The Canadians captured the Canal du Nord, then set to work bridging it to allow the support troops to cross. The Germans, recovering, retaliated with heavy artillery barrage and machine gun fire. The advance continued for another day, with heavy casualties sustained by Canadian battalions. The attack was renewed on September 29, when members of the Black Watch had to cut through hundreds of metres of barbed wire on the Cambrai-Douai road to claim Tilloy Hill. A shell exploded close to Walter, tearing into his arm and thigh.

September 29, 1918

Dr. Lowell Foster is making his way through the military compound referred to locally as the "hospital," set up to the northwest of the Cambrai Road in France. Canadian wounded are coming in fast, and many more are said to be on their way. Ambulatory cases are sent directly on to the trains, possible surgical cases are brought to the operating tents, and those deemed "the hopeless cases" are laid in a big marquee tent.

Dr. Foster enters the marquee tent. As his eyes adjust to the shadows, he is able to see rows of closely packed stretchers that completely fill the room. He tries to disregard the sounds as he scans the men for signs of life, and squats down to assure a man quietly that the chaplain is on his way. A few nurses move among the wounded, offering water.

Foster hesitates, about to step over a pair of feet that are sticking out into the passageway. He looks at the man and sees that he is wearing the uniform of an officer in the Black Watch, his own old regiment. So little of the man is visible–he seems to be completely swathed in blood-soaked bandages–that at first Foster doesn't recognize Walter Molson. He is not moving. Foster picks up the officer's wrist and can feel no pulse. He speaks to him.

Walter opens his eyes. "Is that you, Lowell Foster?" He gives his friend a weak, teeth-chattering smile.

"Nurse!" is Foster's next word. He fears that Walter doesn't have long to live–his wounds are numerous. Already he has gone into shock, his body is covered with a cold clammy sweat, and his skin looks bloodless and pale.

"There's an officer here–he's in a bad way–get him out of here in double-quick time!"

"Yes, doctor." The nurse runs from the tent. Foster strides after her to the door and calls her back.

"Get me a cot in the resuscitation tent," he demands.

"There are only six cots, and they're all–"

"Get me a cot *now.*"

The cot is procured, and Walter is immediately administered stimulants and wrapped entirely in hot blankets. Nurses pack hot-water bottles about him and get the oven going "full blast" underneath his cot. After some time Walter's pulse is stronger, his body heat becomes normal, and a surgeon (whose name has not been recorded) has him brought into the operating tent "to be patched up."

Dr. Foster watches while the surgeon prepares to operate. At first he is horrified to see the extent of his friend's wounds. His right hand is badly mangled by a fragment of shell. The right elbow is completely shattered; in fact, a large hole is visible through the elbow joint. A very large wound has marked his leg; another hole, in the muscle at the back of his thigh, is "large enough to admit a closed fist."

When the surgeon prepares to amputate Walter's arm above the elbow, Dr. Foster objects.

"If the shattered ends of the bone were trimmed and the wound packed," Foster says, "an amputation could be done later at the base, if it's found necessary."

The surgeon follows Foster's suggestion. Walter, who seems to withstand the anaesthetic well, is on the operating table for two hours. He is then taken to the recovery tent.

Foster has to rush to his work, as the wounded are coming in by the hundreds. He is unable to visit Molson again until the next day, a few minutes before he is taken off to the train.

When Walter's wife, Mary Kingman, is told about her husband's injuries she is warned that he may not live through surgery. Mary, who has taken nursing courses through the Red Cross in Montreal, immediately applies to be transferred to the hospital in France where Walter is recuperating.

While Herbert was overseas during the war, Fred ran the brewery with his eldest son, Bert. Beer consumption in Montreal rose during the war years, particularly among those entering the work force. But increased sales did not mean that all went smoothly at the brewery. Difficulties included staff shortages, higher costs, scarcity of raw materials and, perhaps most significantly, a prohibition movement again on the rise.

Fred's annual fishing trip down to the lower St. Lawrence was not interrupted during the war. He would always send a box of salmon as a gift to the executives. In the summer of 1914 he'd had a house built at Métis for his wife Catherine, and called it "Birchcliffe," which became better known as "Mother's Rest."

Fred looked forward to these forays so much that as the season approached he would overhaul his tackle, order newfangled fishing equipment from England, and pore over his collection of flies. He would take the coastal steamer from Quebec to Rivière du Loup, drop Catherine off at "Mother's Rest" in Métis, and then cross to Godbout. The steamer was often packed with tourists. On one occasion it was so full, the captain apologized to Fred and offered him his own cabin. Fred turned to a friend who had arrived behind him. "I've just acquired the captain's cabin, and I'll rent you the floor," he joked. By 1916 Fred had purchased his own yacht, the *M.V. Edamena.* He joined his brother as a member of the Royal St. Lawrence Yacht Club, and sailed to Godbout himself every year thereafter.

Temperance brews were introduced in Canada by law in 1918. Beer could not exceed 4.4 percent alcohol (volume). Early in the year, the most comprehensive prohibition bill ever introduced in Quebec was tabled by Lomer Gouin, and passed soon afterward, to take effect in fourteen months.

Fred and Bert feared they'd have to close the brewery. One story claims that a seminary in Montreal suggested to Fred that if they gradually increased the strength of the beer back to its former level, the authorities would never know. Fred refused. Tom, now in his final year at Bishop's College School (BCS), wrote to his father, Herbert. Would he still be able to attend the Royal Military College in Kingston, as he had hoped? Herbert's reply has survived:

> *Don't worry about going to college; Daddy has enough to educate his children & take care of them even if the brewery closes but we may not be able to do all that we like to do, and if the business was closed we would have to decide what to do with you and Hartland after the war as you have to work and can't be idle.*

In June 1918, Tom graduated from BCS, winning the Governor General's medal, the Pattee Shield, the Old Boy's Prize, the Classics Prize and the Sixth Form French Prize. He wrote the entrance exam for the Royal Military College, placing second out of 138 applications from across Canada.

Many of the women in the Molson family were actively supporting the war effort in Montreal. Not only Walter's wife Mary Kingman, but also John Thomas's daughters, Evelyn and Mabel, had enrolled in Red Cross courses. In 1915 their cousin Mary, wife of Dinham Molson, a grandson of John Molson Junior, founded the Khaki Club, a volunteer-run agency that arranged accommodation for soldiers in Montreal. Mary made sure that the Khaki Club's headquarters, first on Dorchester Street and later on Bishop Street, provided an atmosphere in which the men would feel at home. Dinham, who was manager of a local branch of Molsons Bank, helped his wife at the club as well.

With Jack away at boarding school, Mabel Molson did volunteer work at the club with her cousin Mary.

November 9, 1918

Mabel Molson opens the door of the nondescript house on Bishop Street. A handsome soldier with a bright spark of amusement in his eye is standing on the step. Colonel Bill Sutherland takes his cap off to address her.

"Good afternoon, Miss. They told me at the station that I could find comfortable quarters if I called at this address."

Mabel, like Mary and the other volunteers, wears a blue linen uniform with a veil.

She smiles from under the veil at the soldier as she admits him and explains, "This is a meeting place, and we can find a bed for you at a home nearby, if that is what you need. I'll get 'Mother Molson' for you."

Sutherland is one of thousands of soldiers spending their leave in Montreal to have come to Mary Molson. Beginning with a few beds, mostly offered by local families, the club now provides some 500 beds.

Colonel Sutherland meets "Mother Molson" in the drawing room. Large comfortable chairs are arranged around the room, and he can see some uniformed men playing cards in one corner. A fireplace glows warmly. Mrs. Molson nods a greeting at him as he enters the room. Some of the soldiers had been having a conversation with her. Sutherland listens.

"Now I don't want to lecture you boys, but ...

That Mary cares about them all is obvious. The soldiers respond to her with trust and affection.

"Live honourably on your own money, not idly and dishonourably on others," she continues. "You must remember to stay away from strong drink, which has been a pitfall for many returned men. God has spared you boys."

It is impossible for Mary to describe her feelings about her "boys," impossible to tell them how grateful she is to them or how proud she feels of them, as though she had some claim to pride. Sometimes she sits with them for hours and listens to their troubles. In three years, one hundred thousand men have come through the club.

"I am only the old woman who lives in a shoe," she says to Sutherland later.

Although Mary is described as having "done more for the returned soldier than any single person in Canada," she will gently turn aside King George V's offer of the title "Dame of the British Empire." As she puts it:

> *I am most grateful for the thought behind the offer. However I wish to be allowed to refuse the honour. I cannot accept such a title after all that the men have done on the battlefields. It is reward enough that my boys call me 'Mother Molson'–I need no other title.*

Herbert returned from Europe to Montreal to find a crisis developing at the brewery. This was triggered by Quebec premier Lomer Gouin's prohibition bill, finally confirmed (February 1919) to include beer and wine. There was no time to adjust to civilian life; no time for the colonel to ease into his role as a businessman, manufacturer, philanthropist and father; no time to weaken, to be anything but strong and capable.

In Montreal, the aftermath of the war was insidious: there had been an undeniable shift in people's sensibilities, in their morality, in their household economy. The cost of raw materials had risen. Returned employees wanted their jobs back; in accommodating them all,

Herbert had also to shorten the work week and increase wages, which had almost doubled–all in the shadow of the brewery's possible closure in May 1919.

Beer production was suspended in February. Molson's continued to sell their old stock but the brew kettle remained empty, and the mechanical equipment that had been installed five years earlier ceased operating. Herbert put his full attention toward organizing a Moderation Committee to define (and influence) the public position and fight the passage of Gouin's bill. He became the committee's chairman and conducted a poll in the city to gauge public opinion. The poll revealed that 75 percent were against the prohibition of beer and wine. The Brewer's Association launched an unprecedented public campaign. Their first advertisement read: "Is the Oldest Manufacturing Business In Canada To Be Legislated Out Of Existence?"

Less than a month before Quebec was scheduled to go dry, the premier agreed to put the matter to a vote. A referendum was scheduled for April 10. "Is it your opinion that the sale of light beer, cider and wine as defined by law, should be allowed?" Seventy-eight percent of Quebecers answered yes. Brewers had won, but they had to stick with their temperance brews.

The Brewers' Association and Herbert's moderation committee were victorious and relieved. They resumed production of temperance beer, and their output soon exceeded prewar levels.

September 22, 1919

At precisely the same minute every afternoon outside the brewery's main entrance on Nôtre Dame Street, a four-cylinder Packard sweeps up to the threshold, and a chauffeur emerges to open the passenger door for Fred Molson. It is unlikely Fred is contemplating that more than a hundred years ago on this very spot, his great-great-grandfather had stood to hail the farmers heading into town. For, when Fred's chauffeur isn't on time, like today, Fred becomes agitated, pacing to and fro, frequently and conspicuously consulting his very accurate timepiece.

"Mr. Fred," as the brewery employees have long called him, is particularly anxious to leave this afternoon, for he will be meeting his friend Richard White (president of the *Gazette,* and recently named senator) to take the six o'clock train up to Nantel, in the Laurentian Mountains north of Montreal, where Fred owns a 1,200-acre property and a house his family calls Father's Rest. He would prefer to not be dependent on a chauffeur, but the one time he had taken the wheel of the Packard, he manoeuvred the vehicle into a ditch–walking away in disgust and vowing never to drive again.

The automobile arrives, and Fred Molson speaks sharply to the driver as he steps in. His annoyance will hang about him like a cloud until he is safely settled in his suite and the train is chugging out of the station. Then his mood will start to lift, and he will begin to relax.

Father's Rest was Fred Molson's own retreat, where he could go to fish on weekends during the year. Fred's friend, and the superintendent of Molsons Bank, A.D. ("Gus") Durnford, had introduced him to the area many years earlier. The Durnford family owned 2,000 acres, encompassing seven lakes. Likewise, John Thomas Molson's family had purchased property in the area. When a generous lot adjacent to the Durnford property, on Lac de la Brume, went for sale in 1911, Fred could suddenly imagine owning the land surrounding the whole lake. "If I can gain control of all this lake's access points, we will stock it with trout," he had vowed to Gus and his other friends.

Fred arrives at the station today fifteen minutes early. Although Gus had died in 1912, Fred frequently catches himself searching for his friend's face in the crowd. Now, he sees and greets Richard White.

The Friday afternoon light falls into evening, the train leaves the city, and the buildings, the bustle and the heat fall away as the countryside becomes visible. Trees–maple, birch, spruce and balsam–close in as the train cleaves into the mountains. Bruneau, his caretaker-farmer, will be there with the carriage and team to take him to his retreat. Fred has ingratiated himself to the villagers by making sure the three miles of road between Nantel's railway station and the lake are in top condition.

This afternoon Fred's satchel is full of packages of sweets, which he will toss to any children he sees along the route. He looks up at the sky. If he asks Lina, his maid, to serve the tea on the lawn, he and White will have no trouble completing a set of croquet before the sun sets.

The irony of the Molson family's position toward her was not lost on Isabel: the fact that they were brewers who disapproved of alcohol seemed to her beyond belief.

Chapter Thirty-One

Tradition and Innovation

Of Fred Molson's three sons, Bert, sometimes called "Bertie," was the most like his father. He was obsessively punctual, excessively frugal. Described by one family member as "picky" and "a fuss-pot," he not only conducted a ritualistic tour of the brewery every morning, but would stand by the door for thirty minutes twice a day to make sure no employees arrived late or left early. He opened all the mail that came to the office, no matter to whom it was addressed. He had a different set of clothes for each of his roles and activities: one for brewery tours, one for fishing, one for board meetings, another for taking the train. He rarely spoke, though he knew most employees by their first names.

Herbert, Fred and Bert Molson invited John Henry to join the company in 1919 and asked Tommy Molson three years later. For the two cousins of the younger generation, entering the family business under the guidance of those formidable three could not have been easy. Each of the principals was as inflexible, eccentric and intractable as the other, yet the hierarchy was respected by all; the elders unquestionably made all the decisions, and business always came before any personal considerations. Each of the Molsons preserved his own privacy, each had high standards and each was respectful of the others. Much of what John Henry and Tom learned at the brewery reflected the very principles that the younger generation had learned through example at home.

In 1920, beer sales catapulted to five million gallons. Prohibition restrictions had been lifted the year before; already the issue seemed to have faded from the public's consciousness. Molson's, National, and newcomer Frontenac Breweries in Montreal were brewing year-round. Increased tourism, a result of the growing automobile industry, was largely responsible for the growth in overall beer sales. Americans and Ontarians crossed the border to Quebec time and again just for the beer.

Frontenac Breweries had introduced a light lager, drawing many converts from the familiar heavier ales and creating a new demand. In 1921 Frontenac initiated a bold advertising campaign in the form of a "treasure hunt." "Hundreds of $1 and $5 cash coupons have been placed under the caps of the bottles," promised the bold print in the newspapers. Herbert was enraged at this tactic and accused Joseph Beaubien, the owner of Frontenac, of unfair trade practices. A court found Beaubien's actions illegal. Meanwhile, the rival brewers were finding other ways of competing for the market's favour. Frontenac's twenty-by-sixty-foot billboards appeared on roadside fields, and wooden Black Horse silhouettes (National Brewery's logo) dotted every vista between the mountains and the river. Molson's mark on the landscape was the phrase "La Bière Molson," in large white script painted across the most conspicuous red barns between Montreal and Quebec City.

Herbert and Fred were glad to have the younger family members along to share the risk and the work. Fred, who had assumed presidency of Molsons Bank in 1921, had less time these days for the brewery. Commitments to the Montreal General Hospital and McGill University took up a lot of Herbert's time and energy.

Exceeding five million gallons in a year had spurred the Molson cousins to realize it was time to replace their ten thousand gallon brew kettle with a larger one. If they were to get a larger kettle at all, it was logical then that they obtain one twice as large, doubling their capacity while working toward doubling their sales. Yet the impact of the decision was staggering: all their existing equipment would have to be replaced to handle the increased volume, and they would need a new building to accommodate such a large kettle and the correspondingly vast bottling facilities. They would have to tear down Molson Terrace and the old St. Thomas's Church, and build, over the site, a single four-storey building of concrete and stone. The financial commitment to the new building alone was $2.5 million.

Tom would distinguish himself with his ability to reason empirically in every situation. More conservative in some ways than his elders, it was Tom who questioned whether the brewery expansion was too huge a risk to undertake in light of the business's near closure. Tom would always champion improvement over sentiment. The youngest of the five Molsons working at the brewery in the 1920s, if Tom had ideas that would challenge business tradition, he learned early on to bide his time; most changes in the family business were manifested slowly and thoughtfully.

In 1922, the year the new building was completed, Tom Molson finished his course in brewing in Birmingham, England, and returned to Montreal to join his father Herbert, uncle Fred, and two cousins, Bert and John Henry, at the brewery. The company incorporated an interesting balance of old and new, of tradition and innovation. Though Molson's had been using automobile delivery trucks since 1910, in 1922 horses were still kept in the stables and dreywagons lined the old courtyard.

For Isabel Meredith Molson, being the second wife of a divorced man was a difficult role to bear, especially in the puritanical, proper and prudish circles in which she and Kenneth mingled. Disapproval of Isabel emanated from the Molsons in many silent ways. Mabel was particularly frosty toward her. When Isabel offered to take Kenneth's son Jack (then age twelve) into her home, the well-meaning gesture was spurned as outrageous. Jack had come to mean everything to Mabel; she wouldn't hear of it.

Whether Isabel's drinking began before or after her marriage, whether it was cause or effect of her internal discomfort, we will likely never know. Her habit might not have become excessive or out of control until after May 1914, when her first child was delivered stillborn.

On her best days, she laughed too loudly, and her ankles wobbled in her fashionable shoes. On her worst days, she was incapacitated. Kenneth referred to her recurring latter states as "illness," not really believing that's what it was. To label Isabel's problem thus was, for Kenneth, not a term of extraordinary understanding. It was a discreet way to avoid referring to something then widely considered a serious character flaw.

The irony of the Molson family's position toward her was not lost on Isabel; the fact that they were brewers who disapproved of alcohol seemed to her beyond belief. How could they condone the practice outside but not inside the family? Feeling that her husband's family expected so much of her, judged her and found her less than adequate only made her want to reach for another glass. In those days, in her circles, everybody drank, ever since she could remember. Since the times of Sir John A. Macdonald's summers in St. Patrick, some things–like the cocktail hour called *cinq-à-sept* and the merry games of ten-cent poker carried on at the Meredith cottage–were just traditional.

In what must have been an act of desperation, Kenneth had his wife committed to McLeans Hospital in Waverly, Massachusetts, in September 1914. It was the same month that troops, including Isabel's father, were assembling at Valcartier for the Canadian Expeditionary Force.

Kenneth had had huge expenses for some time. He paid his mother, Jennie, room and board for Jack's upkeep as well as his private school education (first at Selwyn House in Montreal; then at Ashbury College near Ottawa) and reimbursed Mabel for the boy's other expenses. His divorce costs had been astronomical. The 1912 bill to Kenneth from Pentland, Stuart & Brodie, advocates in Quebec (representing fees from January 1911 to April 1912), totalled $4,000. His trip to England and the private detective fees and expenses were in addition to that. Moreover, he liked to live well. The engagement ring he bought for Isabel at Henry Birks was the most valuable that had ever been sold in the city's history. He owned a car (a Schadt) and a share of Ivry. The house he was building in 1914 and 1915, 576 Pine Avenue, was six storeys high and boasted a billiard room, a conservatory and an indoor rifle range. Including servants' quarters, the house had forty-seven rooms, an elevator, and a built-in vacuum-cleaning system. There was a verandah on every floor, and the servants had their own verandah and sitting room.

Kenneth was listed in *Dau's Blue Book* (an upper-class social directory), in which his memberships were named: Forest and Stream Club, University Club, Garrison Club (in Quebec), Royal Montreal Golf Club, Montreal Amateur Athletic Association, Mount Royal Lawn Tennis Club, Quebec Golf Club, and Montreal Racquet Club. The clubs' yearly fees totalled a fair sum. He had his domestics' wages to pay. Then, beginning in 1914, and continuing on and off for years, there were Isabel's hospital expenses.

In April of 1913 Kenneth had taken out a loan for $15,000 from Molsons Bank. He had it paid back within the year. In 1914 he took out another loan from the same bank, this time for $150,000. In June of 1915 he borrowed another $150,000 from Herbert, giving the right, title and interest of his share in the residue of John Thomas's estate as collateral.

Kenneth stayed at home in Montreal for the duration of the war. "We need him to look after our investments," his brothers said. It was as though his brothers had made a tacit pact to protect him. Were they considering more than his domestic stresses (his new marriage, his son Jack and now Isabel's hospitalization)? His brothers seemed to recognize that in spite of his physical health and strength, there was something indefinably fragile about him. Perhaps what Kenneth needed was the chance to begin his new life; to build his house, establish his business, look after his children.

As the war progressed, suffragettes handed white feathers to able-bodied men in Montreal who were not in uniform. Kenneth went to his brokerage office at Molson and Robin every day clad in his Grenadier Guard uniform. Though he was a local member of the 1st Regiment, while passing the suffragettes' alert countenances he felt like an impostor. He worked extra hard at his office and on his brothers' behalf to compensate for perceived personal "failures." That he continued to borrow money was at some level a means to gain ground, to achieve perceived personal "successes."

Kenneth supervised the gardener Weston's planting of a *potager* garden at 576 Pine Avenue. From spring until fall, as the end of each day approached, he would glance at the clock to see how much more time was left before he could join Weston in the garden, deadhead the peonies, mulch the asparagus, or trellis the sweet peas.

"Truly a noble pursuit, gardening … how it invigorates one, somehow, gives one hope, teaches one … to be patient," Kenneth commented one day. "Yet one cannot help but consider that while our hands tend the earth here, the earth over there–" he gestured east, "is being blown apart."

"Yes," agreed Weston, "while we are digging these beet rows, our brothers are digging trenches."

Kenneth's garden was his panacea. Colours soothed him; here, his mind grew clear and he began to feel that his life could become as orderly and as predictable as these hedges of spirea, these rugosa roses; as tenacious and rewarding as these herb beds.

At the end of the war, at the age of forty, Kenneth took an extended leave of absence from work to enroll as a student at Macdonald College, which had been recently established as McGill's Faculty of Agriculture. Isabel had come home from hospital in the spring of 1915; for the next several years she would spend alternate seasons between hospitals and home. She and Kenneth had three healthy children; Kenneth Meredith (called Meredith), born in 1916; Winnifred, born in 1919; and Jane, born in September 1921.

In 1920, Kenneth sold his share of Ivry to his brothers Walter and Herbert, and had a summer home built in St. Patrick, next to Belle Rivière, which had been built by Sir William Meredith as a wedding present for Isabel's father Ned. Isabel was delighted. Kenneth's cottage now joined the distinguished row of summer homes overlooking the river, among them Les Rochers, which had belonged to Sir John A. Macdonald.

Kenneth never lost his fascination with agriculture. Since finishing his course at Macdonald College, he had been thinking about how he would implement some of his ideas for agricultural experiments. Within two years he had worked out a way to accomplish his goal. In the summer of 1922 he purchased a farm across from his and the Merediths' homes, and began to cast about for someone to manage it.

Jennie broached the subject of her son's interest to her gardener. Adelard Jutras visited the farm in September and then, in the spring of 1923, moved his wife and three children to St. Patrick.

Kenneth's mind bristled with ideas. Since there was a brook on the farm, he decided he could pipe the water in to supply his and other summer homes, and they could all jettison their unsightly and inconvenient outhouses. Not only did Kenneth design the pump and direct the installation of the pipes himself, but he also fashioned a way to charge every household for the amount of water they drew, applying the rate proportionally to the costs. He then set about developing his own working septic system that siphoned itself empty.

Kenneth had an agreement with Jutras that no money would be exchanged between them. Jutras had agreed that in place of rent, he and his family would work Kenneth's farm for him. Kenneth improved and expanded the farm every year. He constructed a cattle barn, an implement shed, a chicken coop, a pig barn, and a bridge to cross the brook, all from wood that Jutras had felled on the property. He bought chickens, pigs, sheep, cows, and a registered bull from Macdonald College. Two cart horses were used for all the ploughing and to cart wood, move rocks, and harvest crops. Then Kenneth bought a tractor, the first one seen in Rivière du Loup. Soon his innovative farm drew visitors from as far away as Quebec City.

When Kenneth and Isabel's children were not at home, they could be found either next door at the Merediths' cottage, or across the road at the Jutras farm. Every morning, after farm chores were completed, the Jutras children (Leyone, Georges and Lucienne), the Meredith children (Joan and Clive) and the Molson children (Meredith, Winnifred and Jane) played together at the farm. Adelard Jutras hung ropes from the trees so the children could swing like Tarzan. Leyone recalls that there were twenty-two children swinging among the trees one afternoon when a convoy approached on the road–a travelling circus and all its supplies. The lead car, a black Packard, stopped, and a man who looked like P.T. Barnum himself emerged. "I'll take the lot of them!" he called out jovially to Jutras, gesturing at the children.

Kenneth had his Montreal gardener, Edward Weston, prepare a grass tennis court behind his house, and he frequently invited the Merediths and others to join him in a game. He bought another portion of land west of the farm, bringing his land all the way to his neighbour Stanley Coristine's property. With Coristine's and Kenneth's consent, a group of their mutual friends set about creating an 18-hole golf course that sprawled across both properties. An existing building became a club house, and Jutras's sheep kept the grass trimmed. Kenneth didn't often join his friends at golf, preferring tennis. He made time to find books to give Leyone, whose father was illiterate, and help her read them. He took his children to swim in freshwater lakes and taught his son Meredith to shoot ducks in the swamp and to fish for tommycod and flounder down at the rocks.

Once or twice a summer, Kenneth would hail the old familiar pioneer from the hinterland who passed through town in a shaky buck-board truck, and buy one of his ten-pound blocks of maple sugar wrapped in birch bark. Some days he would take Winnifred out to see the moving picture matinees in Rivière du Loup, four and a half miles away. They would both get all dressed up, while Jane, told she was too young to go, would stand at the window and wistfully watch them leave.

Isabel would rally for a while, relapse, then rally again. On her good days, she would choose cuts of meat from Labbé, the butcher from Le Portage who brought his covered cart right to the door, or select fresh herring and salmon from the fish man. On her bad days, she joined neighbours for *cinq-à-sept.* By the time she was five, Winnifred had her own way of fighting her mother's addiction: she would attack the liquor delivery man who came to the kitchen door–flying at him with her fists, then throwing dishes at him from across the room.

Kenneth's investment company was doing well. Its success and his inheritance from his father enabled him to pay back all his loans. The war was over, and he joined his brother Walter, cousin Bert and uncle Fred to form the Concord Realty Company, which dealt in real estate, insurance and property management. Except for his strained marriage, Kenneth was living a perfect life: he had three healthy children and was financially secure.

The structure of Canada's banking industry shifted dramatically during the years that followed the war. Between 1918 and 1925, ten of the twenty-one Canadian banks vanished, swallowed up by larger institutions. The Merchants Bank and the Bank of British North America were acquired by the Bank of Montreal, whose president was Isabel's uncle, Sir Vincent Meredith.

When Fred Molson had become president of Molsons Bank in 1921, the institution had 125 branches throughout Canada. With $68 million in assets, it was considered a middle-sized player on the stage of Canadian banking. The three "giants," the Bank of Montreal, the Canadian Bank of Commerce and the Royal Bank, vied for primacy. Merging with Molsons Bank would put the Bank of Montreal securely in the lead. Fred could see that there was much to be gained by the Molsons as well, letting go of a business that had nowhere to grow, and funnelling all their energy and resources into the brewery.

In 1923 a series of financial events affected Molsons Bank. Bay Sulphite Companies and other large clients connected to them were forced into liquidation. The failures affected all banks investing in Saguenay; the Molsons Bank had to appropriate its reserve fund of $2 million. In 1924, Fred Molson thought the time was right to seek a merger with the Bank of Montreal. The latter approved the merger the day before Christmas that year.

It was agreed that current Molsons Bank shareholders would receive two shares of Bank of Montreal stock plus $10 to every three shares of Molsons Bank stock (the equivalent of $170 for each Molsons Bank share). Moreover, as Fred had insisted, all Molsons Bank employees were to receive alternative posts or a life pension. The merger took effect in January 1925; the following year, Fred joined Herbert on the board of the Bank of Montreal.

In 1925 Herbert and Bessie bought Villa Medea, a house in Métis Beach that stood on the property next to Fred and Catherine Molson's Birchcliffe. Bessie was enchanted with Villa Medea and its setting, especially its garden possibilities. She had the landscape arranged in her mind before the final papers were signed.

Renovations cost $25,000 and took two years to complete. Herbert added a wing to the house which included a spacious dining room panelled in B.C. pine, a new kitchen on the main floor, and a master bedroom that overlooked the sea. The sitting room became a library. A pink granite fireplace in the drawing room was built from one enormous boulder on the beach. Bessie ordered plants to be brought in from the city on railroad flatcars and hired gardeners to help her.

The fourth floor of Villa Medea was the staff's quarters, where all except Mary and Michael O'Neill, Bessie's private maid and her head gardener, stayed. Mary, in a white starched uniform and cap, would light the fire in Mrs. Molson's bedroom every morning at five o'clock, and go out later in the morning to fill baskets with cut flowers, arranging vases in every room. Michael installed wire and copper trellises over Villa Medea's cedar shingles and planted sweet honeysuckle vine to climb them.

Crawley, the chauffeur, lived in what is still called the "chauffeur's cottage," closer to the beach. To the amusement of the Molsons next door, Crawley would need at least a half-hour's warning before Herbert's Dodge was required, for it took twenty minutes to get it out of the little garage and positioned in the right place so it could descend the narrow laneway.

The two Molson properties in Métis–Villa Medea and Birchcliffe–were separated by a cedar hedge lined with raspberry canes and connected by a zigzagging footpath. Catherine continued to stay at Birchcliffe every summer. When John Henry married Hazel Browne in 1920, they were offered the chauffeur's cottage at Herbert Molson's, next door. The couple gratefully accepted.

September 2, 1925

Fragrance fills the cottage as Bessie glides like a duchess through the bottle-green, uncluttered sitting room into the pale yellow library. Bureaus are draped with lace, and windows trimmed with dotted Swiss and hung with glazed cotton edged with sheer organdy ruffles. Glass vases containing bouquets of sea lavender decorate windowsills.

Petite, gracious and radiant, Bessie seems to balance her husband's dour side perfectly. With unselfconscious grace she gestures guests to sit down, pushes her hair out of her eyes, or adjusts china and seashells on the table. Her demeanour is usually optimistic, but briskly so; some find her "bossy." Yet she blushes a lot, steers conversations away from herself, and in her relaxed moments scatters laughter.

Bessie is going outdoors to place the half-oranges her family has saved at breakfast between the violas in the garden to collect the slugs. Bessie's garden includes white lilies, roses, delphiniums, monk's hood, and sweet peas that sprawl along the edges of paths and hedges. She is happiest when the weather is fine and she can meander in her Liberty-linen flowered garden smocks and red straw hat.

Herbert divides his summers between Métis and Montreal. When the *Curlew* arrives, Bessie orders the British flag to go up on the flag-pole. The colonel spends his leisure time in Métis golfing, playing tennis and sailing. He and Bessie host afternoon tea on the verandah, where they nibble on seed cake, hot cheese biscuits, and cucumber sandwiches. From there they can see Lighthouse Point, where the ruins of the old manorial house still stand on the other side of a copse of trees. They talk about the legends associated with the marks on the stones there. They watch the seagulls circle Bull Rock as the tide falls, exposing seaweed, mussels and tangles of driftwood along the shore. They wave at the people they recognize on the beach below.

For Kenneth Molson, the economic downturn was particularly devastating. His personal financial circumstances were hardly affected... However, his career in the investment business, in which one's reputation meant everything, suffered in proportion to the devastating economic times.

Chapter Thirty-Two

The Great Depression

Tom Molson and his cousin Jack had remained close over the years. Before Jack was sent to Ashbury College in Rockcliffe Park (then just east of Ottawa), they had both attended Selwyn House in Montreal. Between 1918 and 1921 Tom was at Cambridge and Jack at McGill, but they continued to see a lot of each other in Métis in the summers, where they would enjoy sailing excursions. When Tom returned from England to join the family brewery, Jack was beginning his career as a chartered accountant with McDonald Currie in Montreal. But Jack was soon moved to Quebec City to become assistant to the partner there.

In the summer of 1924 when Jack was twenty-two years old, he met Doris Carington Smith at a debutante party on board the *HMS Hood*, in the Quebec harbour. Her family lived in Les Falaises, an elegant house at the top of Montmorency Falls. Jack began to pay visits to the Carington Smiths to see Doris, and they soon joined parties of mutual friends for scavenger hunts and tournaments of golf. By November they were engaged.

Jack passed his final chartered accountant examinations and received his degree in December 1925. Now he could become a full partner; his future was assured. As a wedding gift, Kenneth offered to have a house built for the couple on Belvedere Circle in Westmount. When Jack took Doris up to the lot, she, long familiar with the view of the St. Lawrence River from the heights of Montmorency, stood still, engulfed in wonder at how vast Montreal looked from Westmount Mountain. At that moment her happiness was so broad it seemed that if she stretched out her arms she could gather and embrace the whole, radiant city.

Jennie, "Grannie" to Jack, died of natural causes in July 1926. She had spent the declining few years of her life ensconced in lace and pillows in her bedroom on Pine Avenue. Her funeral was in Montreal, two months before Jack and Doris were married at St. Mary's Church in Montmorency. The Carington Smiths hosted a wedding reception afterward at Les Falaises. The young couple left the following day for Europe, on a two-month honeymoon that would include skiing in Switzerland.

But first, Jack wanted to find his mother, Mary Letitia Snider. She was now Mrs. Harold Tinker, and was reportedly living in Harrogate, in the county of Yorkshire.

September 22, 1926

Jack takes Doris's arm as they walk along Cambridge Crescent in Harrogate. This town, close to the city of York, has long been famous for its natural springs and mineral baths. The trees cast dappled shadows on the swept wooden sidewalk. The streets are pretty and clean, the parks well maintained.

Jack has found his mother's address in a directory. He unfolds the piece of paper and shows it to Doris.

Jack has felt his mother's presence from the moment they arrived in Harrogate, and now, walking along Cambridge Crescent, he suddenly thinks he can smell lavender in the air. He stops. Can he really have remembered, after all these years, what she smelled like? They are standing outside Betty's Tea Room and Cake Shop. He looks around, confused. "Let's stop here and have some tea," he says to Doris.

Jack is glad and grateful that Doris is there with him. He opens the menu. He knows Doris loves everything English. Her family is from the Channel Islands; her brother Noel has settled in Perthshire; she is well-travelled, and knows about things that are foreign to him like lemon thins, mince pies and cream scones.

"What's a hot buttered pikelet?" he asks her.

"I believe it's a Yorkshire specialty ..." she begins.

A violinist and piano accompanist begin playing a divertimento. Jack listens for a while and his mind starts to wander.

It occurs to Jack that his mother may be here. She may even be the woman in the pearls and hat at the next table, having the spiced tea-cake. He wonders what kind of a person Mary is now. Has she become nonchalant and hardened, or contrite, soft and full of regrets? He tries to imagine what kind of dress and hat she would wear. He looks at the other women in the room and wonders if any of them know her.

He wonders what he will say to his mother. What will he tell her? That his father has three more children now, that his youngest half-sister is five years old today?

"Will you take cream with your tea, sir? A lump of sugar?" asks the waitress.

"Thank you."

When they are finished and ready to leave, Jack checks Mary Tinker's address again. "Excuse me, could you tell us how to find East Parade Street?" he asks the waitress.

"Oh, yes," she says, "it's just around the cor-ner!"

Smiling, Jack thinks to himself, "I have a beautiful new bride, it's a sunny day, we are on our honeymoon, and I am about to meet my mother. Life doesn't get any better than this."

A few minutes later they are standing on the doorstep of an elegant stone house at number 67 East Parade. Jack has tried to imagine every scenario that might play out–but he has never imagined *this.* Just days before the young couple had come to Harrogate to find her, Mary had died, at the age of forty-six. "Hypostasis–congestion of the lungs," the stranger on the threshold tells them.

After the finalization of the Molsons Bank/Bank of Montreal merger, Fred and Herbert purchased another block of land west of the brewery, anticipating a future expansion. In 1927 prohibition was lifted across Canada, and Molson's Brewery annual output rose to seven and a half million gallons. In the first twelve months post-prohibition, Ontario sales accounted for a million gallons alone. By early 1929, Molson's was serving 32 percent of the Quebec beer market. Sales in Ontario alone were nearing 3 million gallons, and the company's total annual beer sales were rapidly heading toward 10 million gallons. Herbert's second son, Hartland, was six years younger than Tom. As a boy he had attended Bishop's College School in Lennoxville, Quebec, then Charterhouse School in London, England. Hartland was always first or second in his classes, where competition was sharp. At Charterhouse he was described as a "manly boy, with honesty and character which should bring him through well," echoing the sentiment expressed by schoolmaster William Nelson, who had written about John Junior in 1797. At nineteen in 1926, Hartland entered Royal Military College, where his conduct was recorded as "exemplary" and his character as "keen, smart, and dependable."

Hartland joined the football team at RMC, which won the Dominion Intermediate Championship in 1926. He also participated in rugby and track, but it was hockey that most captured his imagination. He joined the Kingston Hockey Club and played in the Memorial Cup finals.

When Hartland left RMC, Herbert encouraged his son to travel in Europe before settling down to a career. In September 1928 the young man wrote to his father from a hotel in Amsterdam:

> *My Dear Dad,*
>
> *This note is just to tell you how much I really appreciate this trip. I have a real lack of effusiveness which sometimes makes the family think that I take everything for granted and don't realize how lucky I am, and how good you are to me. That is my nature, but I do appreciate your great generosity & especially in this case …*

By Christmas, Hartland's first away from home, he was living in Paris and working at the Banque Adam, a job that allowed him to become proficient in French and banking at the same time. At twenty-one, his interests were many and he liked to challenge himself. Later, in Switzerland, he took a military engineering course and became involved in a local hockey club, coaching a young team for the Olympics. Hartland would describe his time in Europe as "a most pleasant year." It ended in July 1929, when he returned to Montreal to work for McDonald Currie, the chartered accounting firm where his cousin Jack had been working for five years. Hartland had been there less than three months when the stock market collapsed. "That," he said in his typically understated way, "was quite an experience."

Fred Molson died on February 5, 1929, nearly nine months before the stock market crash. He had a private and a public funeral, the first at his home and the second at St. George's Church in Westmount. Tributes to his business ability, his initiative and his "marvellous executive acumen" were numerous. The *Financial Post* described him as "one of the half a dozen wealthiest men in Canada." Senator White, president of the *Gazette*, printed his friend's obituary and photograph on the front page. (It was said that Fred had challenged White at a cocktail party, asking him why he never published photos in his newspaper of those who had died. White had responded by laughingly promising to publish his.)

Fred's three sons, Bert, Stuart, and John Henry, were willed their father's brewery shares. He left the Drummond Street house, Father's Rest in Nantel, and Birchcliffe in Métis directly to Catherine. He also provided her with an account to maintain the houses, in addition to an annuity of $40,000. (Her death, only six months later, created a significant financial difficulty. It meant that succession duties had to be paid twice on the same estate that year. Although the estate's assets had been evaluated at pre-crash value, duties were payable post-crash, when assets were worth far less than they had been. These succession duties spurred the brewery to become incorporated under the Dominion Charter, allowing it to narrow its possible future liabilities.)

Herbert, at fifty-five, became president of the brewery. For the past ten years he had been able to pursue leisurely ambitions such as salmon fishing, golf and bridge. He could drop into the Mount Royal or St. James club for luncheon, sail to Métis in summer, take long holidays at

Ivry in the winter. Now he would have much less time for such activities. He took over the big corner office overlooking Nôtre Dame Street and Papineau Square, while Bert and John Henry retained their old offices and Tom took over the smaller office that had been Fred's.

The stock market collapse had a dramatic effect on brewery sales, which plunged from a peak of nearly ten million gallons annually to five million. For most members of the Molson family, however, especially those connected directly to the brewery, lifestyles were largely unaffected by the crash. Their most conservative, secure investments, such as government bonds, provided their sound financial foundation.

There was only one Molson whose personal assets did not remain intact after the Depression. Stuart Molson was one of four investors in the Beauharnois Power Project. This was an enterprise involving diverting water from the St. Lawrence River into a canal and harnessing its power through a 25-metre fall, which generated electricity to be sold to Ontario and Quebec. The project itself was sound (and would, eventually, be a success), but a political scandal that was exposed during the Depression weakened it. Rumours of influence-peddling in the Senate on behalf of Beauharnois were investigated by a House of Commons committee, which concluded that charges were justified against three Senate members. After this setback the company borrowed money, and then fell into arrears. In 1936 the Royal Bank called its loan.

Of the four "joint and several" guarantors of the company that owned Beauharnois, Stuart was the only one who had not taken steps to protect his personal assets. Subsequently he lost almost everything, excluding only (thanks to a clause in his father's will) his brewery shares. Stuart's new house on Redpath Crescent, his stocks and bonds, his boat, and even his automobile were seized. Stuart and his family moved into a rented house on Chelsea Place. Bert and John Henry promptly offered their brother long-term, interest-free loans, with which he soon started a small brokerage firm.

Herbert still had the *Curlew,* Walter maintained his own diesel yacht, *Caprice*, and John Henry had the *Red Hackle.* Tom also continued to go sailing with friends and crew and owned a series of boats that he kept at the St. Lawrence Yacht Club. Before and after the stock market crash, Tom continued to work at the brewery, go to Ivry on odd weekends and sail down to Métis in the summer, and he even took a trip to Europe to tour breweries.

Molson Brewery's market share declined to 27 percent. Hartland was laid off at McDonald Currie, but was immediately hired by Herbert as a consultant on behalf of McGill University, which was experiencing a financial crisis.

While queues were becoming a familiar sight outside soup kitchens and relief offices in Montreal, the Molsons and their friends continued to enjoy the privileges of their class. The glamour of dinner parties, theatre and hockey games persisted. Hockey was infused with excitement and mystique. The young ladies always dressed in their best formal evening wear and long white gloves. Herbert (in his velvet smoking jacket or fur-lined coat) and Bessie (in her mink cape) for discretion's sake had their driver pick them up at the back door more often than the front.

The Cantlie family–friends and neighbours of Herbert and Bessie's for many years–bought the house next to their own new house on Sherbrooke Street and set it up as a soup kitchen. Colonel George Cantlie forbade his daughter Celia to leave their Sherbrooke Street house by the front door if she was dressed to go out for an evening, clad in her "Paris clothes"; nor was she to be seen getting into their chauffeur-driven car.

In the way that the misfortunes of some can create opportunities for others to build power empires, the Great Depression brought about at least one such prospect for the Molsons. Hartland drew his father's attention to the fact that the brewery was in a position to call in notes backed by National Breweries shares, and thus gain control of the much larger company. Herbert declined to act, dumbfounding Hartland, who regretted the tremendous lost potential.

Herbert's active decision not to take over National Breweries was a well-evaluated one. Though it was a balanced and honourable choice, it wasn't entirely altruistic. He knew such an action would set a precedent and wasn't interested in creating a monopoly. He consulted his friend, Prime Minister R.B. Bennett, about other connected risks. What would the market future be like, following the Depression? He considered how his ancestors would have acted in the same situation. Following their lead, in his public and his private life, Herbert had always applied the same principles of decency to everything he did. His attitude influenced and inspired his descendants, who learned from him that when one had an opportunity to choose between power and honour, honour was more important.

Herbert frequently aided others financially, as would his son Tom. Neither ever refused a friend in need, nor asked anyone to sign a promissory note. Both would say, "I don't lend money, I give money," meaning simply that they would not regret having given it, even if it never came back to them. Their particular kind of generosity was private and subdued; any expression of gratitude might have elicited mild embarrassment.

For Christmas in 1934, Herbert sent his son Hartland a cheque, with an accompanying letter:

> *I will be disappointed if [the money] is not wisely invested and conserved. Perhaps you think your father old-fashioned and conservative but at least he has been able to save something for his children when many others have made an unholy mess of things. This amount of money is what, I believe, you call in accounting circles "non-recurring profits" and must not be counted upon in future years or as a precedent. The till wouldn't stand it. So invest it wisely if you can and do not disappoint me.*

The following Christmas, Herbert sent Hartland another cheque. "It is unnecessary for me to enlarge on the importance of its wise investment by you," he wrote,

> *as it will probably be increasingly difficult and expensive for me to give substantial sums to my children at my death; the succession duties will make a huge hole in the results of a lifetime of work.*

During the Depression, Herbert commissioned historian Bernard K. Sandwell to write a history of the Molson family. As 1936 would mark the brewery's 150-year anniversary, Herbert believed it would be a good time to publish a commemorative biography for family members. A growing collection of personal and business records had been safely stored at the brewery for fifteen decades, documents that would provide more than enough information for a biography. Not all the information would be suitable for publication, however, and the family must be portrayed in positive terms only. "There is no need to write anything negative, of course," Herbert cautioned Sandwell. He expressly instructed the writer not to refer to the first generation's illegitimacy, or to Thomas Molson's second marriage to Sophia Stevenson.

Five hundred copies of *The Molson Story* were printed in 1933 and distributed among family members.

In 1931, in the middle of the Depression, Tom Molson and a Cambridge friend were returning to Canada from a holiday in Europe aboard the luxurious, newly completed *Empress of Britain.* The launch, her maiden voyage, was a memorable and festive occasion. The Prince of Wales (later Edward VIII) came down to Southampton to see the ship off. Among other passengers on the first-class deck that morning, waving to the crowd, were two whom Tom recognized from Montreal: Lady Mount Stephen and her niece, Celia Cantlie.

Tom and Celia had known each other when they were children, though Tom, twelve years older than she, would often be away at school when Celia visited. She and her mother frequently went to tea at Herbert and Bessie's Ontario Avenue house. Celia remembers that Herbert, whom she called "Mr. Moley," would take her up to the nursery to see the toys and play there with the Molson girls' magnificent dollhouse.

Before their encounter aboard the *Empress* in 1931, Tom hadn't taken much notice of Celia. He was thirty years old that year and she a debutante of eighteen. He spotted her with her aunt again after dinner the following evening. Cheerful band music was whirling through the room and moonlight reflected across the water all the way to the horizon. Celia's eyes sparkled as she spoke to her aunt. Tom found himself irresistibly drawn to her graceful manner and unflinching gaze, but his interest did not seem to be returned. When he asked if she would like to dance, she replied politely, "No, thank you, I'd rather sit with my aunt."

In Montreal in 1931 there were fewer balls than usual because of the Depression. But later that year Tom saw Celia again at the St. Andrew's Ball at the Black Watch Armoury and determined to ask her again to dance. This time she obliged.

As Celia pointed out later, there was nothing not to be attracted to about Tom Molson. He was handsome, self-possessed, educated and worldly, and he had a solid future. Both sets of parents were pleased to see the attention Tom was paying Celia. At a charity ball at the Montreal Maternity Hospital, the two met again. Before long Tom had called on her and asked her if she would like to join him and his family for a weekend at Ivry. Bessie put her at ease by asking, "Do tell us everything that you did in England," causing others to laugh at the improbability of the question. Soon Celia and Tom were engaged.

Throughout the Depression, John Henry and Hazel hosted garden parties at their house in Métis. After his parents' deaths in 1929, John Henry and his family had inherited Birchcliffe. Blonde, vivacious Hazel was irrepressible, even mischievous. Bessie, by comparison, seemed stern; some felt she emanated a cool reserve toward the older woman.

The John Molsons and their uninhibited friends enjoyed making moving pictures, playing tennis and entertaining friends. They kept a different set of friends than Herbert and Bessie. John and Hazel's garden parties at first drew only Protestants, but soon also included the Catholics in the village. In 1932–the summer overshadowed by news of the Lindbergh baby kidnapping–John Henry had two tennis courts installed on the grounds and began to organize matches among the locals. The first time the village priest came to play tennis with him, he appeared in his cassock. At once Hazel exclaimed, "Oh, we can't have that!" and insisted that next time he had to wear a pair of white shorts. The priest came to Birchcliffe regularly after that in white shorts and shirt; and he drank a double scotch after each set of tennis.

Hazel began organizing summer cabarets during the Depression years. Multi-talented and experienced in theatre, she wrote and produced shows that would amuse Métis's summer residents. Dozens of people became involved. The immensely popular shows, well rehearsed and rich with music, witty scripts, choreography and elaborate costumes, provided a showcase of talent and fun in the exclusive community. Two productions were presented every summer. Hazel's four children, and other Molsons including Walter's son Chip, were always involved.

John Henry, anxious about the safety of the children on the beach across the road from Birchcliffe, fashioned what was later called "the Molson pool" by moving rocks and pouring concrete to define the edges of a swimming hole which would contain water at low tide. Also for the children's safety and shelter from the wind, he built a stone wall on the beach. He adored his wife and family and was content always to stay at home, where Uncle Harry's mantel clock chimed in the dining-room every hour and half-hour. Often he would sit in one of the upholstered brown wicker chairs on the verandah, from time to time exclaiming, "Why would I go anywhere else in the world, when I could be here?"

Up to and including Fred Molson's generation, every male Molson had spent at least some time in the executive offices of the brewery. Walter and Kenneth were the first of the following generation not to.

For Kenneth Molson, the economic downturn was particularly devastating. His personal financial circumstances were hardly affected; his bonds and other conservative investments had continued to yield a healthy $30,000 in annual income throughout the Depression. However, his career in the investment business, in which one's reputation meant everything, suffered in proportion to the devastating economic times.

We will never know when Kenneth first began thinking about ending his life. He was not a man who was prone to depression, yet he had come to believe that over the years he'd made a series of bad decisions, for which he felt disgraced. Within the family his own record had been less than estimable. His self-esteem was battered. It wasn't just that the scandal with Mary had overshadowed the formative professional years of his life; his second marriage had turned out to be similarly doomed. Isabel's "illness" persisted. Was he, he wondered, simply a failure at being a husband? Kenneth's children, work, farming and gardening had always kept his spirits up. But now, in the spring of 1932, gloom hung about him like a persistent fog. Every day it became heavier, harder to dispel.

Kenneth contemplated suicide long enough to have his will drawn up. He had a substantial estate worth approximately $400,000; he prepared a list of his debts and liabilities, which amounted to $160,000. He needed to secure an appointment with his lawyer, prepare a first draft, survey the final one, and sign the documents. By the time the paperwork was completed and registered, the children's Easter holidays had just ended. On April 8, Winnifred and Jane returned to The Study, where they were day students, and Meredith returned to Ashbury College, where, like his half-brother Jack before him, he was enrolled as a boarder. That afternoon Kenneth drove his son Meredith to the train station to see him safely off to Ottawa.

Kenneth left the train station and drove slowly in his gleaming black Schadt to his brother-in-law Dr. Colin Russel's house on Bishop Street. He parked next to Russel's front gate, crossed the walk and ascended the steps to the door. Declining his brother-in-law's invitation to come in, Kenneth stood on the step and spoke with him for a while. Colin's six-year-old daughter Marnie came outside to join them and moved to stand next to her uncle Kenneth. Sensitive and compassionate, Marnie at once felt something of his detachment, something too terrible to articulate but so powerful that she instinctively slipped her small hand into his large one, and curled her fingers lightly around his fingers. Kenneth returned the squeeze on her hand. When Marnie remembers this, fifty-five years later, her eyes fill with tears.

The following day, April 9, 1932, Kenneth entered his bathroom, closed the door and shot himself in the head. No one heard the shot. Isabel found him and, it was agreed afterward, was "never the same after that."

Family members, shocked and shaken, determined to keep the circumstances of Kenneth's death utterly private. The *Gazette* solemnly reported his "passing" as having come "after a long illness." An executors' meeting took place three weeks after his death to discuss the estate. Walter, Jack, two representatives from the National Trust, and friend William Leggat were at the meeting and decided which stocks to sell to pay off the debts, and which ones to keep in the portfolio. Kenneth's house in Montreal and his house in St. Patrick would be sold. Although Kenneth had promised Jutras that the farm would be his after twenty years of work, the executors of Kenneth's estate arranged instead to sell it to the farmer. They established a price and instructed Jutras that he would be required to make a payment on the principal every fall.

Kenneth left his old servant, Emma Larabie, and his gardener, Edward Weston, annuities of $420. Weston was kept on as a gardener with the family until his own death in 1950. Kenneth also left Isabel an annuity of $7,500, secured by separate stocks.

Isabel tried her best to persevere, but having to cope with the children, having to learn to drive, and trying to manage her drinking bouts were all too much for her. She ate too much and gained much weight. She was frequently depressed, during which times she would cry or sit perfectly still. She became more and more dysfunctional. By 1936 Herbert Molson and Jack, who had power of attorney, agreed that she needed to be put into chronic care. Isabel was admitted into the Neuro-Psychiatric Institute at the Hartford Retreat, a private not-for-profit hospital. Her children were left in the guardianship of one of her sisters.

May 7, 1936

Herbert Molson's office at the brewery is a modest one. It contains an old-fashioned roll-top desk, a chair, a single black telephone, a plain table with a lamp on it, and a few scattered papers. A painting of the *Curlew* hangs on his wall.

This is the first year stenographers have been hired at the brewery offices. There are no secretaries, no modern accoutrements such as an in-house telephone system, no battery of Dictaphones. "In short," wrote Grattan O'Leary in his panegyric on the Molsons for Maclean's magazine, "the surroundings reflect solidity, taste, and common sense."

Herbert is proud of the way he keeps the conduct of business at Molson's simple. He continues to use the same bound notebook that he has used since 1912 for all his accounts. There are no shareholders, no dividends to be distributed. The directors' meetings are so casual that they are seldom prearranged. Herbert, Bert, John Henry, and Tom simply stop by the same office and "chat pleasantly," deciding what must be done. Every detail of business is shared by each of them.

The fourth and fifth generations of Molsons are, like their predecessors, more than brewers. Herbert is head of the Montreal General Hospital and a governor of McGill University. Described as a modern-day "elder statesman of sport," he is governor of the Dominion Rugby

Union and attends all of McGill's football matches. He continues to attend hockey matches and is a founder of the Canadian Arena Company, known as the Forum.

Herbert calls all employees by their first names. They call him "Colonel Molson." No one can remember a single labour dispute. During the Depression Herbert had allowed no dismissals: hours of work were distributed, but no one was let go. Not only does Herbert remember how important this had been after the Great War, but he also knows that for generations a trust has existed between the Molsons and their employees. Many employees have been with them for decades, and sons frequently follow their fathers into the company. Ill employees take their regular pay, a policy carried out since his great-grandfather John Molson Senior first hired help. Those in hospital are sent flowers; when an employee dies, Molson's provides for his family.

Tonight a celebratory dinner is underway in the new reception room, which has been designed to resemble the Molson vaults. All share the pride in the celebration of their 150 years of brewing history. Molson's market share has grown. By 1936, annual production is up to 6.7 million gallons. Within the past year Ontario breweries have been entering and establishing themselves in Quebec, but sales had burgeoned nonetheless.

A happy toast, proposed at the dinner that evening, would have brought a smile to John Senior's face:

> *You have not laid sufficient stress on your peerless product, which nourishes the sick, sustains the feeble, solaces the troubled, cheers the despondent and brings that sense of supreme well-being to those epicurean palates which can and will accept no substitutes and automatically reject any other so-called beers which may be offered under the guise of Molson's. Long may it flow!*

She became so vehemently opposed to drinking alcohol that no one who met her dared to drink in her presence. To Mabel, the family business was a noble one only as long as the family members didn't indulge in the product themselves.

Chapter Thirty-Three

Flying Lessons

FROM THE crucible of the 1930s in Montreal, Molson's Brewery was emerging not only unscathed, but in a stronger position than ever. Herbert, Bert, John Henry, and Tom Molson, different as they were in temperament and views, operated as a conservative, efficient team. A hundred and fifty years of running a family business was an unmatched achievement in Canada, adding immeasurable prestige and authority to the name "Molson" in Montreal.

Of the four Molsons running the brewery, only Bert remained a bachelor. John Henry and Hazel had children Billy, Mary, David and Peter. Tom, who had married Celia in 1933, also had four children by the end of the thirties. Tom's sisters Dorothy and Betty had both married and started families as well. In 1926 Stuart Molson married Claire ("Tootie") Jeffrey, and they had two daughters: Lucie in 1927, and Katie in 1935. Hartland married actress Helen Hogg in 1934; their daughter Zoe was born in 1935.

Hartland's mission to design a plan to steer McGill away from bankruptcy and place it in a secure financial position had been successful. Herbert could not verbalize how proud he was of Hartland, or of any of his children–each of whom saw him as the embodiment of strength of character, the champion of deep-rooted reserve, a man who regarded even laughter as a weakness that invariably ought to be suppressed. But Hartland knew when Herbert was pleased. He could always tell by the set of his father's jaw clamped around his pipe, or by the direction in which he turned his frown.

Understandably, as a young man Hartland had learned not to reveal sensitivity or emotion. He readily admitted that he had "a real lack of effusiveness," which could lead to being misunderstood. But unlike his father, he would never hesitate to laugh.

Hartland wore a ring on his right hand, a bloodstone left to him in 1917, when he was ten, by his uncle Percy. Only once, to have it repaired, did he take it off. And because the setting had traces of dried mud from France, Hartland never had it cleaned. He cherished his memories of Percy, who had been, according to his sister Evelyn, "too sweet for words with children." Hartland had felt the loss of his favourite uncle as poignantly as young John Molson Senior had felt the loss of his uncle, Robinson Elsdale, in 1785.

Hartland was an ambitious young man who possessed John Senior's versatility and foresight. One of his interests was soya beans, the mainstay of life in China for thousands of years but in the 1930s virtually unknown in North America. One champion of the protein-rich bean was old Henry Ford. Hartland arranged to meet Ford in Detroit in 1933. He bought patented soya-processing plans and equipment from Ford, and early the following year established Dominion Soya Industries in Montreal. Hartland's plant was the first in Canada to produce soya oil, meal and flour. But, the market wasn't yet ready to embrace the unfamiliar product, and the company lasted less than a year.

In 1934, at the suggestion of friend and mentor Lieutenant-Colonel W.A. ("Billy") Bishop, Hartland took flying lessons at the Montreal Aeroplane Club. He received his pilot's licence and in December went into the flying business, buying a private company in partnership with his brother Tom, father Herbert, and Billy Bishop. Operating in the far north, Dominion Skyways transported supplies and equipment for mining, prospecting and surveying parties. The partners began with three planes; a year later they had eight, and by 1938, twelve. For a time, their main base in Rouyn, Quebec, was one of the most active airports in North America. The company was an unequivocal success.

Hartland continued to travel to Métis every summer. In June 1936 he wrote to F.J. Astle, proprietor of the Seaside House:

> *My chauffeur, James Lowther, is leaving here tomorrow with the cook and should arrive in Métis about noon Friday the 26th … Would you be good enough to have the stove going on Friday morning and to take care of their meals until they have time to buy some food … Mrs. Molson & I will arrive with the Baby [Zoe] and Maids on Saturday morning the 27th, by train and would like to have a car to meet us in addition to our own.*

In many ways, Mabel Molson was the central female figure in the family in the 1930s. All the other Molsons looked up to her as a living example of service and devotion to Anglicanism, the royal family, temperance and good causes. By now she was considered an old maid, too old to marry. Her raising Jack while still a young woman had been more of a sacrifice than anyone had realized. She lived alone with few servants, in a Victorian three-storey brick house on Cedar Avenue next to the Montreal General Hospital. Although she had a chauffeur, Mabel often hired a taxi to take her to Sherbrooke Street so she could browse in the bookshops at her leisure.

When she wasn't reading books or writing letters, Mabel was with her nieces and nephews, taking them to museums and galleries on weekdays and engaging in earnest conversations with them over tea on Sunday afternoons. She loved children, though sometimes they got the better of her. One unforgettable summer in Métis she had volunteered to mind her brother Walter's children, so that he could take his wife, Mary, with him to Paris, where he was to attend a Board of Trade meeting.

There were four children: Caro, fourteen years old in the summer of 1925; Naomi, eleven; Chip, nine; and four-year-old Percival Talbot, called P.T., or simply Pete. The middle two, closest in age, were closest also in temperament. Naomi and Chip would go off on their bicycles every fine evening, heading across the golf course once all the players had deserted the links. They made their own fun and were never bored. One game began on their first day in Aunt Mabel's charge: they decided to try bicycling together three-legged style. At first they practised along the road in front of the house to master the art of side-by-side leg-pumping. Then, ignoring Aunt Mabel's cautions and reproaches, they began to wonder what other activities they could manage to do with their legs tied together. It was an added benefit when they found their antics flustered their aunt Mabel, who was especially perturbed when the brother and sister entered the bathroom together. That night, the children slept in their bunk beds one above the other, their ankles determinedly fastened: Naomi on the top, dangling her leg down; and Chip on the bottom, with his leg propped up. For three days and nights they kept up the game, until Mabel, who couldn't bear it any longer, sent a cable to Walter and Mary, which arrived aboard the Cunard ocean liner in mid-Atlantic:

> *Naomi and chip tied together three-legged style stop impossible to separate them stop am truly anxious stop please advise stop mabel*

Walter's reply evidenced both his pragmatic side and his sense of humour:

> *Try scissors stop Walter*

Mabel's efforts on children's behalf didn't stop with her own family. She was a generous supporter of charities, including the Boy's Farm and Training School, a home for underprivileged boys in nearby Shawbridge. One day early in the 1930s two young boys came to her door on Cedar Avenue with a grocery delivery. Noting that both boys had eye infections, Mabel gave them some money and urged them to go next door to the hospital, where they could see a doctor and get some medicine to clear up the infections. A few days later the boys were back with another delivery, and Mabel noticed that their eyes were worse. They had given the money to their mother, the brothers admitted, to purchase food for their family. This time, Mabel took them to the hospital herself. Later, with the mother's permission, she arranged for them to be boarded and educated at the Boy's Farm. Mabel kept in touch with the brothers and eventually financed their higher education.

Jack's wife Doris did not appreciate any of Mabel's good qualities, nor did Mabel feel charitable toward Doris. The two women saw each other as rivals for Jack's affection. To Doris's indignation, after they were married Jack continued to spend a lot of time with his aunt, not only preparing her income tax returns and managing her financial portfolio, but also helping her with chores and household repairs.

As much as Mabel was loved for her generosity, she also inspired anxiety in many, for her personality could be quite imposing. Before the terrible blow of Percy's death she challenged the conventions of her day, but in the years following 1917 she became quieter, more dour, and formidably resolute. The days of swimming nude at Métis were long over. Life, death, and one's health were serious subjects. She began eating a clove of garlic every morning, said to make one live longer. She became so vehemently opposed to drinking alcohol that no one who met her dared to drink in her presence. To Mabel, the family business was a noble one only as long as the family members didn't indulge in the product themselves.

Mabel had lost one brother to war in 1917, and another to suicide in 1932. In 1936, Herbert, Mabel's eldest brother at age sixty, was operated on for cancer. True to his nature, he refused to discuss his illness with any family member other than Bessie. He seemed to improve for a while, then in December 1937 became ill again. Herbert continued to be stoical about his failing health, not expressing denial, but his own kind of private, wordless acceptance. He updated his twenty-two page will, arranged inventory to be carried out in his house in February, and resigned as president of the Montreal General Hospital at the beginning of March. Herbert died at home in Montreal on March 21, 1938.

For the afternoon of Herbert's funeral, McGill cancelled all classes, while Birk's, Eaton's and Morgan's closed their stores. Outside Christ Church Cathederal, mourners stood six deep and strained to listen to the two bishops who conducted the service.

Bessie received letter after letter of condolence. George McDonald, senior member of McDonald Currie, wrote:

> *My dear Mrs. Molson,*
>
> *Looking back over forty years I think of my extraordinary good fortune in being brought into close contact with members of the Molson family. In school and college days the sterling character of Walter had a greater effect in raising the standards of his classmates than any other influence that came into our lives. After graduation it was my lot to work closely with Percy in business affairs, in graduate activities and later in the war. I think the word "gentle-man" was made for him and I know of none more gallant. From the earliest years we all looked up to Herbert for guidance and counsel. After the war, as my associations with him increased, so did my admiration and affection. He has given to Canada a standard of good citizenship that few may achieve but I believe that his example will inspire others to try harder.*

Colonel Hamilton Gault, founder of the Princess Patricia's Canadian Light Infantry, wrote:

> *To us all he ever stood sans peur et sans reproche for every thing that was fine, and great, and true the very best that Canada produces. As you know we all loved him …*

Governor General Lord Tweedsmuir (John Buchan) wrote from Rideau Hall in Ottawa, on plain stationery:

> *With him goes one of the great figures of Canadian life, for Canada had no finer citizen. There was no good cause to which he did not lend a hand. It is a hard fate for Canada that in the last year she has lost so many of her leading men. But the chief loss is your own. I want you to know how deeply my wife and I sympathise with you in your great sorrow.*

Herbert's will provided Bessie with the use of their houses in Montreal and Métis, and a $40,000 annuity. The bulk of Herbert's estate was divided into seven parts, distributed three to Tom, two to Hartland, and one each to Dorothy and Betty. Tom and Hartland inherited their father's brewery stock. Herbert left endowments of $250,000 each to the Montreal General Hospital and McGill

University. Other legacies included those to the Shawbridge Boy's Farm, several friends, employees, and various household servants including gardeners, chauffeurs, and a former governess to his children.

Even after his death, Herbert's life continued to be held up as exemplary among family members. Walter described Herbert's philosophy in a letter to his nephew Jack in July 1939. (Jack had recently been diagnosed with ulcers, which Walter suspected was caused by "worrying.")

> *Worrying does nobody any good ... it is helpful to take Uncle Herbert's example who had plenty to worry about except his own financial affairs ... [I remember] years ago asking him how he managed to carry on handling vast problems & difficulties of the Hospital & other institutions, as well as troubles of many relatives and friends. He merely shrugged his shoulders, laughed and said "I never worry. If I did I wouldn't be alive. When I have done the best I can on anything the outcome must take its course as it may, so what is the sense of worrying, and I don't."*

Following Herbert's death in 1938, Bert was named president of the brewery. Bert invited Hartland to enter the family business. Hartland promptly sold his interest in Dominion Skyways Limited and joined his brother and his cousins in the office.

Hartland was divorced from Helen Hogg in 1938. In the summer of 1939 he married Magdalena (Magda) Posner, a Hungarian emigrant from the United States.

When war was declared in Europe in September, Hartland, though he had just settled into his brewery position, knew that as a qualified pilot he would be a valuable asset to the Allies. Thirty-two years old, he joined the RCAF, and at his request was soon transferred to the No. 1 Fighter Squadron (later renamed Canadian 401 Squadron). By June 1940 they were in Liverpool. France had fallen, and Hitler had announced that he would destroy the Royal Air Force. Hartland's squadron was the only Canadian unit supporting the RAF in the Battle of Britain. Six days after Winston Churchill declared, "Never in the field of human conflict has so much been owed by so many to so few," the Canadian 401 Squadron joined the air battle. Hartland would later describe his feelings to Magda:

> *The speed with which the whole affair happens is unbelievable and one has nothing but sensations and instincts while the scrap is on. It doesn't feel real somehow, and one certainly hasn't time to be frightened. Afterward, thinking back on things which come to mind is really a bit worse than the actual affair.*

As bombing raids continued into September, Hartland and the other members of the RCAF became engaged in larger and fiercer air battles. Hartland described how the collective morale buoyed and moved him: "The police, fire services, and thousands of volunteers in the auxiliary services are on the job at all times doing their work with an earnest will, coolness and cheerful bravery that makes your heart ache."

By October 5, Hartland had survived sixty-two combat missions. That day he was hit by a single-engine Messerschmitt 109, which was flying directly behind him while he was firing on another. His instrument panel shattered; at the same time he felt a ringing blow on his leg. His Hurricane spinning out of control at 20,000 feet, Hartland bailed out, pulling his rip cord when he estimated he was at 7,000 feet. Reports had warned the pilots not to pull their rip cords too early, for they might be shot at while they were parachuting down. As Hartland would recall:

> *I landed with a plunk … on some nice damp ground. I hobbled about 30 yards to a wide path and sat down, then started to call every minute or so. Soon I heard an answer and about 10 minutes from landing half a dozen Cockney soldiers were mothering me wonderfully. They put field dressings on my wounds, covered me with all of their tunics, lit me a cigarette, sent off for a truck and advised their M.O. They handled me like a baby, made me very comfy in the truck and took me to their billets where their M.O. checked the dressings and arranged for me to go to a Casualty Clearing Station … where they could not have treated me better. From 2:30 to 5:15 they kept about 4 blankets and a big heater on me to get all the chill off, then X-Rayed, gave me an anaesthetic and removed pieces and fixed me up beautifully.*

Hartland convalesced from his injuries at Lady Astor's estate and returned to Canada in November. He received a promotion to wing-commander, but never went back overseas. At first he was posted to Number 118 Squadron at Rockcliffe, Ontario, where in January 1941 he was promoted to squadron leader. His squadron was transferred to Moncton, New Brunswick, in July, and the following year he became director of personnel at the RCAF headquarters in Ottawa.*

Between 1943 and 1946 Hartland took the position of honorary aide-de-camp to the Governor General, the Earl of Athlone. In March 1944, a letter addressed to "Wing-Commander H. de M. Molson" arrived from the principal aide-de-camp at Rideau Hall:

> *I notice by the press that you have been moved from Moncton to Montreal. The Governor General would like you to remain on as his Honorary Aide-de-Camp for Montreal. I have written to Air Vice Marshal Sully telling him about this. Do let us know if you happen to be coming to Ottawa any time. I would like to have you to lunch, and I am sure that the Governor General and the Princess Alice would like to see you …*

When war broke out in 1939, John Henry Molson was forty-four years old and vice-president of the brewery. He held the rank of major in the Black Watch, but opted to revert to the lower rank (midshipman) so he could join the Royal Canadian Navy. After less than a year he returned to the Black Watch to command the regiment's training depot at Huntingdon, outside Montreal. He remained in Huntingdon for the duration of the war and retired with the rank of lieutenant-colonel.

Tom Molson, like Hartland, had been commissioned into the Canadian Artillery upon his graduation from the Royal Military College. He left for training in Petawawa not long after Hartland and his squadron had left for Europe. Tom, thirty-eight and considered too old for combat, was never sent overseas.

C.D. Howe, minister of munitions and supply, commissioned a number of wealthy Canadians to purchase luxury yachts in the United States, which the navy could convert for wartime use. To avoid being

*When Hartland was there he persuaded the provincial Liquor Board to allow carloads of beer from Molson's Brewery to be transported to Moncton station.

perceived as partisan, the "neutral" United States allowed private citizens (rather than commissioned officials) to carry out these small but significant acts of support for the Allies. Tom and two of his friends were asked to travel to Quincy Harbour, Massachusetts. There they would purchase the 260-foot *Aztec,* sail her to Halifax, and deliver her to the navy. Tom, R.B. (Dick) Angus, and Charlie Creighton, finding the *Aztec* had been recently damaged in a hurricane, negotiated a fair price, and had the ship towed to Boston for repairs. As Tom remembered:

> *We had trouble in Boston with the Gyro Compass and the radio direction finder, and being unable to get a Sperry man in Boston the U.S. Coast Guard very kindly repaired them for us … I decided to run to Halifax through the night on account of the possibility of U boats being off shore. We ran through the night with all lights out … The next day I went ashore and turned her over to the R.C.N … A total account for purchasing, drydocking, repairs, customs duty and sales tax … came to $73,000. I think the* Aztec *was the cheapest, largest, and best buy that was made in our joint venture. It was a lot of trouble for me but looking back on it, it was in a way fun.*

Tom's first cousin P.T. (Pete) Molson joined the Royal Canadian Navy in 1941. He had just graduated from McGill with a Bachelor of Arts and a First Class Honours in Economics and Political Science. He was both a University Scholar and winner of the Rhodes Scholarship to Oxford. On account of the war, Pete declined taking his place at Oxford. He served in the navy from 1941 until 1945, was given the rank of lieutenant, and did well enough that he eventually became a lieutenant-commander in charge of a frigate. His was one of a flotilla of vessels shepherding and protecting the Atlantic freighters that transported victuals, equipment and ammunition to England from Canada, providing a life-line between the two countries.

The war years in Montreal, though fraught with grim news and unrelenting tension, had brought about a rapid and welcome end to the debilitating Depression. The city had suffered more than its share of Canada's poverty and unemployment, but a strong loyalty to the

British Empire prevailed. Crowds of French, English and Iroquois Montrealers had taken to the streets and cheered in an emotional show of support for King George VI and Queen Elizabeth when they came to Montreal in the spring of 1939. When war was declared, some had felt a sense of anxiety and dread, but others felt a sense of purpose. The unemployed lined up to enlist at regimental headquarters. Troops carried out drilling exercises and artillery demonstrations on the Champ de Mars; Red Cross workers trained nurses and recruited volunteers.

Social events such as debutante balls, dinner dances and concerts were cancelled; people gathered instead around posted newspapers to read accounts of the fighting in Europe and to scan casualty lists. Soon the hovering possibility of conscription divided the city into French and English factions. Demonstrations became riots.

Householders in Montreal were urged to prepare for possible air raids by stocking basement shelters with food and first-aid provisions. Ration books for tea, coffee, sugar, butter and meat were issued in 1942. Families who employed full-time labourers faced multiple inconveniences when their help left to work in munitions factories. Many wives whose husbands had joined the forces, including Mrs. Tom (Celia) and Mrs. Hartland (Magda) Molson, had to cook, clean, mind their children and otherwise fend for themselves for the first time.

In 1941, when he was forty-eight years old, Stuart Molson entered the brewery, becoming a director and assistant-secretary. While Stuart had been pursuing other interests, including his brokerage firm, his brothers Bert and John Henry had for many years been involved in the brewery. When war began, Stuart had enlisted with his old regiment, the Black Watch, and was sent to England as paymaster. But he continued to suffer from stomach ulcers, and was invalided out of the service and sent home in November 1940.

Barley malt was required in the manufacture of explosives, yet in spite of the government's war-time restrictions beer production was higher than ever at Molson's between 1940 and 1945, when the brewery averaged 14.7 million gallons per year. More women were hired. Fast upon the heels of higher production and employment came higher taxes and a new economic sensibility. At Stuart's suggestion and with his encouragement, the employees formed a union. The first contract between Molson's Brewery and the Molson's Brewery Employees Association was signed in 1944.

Late that year, news came to Montreal that the German army was retreating from the Allies. Confirmation of Germany's surrender came in May 1945, and the city celebrated with a joyful cacophony of horns, whistles, cheers and singing.

National Archives Canada

John Thomas Molson (1837-1910), his second wife Jennie (née Butler) and family, 1890. From left to right, back row: Naomi, Walter (on mother's lap), Jennie, Herbert, John Thomas, and Lillias. Front row: Percy, Evelyn, Kenneth, and Mabel.

Molson collection

Molson collection

Molson collection

Above: Hobart and Edith Molson, children of Dr. Wm. Alexander Molson and Esther Shepherd, in 1889.

Top left: Dr. Wm. Alexander Molson (1852-1920), c. 1911. A contemporary of Dr. William Osler's at McGill, Dr. Molson became a remarkable figure in the community, playing a leading role in fighting Montreal's smallpox epidemic of 1885. He waived his fees for families who were struggling to live within their means.

Bottom left: Esther Shepherd, c. 1890, who married Dr. Wm. Alexander Molson but had also attracted the amorous attention of the renowned Dr. William Osler. Her marrying Molson irked Osler, who played practical jokes at the expense of his rival for many years.

National Archives Canada

Above: On April 11, 1899, Herbert Molson (1875-1938) and Bessie Pentland were married. Their wedding was deemed "the social event of the season in Quebec City." Bridesmaids were Naomi Molson, Mamie Pentland, Hilda Pentland and Louise Casault. Best man was Stuart Wotherspoon; ushers were John F. Savage, Archie Russell, and C.F. Pentland. At the time of his wedding Herbert owned one-eighth of the brewery. Kenneth Molson (1877-1932), his brother who can be seen in the background, would be married four days later to Mary Snider at a quiet, private ceremony.

Right: Herbert Molson's wife, Bessie Pentland Molson, with their first child, Tom, in 1901. Bessie's father, prominent advocate Charles Pentland, acted on Kenneth Molson's behalf during his divorce in 1912. Bessie, who would be remembered by some as gentle and gracious, and by others as bossy, spent her happiest hours in her garden.

National Archives Canada

Michael Stewart

The Snider family, of Hamilton, Ontario, in 1896. From left to right: Winnifred, Kathleen, Judge Colin Snider, Edith, Hedley, Helen Senior, Helen, and Mary. Judge Snider's daughter Mary, whose first husband was Kenneth Molson, led a life that disgraced and so enraged her father that he eventually disowned her.

Molson collection

Mabel Molson (1878-1973), with her nephew (and beloved charge) Jack Molson (1902-1997), c. 1910.

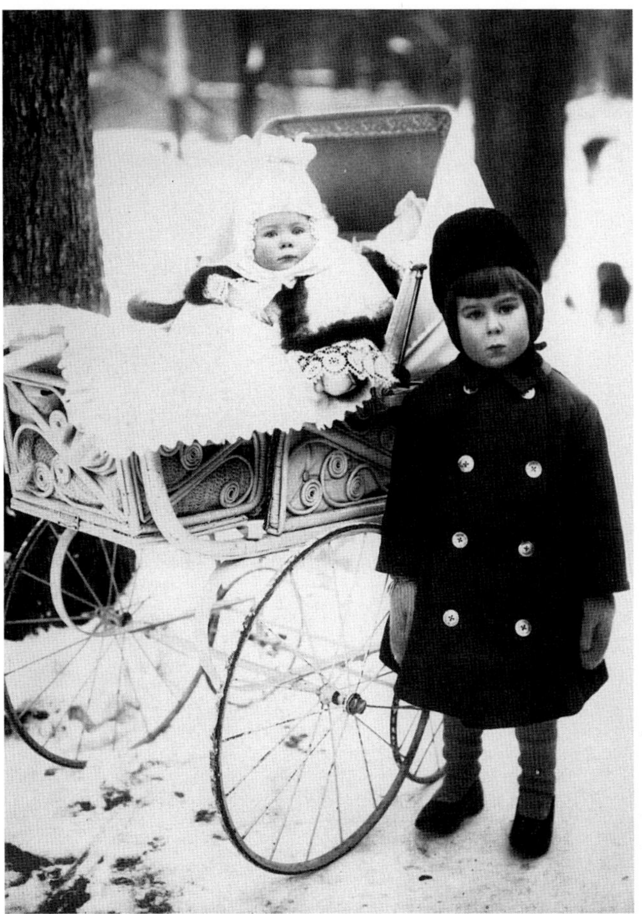
National Archives Canada

Tom Molson (1901-1978), in 1905 with his younger sister Dorothy (1904-1992), outside their house on Sherbrooke Street. Herbert and Bessie's children's solemn expressions belie their surroundings, a privileged world that included such opulent touches as this fancy wicker carriage, double-breasted worsted coat, and lace- and fur-trimmed cape.

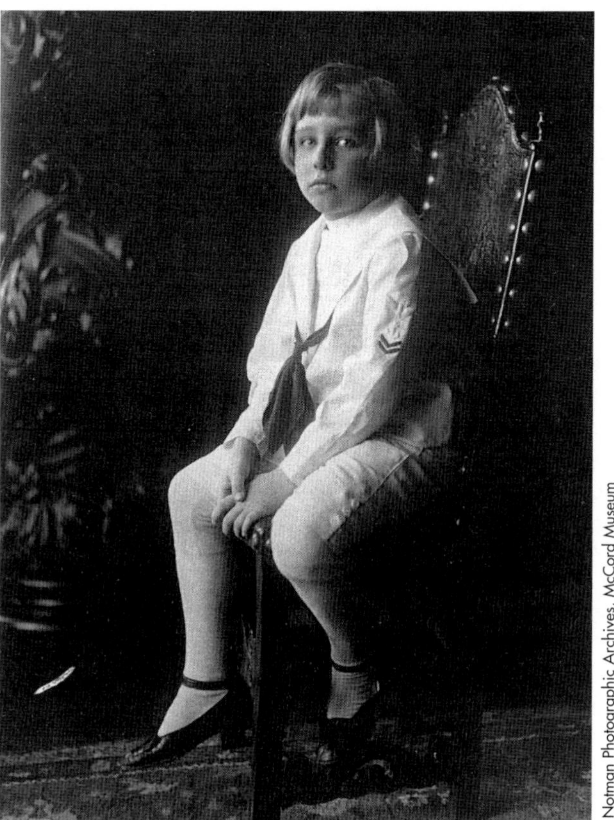

Notman Photographic Archives, McCord Museum

Above: Billy Van Horne (1907-1946) was the only child of Bennie Van Horne (1873-1931) and Edith Molson (1877-1960). Billy was pampered and spoiled, especially by his grandfather Sir William Cornelius Van Horne. At age 7, in 1914, his playthings included a pony, a room-size electric train set, and a child-size replica of a Model T Ford. Raised in the Van Horne Mansion on Sherbrooke Street, Billy was enrolled at nearby Selwyn House, a private day school for boys.

Facing page, top: Brothers Percy **(left)** (1880-1917) and Walter **(right)** (1883-1952) in 1897 and 1899, respectively. Both attended McGill University and both became members of the Montreal Amateur Athletic Association. The only all-round-athlete award winner for three consecutive years at McGill, Percy held many other records that remain unbroken, including the distinction of being the youngest player ever to win the Stanley Cup. When war came, Percy enlisted in the Princess Patricia's Light Canadian Infantry, and Walter joined the 42nd Battalion Royal Highlanders, known as the Black Watch.

Bottom right: Walter Molson and Mary Kingman had four bright and boisterous children, the first three of whom were Caro (right), Naomi (left), and Walter ("Chip"), centre. This photograph, taken in 1917, was likely a memento for their father, who was serving in France at the time.

Molson collection

Ian Angus collection

Ian Angus collection

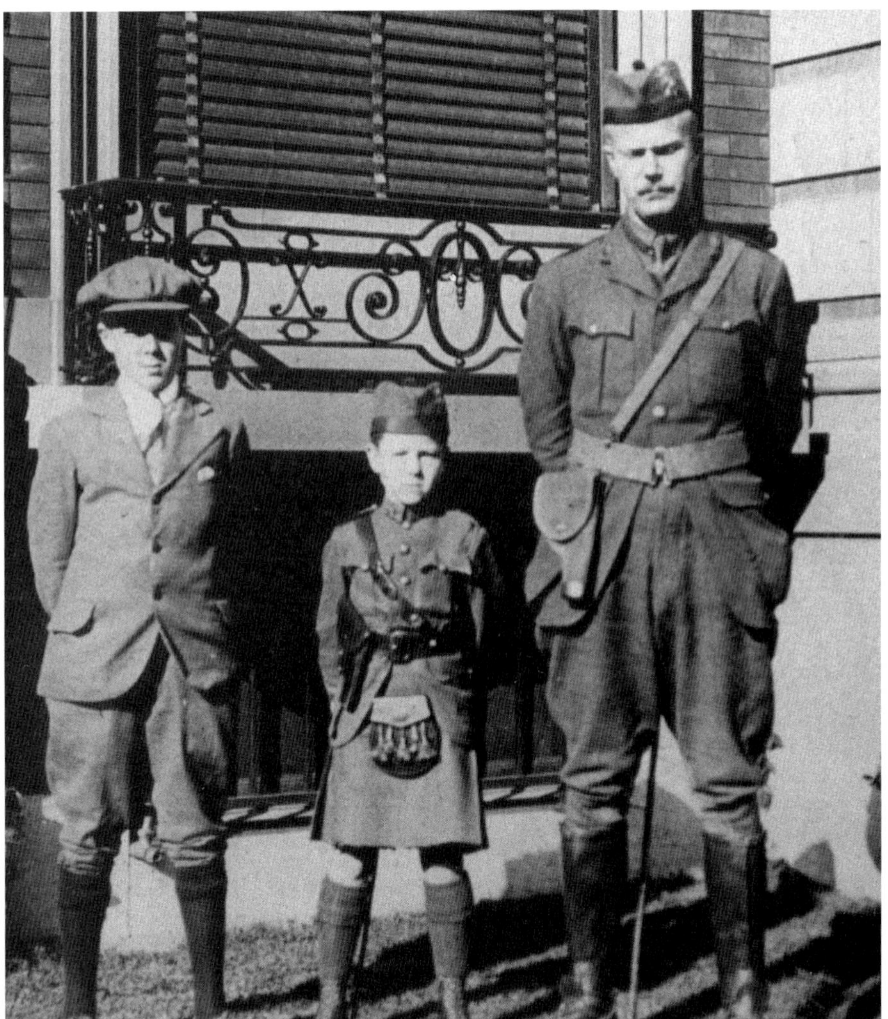

Molson collection

Above: Herbert Molson (1875-1938), with sons Tom **(left)** and Hartland **(centre)**, in October 1915, shortly before he left for Belgium with the 42nd Battalion, Royal Highlanders. Hartland, recalling this time when the children of Black Watch officers in Montreal were issued imitation uniforms and invited to take part in "important and serious" events at the armoury, today jokes about his part: "We were probably the biggest nuisance the army ever created." In time Hartland would join the air force and fight in the Battle of Britain in World War II. Tom would join the brewery in 1922.

Right: F. Stuart Molson (1893-1983), brother of John Henry and Bert, always wanted a military career. He joined the Black Watch during World War I, and he acted as paymaster for his regiment in England in World War II. Stuart entered the family brewery in 1941 when he was 48 years old, becoming a director and assistant secretary, and eventually secretary-treasurer.

National Archives Canada

Stuart Iversen

Five children of Fred W. Molson (1860-1929) (left to right, Brenda, John H., Bert, Louisa, and F. Stuart) enjoy a light moment aboard John H. Molson's sailboat, *The Heather II,* on the St. Lawrence in the summer of 1951. Though the adult siblings rarely spent time together as a group, they always enjoyed one another's company.

Molson collection

Doris Carington-Smith and Colin John Grasset (Jack) Molson (1902-1997) met in 1924 at a debutante party on board the *H.M.S. Hood,* anchored in the St. Lawrence. This is their engagement photo, taken in 1925. They married in 1926.

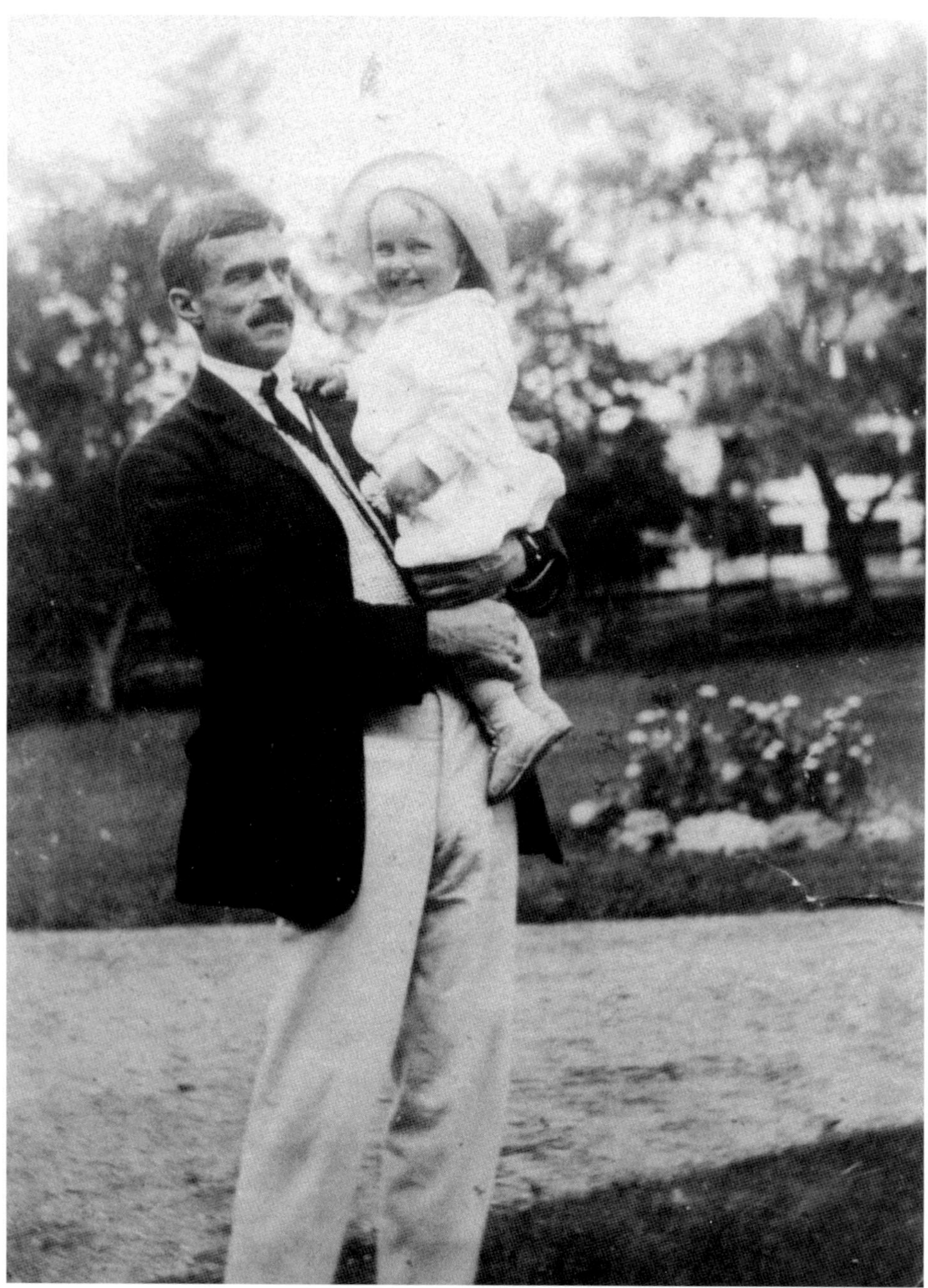

Molson collection

Kenneth Molson (1877-1932) at St. Patrick, holding his daughter, Jane, in the summer of 1923. Jane was the youngest of three children Kenneth had with his second wife, Isabel Meredith. The children adored playing with their Meredith cousins next door and the Jutras children across the road.

Above: John Henry Molson (1896-1977), a member of the Black Watch in World War I, was taken as a prisoner of war in 1918 and liberated after armistice. In 1919 he returned to Canada and soon joined the family brewery. Over the next 20 years he worked his way up to become vice-president of Molsons. Shown here in 1949, John Henry was two years away from retirement.

Top right: Five Molson family members were actively involved in Molson's Brewery in 1965. From left to right, Hartland, William (Billy), Thomas H.P. (Tom), Percival Talbot (Pete), and Eric Molson pose beneath portraits of John Molson Senior and John Molson Junior. Molson Senior noted, in his 1836 will, that he wanted his portrait to hang in the boardroom for as many years as his descendants continued to own and operate the brewery.

Bottom right: Brothers Eric (b.1937) and Stephen Molson (b.1939) and their uncle (centre) Hartland Molson (b.1907) photographed in 1996. While Hartland entered the brewery after a career in the military and in aviation, Eric joined directly after graduating from Princeton University. Stephen was invited to work for the Molson Foundation in 1971.

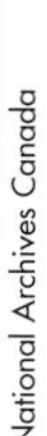

National Archives Canada

Bob Fisher/CHC

Molson Inc.

Members of the sixth- and seventh-generation of Canadian Molsons who control the brewery. In reverting back to the core business, which is brewing, Eric, Stephen, and Ian Molson are looking at the past as well as to the future. In 2001, they steer the course at Molson Inc.

Hartland wanted to be able to promote Molson's beer on the televised "Hockey Night in Canada." Imperial Oil, however, had signed on as the primary sponsor.

Chapter Thirty-Four

Hockey Night in Canada

After his convalescence at Lady Astor's estate, Hartland returned to Canada a hero. He had survived sixty-two combat missions. For the remaining years of the war he delivered lectures to audiences across Canada, accepted invitations to speak to clubs in New York City, and was promoted several times. He also flew training missions and worked in personnel at various air bases. He retired from the RCAF in 1945 with the rank of group captain.

When Hartland returned to the brewery, he became vice-president and secretary. John Henry and Tom also returned and resumed their old places in the office and on the board. Monumental shifts had occurred in their absence. John Henry, Tom and Hartland no sooner acclimatized to peacetime and the presence of the new employees' association, than they found themselves gearing up for a transition from private to public company.

In 1945 the brewery's common shares split 25 for 1, into 750,000 shares. In February, 150,000 twenty-dollar shares were listed on the Montreal Stock Exchange. The shares sold rapidly. The board confidently directed Hartland to oversee a $10 million expansion that would double the brewery's capacity.

Tom returned from war service to a home and family that had altered greatly, and a relationship in which his place was no longer definable. In the years following the war, the strain of adjustments within and without the brewery would take a heavy toll on his marriage to Celia.

Pete (P.T.) Molson was offered an extension to take up his scholarship at Oxford in 1945, but decided instead to sit for the External Affairs exam, which he passed. He joined External Affairs as a Foreign Service Officer, and was appointed private secretary to Vincent Massey, Canadian ambassador in London. Following his tenure with Massey, Pete was recommended for a position under External Affairs' Secretary of State Lester (Mike) Pearson. While working for Pearson, Pete travelled often between Montreal and London, England.

In London in 1947, Pete was introduced to an elegant, bright twenty-year-old debutante, Lucille Holmes. They were married in Montreal in the spring of 1949, then flew back to England, where Pete continued to work for the High Commission. Soon after he was stationed to Berlin, a city with no official diplomatic missions, and half of it blockaded by the Russians.

When Lucille became pregnant with their first baby, Pete arranged to have her secretly flown to England on a Lancaster bomber aircraft, which was making a scheduled flight to transport sacks of flour. Lucille, age twenty-three, was longing for the comforts of home in which to give birth.

Baby Peter was born in London, and afterward Lucille returned to Berlin with the infant. By then the Russian Entente had been established. In 1951 Pete was transferred to Ottawa to head External Affairs' South American desk.

In 1949, Bert Molson wrote to Whitbread's Brewery to let them know Hartland would be travelling to London and would like to call upon them "to get some view of contemporary British practice." Family-run Whitbread's had long been the Molsons' business mentor; it represented the epitome of brewing tradition and was, like Molson's, the largest and longest-established brewery in its country. As his great-

great-grandfather had done at the beginning of the previous century, Hartland toured the London brewery and purchased hops in England. In 1949, even the most "traditional" industries could improve production without sacrificing quality. In the light of post-war prosperity, industrial expansions, and mechanization, Bert and Hartland knew that to stay competitive, it was important to stay abreast of innovations.

Hartland stopped at the High Commission and had a pleasant visit with his cousin Pete. He told him that the area occupied by the family brewery was now twice what it had been two years earlier. The old brewery stables had been dismantled, and the last horse finally retired to pasture. Production had risen to over 21 million gallons of ale. Unsurprisingly, in the new bottling plant, labels that were glued to the bottles still read "John H.R. Molson and Brothers."

In 1949 Molson's shares were subdivided: one "A" (non-voting) and one "B" (voting) share exchanged for each common share. Authorized capital increased to one million A and one million B shares. A year later, production surged to 31,250,000 gallons.

Unlike Molson's, National Breweries had suffered a decline in the years after the war. National's owner, Norman Dawes, offered to sell control to Molson's in the mid-1940s. Herbert had forgone the opportunity in 1932; Bert declined for many of the same reasons.

Times had never been better for the beer industry. The ancient beverage now had a revived, modern appeal. Sales of beer in Ontario and Quebec had doubled between 1936 and 1950, largely due to the consumption of beer by women.

In 1950, Molson's faced competition with National Breweries and relative newcomer John Labatt. In 1951 and 1952, National Breweries' lighter brands dominated the market. The three competitors' efforts to outdo each other in those years were marked by major advertising campaigns and promotional giveaways. Molson's brewery introduced Golden Ale and lightened their Export Ale, the popular brand name for the past fifty years.

Bert Molson, at seventy years of age, had no inclination to embark upon new marketing strategies. In fact he wanted to retire, and did so, but not before he had ensured that his successors were well chosen. Tom was named chairman of the board and Hartland president–on the advice of an impartial professional advisor–while John Henry became vice-president and Stuart secretary-treasurer.

Meanwhile, the financier/industrialist E.P. Taylor, president of Toronto-based Canadian Breweries Limited, completed his methodical takeover of National Breweries. The younger members of the board at Molson's once again advocated buying an existing brewery in Toronto, or establishing a new operation there.

Toronto's market was then growing faster than Montreal's, and it seemed that if they were ever going to expand out of Quebec, Molson's should do it now. A ten-acre site on Toronto's lakeshore was purchased for the new brewery, and Tom and Hartland led the $12-million construction. Tom designed the premises, which were working at full capacity by the end of 1954.

The Molsons' Toronto enterprise was designed to brew only lager, a brand they called Crown and Anchor. Dave Chenoweth (formerly with Pepsi Cola) joined Tom and Hartland to work at the site in Ontario. With the gala opening of the new plant, Molson's became a national brewery, competing successfully for the same market as E.P. Taylor (who had changed National's name to Dow Breweries).

Brothers Tom and Hartland were now the controlling shareholders at Molson's, and their new titles and duties soon required their full-time presence in Montreal. Chenoweth's duties required him to divide his time between the two cities. Who, they wondered, could run the Toronto operation? Who could be the next Molson successor? Hartland thought he had the answer when he suggested they ask P.T. Molson. Lester Pearson was reluctant to let Pete go.

With reluctance, Pete agreed to Hartland's plan. He loved working in External Affairs and didn't want to leave. But Walter was dying and his fondest wish was that his son would accept. Pete, who had always tried to be perfect, could not say no to his father's request.

Pete had been a gifted child, but the expectations placed upon him had been extraordinary. His mother had doted on him excessively; his uncle Herbert singled him out for scrutiny many times. Sensitive to the extreme, Pete felt a tremendous need to live up to his reputation and deeply feared disappointing those who had such faith in him. But these pressures took their toll, and Pete had a mental breakdown in

Berlin in 1949, where he was hospitalized. He was well again for three years, but in 1952, while living in Ottawa, was in hospital again. At a time when the medical profession knew less about mental illnesses than it does now, P.T. was diagnosed as manic depressive.

"The world was very difficult for Pete," Lucille would say later. Members of his family in Montreal persistently refused to believe that Pete could be ill. Those who didn't understand the disorder simply denied it was there, and there were many including his mother who didn't understand it. This left Pete feeling isolated, depressed, moody and unstable. He'd always managed to channel the best of his abilities into his professional career, but his marriage suffered considerable strain, and his and Lucille's children, in turn, absorbed the tension of the situation.

Lucille knew Pete's vulnerabilities and knew how unsuited he was to working at the brewery. She advised him to turn down Hartland's proposal. Not only had he had no business experience, but he was also non-confrontational, too gentle, too acquiescent to be an executive in a large competitive industry. But many elders in his family, as well as Walter, encouraged him to accept. In March 1953 Walter died, and in May, Pete presented himself at Molson's to begin the "grooming" for his future.

In 1953, Molson's produced 41 million gallons of beer in Montreal. This meant that every day the company filled and shipped 1,750,000 bottles of ale, which they sent by truck and by rail to their customers. More than a thousand employees were on the payroll.

Less than eighteen months after Bert retired in 1953, he died of a stroke. A bachelor, he willed his long-time friend Margaret Villeneuve an annuity. His brewery stock went to his cousin John Henry's three sons, Billy, David and Peter.

In July 1955, Prime Minister Louis St. Laurent asked Hartland if he would accept an appointment to the Senate. Though he was honoured by St. Laurent's offer, Hartland had serious misgivings about entering politics. He had never been partisan to any party, and didn't see what benefit would come if he declared allegiances now. He spoke to his brother Tom to solicit another opinion, and to discuss what effect his regular absences might have on the brewery. The following day, he telephoned the Prime Minister to say that he would accept the appointment if he would be permitted to sit as an independent. St. Laurent agreed, and on July 29, Hartland was formally inducted into the Senate.

Long-time senator Donat Raymond was president of the Canadian Arena Company. Hartland was an old acquaintance of Raymond; they had known each other since Donat had bought the Canadiens hockey team in 1938. The owner's box and the Molson family's box (a vestigial privilege of Hartland's father's and uncles' involvement in founding the arena) had been side by side behind the players' bench since the Forum's construction in the 1920s.

The family's box was occupied by ardent Molsons and their guests, game after game. Yet since Percy's years of playing for the Montreal Victoria's, no other Molson had pursued a love of hockey as Hartland had. On his father's advice he was careful not to jeopardize his amateur status: as a young man Hartland had played for the Kingston Frontenacs, later he coached the game in Switzerland, and during the Depression he even played as an extra with the Montreal Maroons, many times against the Canadiens. In 1955 the Canadiens were the best team in the world, and Hartland especially appreciated the skill with which these professionals made the game look like a beautiful and brilliantly executed dance.

Even when his commitments at the brewery consumed most of his energy, Hartland worked to establish a connection to the sport about which he cared so passionately. The company already endorsed broadcasts of hockey games on the radio. Now the number of national hockey fans was growing, as more householders were buying televisions. Hartland wanted to be able to promote Molson's beer on the televised "Hockey Night in Canada." Imperial Oil, however, had signed on as the primary sponsor.

In 1951 Hartland sent Zotique L'Esperance, vice-president of public affairs, to Quebec City to make Jean Béliveau a proposition: skate for the Canadiens and work for Molson's as a public relations representative. Only twenty years old, Béliveau's future looked infinitely bright. Could the star of the Quebec Aces be persuaded to come to Montreal?

Béliveau considered Hartland's offer but didn't meet with him until 1953, once his contract with the Quebec Senior Hockey League had ended. Over a handshake in Hartland's office the two agreed to a deal that seemed too sweet to be true. In return for bringing Béliveau to Montreal, Frank Selke, the Canadiens general manager, had promised to get Molson's the television rights to the senior league games at the Forum. The young PR rep began work for Molson's on the first of October 1953, the same day he signed a five-year contract to play for the Canadiens. As Béliveau explained, "I was a full-time Molson employee who happened to have special dispensation to play hockey for the Montreal Canadiens." Béliveau proved to be both articulate and unfailingly polite off the ice. Hartland knew, the moment he met him, that the young hockey star would be the perfect representative for the brewery. He was exactly what he was looking for: the embodiment of words and actions, strength and agility, cadence and harmony ... beer and hockey.

In September 1957, Hartland and Tom bought the Montreal Canadiens and the Arena Company from Donat Raymond. Tom and Hartland's decision to buy the team was considered much more than a $2 million investment; it was part of a Molson family tradition. The aging Raymond recalled that the late Herbert Molson had been one of the founders of the arena who also supported both the Canadiens and the Montreal Maroons through the Depression years. Here was an opportunity for the Molsons not just to support a sport they loved, but also to direct it, be a leading influence in its advancement, and, finally, become a corporate sponsor of "Hockey Night in Canada," creating unprecedented advertising exposure and goodwill for the brewery.

As Hartland put it shortly after the sale, "We don't own the Canadiens, really. The public of Montreal, in fact the entire province of Quebec, owns the Canadiens. This club is more than a professional sports organization. It is an institution and a way of life." Béliveau, who understood many of the things that Hartland never articulated, years later would say, "When the Molsons walked into the Forum I always had the feeling that they loved the game so much, and the Canadiens so much, that they forgot that they owned the team."

The first step would be to pursue full ownership—to move the brewery back into Molson family hands. This would mean ending diversification. The second step, facilitated by new European Union trade rules, would be to market Molson's beer worldwide.

Chapter Thirty-Five

Heirs to an Empire

Like many of his forebears, Hartland Molson seemed to have the Midas touch. In 1958, the Montreal Canadiens won their third consecutive Stanley Cup. Later that year, Molson's Brewery stock split two for one for the second time. Expansion into Ontario had been so successful that construction crews were continually enlarging the Toronto plant. In 1959, Molson's bought Sicks' Breweries, fanning into the west. They paid $31 million to acquire Sicks' plants, including those in Regina and Prince Albert, Saskatchewan; Edmonton and Lethbridge, Alberta; and Vancouver, B.C. By the end of 1960 Molson's had acquired the Fort Garry Brewery in Winnipeg, Manitoba, and by 1962, the Newfoundland Brewery in St. John's. All these breweries were converted to Molson plants.

Consumers across Canada responded positively to Molson's beer. As volume grew, plant capacities were increased and every enlargement incorporated the most modern equipment and technology. Molson's focused on marketing more than ever before. The company sponsored research, improved advertising, introduced promotions and reaped steadily increasing profits.

Hartland and Tom continued to carry out philanthropic works, as had their ancestors. In November 1958, the brothers formed the Molson Foundation, whose purpose was to support "innovative projects in the fields of health and welfare, education and social development, and the humanities." One of the foundation's first actions was to present $900,000 to the Canada Council to establish the Molson Prizes: three annual awards of $20,000 each, given to individuals recognized for exemplary contributions to arts, social sciences, humanities or national unity. (Since the inception of the family foundation, thousands of gifts–totalling tens of millions of dollars–have been distributed to universities, research groups, hospitals and other institutions.)

In 1959 Tom's eldest son, twenty-two-year-old Eric, accepted a position in the brewery. He had graduated from Princeton with a degree in chemistry. In April 1960 he was transferred to the new Vancouver brewery, where he worked first as an assistant in the laboratory and then as a chemist. There he began to get to know all aspects of brewing, including mashing, bottling and marketing operations. In 1962 Eric left the brewery to take an economics course at McGill, then returned in 1963 as Hartland's assistant.

David Molson, who had previously been personal assistant to the president, was promoted to manager, and eventually vice-president, of the Quebec division. Hartland was well aware that his cousin's enduring interest was hockey; in fact, like Hartland, David had some years earlier considered a professional career in the game. Hartland was now forming a plan for David that he was certain would suit his ambitions perfectly. In 1964 in Montreal, Hartland arranged a general reorganization of the Canadian Arena Company, which included a physical refurbishment of the building as well as an executive shuffle. Sam Pollack replaced Frank Selke as general manager of the Canadiens; Hartland announced his retirement as president of the Arena Company in order to become chairman of the board at Molson's; and David became president of the hockey team.

David loved his role within the world of hockey so much that he was happy to leave his brewery office and devote all his time to his new position. He wrote his cousins a formal letter in April 1966, in which he suggested that he and his brothers, Peter and Billy, buy the Canadiens from Tom and Hartland. He pointed out that it would be reassuring to them to have a serious investment upon which they could mould their own careers and reputations. He added, "As long as the family is predominant in both organizations, and particularly in the Hockey Club, then this will ultimately work to the advantage of each, both through overall policy and long-term benefits."

Hartland, nearly sixty years old in 1966, had more matters than usual on his mind. He had begun to consider who might best succeed him as president when he moved on. His nephew Eric (who married Jane Mitchell that year) was now brewmaster of the Montreal plant. His cousin David was ensconced in the hockey club. Brewery manager David Chenoweth had the most experience and was most qualified, but when the board asked him to become president Chenoweth demurred, protesting that the brewery's new leader should be a family member. It didn't take long for Hartland to concur with other family members that P.T. Molson's was the next most deserved name to grace the position. Surely Pete could carry the torch into this new era. He had done well in Toronto and had won praise in External Affairs. It was his turn now to do the family proud in Montreal.

When Pete agreed to take the position as president of Molson's brewery he moved into a house on Grovesnor Avenue, in Westmount, noticeably without Lucille, who stayed in Toronto. She who had argued vehemently, but in vain, against his taking the position, had now, as Pete knew, fallen in love with someone else. On July 1, 1966, P.T. Molson was named president of Molson's Breweries Limited. He was 44 years old, a brilliant academic and diplomat, and completely unsuited to the position in which he found himself. Those around him sensed this and took the reigns of decisions from him, often leaving him to deal with the residue of accountability. Eric puts it flatly: "Pete got kicked around."

Hartland did not know that Pete had been treated for mental illness during the thirteen years he had been living in Toronto, nor that, after coming to Montreal in the spring of 1966, he underwent more treatment at the renowned Allan Institute. This institute, located in the former home (known as Ravenscrag) of Sir Montague Allan, was funded by McGill University (and, for a time, the CIA) and undertook behaviour-control research projects. The psychiatric hospital was known as progressive and even visionary, and Dr. Ewen Cameron was its champion and chief psychiatrist. In his misguided efforts to control schizophrenia and depressive disorders by wiping out a patient's memory, he used sensory deprivation, sleep induction, LSD treatment and intensive electroshock therapy. The particulars of Pete's treatment remain locked up to this day among the institute's surviving records. Suffice it to say that Pete was one of many who was done more harm than good.

By September of 1966, Pete's emotional, personal and professional distresses combined to besiege his equilibrium one final time. No one was aware of the turmoil he was carrying with him on Friday, September 10, when he went up alone to Ivry. When he didn't report to work on Monday, Hartland alerted the caretaker, who found his body in the solarium of the house. Police and the coroner grimly noted that Pete had been shot "in the face," most likely with the 20-gauge shotgun that was lying next to him. A freshly opened box of shells sat on a table close by. Later investigation revealed that Pete, who was not a hunter, had only recently bought the gun and its ammunition. Dr. Jean Louis Taillon, the district coroner, concluded there could be "no other verdict but accidental death," the common euphemism for suicide.

Numerous tributes were publicized when the tragedy became known. "In diplomacy, he was something rather special," remembered one editorial. "Everything he touched, he adorned." The *Gazette's* lengthy obituary concluded:

> *As was to be expected, [P.T. Molson] was also active in the welfare of the community, notably in the work of the Montreal Children's Hospital. He was a valued member of any committee, helpful, constructive, dependable. That he was a man of high intelligence and practical competence, his long list of achievements shows. But more than this, the friends he made wherever he went will remember him for his graciousness and tact–a rare blending of an innate dignity with an instinctive sympathy. Percival Talbot Molson was a great gentleman.*

Within the family, the aftermath of Pete's suicide was inexpressible. Even more than thirty years later the discomfort has not lessened, only blurred. Those who had been closest to Pete–who shared an unspoken responsibility–could cope with his tragic death only by placing blame, and the most obvious target for such was his estranged wife, Lucille. She and her children moved to England, but no place could be far enough away for them to escape the horror of the past.

After Pete's death Dave Chenoweth became the new company president. The presidency of Molson's Brewery would now be viewed as an office distinct from ties of ownership and be given to the person most experienced and capable of assuming it. No family member has been president of the brewery since then; instead, Molsons fill board positions and sit as executive officers, such as chairman, vice-chairman and honorary chairman.

The company and its subsidiaries continued to evolve with the times and economics. In 1968, Tom and Hartland agreed to sell the Canadiens and the Forum–valued at $5.5 million–to their cousins David, Billy and Peter, for $3.3 million. Hartland explained his philosophy when he said these words at a press conference at the arena on August 15, 1968:

> *I believe that this approach which places exciting colourful hockey ahead of financial return on investment has been the main factor in creating the unique sports position that Les Canadiens enjoy with their fans in this city and province … In expressing my best wishes for the future to David, Peter and Bill, I cannot wish them anything better than the same friendship and support I received from all the people connected with hockey. May the Canadiens continue their winning ways for many years to come.*

In the 1960s, after decades of political calm in Montreal, a resistance movement emerged in the form of the Front de Libération du Québec (FLQ). Demands for the release of the FLQ members convicted of violence, or "political prisoners," were followed by plans to overthrow the provincial government. A campaign of terrorism began. Between 1963 and 1968, thirty-five FLQ-planted bombs detonated in Anglo neighbourhoods; in the next two years, fifty more bombs exploded. The group published a list of prominent residents whom they intended to single out as targets. On October 5, 1970, British trade commissioner James Cross was kidnapped. The FLQ's manifesto was read on CBC radio the following day–an invective in which Molson's beer was referred to as "horse piss." On October 10, Pierre Laporte, the provincial minister of labour and immigration, was kidnapped. Prime Minister Pierre Trudeau enforced the *War Measures Act,* giving the government emergency powers. It was the first time the statute would be in effect in Canada during peacetime. Then Laporte's murdered body was found. Widespread arrests were carried out. Members of the military were summoned, many of them assigned to act as bodyguards for potential targets. Quebec premier Robert Bourassa booked a suite in the Queen Elizabeth Hotel. Such times had not gripped Montreal since the 1837 Rebellion.

Both Hartland's and David's names were on the FLQ "hit list." Neither would accept bodyguards, and each continued to go to work as usual. Hartland left for Jamaica in November, but not before he delivered a widely quoted speech in the Senate. His conclusion, supporting a supplementary bill to the *War Measures Act,* was memorable:

> *I am Québecois. Although Anglophone, I have French blood in my veins and can claim to be truly, wholly, Québecois. I say this not only because I am proud of it, but because I must point out that a Quebecer follows events in his Province with an understanding and a sensitivity which at times seems to escape other good Canadians brought up in a less complex, unilingual part of the country.*

David, who stayed in Montreal, felt particularly vulnerable. Whether in public attending televised hockey games or at home on the lakefront of Baie d'Urfé, he and his family–wife Claire and their three small children–presented open targets to terrorists. Their high profile in the community had become a dangerous liability. During this time, armed and uniformed RCMP officers would show up at David and Claire's house–at different hours of the day and night–to search for bombs. Much as he loved his career, David began to think that relinquishing the hockey team might take him and his family out of the spotlight. (But first the current season had to be played out: the Canadiens were on their way to winning another Stanley Cup.)

Meanwhile, David Chenoweth and the board members were leading Molson's metamorphosis from a brewery into an industrial conglomerate. Diversification had begun in 1967, when Molson's bought two-thirds of Vilas Furniture for approximately $4 million. In 1968 the company's name was changed to Molson Industries Limited (M.I.L.); that fall, it acquired Anthes Imperial–the largest conglomerate in the country, manufacturing pipes, scaffolds and furnaces–for approximately $80 million. Bud Willmot of Anthes became the new president of M.I.L., while Dave Chenoweth moved aside to vice-president.

The wisest direction in which to grow in the 1960s seemed to be to diversify into industries other than one's core business. Many companies were doing the same; a strong investment plan meant building a conglomerate. Thus the brewery corporation continued to expand, taking on distributing and warehousing operations, lumber businesses, office supply companies, printers and chemical manufacturers. In the light of the growing consumer economy, all the consultants agreed: diversification was the way of the future.

David, Billy and Peter Molson saw their future in the stock market. John Henry's three sons maximized their earnings by splitting shares of the Canadian Arena Company fifty to one before listing them on the Montreal Stock Exchange. As they had anticipated, the price of the shares rose rapidly. By 1971 the brothers were collecting dividends that were six times greater than they had been three years earlier. The idea to act now, to "sell high," was supported by one more factor. Capital gains tax, announced in November, would take effect on January 1, 1972. David and his brothers relinquished control of the arena company and the hockey team to the Bronfman family in Montreal for $13.1 million on December 31, 1971. (The Bronfmans controlled Seagrams, an international distilling corporation.) This transaction enabled them to pocket a nearly $10 million net profit on a $3.3 million investment, over only three and a half years.

"The group to whom we are selling," wrote David to Hartland in December 1971, "first approached me some months ago, and negotiations have been on and off until this week, when they expressed a desire to close immediately. They are totally Canadian and have good French Canadian representation. The principals are Jacques Courtois and Peter Bronfman, with minority financing from the Bank of Nova Scotia."

Hartland met news of the sale with disbelief. On January 5, 1972, he released a blistering statement to the media. In his view, the Montreal team and the Molson Brewery were synonymous. The sale ended a decade and a half of Molson ownership of the team. In those years, eight first-place finishes and six Stanley Cups had given the Canadiens and their owner-sponsors immeasurable gratification and glamour. It was a "trust" he had sold, not just a hockey team. Hartland stated that he "couldn't understand the reason for the sale and was bitterly disappointed by this move on the part of David Molson and his brothers."

In the last decades of the twentieth century the Molson brewery no longer resembled the traditional institution it once was. Having abandoned the ancient ideals of family management and control, as well as the steadfast policy of avoiding long-term debt (in the first ten years of diversification, Molson's long-term debt had climbed from zero to $100 million), it had become a brewery that had turned away from beer. Companies–including Vilas and Anthes–were broken up so that their components could be sold, but many were divested at a loss. Was it a run of bad luck, or the unpredictable economy? Had this player ventured too far afield–or forgotten how to win the game?

Molson Stock was declining when Tom Molson, who had been diagnosed with lung cancer, retired in 1974. Hartland became honourary Chairman of the Board. In April 1978 Tom died, age 76. His shares were willed to his children; the main beneficiaries were his sons Eric and Stephen, who now headed the Molson Foundation. Before and after Tom's death, discussion in the boardroom over how to revitalize the company continued to revolve around which businesses to sell and which next to acquire. Willson Office Specialty and Beaver Lumber became Molson subsidiaries. In 1978 Hartland thought he had the answer, or at least part of it. He led negotiations for the brewery to buy back the Canadiens from the Bronfman family, for $20 million.

Hartland Molson, who that decade had been profiled by *Canadian Magazine* as "one of Canada's ten wealthiest men," had been inducted into the Hockey and Aviation halls of fame, and had been awarded honourary degrees from four universities. He found one transition more subtle yet more significant than the rest: upon Tom's death, he became the family patriarch. At seventy, he may have been ready to step out of the limelight somewhat, but he wasn't about to alter his pace. His seasons would include winters in Jamaica and salmon fishing trips on the Bonaventure River. He would retain his position as Honourary Chairman at Molson's, and uphold his seat in the Senate.

Prospects for the company seemed to be taking a turn for the better. In 1979 Molson's sales exceeded a billion dollars. Other things were going its way: the Canadiens won the Stanley Cup again. In 1981 Eric, by then chairman of the board, asked Bud Willmot, who was planning to retire soon, if he would be willing to trade his half-million "B" shares for an advantageous equivalent in their "A" shares. Willmot agreed. By November 1981, the Molson family held 55 percent of the company's voting shares.

Molson Industries Limited in the 1980s had to contend with the severe economic recession that rippled through the decade. Though at first, record earnings were again reported at Molson's, 80 percent of the profits came from the brewing group. The restored alliance between hockey and Molson's beer notwithstanding, the recession was affecting the other divisions, and now, as the company struggled to rebalance itself, Molson began to lose market share to its national competitor, Labatt. Production capacity was almost immediately diminished to meet falling volumes: two western breweries were closed and employees were laid off. The shareholders' report drew attention to the millions of dollars the company would save. Yet market analysts were quick to point out that downsizing and lower production volume would "meaningfully impact profits."

Through the 1980s, Billy Molson's son Ian was paying careful attention to the direction of Molson brewery. He had been born in Montreal in 1955, excelled in economics at Harvard University, and was, by the 1980s, a managing director for Credit Suisse First Boston in London, England, one of the leading investment banking and securities firms in the world. He had married and started a family in England, though he never left Canada behind. Ian rarely missed a summer visit to Métis to be with other members of his family. Moreover, he harboured a conviction since childhood that he would one day join the brewery.

Ian was not the only one to notice that the company had been gradually restructuring itself, paying down debts and redefining its purpose. Beginning in 1988, it sold blocks of brewery shares to Miller Brewing Company and, in 1989, it "merged" with Foster's Group of Australia. For nearly ten years, the Molson family would not control Molson's Brewery.

Eric Molson and new president James Arnett, who joined the company in 1997, initiated an intensive program to turn around Molson's fortune by refocusing on what it did best: brewing beer. The first step would be to pursue full ownership–to move the brewery back into Molson family hands. This would mean ending diversification. The second step, facilitated by new European Union trade rules, would be to market Molson's beer worldwide.

Reflecting their faith in the link between hockey and Molson, the executives were at first unanimous that the Sports and Entertainment Division be considered a core asset of the brewery. In fact, in 1996 the colossal Molson Centre stadium, with more than 21,000 seats, was completed at a cost of $265 million. The new home for the Canadiens was a coup for the team, for the Molson family business, and for Montreal. Then in 1998 the hockey franchise and the Molson Centre reflected an uncharacteristic drop in its earnings, the result of a combination of increased player costs and high realty taxes.

Molson's and Foster's repurchase of Miller's 20 percent was executed smoothly. But Foster's 50 percent stake, worth approximately $1 billion, might, Molson's feared, pose a problem. The problem wasn't the money; the sale of Beaver Lumber to Home Depot brought almost enough cash in early 1998 to finance the transaction. But Foster's was under no obligation to sell. The value of the brewery's shares slumped while the market speculated on the merits and demerits of the deal. Since Molson's had more to gain than anyone by buying back control, might they be inclined to pay more for the shares than they were worth? Then, on June 23, 1998, the Foster's repurchase was finalized, and Molson's became 100 percent family-owned again.

In 1996 Ian Molson purchased his first blocks of Molson company shares and was invited to sit on the brewery board. In December 1997, he announced his resignation from First Boston, where he'd headed their investment banking department in Europe. This member of the seventh generation of the Molson family, who had become a reverse emigrant, was returning to Canada. If John Molson Senior was *"le père Molson,"* then Ian may be *"le fils Molson,"* who will play a large part in leading the ancient brewery into the new century.

In the boardroom of the brewery on Nôtre Dame Street, Montreal, John Molson Senior wears a somewhat self-conscious but nevertheless impenetrable expression in the one portrait that has survived of him, giving the effect of an intriguing clash of convictions: benign determination perhaps, or dignified amusement. It is an expression still apparent in many in the family today: inscrutable, protective, guarded, alert. A hint of amusement lurks behind the formality on the surface.

John Senior's innovative and practical achievements instilled a legacy his sons and grandchildren admired and felt compelled to emulate. More than his genius had made him an enigma, and more than his quiet convictions of honour and responsibility had made him an ordinary man. John Molson Senior was, as leaders of the family in succeeding generations have described him, a "deviant conformist." Maintaining that balance between those opposite sides of his nature was his greatest strength.

At the beginning of the twenty-first century, the company's direction is clear again. It has a new name, Molson Inc., to better reflect its single focus on brewing and make it easier to position the trademark beer internationally. In the year 2000, Molson Inc. employs 3,800 people, owns and operates seven breweries in Canada, owns 49.9 percent of Coors Canada and 24.95 percent of Molson USA (which markets and distributes Molson's and Foster's in the United States). Molson reports annual sales of over $2 billion. And the hugely successful Molson advertisement "I Am Canadian" tapped into latent Canadian patriotism and gained the company further worldwide recognition.

Today, in Eric Molson's facial expressions, his manner, his body language and stride, the portrait of John Senior comes to life. "We are not wealthy," Eric says characteristically, "we are merely guardians of wealth … guardians of culture, not just finance." He bought an old farmhouse, where in his spare time he raises Highland cattle, donkeys and Jack Russell terriers.

He believes the future of the brewery lies in the promising ability of the coming generation of family members: people like Ian Molson, who can adapt the age-old principles of the brewery and align them with modern production and marketing strategies on a global scale. The man who in 1787 had written "MY COMMENCEMENT ON THE GRAND STAGE OF THE WORLD" has remained near enough, spiritually and physically, to his descendants to pass on his conviction to Eric, Stephen and Ian Molson, now continuing their ancestor's vision.

Bibliography

Ackroyd, Peter. *Dickens* (London: Sinclair-Stevenson, 1990).

Anonymous. *A History of the Montreal Ladies' Benevolent Society 1815-1920* (Montreal, 1921).

Aubert de Gaspé, *Canadians of Old* (translated by Jane Brierley; Montreal: Véhicule Press, 1996).

——. *Mémoire de Gaspé* (translated by Jane Brierley; unpublished university thesis).

Baldwin, Alice. *High, Wide and Handsome* (Montreal: Price, Paterson).

Belisle, Jean. *Bâteau à Vapeur* (Quebec: Editions Hurtubise, 1994).

Bethune, A.N. *The Memoirs of Bishop Strachan* (Toronto: Henry Boswell, 1870).

Bliss, Michael. *A Canadian Millionaire* (Toronto: Macmillan, 1978).

——. *A Life in Medicine* (Toronto: University of Toronto Press, 1999).

——. *Plague: A Story of Smallpox in Montreal* (Toronto: Harper Collins, 1991).

Borthwick, Rev. J.D. *History and Biographical Gazetteer of Montreal to the Year 1892* (Montreal: John Lovell and Son, 1893).

Bosworth, Newton. *Hochelaga Depicta* (Montreal: William Grieg, 1839).

Bowen, Frank C. *A Century of Atlantic Travel: 1830-1930* (Boston: Little, Brown, 1930).

Bowering, Ian. *The Art and Mystery of Brewing in Ontario* (Burnstown, ON: General Store Publishing House, 1988).

——. *In Search of the Perfect Brew in Ontario and Quebec* (Burnstown, ON: General Store Publishing House, 1993).

Brown, Craig. *The Illustrated History of Canada* (Toronto: Lester and Orpen Dennys, 1987).

Call, Frank Oliver. *The Spell of French Canada* (Boston: LC Page, 1923).

Campbell, M.W. *Northwest to the Sea: A Biography of William McGillivray* (Toronto: Clarke, Irwin, 1975).

Campbell, Robert. *A History of the Scotch Presbyterian Church* (Montreal: publisher unknown, 1997).

Choko, Marc H. *The Major Squares of Montreal* (translated by Kathe Roth; Montreal: Meridian Press, 1990).

Christie, N.M., ed. *Letters of Agar Adamson* (Ottawa: CEF Books, 1997).

Cooper, Cynthia. *Magnificent Entertainments, Fancy Dress Balls of Canada's Governors General 1876-1898* (Fredericton: Goose Lane Editions and Canadian Museum of Civilization, 1997).

Craig, Gerald M. *Upper Canada* (Toronto: McClelland and Stewart, 1963).

Creighton, Donald. *The Empire of the St. Lawrence* (Toronto: Macmillan, 1956).

Cruise, David, and Alison Griffiths. *Lords of the Line* (Toronto: Penguin Books, 1988).

Denison, Merrill. *The Barley and the Stream* (Toronto: McClelland and Stewart, 1955).

——. *A History of the Bank of Montreal* (Toronto: McClelland and Stewart, 1966).

De Volpi, Charles P. *Montréal. A Pictorial Record: Historical Prints and Illustrations of the City of Montréal, Province of Québec, Canada, 1535-1885* (Montreal: Dev-Sco. Publishing, 1963).

Dickenson, John A., and Brian Young. *A Short History of Quebec* (Toronto: Copp Clark Pitman, 1993).

Dickens, Charles. *American Notes for General Circulation* (London: Chapman and Hall, 1842).

Ellice, Jane. *The Diary of Jane Ellice* (ed. by Patricia Godsell; Ottawa: Oberon Press, 1975).

Frost, Stanley B. *McGill Milestones 1744-1999* (Quebec: McGill Development Office, 1999).

Fry, Henry. *The History of North Atlantic Steam Navigation* (London: Sampson Low, Marston and Company, 1896).

Galbraith, J.K. *The Great Crash, 1929* (Boston: Houghton Mifflin, 1954).

Gillet, Margaret. *We Walked Very Warily: The History of Women at McGill* (Montreal: Eden Press, 1951).

Glazebrook, G.P. de T. *A History of Transportation in Canada, Volumes 1 and 2* (Toronto: McClelland and Stewart, 1964).

Gooch. *A History of Spalding* (Lincolnshire, England: Spalding Free Press, 1940).

Good, Mabel Tinkiss. *The Bridge at Dieppe* (Toronto: Griffin House, 1973).

Gourvish, T.R., and R.G. Wilson. *The British Brewing Industry 1830-1980* (Cambridge: Cambridge University Press, 1994).

Graham, Conrad. *Eclectic Tastes* (Montreal: McCord Museum, 1992).

Greenhill, Ralph, and Andrew Birrell. *Canadian Photography: 1839-1920* (Toronto: Coach House Press, 1979).

Greenwood, F. Murray. *Legacies of Fear: Law and Politics in Quebec in the Era of the French Revolution* (Toronto: Osgoode Society, University of Toronto, 1993).

Gubbay, Aline. *A View of Their Own: The Story of Westmount* (Montreal: Price, Paterson, 1998).

Guillet, Edwin C. *Pioneer Travel in Upper Canada* (Toronto: University of Toronto Press, 1966).

Grun, Bernard. *The Timetables of History* (New York: Simon and Schuster/Touchstone, 1946).

Hall, Roger, et al. *The World of William Notman: The Nineteenth Century Through a Master Lens* (Toronto: McClelland and Stewart, 1993).

Hitsman, J. Mackay. *The Incredible War of 1812: A Military History* (Toronto: University of Toronto Press, 1965).

Hodgson, Adam. *Letters from North America* (London: Hurst Robinson, 1824).

Hopkins, J. Castell. French Canada and the St. Lawrence (Philadelphia: John Winston, 1913).

House, Madeline, et al., eds. *The Pilgrim Edition: The Letters of Charles Dickens* (Oxford: Clarendon Press, 1974).

Jeffreys, C.W. *Picture Gallery of Canadian History,* Volume 2 (Toronto, 1945).

Lafrenière, Normand. *Lightkeeping on the St. Lawrence* (Toronto: Dundurn Press, 1996).

Langton, Anne. *A Gentlewoman in Upper Canada* (edited by H.H. Langton; Toronto: Clarke Irwin, 1950).

Leach, Campbell W. *Coopers and Lybrand in Canada* (Toronto: Coopers and Lybrand, 1976).

Lepine, Luc. *Les officiers de milice du Bas-Canada 1812-1815* (Montreal: Société généalogique canadienne-française, 1996).

Leveritt, Norman, and Michael J. Elsden. *Aspects of Spalding 1790-1930* (Spalding, England: Chameleon International, 1986).

——. *Aspects of Spalding: People and Places* (Spalding, England: Chameleon International, 1989).

McCloskey, Dennis. *Son of a Brewer* (Burnstown, ON: General Store Publishing House, 1997).

MacKay, Donald. *The Square Mile: Merchant Princes of Montreal* (Vancouver: Douglas and McIntyre, 1987).

Mackey, Frank. *Steamboat Connections* (Montreal: McGill-Queens University Press, 2000).

MacLennan, Hugh. *McGill: The Story of a University* (London: George Allen and Unwin, 1960).

May, Trevor. *The Victorian Undertaker* (Buckinghamshire, England: Shire Productions, 1996).

Miller, Pamela. *The McCord Family* (Montreal: McCord Museum, 1992).

Mitchell, Doug, and Judy Slinn. *The History of McMaster Meighen* (Montreal: McMaster Meighen, 1989).

Morton, Desmond, and J.L. Granatstein. *Marching to Armageddon* (Toronto: Lester and Orpen Dennys, 1989).

Neilson, Helen R. *Macdonald College of McGill University 1907-1988* (Montreal: Corona Montreal, 1989).

Nicholson, Col. G.W.L. *Canadian Expeditionary Force* (Ottawa: Queen's Press, 1962).

O'Shea, Stephen. *Back to the Front* (Vancouver: Douglas and McIntyre, 1996).

Ouellet, Fernand. *Histoire Economique et Sociale du Québec, 1760-1850* (Montreal: éditions Fides, 1966).

Parks Canada. National Historic Parks and Sites Branch Manuscript #186 (The Fort at Coteau du Lac, 4 reports, 1978).

Percival, W.P. *The Lure of Montreal* (Toronto: Ryerson Press, 1945).

Remillard, François, and Brian Merritt. *Mansions of the Golden Square Mile, Montreal* (Montreal: Meridian Press, 1987).

Richardson, John. *Theoretic Hints on an Improved Practice of Brewing* (London, 1777).

Roberts, Leslie. *Montreal: From Mission Colony to World City* (Toronto: Macmillan, 1969).

Robertson, J. Ross, ed. *The Diary of Mrs. John Graves Simcoe* (Toronto, 1934).

Roy, James A. *Kingston: The King's Town* (Toronto: McClelland and Stewart, 1952).

Rubinstein, W.D., ed. *Wealth and the Wealthy in the Modern World* (London: Croom Helm, 1980).

Ruddel, David T. *Quebec City* (Ottawa: National Museums of Canada, 1992).

Sandham, Alfred. *Ville-Marie, Past and Present Montreal* (1870).

Sandwell, B.K. *The Molson Story* (Privately published limited edition; Montreal, 1933).

Senior, Elinor Kyte. *Roots of the Canadian Army: Montreal District 1846-1870* (Montreal: The Society of the Montreal Military and Maritime Museum, 1981).

Schull, Joseph. *Rebellion: The Rising in French Canada in 1837* (Toronto: Macmillan, 1971).

Scott, Frederick George. *The Great War as I Saw It* (London: Good Child, 1922).

Shortt, Adam. *History of Canadian Currency and Banking* (Toronto: Canadian Bankers Association, 1986).

Snell, John Ferguson. *Macdonald College* (Montreal: McGill University Press, 1963).

Stanley, George F.G. *The War of 1812: Land Operations* (Ottawa: National Museums of Canada, 1983).

Stevens, G.R. *History of the CN Railways* (Toronto: Macmillan 1973).

Stone, Lawrence. *Broken Lives: Separation and Divorce in England, 1660-1857* (Oxford: Oxford University Press, 1993).

Sweet, Richard. *The Dictionary of Canadian Breweries* (second edition) (Saskatoon, 1996).

Triggs, Stanley G. *The Composite Photographs of William Notman* (Montreal: McCord Museum, 1994).

——. *William Notman's Studio* (Montreal: McCord Museum, 1992).

Uden, Grant, and Richard Cooper. *Dictionary of British Ships and Seamen* (New York: St. Martin's Press, 1980).

Upper Canada College Old Boys' Association. *Roll of Pupils of Upper Canada College from 1829 to 1900, with Appendices* (Toronto: Warwick Bros. and Rutter, 1901).

Vaillancourt, Emile. *The History of the Brewing Industry in the Province of Quebec* (Montreal: G. Ducharme, 1940).

Ward, Peter. *Courtship, Love, and Marriage in Nineteenth-Century English Canada* (Montreal: McGill-Queen's University Press, 1990).

Weintraub, William. *City Unique* (Toronto: McClelland and Stewart, 1996).

Williams, Jeffery. *Princess Patricia's Canadian Light Infantry* (London: Leo Cooper Ltd., 1972).

Winslow-Spragge, Lois. *No Ordinary Man* (Toronto: Natural Heritage/Natural History Inc., 1993).

Whipple, A.B.C. *Fighting Sail* (New York: Time-Life Books, 1978).

Whitelaw, Marjory, ed. *The Dalhousie Journals* (Ottawa: Oberon Press, 1982).

Wood, William, ed. *The Storied Province of Quebec,* Volumes 1-5 (Toronto, 1931).

Woods, Shirley E., Jr. *The Molson Saga: 1763-1983.* (Toronto: Doubleday Canada, 1983).

Archival Sources

Archives Nationales du Québec: Montréal; Christ Church Cathedral Archives: Montreal; Lincolnshire Archives: Lincolnshire, England; McCord Museum: Montreal (Molson Papers, Badgley Papers, Notman Photographic Archives); National Archives of Canada: Ottawa (Dorwin Diary; Journals of the Legislative Council of the Province of Lower Canada (extracts); Meredith Papers; military and census records; Molson Archives; Van Horne correspondence); Public Records Office: York, Yorkshire, England; St. Thomas's Church Archives: Montreal; Spalding Public Library: Spalding, Lincolnshire, England; Unitarian Church Archives: Montreal

Newspapers and Periodicals

Canadian Courant, Canadian Magazine, Canadian Times, Kingston Chronicle, Lincolnshire Free Press, Montreal Gazette, Montreal Herald, Montreal Pilot, Quebec Mercury, Upper Canada Herald

Dictionaries, Indexes, Directories

Dictionary of Canadian Biography, International Genealogy Index (IGI), Lovell's Historic Report of Census of Montreal (1891), Montreal city directories, including Lovell's

Index

N

O